PRINCIPLES OF RETAILING

PRINCIPLES OF RETAILING

2ND EDITION

ROSEMARY VARLEY

LONDON COLLEGE OF FASHION, UNIVERSITY OF THE ARTS, LONDON

MOHAMMED RAFIQ

PROFESSOR OF MARKETING AT UNIVERSITY OF ROEHAMPTON BUSINESS SCHOOL

BLOOMSBURY

NEW DELHI • LONDON • OXFORD • NEW YORK • SYDNEY

BLOOMSBURY INDIA
Bloomsbury Publishing India Pvt. Ltd
Second Floor, LSC Building No. 4, DDA Complex, Pocket C–6&7,
Vasant Kunj, New Delhi 110070

BLOOMSBURY, BLOOMSBURY ACADEMIC INDIA and the Diana logo are trademarks of Bloomsbury Publishing Plc

First published in India 2023
First published 2014 by PALGRAVE MACMILLAN
Now published by Bloomsbury Academic

ISBN: 978-93-56403-30-7

10 9 8 7 6 5 4 3 2 1

For sale in the Indian subcontinent only

Printed and bound in India by Thomson Press India Ltd

To find out more about our authors and books visit www.bloomsbury.com and sign up for our newsletters

CONTENTS

VIGNETTES, FIGURES AND TABLES

VIGNETTES

FIGURES

TABLES

1 AN INTRODUCTION TO RETAILING

LEARNING OBJECTIVES

- To understand the meaning of the term retailing.
- To understand the relationship between the retailer and the consumer, in terms of the distribution of goods.
- To understand the contribution that the retail industry makes to an economy and a society.
- To examine the structure of the retail industry and the recent trends within it, in order to appreciate the relationship between retailers and the business environment within which they operate.
- To appreciate the diversity of the retail industry.

INTRODUCTION

Retailing is the activity of selling goods and services to final consumers for their own personal use. It is concerned with getting goods in their finished state into the hands of customers who are prepared to pay for the pleasure of eating, wearing or experiencing particular product items. Retailing is all about the distribution of goods and services, because irrespective of how a consumer makes a purchase, be it in a store or via a mobile Internet device, retailers play a key role in the journey that products make from a manufacturer, grower or service provider to the person who consumes. Retailing is also one of the key elements of a marketing strategy; it facilitates the targeting process, making sure that a product reaches particular groups of consumers. It is important in a marketing strategy because it is concerned with matching the arena in which a product is purchased to the benefits and characteristics of the product itself and its price. Retailers provide a collection of service benefits to their customers such as being located in convenient places, editing product choices according to shopping tasks, providing information and recommendations to ensure the best match of product to customer need and selling goods in quantities that match personal consumption levels. Ensuring that this process runs smoothly presents a host of managerial challenges. Retailing is therefore a deceptively simple management process – yet fascinatingly complex in its detail.

RETAILING DEFINED

The word retailing has its origins in the French verb *retailler*, which means to cut up, and refers to one of the fundamental retailing activities, which is to buy in larger quantities and sell on in smaller quantities. For example, a convenience store would buy tins of beans in units of two-dozen boxes, but sell in single-tin units. However, a retailer is not the only type of business entity to 'break bulk'. A wholesaler also buys in larger quantities and sells on to their customers in smaller quantities. It is the type of customer, rather than the activity, that distinguishes a retailer from other distributive traders, the distinction being that a retailer sells to final consumers, unlike a wholesaler, who sells on to a retailer or another business organization. Baker (1998) defined a retailer as 'any establishment engaged in selling merchandise for personal or household consumption and rendering services incidental to the sale of such goods'.

There are, however, many businesses that carry out retailing activity that are not in themselves classified as retailers; for example a factory may engage in retailing activity by selling 'seconds'-quality goods in the shop attached to its manufacturing premises. In the UK a retailer is only classified as such for government reporting if the business gains over half of its income from selling to the final consumer.

The term retailing applies not only to the selling of tangible products like loaves of bread or pairs of shoes, but also to the selling of service products. Companies who provide meals out, haircuts and aromatherapy sessions are all essentially retailers, as they sell to the final consumer, and yet customers do not take goods away from these retailers in a carrier bag. The consumption of the service product coincides with the retailing activity itself.

The Internet has facilitated retailing to such an extent that almost anyone can now become a retailer. Online market places such as eBay have opened up selling to consumers by individuals, while direct selling by producers to consumers across a wide geographical area is now eminently possible via a website that is accessible to all. The term retailer has therefore less relevance now, but the activity of retailing retains its status as the generator of wealth for businesses of all sizes, and the principles of retail management still apply.

THE RETAILER WITHIN THE DISTRIBUTION CHANNEL

From a traditional marketing viewpoint, the retailer is one of a number of possible organizations through which goods produced by manufacturers flow on their way to their consumer destiny. These organizations perform various roles by being a member of a distribution channel. For example, a chocolate producer like Cadbury will use a number of distribution channels for its confectionery, which involve members such as agents, wholesalers, supermarkets, convenience stores, petrol stations, vending machine operators and so on. Channel members, or marketing intermediaries as they are sometimes referred to, take on activities that a manufacturer does not have the resources to perform, such as displaying the product alongside related or alternative items in a location that is convenient for the consumer to access for shopping. Figure 1.1 shows a number of alternative distribution channels that a chocolate confectionary producer might choose to use.

Intermediaries facilitate the distribution process by providing points at which deliveries of merchandise are altered in their physical state (for example being broken down into smaller quantities, or being repackaged) and are made available to customers in convenient or cost-effective locations. Figure 1.2 illustrates how marketing intermediaries (or 'middlemen') make the distribution of goods from producer to consumer more efficient.

Over time, and particularly since the laws that allowed manufacturers to set prices (RPM – resale price maintenance) were abolished in the mid-1960s, retailers in the UK became more dominant in the distribution channel. Their passive distributor status has been transformed into a more proactive one, using price as a competitive weapon, introducing ranges of own-branded goods and developing shopping environments that engender loyalty to an outlet rather than loyalty to a product. The shift in power from the manufacturer to the retailer was further enhanced by information technology, which enabled retailers to gain a greater understanding of their customers' purchasing patterns and preferences. The advent of online shopping however has been disruptive; producers are now able to reach limitless consumer markets, and consumers have limitless product information at their fingertips, transforming them from passive recipients of marketing communications to informed co-creators of the retailing experience.

THE VERTICAL MARKETING SYSTEM

Although Figure 1.1 illustrates the traditional distribution channels that are used in many instances to get products to consumers, there are a large number of marketing approaches that do not fit neatly into this model. Levi Strauss, for example, have a large network of shops through which only their own merchandise is sold. Their retailing activities are, in a marketing sense, of equal importance to their manufacturing activities (irrespective of the financial contributions of each activity), and the two facets of the business are highly integrated. In order to reflect this type of situation,

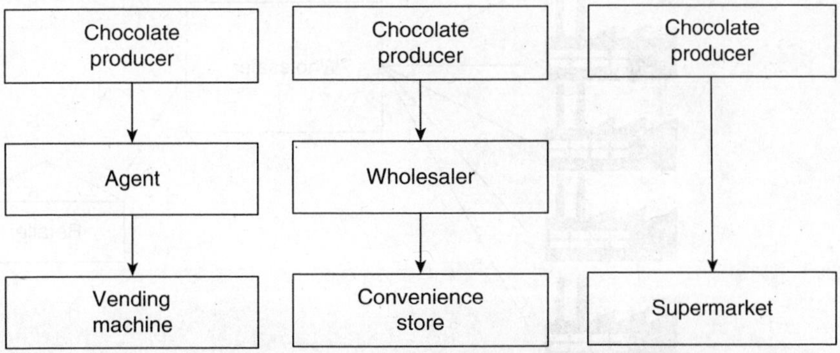

Figure 1.1 Alternative distribution channels for a chocolate confectionery producer

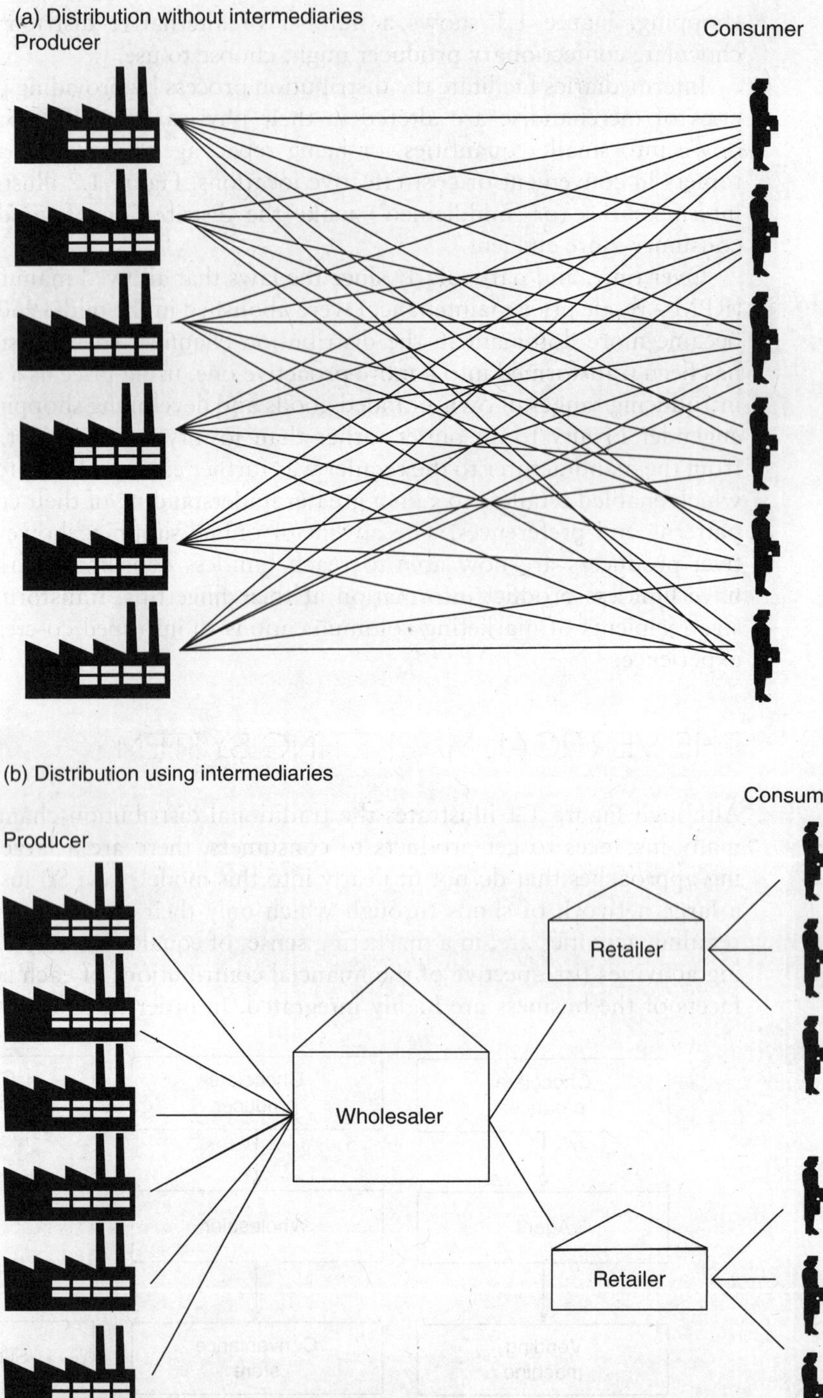

Figure 1.2 The efficiency of the marketing intermediary

the notion of a vertical marketing system was developed (Walters, 1979), as shown in Figure 1.3.

The vertical marketing system usefully depicts a more realistic view of the retail industry in developed economies. Many large multiple retailers like J Sainsbury, Marks and Spencer and Wal-Mart are actively involved in marketing functions that were at one time left to producers, such as product development, branding and advertising. Some retailers even have their own manufacturing facilities. Conversely, many producers are involved in retailing activities, either by running retail outlets dedicated to their own merchandise or by performing functions that at one time were the preserve of the retailer, such as allocating shelf space to their range of products in a process commonly referred to as vendor-managed inventory. The Internet in particular has allowed producers, many of whom are small niche players, to thrive as they take on retailing activities themselves. By setting up their own online shop, they do not have to rely on being 'stocked' by retailers in order to reach consumers and they can engage with customers themselves without the expense of running a physical store.

One of the results of the adoption of the vertical marketing system is the demise of the wholesaler within the distribution channel. Vertically integrated manufacturers do not need to rely on wholesaling activities when they have their own network of retail outlets to distribute their products (see Vignette 1.1), and vertically integrated retailers gain the benefit of cutting out the wholesaler's profit margin when they go directly to the producer. The contracting wholesale industry is one of the many structural changes that make the survival of the small, independent shopkeeper increasingly tenuous. Even though the demise of the wholesaler was inevitable, as retailers placed orders directly with producers, the function that the wholesaler performs is still required in order to move products from a widespread (often global) supply base to a national or even international network of outlets in an efficient way.

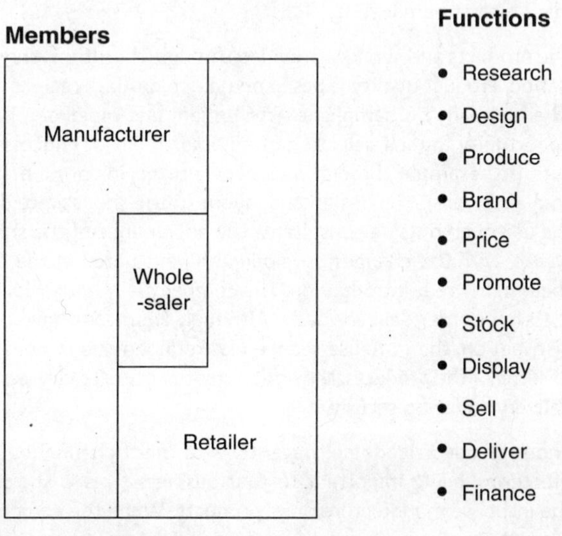

Figure 1.3 The vertical marketing system

The large retailers have therefore developed a dedicated infrastructure of warehouses, distribution centres and transportation fleets in order to replace the network of independent intermediaries.

VIGNETTE 1.1 THORNTONS

Thorntons, the UK's only dedicated high-street retailer of confectionery, was founded in 1911 by Joseph Thornton, who was a commercial traveller engaged in selling confectionery. From the outset the company devised its own recipes and manufactured and retailed the product, a pattern of vertical integration through ownership that has been maintained throughout the company's development. In 2013, Thorntons had a turnover of £221 million. In the 1990s the company went through a significant expansion of their retail network to around 350 shops and a small number of cafes; however, the economic downturn of 2007–10 hit Thorntons hard as customers cut back on discretionary treats. The company scaled back their own retail outlets to 296 directly run stores; however, they continued to grow the number of franchised outlets. The stores are supported by an online shop, and more recently demand has improved as consumers have returned to chocolate as an affordable gift. Meanwhile, the company retained their in-house manufacturing of the core product (chocolates) whilst introducing outside suppliers for peripheral ranges such as solid chocolate bars and ice cream.

Thorntons primarily compete in the boxed chocolate market, where their 'Continental' brand has a 6 per cent share. As a gift, Thornton's chocolates compete with a wide range of products, such as toiletries, lingerie, flowers and wine provided by other retailers, but as a retailer dedicated to specialist confectionery, the company has no large competitors in the UK, although to an extent the supermarkets Boots, Marks and Spencer (to whom Thorntons is a supplier), BHS and Woolworths offer competing products. In some locations, smaller luxury chocolate retailers such as Paul A. Young and Leonidas would be considered to be competition. The company describe their market position as mass premium, operating between the premium luxury and mass mainstream levels.

The products and services provided through Thorntons' shops are developed to achieve differentiation. Product quality is based on unique product recipes and the use of high-quality materials (the company's Champagne Truffle contains Moët et Chandon). The retail outlets offer the opportunity for self-selection of an assortment of chocolates and the personalization of products (for example through messages written in icing on the company's 2 million Easter eggs sold each year). The design and layout of the shops were developed by an in-house team, with the use of an outside consultant. The appearance of the shops is changed as often as every two weeks, with the changes developed and evaluated in the company's two mock shops, prior to their high-street introduction. The company's in-house delivery fleet serves the outlets through a 48-hour order delivery cycle. Although Thorntons have considered outsourcing their physical distribution, the in-house service was retained due to considerations that included the fragility of some of the products, the difficulties of access to city-centre sites and issues concerning night delivery and shop security.

Thorntons described itself recently as a multi-channel business, with both retailing and manufacturing being important to that business. This is shown in the continued commitment to the in-house manufacture of its products. While the equipment for the company's manufacturing is generally available, the company has over time developed knowledge and routines that ▶

are particular to the organization and provide the required product characteristics. Packaging is an important part of the product, for the appearance and to maintain the product in good condition, and so is designed in-house. In contrast, the basic liquid chocolate is supplied by a larger manufacturer who is able to achieve larger economies of scale in what is capital-intensive commodity processing.

Thorntons has recently revamped the brand identity of both its products and its stores, and has renewed efforts to make own-brand supply to other retailers a significant part of the business. Selling through its own and other retailers in new international markets is central to the company's plans for the future. Thorntons' ownership of retail outlets provides market access and higher margins than those achieved by selling through other retailers; however, the costs of running stores have risen against stagnant sales and so those other retail partners are now seen as an important part of future expansion plans. The strategy of vertical integration provides a number of differentiating factors, helping to distance competition and limit the possibilities for other companies entering a part of the confectionery market that Thorntons has helped to develop. The company also gains benefit from multi-channel integration of activities and is able to access customer feedback to assist the processes of product and service innovation. The in-house manufacturing can be seen as determined by the characteristics of the product and the unique aspects of its associated technology (chocolate enrobing). The specific nature of the manufacturing technology greatly reduces the opportunity for outsourcing from a competitive supply market, and self-manufacture avoids the risk of dependence on outside suppliers.

Source: Jennings (2001), *Thorntons Annual Report and Accounts* (2013)

THE CONSUMER-LED APPROACH TO RETAILING

Although the vertical marketing system adequately models the way in which distribution as a marketing function has developed, it makes the assumption that marketing activity is shared between the channel members and that the final result is offered to the customer. This underplays the extent to which retailers and producers have become customer focused, and in many instances customer driven. The customer is not just the end result (they buy or they do not); the consumer is now an integrated member of the marketing channel. To determine how the customers buy, when they buy, what product combinations are purchased and how they respond to promotional offers is the type of challenge that the members of distribution channels are all looking to meet, and increasingly they are pooling their resources to do so. Information technology enables marketing organizations to build up a wealth of data about customers that can then be used to gear up distribution channels that bring maximum choice and satisfaction to the consumer, but at the same time utilize the resources of marketing channels' members in the most efficient way. This approach to retail distribution is called efficient consumer response (ECR) (Figure 1.4); it puts the consumer at the centre of all marketing activity and aligns all distribution channel members (or, in modern terminology, supply-chain members) around the challenge of maximum customer satisfaction (Fernie and Sparks, 2009, Hines, 2013).

Alignment within the supply chain relies on cooperation and collaboration between members. Manufacturers therefore cannot take the view that retailers are simply

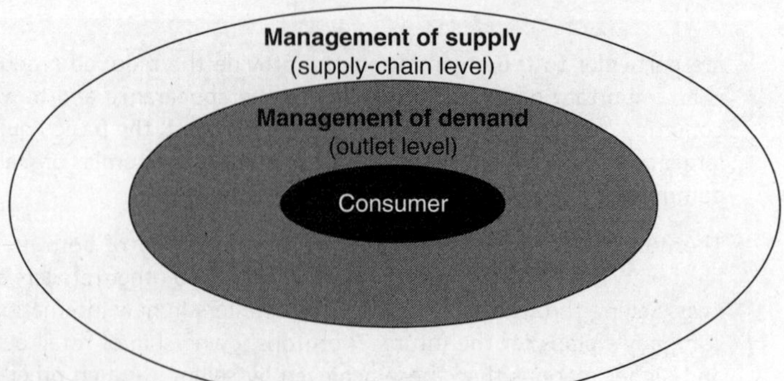

Figure 1.4 Efficient consumer response

intermediaries to distribute products; they have to accept them as powerful sellers, or agents for a group of consumers defined by, for example, an ability to purchase or a geographical location. It is in the producer's interest to develop a relationship with these 'consumer agents' that is one of an ally rather than of an adversary, in order to maximize sales opportunities with the final consumer.

The power of the Internet not only allows retailers, and, when in partnerships with them, suppliers, to gather and analyse information about individual customers' shopping activities, but it also allows retailers to see those customers as 'markets of one'. Theoretically, a retailer can customize product offers, promotions and prices to individual customers, should they wish to do so. Effectively encouraging customers to take part in a co-created shopping experience is a current challenge as well as an opportunity for many retailers.

THE RETAIL INDUSTRY – ITS CONTRIBUTION TO THE ECONOMY

As well as being a vital part of a marketing strategy, retailing activity can also be viewed as a significant contributor to the economy in general. In the last two decades of the twentieth century, the UK and many other countries saw their economies change from being manufacturing led to being service led, in terms of wealth creation, employment and investment. The retail sector in the UK for example accounts for 20 per cent of the country's gross domestic product (GDP) and is the largest private sector employer; around one-third of consumer expenditure takes place through retail outlets, with around 9 per cent of those being online retailers (British Retail Consortium, 2013).

Retail sales monitoring is often used as an indication of the general state of an economy; in the UK the Retail Sales Monitor (operated by the British Retail Consortium in collaboration with business analysts KPMG) collects data from retailers across a number of product categories to establish monthly growth rates and like-for-like comparisons. The Retail Sales Index (issued by the Government's Office for

National Statistics, ONS) measures monthly movement in the average weekly sales of 5,000 British retailers who are legally obliged to submit data. The ONS then releases a seasonally adjusted volume of overall retail sales and detailed information by type and size of retailer. The retail industry thus contributes to and provides a reliable indicator of the economic well-being of the country.

A GLOBAL VIEWPOINT

Retailing is increasingly a global business. A more structured retail industry with more multiple retailers (those with more than one outlet) is a sign that an economy is developing, as organizations specialize and gain economies of scale. Additionally, when disposable incomes rise, retailers play an active part in distributing increasingly discretionary goods to centres of population. Emerging markets are a significant (although highly complex) opportunity for experienced retailers, especially if they are faced with high levels of retail provision and therefore competition in their traditional markets. Brand saturation can also be a strong motivating force for overseas development. Online retailing can support expansion both domestically and internationally, and so evaluation of the optimum representation of a retail brand in terms of store numbers will increasingly require a global rather than domestic viewpoint.

As the artificial barriers to trade, such as import duty and quota restrictions, are removed from the global economy, many retailers view the world as their marketplace and make sourcing and outlet operation decisions on a set of criteria that are relevant across the globe. In the UK some of the strongest players in the market are non-domestic retailers, such as ASDA (owned by Wal-Mart), IKEA and Zara, and some UK-based retailers are having considerable success on a global basis, such as B&Q and Burberry. However, long distances and political and cultural complexities are huge challenges to retailers, which can only be overcome by the strongest contenders. International retailing activities have often stemmed from retailers seeing opportunities for formats that are under-represented in new markets, such as the entry by the 'hard discount' supermarket operators Aldi and Lidl into the UK in the early 1990s.

EMPLOYMENT IN THE RETAIL SECTOR

The retail sector provides a great diversity in the 2.9 million jobs (British Retail Consortium, 2009) that it provides to the UK workforce. Table 1.1 offers a selection of position titles that are frequently found within large retail organizations.

Although the wide variety of employment opportunities in retailing allows for a diverse application of skills and knowledge, the retail industry in the UK has traditionally found it hard to attract the best young people, and so in recent years initiatives have been launched in order to build stronger relationships between education, training and retailing. The National Skills Academy is a UK government-supported body whose vision is that of improved productivity in retail businesses and of their staff through training and development (see Vignette 6.1).

Table 1.1 Selected retail occupations

Store-based occupations	Central-office-based occupations	Combined central office/store-based
Store manager	Buyer	Retail operations manager
Department supervisor	Merchandiser	Visual retail manager
Sales associate	Distribution manager	Store development manager
Checkout operator	Human resource manager	
Visual merchandiser	Financial analyst	
	Product technologist	
	Public relations officer	
	Marketing manager	
	Brand manager	

A RETAILER'S POSITION IN SOCIETY

As well as making a significant contribution to the economy, the retailer has always had a very important place in our personal and social life. From a very early age, we are introduced to shopping environments, and they become familiar and comfortable places in which to spend time. As we get older, we use shops as reference points when learning about the world and its opportunities. We see some outlets as places we like to be at and others as places where we feel uncomfortable, whilst some others might be intimidating or places that we aspire to shop in one day. Retailers therefore play an important part in our own development and the way we formulate ideas about ourselves. Retail outlets have five distinctive roles in addition to the earlier-identified function as a breaker of bulk:

1. *Promotion and communication*. Shops introduce us to new products and remind us of old ones. Without shops, we would have to rely on other, often less suitable, media to discover what is on offer. The retail environment is where a plethora of marketing communications take place about a retailer's own and other brands.
2. *Advice and guidance*. Many shop staff are experts in their product ranges and routinely provide relatively unbiased advice and guidance on what best meets each consumer's specific requirements.
3. *Negotiating sales and forming contracts*. Shops take the risk in what they sell, and in what they may value for part exchange, thereby relieving those further back in the supply chain of many problems of quality, suitability, valuation and legality. For example, the shopkeeper decides whether the alcohol customer is over the required age for purchasing.
4. *Financial management*. Shops take or arrange for payment and accept risk of default. They arrange for the secure transfer of funds, including funding any bridging period, and judge which payment instrument provides the appropriate certainty of completion.
5. *Handling of warranty claims, and after-sales facilities*. Shops provide the local points of responsibility when anything goes wrong and an entry point into repair

and maintenance functions. Online and catalogue retailers provide the additional function of home delivery.

Store-based retailers also provide an arena for us to carry out our social activities. We may go shopping with a group of friends for clothes, or with a partner for home furnishings or with the family for a day out combined with a visit to the cinema. Alternatively we may go shopping alone, in the hope that we can talk to a product expert about a specialist purchase that we are interested in making. Commercially viable small shops have traditionally provided goods and services to local consumers, provided an outlet for local produce, provided local job opportunities and acted as the central hub of a community. Increasingly they are developing their businesses to fulfil the needs of a 'modern society' by providing services such as prepared food and drinks, online ordering and delivery, social information provision, utility payments, postal and money transfer services and so on.

Many retailers state that an important aspect of their business is that of contributing to society. Tesco, for example, may feel that by bringing a huge diversity of good-quality products from around the globe, in a clean and standardized shopping environment, they are making a valuable contribution to society, and, being market leaders in the grocery sector (in 2013), many consumers clearly agree. However, farmers' markets offer customers a different set of values, offering small producers a route to gain direct access to local customers. The unique and diverse range of high-quality produce can create a highly sociable, almost fanatical gathering of customers who care about the origins of their food. Retailers also make contributions to society in other ways. For example, Body Shop were leaders in the field when it came to what many women would feel to be 'enlightened' attitudes towards flexible working arrangements for parents, and B&Q have led the way in providing work to older employees. Retailers contribute to national and local charities, sponsor sporting events, teams and individuals and support educational initiatives, thereby building on the close association with the consumer in the community.

RETAIL INDUSTRY STRUCTURE AND TRENDS

A retail market is characterized by a number of factors that make it more or less attractive to new entrants. These factors are important for considering global market entry; however, here they will be used as the basis for a discussion on the structure of retail markets.

Retail provision and market saturation

Retail provision is generally considered to be the number of shops available per capita, within a measured geographic area. Where a retail market has a high level of retail provision, there are a great number of choices of retail outlets from which consumers can make their personal purchases. As the use of non-store retail outlets has grown, measuring retail provision purely on the number of shops in this way does not give a completely accurate picture. Nevertheless, in most product sectors, retail provision in the UK for example is generally considered to be high, with a large amount of retail space for every consumer. In fact some geographical areas are becoming over-provided with retail space, as the combination of economic downturn and increasing online purchasing reduces expenditure in stores, resulting in closure.

In a buoyant economy, a situation where high provision and saturation looms, markets tend to become highly competitive. Industry players are competing for market share and will use a host of price- and non-price-orientated methods to attract customers to their outlet. In essence, they all attempt to add value to the shopping process for the customer, and some of the ways in which retailers can add value over their competitors are listed as follows:

1. Offer prices that are at a level that is, overall, lower than that of competitors.
2. Offer really good bargains for specific products.
3. Offer a superior level of customer service.
4. Offer a more convenient shopping format.
5. Offer an interesting, congenial or exciting shopping environment.
6. Offer a more relevant range of products.
7. Allow customers more flexibility in the way they shop.
8. Provide a higher or more relevant level of corporate responsibility.

Competition within a retail market, in theory, should promote new ideas and innovative approaches to retailing, as competitors strive for better ways to capture the spend of consumers. However, there is a force within a mature market that can work against innovation, which is the result of organizations' success in the past, and that is the extent of concentration within the market.

Concentration

A market that is characterized by high levels of concentration is one where a small number of competitors share a very large percentage of the sales within a market. Although monopoly and oligopoly markets are highly concentrated, these types of markets are rarely found in their pure form in the retail industry. The most concentrated industry sector in the UK is the grocery sector, where the four companies Tesco, Sainsbury's, ASDA and Morrisons account for around three-quarters of sales in the sector. The clothing sector is overall less concentrated, but is still dominated by large organizations such as Marks and Spencer, Next and Debenhams.

Whilst industry concentration brings certain advantages to the consumer, such as expertise and economies of scale resulting in lower prices, it can also bring potential disadvantages including the erosion of market share of smaller retail organizations, the danger of price fixing between industry leaders, the domination of established retailers in the best shopping locations and the tendency for retailers to lack innovation.

Demise of the independent retailer

As large multiple retailers become more dominant in the industry, the small independent specialists are forced out of the market as they are unable to compete with the prices and assortments that the larger stores can offer. In particular, many independent retailers in small market towns and rural villages have closed when superstores have opened nearby. This not only has negative implications for the less mobile members of society who may rely on local shops for everyday goods and services, but it can also mean the loss of the central hub of a local community. In the clothing sector, the independent retailer has the potential to be more resistant, because they can offer more distinctive branded merchandise in a market where product differentiation is more important.

Price cartels

If there are only a small number of competitors in a market, there is a risk that these companies might enter into informal arrangements with each other to keep prices artificially high. Severe price competition is not in the interest of the industry players' ability to generate high levels of profits, and so they may agree that they will not undercut each other in order to promote a price war, which would result in everybody having to cut their profit margins.

Lack of innovation

Another problem with a concentrated and saturated retail market is that there is a lack of opportunity for new retailers to enter into the market. Shops are often run on leases for a number of years, or they may actually be freehold properties. This reduces the need to make highly productive use of the space, and there is a danger of complacency and the acceptance of lower than ideal standards of trading. Newer and more exciting retailers are therefore less able to obtain good locations in order to give their businesses an encouraging start. Many high streets in the UK have had the same collection of retailers for many years. Some of these could be criticized as being stale and lacking in innovation, yet by occupying the prime space they survive because customers have little alternative. Some of these well-established retailers have been given a real shock when new competition has finally broken into a retail centre or redevelopment programmes have generated new location alternatives. In particular, the clothing sector has been dominated by the likes of Marks and Spencer, Next and the Arcadia Group, which have tended to monopolize UK high streets. New entrants have had to fight their corner in secondary locations (a strategy employed by New Look in the early stages of development) or by taking sites in new shopping-centre developments. In June 2001 it was reported that having successfully broken into the UK market via the regional shopping-centre route, Spanish fashion retailer Zara was targeting prime city-centre locations in order to speed up awareness and acceptance of their retail brand (*Retail Week*, 2001). By 2013 Zara was trading from 75 stores in the UK, including 10 home furnishings stores (www.inditex.com, 2013).

The diversity of retailing

In spite of the lack of innovation in store retailing, the retail industry is a diverse one; successful retail businesses can range from the one-person specialist to the multinational thousand-plus outlet retailer. Even in concentrated sectors such as the food sector, dominated by huge and powerful organizations, an enthusiastic retail entrepreneur can exploit a gap when opportunities for new businesses arise (see Vignette 1.2). The awareness of the importance of retailing to smaller communities and the emergence of consumer support for initiatives like pop-up shops, local enterprises and community-owned shops will help smaller retail organizations resist the continued onslaught of the larger mass market retail operators.

VIGNETTE 1.2 GRAZE

Graze is the epitome of a modern-day retailer. It does not have shops, customers are co-creators of a customized product and the service delivery is convenience based, fast and inexpensive. The retail sector in which this retailer operates, however, is the most basic and traditional one – food. Based in West London, Graze compiles and delivers small boxes of healthy snacks by first-class post across the UK. The simple but attractive packaging is designed to fit neatly through letter boxes, and orders which have to be sent furthest from the factory are packed earliest in the day so that they have the best chance of arriving the next day. When it arrives, the graze box provides tasty combinations of snacking food in a laptop-style recyclable box, perfect for eating in front of the TV or while social networking.

What goes into the box is determined by a sophisticated artificial intelligence algorithm that controls the production and customization of every box using literally millions of combinations of ingredients. The company refers to this as Darwin (Decision Algorithm Rating What Ingredient's Next), which contributes to the production process as follows:

Step 1 – Preferences are recorded: On the graze.com website, customers select types of snacks to try – olives and rice crackers, perhaps. Darwin looks at how customer choices relate to their past orders and feedback ratings.

Step 2 – Snacks are chosen: To decide which four snacks make it into a box, Darwin studies stock levels, a customer's past orders and ratings, nutritional value, new test products and even the colour and texture of snacks to ensure variety.

Step 3 – Robots sort and pack: Off-the-shelf machinery is no good when you're sorting strawberries, so Graze designed its own robots which sort small amounts of fresh food very fast.

Step 4 – Food is boxed: Darwin instructs human pickers on which snacks go into a given box. If a picker's stock runs low, Darwin sends an alert to the devices worn on a replenisher's wrist that a refill is needed.

Step 5 – Boxes are mailed: Darwin does some of Royal Mail's postal sorting itself. For instance, a box going to Scotland from the London factory takes the longest, so Darwin makes sure those are packed first in the day for sending first class.

Step 6 – Feedback comes back: Once the graze box reaches its customer, the system solicits data: post-nibbling, the customer is asked to tell the Graze website – and thus Darwin – which snacks they liked. And the cycle goes on.

The company website puts this complex information processing into simple words for the customer:

What food can I get? We have a range of over one hundred tasty snacks (with healthy benefits), including nuts, dried fruit, dips, olives and seeds, as well as some well-deserved flapjacks, cakes, popcorn and natural treats.

How do I choose the contents of my box? We pick your snacks based on the ratings you select online. For each of our foods, you tell us whether you like, love or would like to try them. Rating only takes a few minutes and it's the best way to make sure you get boxes which are just right for you.

How do I order a box? Ordering is simple. You choose a box type and enter your delivery and payment details. Then all you have to do is sit back and wait to enjoy the food when it arrives, simple as that.

How do I cancel? There's no commitment ever – you can cancel your regular deliveries at any time online. However, because we prepare your boxes in advance, we just need you to give us a few days' notice.

Graze represents a food solution that responds to the social trend of grazing and snacking in place of formal meals. The sophisticated management information system allows customers to use their own preferences and experiences to determine subsequent offers, which are developed using high-quality 'postable' ingredients. The product is received conveniently using an established infrastructure and the price is low. Only time will tell what impact this retailer will have on pizza delivery companies.

Source: Lanxon (2012), graze.com (2013)

Internationalization

The continuing globalization of the world economy coupled with mature and saturated domestic markets for many mean that international activity has become one of the most frequently employed ways to develop retail business. Historically, retailing has been a small-scale, local activity; however, the professionally managed and large-scale multinational retail conglomerates that we see today are a relatively recent phenomenon. Internationalization of retailers in recent years has been facilitated by the Internet and better transportation systems, which have made reaching global markets very easy and the control of international operations relatively straightforward. Nevertheless, the sociocultural barriers can make international retailing surprisingly challenging.

Ethical and sustainable retailing

As in all aspects of business, retailers are facing an increasingly complex and tight legal framework in relation to environmental and social sustainability and they are gleaning from customers who are increasingly informed and ethically aware that it is not sufficient merely to comply with legal requirements, but that they should behave in a socially responsible manner. The growing ethical consumer market is providing niche retailers with an opportunity to provide added-value products for customers who will seek them out and pay a premium for them.

Online retailing

Without a doubt, the most important structural trend to affect the industry, probably ever, is the growth of online shopping. As suggested earlier, this can offer the opportunity for producers to sell directly to consumers, but the more significant impact is the rapid and enthusiastic adoption of shopping via a website. Disintermediation is the term that describes the bypassing of traditional intermediaries in a distribution channel (such as the wholesaler or retailer) to enable producers to sell directly to individual consumers; however, even though intermediaries may be removed from the distribution channels, their functions still need to be performed. A lack of infrastructure behind the website was often the downfall of e-retailers in the early days and is still a challenge for many retailers who are adopting a multi-channel strategy. As mature consumers become familiar, competent and finally institutionalized Internet users, and the digital native generation grows up, the convenience benefits of online shopping are now integrated into modern life styles (see Vignette 1.2). In the UK the negative impact of lower shopper footfall in some traditional high-street retail sectors such as book, music and home entertainment stores is very apparent with businesses failing and shops standing empty, while online retailers in these categories prosper. Wider and mobile access to the Internet means that customers use online retail outlets at various stages in the shopping process and the term 'omni-channel retailing' has been coined. From the retailer perspective, this term means maintaining a fully integrated offer, irrespective of how a customer accesses a retail brand, accepting that could be a combination of static online, mobile online, via social network or affiliate, physical single-brand store or a concession within a department store. From a customer perspective, this means receiving consistent benefits from a retail brand irrespective of how that brand is touched. The impact of the Internet on retailing is considered in depth in Chapter 17.

SUMMARY

Retailing is a vast and fast industry, making a significant economic contribution. It provides a diversity of size and character of business rarely encountered in other industry sectors. Retailers not only contribute to the general economies of nations, but they are also part of the fabric of society itself. In this chapter, the increasingly dominant role that the multi-channel retailer plays in the distribution of products to consumers has been explored. The major trends in retailing such as global expansion and online shopping have been introduced, along with a discussion on the resulting evolution in the general structure of the industry. The modern retail industry provides a challenging arena for dedicated and multi-skilled managers, providing both financial and personal rewards that are only limited by an individual's ambition. This introductory chapter has set the scene for further in-depth study of retailing, beginning with an overview of the various retail formats that constitute the industry in the following chapter.

QUESTIONS

1. Explain how a retailer, as a marketing intermediary, makes the distribution of goods from a producer to a consumer more efficient.
2. Retailing is not just an economic activity, but also one of significant social meaning. Discuss.
3. Explain what is meant by a vertical marketing system. Referring to Vignette 1.1 on Thorntons, identify the advantages and drawbacks of using vertically integrated marketing channels. Identify all the different routes to consumer markets that Thorntons use. Can you think of any other retailers who have successfully used vertical integration?
4. To what extent do you think that multi-outlet retailers have become too powerful? What are the negative aspects of a highly concentrated retail industry?
5. Look through some retail trade journals and find out the types of positions that retail companies are recruiting for. How do these titles compare to those given in Table 1.1?
6. Choose three retail sectors (such as grocery, clothing and DIY). Research and compare the levels of concentration within these sectors. Suggest reasons why there are differences.

REFERENCES AND FURTHER READING

Baker, M. J. (1998) *Macmillan Dictionary of Marketing and Advertising*, 3rd Edition (Basingstoke: Palgrave Macmillan).

British Retail Consortium (2013) 'Stats and Facts' section, available at http://www.brc.org.uk/brc_stats_and_facts.asp [accessed 1 September 2013].

Burt, S. L., Sparks, L. and Teller, C. (2010) 'Retailing in the United Kingdom – A Synopsis', *European Retail Research*, vol. 24, pp. 137–94

Clarke, I. (2000) 'Retail Power, Competition and Local Consumer Choice in the UK Grocery Sector', *European Journal of Marketing*, vol. 34, no. 7/8, pp 975–1002.

Davies, K. (1998) 'Applying Evolutionary Models to the Retail Sector', *International Review of Retail, Distribution and Consumer Research*, vol. 8, no. 2, pp. 165–81.

Dawson, J. (2000) 'Viewpoint: Retailer Power, Manufacturer Power, Competition and Some Questions of Economic Analysis', *International Journal of Retail and Distribution Management*, vol. 28, no. 1.

Fernie, J. and Sparks, L. (2009) *Logistics and Retail Management*, 3rd Edition (London: Kogan Page).

graze.com (2013) 'About Us' section, available at http://www.graze.com/uk/about [accessed 15 September 2013].

Hines, T. (2013) *Supply Chain Strategy*, 2nd Edition (Abingdon: Routledge).

Howe, W. S. (1998) 'Vertical Market Relations in the UK Grocery Trade: Analysis and Government Policy', *International Journal of Retail and Distribution Management*, vol. 26, no. 6, pp. 212–24.

Jennings, D. (2001) 'Thorntons: The Vertically Integrated Retailer, Questioning the Strategy', *International Journal of Retail and Distribution Management*, vol. 29, no. 4, pp. 176–87.

Lanxon, N. (2012) 'Graze Anatomy: The Tech behind Graze.com's Ultra-Customised Snacks Wired Magazine', June 2012, available at http://www.wired.co.uk/magazine/archive/2012/06/start/graze-anatomy [accessed 13 September 2013].

Nielsen (2013) *Retail Pocket Book* (NTC Publications: Henley-on-Thames).

Retail Week (2001), 'Editorial', 8 June.

Thorntons Annual Report and Accounts (2013), available at http://investors.thorntons.co.uk/download/pdf/Thorntons-plc-Annual-Report-and-Accounts-2013.pdf [accessed 15 September 2013].

Walters, D. (1979) 'Manufacturer/Retailer Relationships', *European Journal of Marketing*, vol. 13, no. 7, pp. 179–222.

Wrigley, N. and Lowe, M. (2010) 'The Globalization of Trade in Retail Services', OECD available at http://www.oecd.org/tad/services-trade/46329746.pdf [accessed 15 September 2013].

USEFUL WEBSITES

British Retail Consortium www.brc.org.uk

Local Foods Organisation www.localfoods.org.uk/

Centre for Retail Research www.retailresearch.org

National Skills Academy for Retail www.nsaforretail.com

Office for National Statistics www.ons.gov.uk

2 RETAIL ORGANIZATIONS AND FORMATS

LEARNING OBJECTIVES

- To understand the wide variation of retail organizations in terms of ownership, product orientation and format.
- To acquire knowledge of the characteristics of different retail formats, including both store-based and non-store-based types.
- To appreciate the importance of online retailing in a convenience-orientated consumer society.
- To be able to view large retail organizations from a multi-format perspective.
- To understand the need for retailers to evolve the formats they use in line with market opportunities.
- To appreciate the contribution of retail evolution theories to the understanding of historical retail development and their usefulness in the prediction of future retail developments.

INTRODUCTION

Retail organizations come in a whole variety of shapes, sizes and forms. Having defined the retailing process in the preceding chapter, the aim of this chapter is to present the diversity of the retail industry in terms of the variety of outlets used for retailing activity. Retail outlets can differ in terms of the ownership of the retail business itself, the characteristics of the premises used (the format) and the orientation of the product range. Some types of retailing have been with us for over a century, while new kinds of retail outlets emerge and develop, offering the consumer a constantly evolving choice of shopping modes that embrace a wide range of businesses. Many large retail organizations have evolved using alternative ownership structures, adopting physical and online formats and changing product orientations as part of their growth and development, and so an understanding of the scope of each of these aspects of a retailer is useful when gaining familiarity with the retail industry as a whole.

In spite of the well-documented growth of online shopping methods, store-based retailing is still the predominant section of the retail industry globally, and so this chapter, which is essentially a discussion of all types of retailers, will start by considering the different store-based retail types. It will provide definitions, descriptions and examples of a variety of store formats, including department stores, variety stores, supermarkets, warehouse stores and specialist stores. It will then discuss print-based retail offerings including mail-order catalogues and direct mail. The discussion will then move onto retailing methods that are based on technological applications, with online retailing itself now evolving into various formats. The concluding part of the chapter will consider the evolution of the retail industry as a whole.

RETAIL OWNERSHIP

One way of making a distinction between different types of retailers is by looking at the organization in terms of ownership and control. Most retail organizations can be placed into one of four categories: the independent retailer, the small multiple retailer, the large multiple retailer and the retail conglomerate.

The independent retailer

An independent retailer is a small-scale retail organization owned and managed by private individuals, with less than ten branch stores. Many independents are sole traders, or family-run businesses operating out of a single site. The store may offer a specialized product range, such as a butcher or a shoe store, or it may stock a wide variety of product items as in a village store. They can be located almost anywhere – from single sites to shopping centres – and although the majority of independent retailers operate out of physically small stores, that is not necessarily the case. For example, one of the largest stores in the trendy Meatpacking District of New York is Jeffrey (www.jeffreynewyork.com), one of two shops owned by Jeffrey Kalinsky, who was formally a shoe buyer for the upmarket chain Barneys. The store sells a wide range of designer clothing, but the centrepiece of the store is a magnificent shoe salon, which features both established and emerging designer shoe brands.

Independent retailers are often run by entrepreneurs who prefer to work for themselves and would feel stifled in a large corporation. However, small independent retailers are vulnerable in adverse trading conditions because they do not have the financial support of a large organization. At one time independent retailers accounted for the greatest section of retailers operating in any market sector in the UK; however, many have found it impossible to survive the continuous competitive onslaught of larger multiple retail growth. Defensive strategies, such as reoriented product ranges or niche marketing, have been the key to survival for many, covering product and markets that the large, dominant retailers are unable to serve.

The multiple retailer

Most 'high-street' or mall-based retailers fall into the category of the multiple retailer, which is the term applied to retail organizations that have a central operational headquarters and a collection of branch stores under common ownership. Most, although by no means all, multiple retailers are public limited companies (plc's) and are therefore owned by a collection of shareholders to whom the directors of the companies are responsible. Private multiple retailers are sometimes family-owned and -run businesses, and allow for a greater degree of personal operational control than in a publicly owned business. For example, River Island is one of the largest UK-based fashion multiple retailers in the UK, with 250 stores in Europe, the Middle East and the Far East, yet remains in private ownership. The size of a multiple retail business overall will be related to the number of branch stores and the size of those stores. A small multiple retailer is considered to be one which runs between 10 and 50 stores, after which it is termed a large retailer.

The multiple retailer is a term that can only really be applied to store-based retailers, or to the store side of the business, and therefore this term is beginning to lose relevance in the online retailing era. Online fashion retailer ASOS, for example, has proved to be a major competitor to established UK-based young fashion multiples such as Topshop and River Island. In some sectors, such as music and entertainment, the strength of the online retailer has totally changed the retail landscape. Nevertheless, the multiple retailer has been the success story of global retailing in the later part of the twentieth century, resulting in a concentrated industry in many countries that is dominated by large and powerful corporate entities. Another term that is often used for a multiple retailer is a 'chain store'.

Voluntary retail groups

One way in which independent retailers have been able to fight against the might of the multiple retailer is by becoming a member of a voluntary retail group. Such groups operate in a variety of ways, but the main objective is to gain some of the buying power advantages of multiple retailers by collating orders from a number of independent retailers and negotiating with suppliers through a central buying organization. Members pay a subscription that may also cover the provision of additional retail services such as marketing and training. Some voluntary groups have a strong brand identity brought about by the requirement of members to trade under a common fascia and to stock a range of own-label products. The so-called symbol groups, such as Spar and Londis, are examples of voluntary retail chains in the grocery sector. Other sector examples include Toymaster and Merchant Vintners.

The retail conglomerate

As retailers have become increasingly powerful corporations, there has been a growing amount of financial organizational activity in terms of mergers, takeovers, alliances and joint ventures. In many cases companies have been amalgamated under one retail brand, but in others separate brands or fascias have been retained with the holding company trading as a separate identity, giving rise to the retail conglomerate. Examples of these huge retail entities are given in Table 2.1.

Acquisition and joint venturing have underpinned much of the internationalization of retailing, such as the Wal-Mart takeover of ASDA in 1999 and more recently

Table 2.1 Retail conglomerates

Holding company	Trading companies (selected)
Carrefour	Carrefour, Carrefour Express, Arrefour Montagne, Promocash, Atacadao
Gap Inc	Gap, Banana Republic, Old Navy, Piperlime, Athleta, Intermix
Inditex	Zara, Bershka, Oysho, Massimo Dutti, Zara Home, Pull and Bear
Kingfisher	B&Q, Castorama, Brico Depot, Srewfix, Koctas
Kering (formally PPR – Pinault-Printempts-Redoute)	Gucci, Saint Laurent, Alexander McQueen, Stella McCartney, Sergio Rossi, Bottega Veneta, Christopher Kane, Puma, Volcan, Cobra, Electric, Tretom
Walmart	Walmart, ASDA, Sam's Club, Seiyu, Maxi Pali, Game

Source: Retailers' websites.

the acquisition of Fresh & Easy in the United States by Tesco. Often the customer is oblivious to the international ownership because the domestic brand fascia is retained or an acquisition is only partial in terms of share ownership. Joint ventures are used to combine the expertise of two retail partners, often a local business and an international one. A common type of joint venture is the franchise.

Franchising in retailing

Franchises are operated on the basis of an agreement between two separate business organizations. Normally one partner (the franchiser) provides a product and/or a retail format, whilst the other provides the means by which an outlet is run. The franchisee provides the human resources and the finance required for the premises, is responsible for the operations management of the outlet and pays a royalty to the central organization. The problem with this type of organization is that the issue of ownership and control is often the cause of disputes between the franchiser and franchisee. However, it provides a method by which retailers can expand a successful formula quickly without the need for high levels of investment, and it offers outlet managers more autonomy as they are essentially running their own business (Watson et al., 2005). Franchising has been used extensively by retailers to expand their coverage, both domestically and internationally. It has also been used successfully in the running of multiple food retailers such as McDonald's, Pizza Hut and Costa Coffee.

Cooperative retailers

The beginnings of cooperative retailing in the UK can be traced back to 1844, when a group of men known as the 'Rochdale Pioneers' began a trade in grocery produce based on the 'new' principles of fair prices for reliable-quality goods. A cooperative is managed on the basis that the customers of a business are also the owners of the business. Each customer is entitled to become a member of the cooperative society, thereby receiving the benefits of success via a dividend payout. Cooperative retailing in the UK reached its heyday between the world wars, when the cooperative movement accounted for 11 per cent of total retail sales and a quarter of the grocery trade (Olins, 1997), but the fragmented organizational structure prevented timely reactions to changes in the retail environment, and the cooperative retail movement began to be left behind in the face of strong competition. Following a major restructuring in 2000, the Co-operative Group subsequently took over Somerfield supermarket operations, which strengthened their position to become the fifth largest food retailer in the UK as well as the third largest pharmaceuticals chain and the biggest provider of funeral services (Co-operative Company Report, 2009). In Europe, cooperative retailers also emerge as leading players. In Switzerland, for example, the dominant retail concern, Migros, is run on the basis of a ten-region cooperative structure that includes hypermarkets, large and small supermarkets, department stores and specialist outlets in a number of non-food sectors.

One of the attractions of the cooperatively orientated organizational structure is that it can facilitate a more ethical approach to business, whereby stakeholders become shareholders. The John Lewis Partnership (JLP) in the UK is not owned by customers, but by its staff, who all benefit from bonuses paid from the profits of the organization. JLP owns 28 department stores and the quality-orientated supermarket chain Waitrose, as well as Greenbee, a direct services company and food production concerns. A recent move has been into a home-only specialist store.

RETAIL FORMATS

Many large retail organizations have grown using a particular retail format. Topshop, the well-known UK high-fashion specialist for example, grew using the multiple specialist format, focusing on stores on and in major town and city high streets and shopping centres, with a relatively early move into online retailing. The particular format used, to a certain extent, can be considered to be part of a successful strategy for that retailer, and by adopting a successful format and repeating it on a geographical spread, the retailer obtains economies of scale, efficiency and a strong identity. However, the opportunities for geographic expansion can become limited by available locations, and so diversity in formats used can provide alternative ways to reach customers. Next, also a well-known UK fashion specialist, has used a more diverse range of formats in its expansion, including out-of-town superstores and catalogue and online retailing. An understanding of the different retail formats used in retailing is helpful in understanding successful retail strategies.

Store-based formats

Even though stores are increasingly under threat from online retail developments, they are still responsible for the major part of the retail trade overall, and so the different types of stores will be discussed before other types of retail format.

Department stores

Department stores are the oldest form of large store. The format emerged in the early nineteenth century as a way of offering a collection of personal and home furnishings goods under one roof to the increasingly discriminating and affluent Victorian middle-class customers (Markham, 1998). They are still a powerful presence in today's retailing landscape, providing the focus for shopping centres around the world. A department store is a large store (at one time six or seven storeys were common, but newly built ones tend to be on two or three levels), which is split up into clearly defined areas or departments according to product category. Many department stores offer width and depth in the product range so that almost every shopping need can be met, but other department stores concentrate on fewer categories and aim to offer a great choice within those categories. Mintel (2009a) suggest the range in most department stores would cover clothing, lingerie, fashion accessories, footwear, beauty products and some home-related items. Table 2.2 contrasts a general approach to department store retailing as exemplified by the John Lewis Partnership, with a specialist approach taken by Harvey Nichols.

Department stores in principal cities around the world are not only retailers; they also act as tourist attractions and sources of entertainment. Table 2.3 lists some of the most famous and aspirational department stores around the world.

Department stores have been through something of a revival. In the 1980s many traditional stores found they were faced with stiff competition from increasingly sophisticated retail offerings from a growing list of specialist stores, particularly in fashion, their most important product classification. Many department stores were suffering from outdated shop fits and ineffective operations and systems that gave an old-fashioned image. During the late 1990s, leisure shopping and a fashion trend that favoured designer-branded goods helped the department store sector back onto its feet, and by the end of the decade a number of department stores had undergone regional expansion. Selfridges' second store for example, completed in 1999, provided the iconic anchor store for the revitalized Bull Ring Centre in Birmingham, UK.

Table 2.2 John Lewis and Harvey Nichols: product range comparison

Merchandise characteristic	John Lewis	Harvey Nichols
Price level	Medium	Premium
Fashion orientation	Contemporary	Directional
Own-brand orientation	Medium to high in most departments	Low
Product quality	High	High
Product categories	Diverse	Fashion-orientated
Depth of brand choice within category	Medium	Deep

Table 2.3 Department stores around the world

London	Harrods, Selfridges
Milan	Coin, La Rinascente
Paris	Galeries Lafayette, Printemps
New York	Bloomingdales, Saks Fifth Avenue
Shanghai	Pacific, Shanghai No. 1 Department Store
Tokyo	Seibu, Takashimaya

Many department stores act rather like mini-malls themselves by housing a selection of concessions, or 'shops within shops', where the retail space is leased and operated by a separate company brand. This allows the department store to cut down the risks associated with actually owning the stock, and provides the opportunity for a varied branded offer. However, it reduces control for the department store, in terms of both the nature of the stock, and the way service is carried out in those areas. Nevertheless, successful concessionary arrangements provide a healthy synergy where both parties benefit. The UK's national statistics office does not use the term department store, but categorizes this type of retailer under the term 'non-food dominant non-specialist stores'.

Variety stores

Variety stores emerged as a store concept at the turn of the twentieth century, when Woolworths, an American store chain, opened their first store in the UK. It is the format traditionally used by Marks and Spencer and Wal-Mart, and so is a tried and tested formula. Variety stores are so named because they offer a large variety of goods under one roof, traditionally including both food and non-food items. They are different to department stores in a number of ways as shown in Table 2.4. However, when describing large stores, the boundaries of definition are becoming increasingly blurred. Some variety stores like the larger Marks and Spencer stores are becoming very much like department stores, as increased space allows the width and depth of the product range to be expanded. In contrast, some department stores traded down as a survival strategy in the late 1980s and early 1990s, leading to the evolution of the 'discount department store'. This format combines the product and brand choice of the department store with the low-price orientation of the variety store, with service level and store environment lying somewhere in between. Some of the highly successful value retailers, such as Primark, also use this type of format, although the UK arm of the original variety store Woolworths went into administration in 2008, leaving the retail brand to trade online only.

Table 2.4 Contrasting department stores and variety stores

Department stores	Variety stores
Product Range Wide – Many product categories including clothing, furniture and home furnishings and food; depth in the product range including an extensive choice of manufacturer and designer-branded goods	Product Range Wide – can include clothing, furniture and home furnishings and food; high proportion of own-branded products; limited choice in some product categories
Store Environment Interior store design element and displays used extensively to define departments and provide interest; multi-level; high service level	Store Environment Basic, clearly laid out; usually over one or two floors; product displays are simple; predominantly self-service
Price Traditionally higher to reflect service level and product quality	Price Medium to low, value driven

Specialist stores
Although some department stores might be considered specialist stores because of the restricted product range (for example Harvey Nichols), most specialist retail outlets are smaller, in line with the size of the product range offered. The majority of stores found in shopping centres or central retail areas are specialist stores due to the distinguishing feature of one product area dominating the retail offer (see Table 2.5). However, a retailer that targets a specifically defined customer market segment can also be described as a specialist. Anything Left-Handed traded from a small shop in the centre of London for nearly 40 years, but in 2006 the retailer moved online (www.anythinglefthanded.co.uk), a format that many other specialist retailers have found ideal.

Again, examples of successful retailers that do not fit neatly into the defined terms can be found. Planet Organic is a London small supermarket that only stocks organic foods, so this retailer crosses the boundary between a specialist store and a supermarket. Mamas & Papas is a specialist retailer of nursery products and children's clothing, with a shopping environment that is reminiscent of a small department store. Specialist retailers are not restricted to the selling of products; many speciality outlets offer service products to consumers. Examples include fast-food outlets, cafes and restaurants, banks and building societies, repair centres and dry cleaners and hair salons, nail bars and beauty salons. In terms of brand orientation, specialist retailers span the spectrum, from own-brand fascias such as Zara (international clothing specialist) to multi-brand specialists such as Lane Crawford (China-based luxury brand retailer).

The term category specialist or category killer describes the large specialist retailer that is typically found in an out-of-town or edge-of-town retail park or site. The product range is geared to a restricted merchandise area, but the large size of store allows a very extensive selection within that classification. Comet, IKEA, B&Q, PetSmart and Staples are all examples of this type of retailer. The stores are usually based on a one-level format, and the economies of scale and inexpensive locations allow a value-driven price offer. Many of the stores offer goods that satisfy complex needs (for example a home entertainment system or a carpet), and therefore specialist help is usually available on request, but the service orientation is low key (in comparison to a department store for example).

Convenience stores (C-stores)
The general concept associated with convenience stores is that they are used for 'top-up' shopping, as opposed to a full-scale replenishment shop that would be done at a large store with a wide selection. Convenience stores offer a shallow assortment,

Table 2.5 Examples of specialist stores

Retailer	Sector	Target market
Evans	Clothing	Larger women
Rymans	Stationary	Wide market
Phones 4 U	Mobile communications	Wide market
Blacks	Outdoor clothing and equipment	Active and outdoor enthusiasts

with little brand choice within more categories, but as wide a product range as space will allow. Normally the range would include basic grocery and drink products, confectionery, tobacco and newspapers (CTN) and over-the-counter (OTC) medicines. In order to comply with the suggested concept, a convenience store should have long opening hours. In the UK, stores above 3,000 square feet cannot trade all day on Sunday, so convenience stores are smaller than this threshold. C-stores also need to be easily accessed by customers on foot or by car and may be located on a petrol station forecourt. The convenience store concept has been the saviour of many small retail businesses that saw their trade taken away by large grocery-orientated multi-outlet retailers. By adapting to provide an emergency, impulse purchase and top-up service, many small retailers have found they can make a living with a product range that is reoriented towards convenience or local catchment preferences (including ethnic foods). More recently, however, large UK grocery chains have become active in this sector with dedicated format brands for this type of location: Tesco Express and Sainsbury's Local for example.

Supermarkets, superstores and hypermarkets

Supermarkets, a store concept imported from the United States in the middle of the twentieth century, have been a highly successful retail format. The real advantage that the supermarket offered the customer was self-service, and therefore a much faster method of shopping. Instead of requesting products over a counter, the supermarket allowed the customer to get involved with the product prior to purchase. The ability to peruse the product offering, try new products and impulse purchase appealed to the increasingly affluent post-war customer. In addition, the space and labour-saving factors allowed retailers to offer a wider choice of products at lower prices. The supermarket was therefore quickly adopted as the principal method for acquiring 'everyday goods'. Supermarkets now dominate the retail industry; they have grown into superstores, offering more and more products, adapting to lifestyle changes to provide the most convenient method of shopping for the majority of household goods for the majority of households.

Supermarkets, superstores and hypermarkets can be considered in the same 'family' of retail format, in that the stores are self-service, usually on one level and laid out in a functional grid pattern of aisles and shelving. Supermarkets are the smaller variant, usually located in a town centre or neighbourhood location, with a product range that concentrates on food and household consumables. Superstores would typically be between 3,000 and 5,000 square metres are usually in an edge- or out-of-town location and have an extended product range (featuring non-food product categories such as clothing, home furnishing and home entertainment goods). A hypermarket is a huge retail outlet in an out-of-town location, which offers an extensive range of products with the proportion of non-food items being greater than in a superstore (a hypermarket is typically 60 per cent non-food). Car tyres, bicycles and garden furniture are the kind of product categories that are included in a hypermarket range. Due to planning restrictions, this format is found less frequently in the UK than in the rest of Europe; Tesco Extra and Carrefour are examples. Most of the largest retail companies in the world have their roots in supermarket or hypermarket operations as shown in Table 2.1.

Warehouse clubs

A warehouse club is a retail outlet that stocks a limited range of grocery and household products, some home-orientated goods and some clothing products (usually 3,000–4,000 product lines). The distinguishing feature of a warehouse club is that you have to become a member to shop there. Prices are low, and the store environment is extremely basic. Most warehouse clubs operate in a similar way to a cash-and-carry outlet in that the goods have to purchased in larger quantities, but some (for example Costco) allow customers to purchase smaller quantities of some lines.

Catalogue shops

The best-known example of a catalogue shop (sometimes referred to as catalogue showrooms) in the UK is Argos. These are the store-based outlets for the product ranges of home shopping retailers. Very little product is displayed in the outlet in comparison to the range as a whole, but the catalogues are available for customers to browse through if they wish to. Having specified the product and made a payment, the customer waits for a short time while the product is retrieved from a stockroom attached to the 'showroom' or store front. If the customer wishes, they can arrange for the product to be delivered to their home. In today's era of flexible shopping methods, the catalogue shop is a cost-effective way of providing a 'high-street' outlet. The format, however, introduces some problems in terms of product interaction and display, because of the reliance on the catalogue for representation rather than 'real' products.

Discount stores

Defining a discount store is not an easy task, because the key characteristic is the price of the merchandise, which is subject to individual customer perceptions. However, there has been a thriving interest in the 'discounter' approach to retailing, fuelled by its popularity in the United States and its popularity as a concept with those of lower disposable income. A discount store is a retailer that sells merchandise at a price level that is lower than 'typical high-street stores'. A discounter uses an everyday low-pricing policy, where prices remain constantly low, rather than a high–low pricing policy (see Chapter 13), wherein prices only drop at promotion times. Discount stores are sometimes run on the basis of a product range geared by opportunistic buys by the retailer, or they have planned ranges, sold with an unusually low profit margin. Discount stores can be small in terms of outlet size, such as Poundstretcher, or they may be large departmental stores, like TK Maxx, whilst some of the best-known discounters are supermarkets, for example Aldi, Netto and Lidl. Discount stores can be extremely minimal in terms of store environment and service, but a synthesis of the discounter and the specialist chain store has emerged in the form of the value retailer, who combines carefully planned product ranges, good service and store layout with an everyday low-pricing policy. The success of Primark in the UK clothing sector, where one-third of the population bought clothes in 2008 (Mintel, 2009c), is based on this formula.

Factory outlets

A close relative of the discount store is the factory outlet. Factory outlet retailers offer customers a range of seconds-quality and/or previous season's stock. It gives manufacturers and retailers an opportunity to sell off unwanted merchandise without damaging the image of the main product or retail brand, and allows accessibility to customers who might not normally be able to afford the brands, or who are motivated by bargains. Factory outlets may be single-site retailers, or they may be located within a factory outlet centre or 'village'.

Charity shops
Charity shops are usually run on the basis of selling stock that has been donated, although some also trade new products, for example Oxfam's 'ethical collection', a wide range of ethically sourced products. Charity shops are often located in the 'quieter' areas of major cities or towns, or in smaller town or local precincts. The charity retail sector has grown considerably in the UK, with a more 'professional' approach to organization and outlet operation (Broadridge and Parsons, 2003). The trend for more individualistic and ethical fashion has helped to make the charity shop a desirable shopping destination and has spawned a new kind of second-hand clothing retailer, the 'vintage fashion specialist'.

Flagship stores
Although there is no accepted definition of the term, the concept of a flagship store is one that all multiple retailers will be familiar with. The flagship of a retail chain is normally found in a prestigious, high-footfall location, and it is viewed as the pinnacle of the store portfolio. Flagship stores are likely to be large, are refurbished according to the latest store design concepts and house a full or 'top-end' product range. Many flagship stores can be found in international city centres like London, Paris, New York, Tokyo and Shanghai, or within large regional shopping centres, where the strategic reinforcement of the retailer's brand is as important as the financial performance of the store. The maintenance of a flagship store in a high-profile site may need to be viewed as an investment that the rest of the retail chain (including multi-channel outlets) pays for. Flagship stores perform a public relations function, providing a convenient location for trade and popular press to view new store concepts and product ranges, which is especially important for retailers who are changing strategic direction. A flagship store is also a vital part of a retailer's international strategy as it acts as a reference for further stores and a statement of confidence in a new market. Flagship stores are not restricted to fashion retailers; supermarkets, variety stores and category specialists also use 'model' stores to introduce new design concepts, demonstrate new visual merchandising plans and trial new product lines. Neither are flagship stores restricted to companies that are classified as retailers; many manufacturers use retail flagships to raise the profile of their brands, NikeTown (in London, New York and Chicago) being perhaps one of the best well-known examples.

Pop-up stores
Pop-up stores are retail outlets that run on a short lease for a retail property, 'popping up' to trade for a short period and then disappearing once the lease has finished. Pop-up stores are often run by opportunistic traders, who are able to negotiate a favourable short-term rent deal. They are also used by fashion brands as part of a 'guerrilla marketing' strategy that provides a limited time for brand followers to purchase limited edition or discounted ranges in a surprising or unique shopping setting (see Vignette 2.1).

VIGNETTE 2.1 POP-UP SHOPS

The term 'pop-up shop' is used variously to describe a whole range of retail outlets that are temporary in nature, and as such a pop-up shop can be an opportunistic seller of seasonal merchandise that 'squats' on a short-term lease in an empty retail outlet. However, the idea of the pop-up shop has become a more established part of the retail marketing mix and is often used far more strategically. For example in 2006 UNIQLO used shipping containers to bring its fast-fashion formula to an increased number of worldwide locations, and Kate Spade used an open-house concept in a temporary outlet as a first move into the UK.

A recession can provide opportunities for retailers to pop up into retail space left by failed businesses; however, not all such space is desirable, and pop-ups are often used to test brands in new markets and bring full ranges of merchandise to customers who may not have easy access to them. Doc Martens, the iconic footwear brand, for example, opened a temporary outlet in Spitalfields, which is a popular shopping destination for trendy young Londoners. Previously the company had opened an expensively fitted-out brand flagship in a large store in Covent Garden, London, which had not been successful, so this outlet used a minimalist design concept using wooden palettes and concrete and inexpensive fluorescent yellow Perspex, which was more in keeping with the tough personality of the Doc Martens boot, and cost-effective for the short time frame of the lease.

BOXPARK in nearby Shoreditch, London, refers to itself as a 'pop-up mall', being a multi-level complex of shipping containers which are sitting on vacant land, which will be developed sometime in the future. Meanwhile an interesting collection of lifestyle brands have moved in, with cafes and an art gallery alongside.

Boxpark pop-up mall

Urbanears

Often designed to attract media interest for a brand, pop-up stores tend to be quirky and have surprise features, which appeal to today's shoppers, who seem to have short attention spans and respond to fast-moving visual stimuli.

Source: Ryan (2009), Trendwatching (2009)

Non-store formats

The opportunities for consumers to purchase products using a shopping method that does not include a store at all have increased dramatically in recent years. In particular, growth has been significant through Internet retailing, but direct mail retailing also helped to pave the way towards higher levels of convenience and flexibility in the shopping process. Mobile Internet shopping is in the adoption stage, so that restrictions of when and where to shop are disappearing. It is also becoming apparent that consumers are not only shifting to new formats, but they are combining these with established ones to become truly multi-channel, or 'cross-channel' shoppers. The main benefits and drawbacks of store and online shopping are summarized in Table 2.6. Although online retailing has become the dominant force in non-store retailing and as such will account for the major part of the discussion in this section, some of its forebears in home shopping remain important formats for some retailers and so will be briefly introduced.

Table 2.6 Store shopping and home/mobile shopping comparison, from a consumer perspective

Store shopping	Home/mobile shopping
Advantages • Goods can be touched and tried out • A leisure activity or diversion • Store environments are more interesting, entertaining and stimulating • More opportunity to combine with other social activities, such as eating out • Ability to interact with knowledgeable sales consultants • Acquisition of product is instantaneous	Advantages • Can be performed anytime, and with mobile anywhere • More comfortable and less physically demanding shopping process • Increased privacy • Prices easily compared
Disadvantages • Can be crowded, with time consuming payment processes • Lack of privacy, for example in changing rooms • Parking charges and transport costs • Physically demanding	Disadvantages • Social interaction less likely although virtual social shopping and party plan make this possible • Requirement to return unwanted products • Delivery charges and time lag • Lacks opportunity to consult sales personnel although customer service phone lines can overcome this

Mail order

Mail-order retailers rely on printed media as the basis for their format. Catalogues are sent to consumers, who order from the catalogue either by telephone, by post or online. Alternatively, catalogues may be sent speculatively to consumers who appear on databases that have been sold or exchanged by third-party organizations. In agency mail order, the consumer is offered the chance to order on behalf of friends and family, and to obtain a commission on those sales, but increasingly catalogues are issued on a direct basis, whereby customers simply order for themselves and their families. In Europe there are a small number of large players who dominate the generally shrinking general catalogue retail sector, for example Shop Direct Group, Freemans Grattan/Otto and La Redoute. The rest of the mail-order sector is made up of an increasingly wide variety of specialist retailers who issue smaller catalogues to consumers via the postal system, or as enclosures with other publications. At one time catalogue retailers might have had a website to back up their offer whereas now the catalogue is more likely to be viewed as an alternative way of communicating a product offer that is ordered online. Mail order also includes printed media-based advertisements that rely on consumer response for the transaction to be completed.

Direct selling

Direct selling is the term used to describe person-to-person proactive offers from producers to consumers, and may take the form of direct mailing (to individual consumers), telesales and personal retailing. It would also include any approaches made to individual consumers via e-mail. Direct mail has become a commonly used part of a direct marketing strategy that builds on one-to-one relationships between goods and service sellers and their database-captured customers (see section on online retailing).

Personal retailing

Personal approaches are perhaps the oldest form of retailing, grounded in the activity of the 'peddlers' who travelled from house to house with their wares. Door-to-door selling is rarely seen nowadays, but more organized approaches to direct selling have emerged. The party-plan formula is one example of this type of retailing, used successfully by lingerie retailer Ann Summers. Another example is pyramid selling, used famously by Amway cleaning products, where sellers earn commission not only on sales, but also on the people they persuade to join the organization.

Technology-based retailing

Technological developments in the industry are often the basis of the most significant evolutionary developments in retailing, and over time have provided the means by which entirely new methods of shopping have been introduced. The popularity and sophistication of virtual retailing continue to grow; however, we start this discussion by looking at some of the earlier shopping formats that have been dependent on non-store technology.

Vending The oldest form of technology-based retailing is vending. Vending machines first appeared in the United States in the 1880s, selling gum to New York City travellers, and have since grown increasingly sophisticated as technology has improved. The UK market for products sold via automatic vending machines was estimated to be close to £2 billion by Key Note (2010), with items such as electronic accessories being added to the growing list of convenience products sold in this manner. In a 24-hour society, vending provides an opportunity for on-the-spot convenience and emergency retailing without the need to employ sales staff.

Telesales Another well-established method of retailing that is based on the application of technology is telesales, where product offerings are made by a personal telephone call from a seller to a consumer. Regarded by many as intrusive, telesales has a further, serious disadvantage of not being able to provide any product representation, and therefore its usefulness in many product categories is limited. However, the telephone is a common method of consumer response to non-store retail offerings, and so call centres can play a major part in many retail transactions and remain an important part of both inward and outbound communications between customers and retailers.

TV shopping The earliest form of shopping via television was by means of information provider networks such as Ceefax. This method of retailing suffered from the same product presentation drawback as telesales, but had some success for services retailing (travel, entertainment, insurance) when the product is intangible and information based and the price offer is variable. However, the Internet, with its combination of real-time information and high-quality images, made these more limited media redundant. TV shopping first developed by using the three-dimensional visual representation abilities of a screen image to provide dynamism to print-based retail offerings, first in the form of videos, and soon after in the form of a shopping channel,

QVC, which was launched in the United States in 1983. One of the difficulties of early programmed retail offerings was the need to provide the consumer with the opportunity to skip through unwanted product categories. However, interactive TV now allows this, and TV shopping can now be considered more like a 'live catalogue'. Although the more mainstream popularity of online shopping has meant that TV shopping has remained a specialist market, the opportunities to blur the lines between home computers and TVs in terms of technology hardware will mean that TV shopping will continue to evolve.

Online retailing When the first edition of this book was published, we described Internet shopping as a sophisticated and interactive medium, showing every sign of being accepted as a mainstream shopping mode by an increasingly computer-literate society. What is different as this new edition goes to press is that online retailing is now on the move. Once restricted to the personal computer, shopping is now possible via mobile networks and hand-held devices, so that anywhere, anytime shopping is now becoming mainstream.

Using the Internet to access information has been accepted as part of everyday life, and in the process of shopping it is useful to customers as a way of accumulating information about retailers' product and service offerings in a fast and convenient manner. As a way of accessing specialist retailers that might be geographically remote from consumers, the Internet provides a channel of discovery for the consumer, and a way of providing home shopping services for a wider market for the retailer. The Internet is an efficient home-shopping device, enabling time-poor or less mobile consumers to order and take delivery of routinely purchased items such as basic groceries and household items.

The online retail industry has not only burgeoned new and powerful retail players such as Amazon, ASOS and eBay, but a transactional website is fast becoming ubiquitous for retailers in all sectors. In the clothing industry, for example, where many commentators assumed online shopping would have a small impact because of the so-called need to touch and try on, small independent boutiques are finding that a transactional website is a way of increasing sales without incurring much additional cost. Highly specialized retailers in a diversity of sectors have been able to use Internet retailing to spread catchment areas infinitely, thus enabling a more viable business with or without stores to enhance reputation. The presence of well-established and trusted brands on the Web is generally acknowledged as one of its key growth drivers, however, and many retailers that have been slow to open an online store have been pleasantly surprised by positive results when they have done so.

The role of the 'store' is changing; in today's business world, retailing is an operation that brands engage with in many different ways, rather than retailers being business entities that operate in a prescribed way, and this is permeating through all retail activity. However, just like the plethora of 'bricks-and-mortar' retail formats, it is possible to devise a broad distinction to understand different approaches to virtual retailing.

Pure play

Retailers who only trade online fall into this category, although interestingly they are classified by the UK Office for National Statistics as mail-order companies. Once niche retailers in terms of both customer market and product range, the three online giants mentioned above (Amazon, ASOS and eBay) are demonstrating the ability to expand their product offerings to a customer base that grows in size and confidence, both in the shopping method and in the expertise of the retailer.

Multi-channel

These retailers trade online and through stores and/or catalogues. Catalogue retailers that supplement their offer with a transactional website remain in the mail-order classification, and unless a multi-channel retailer takes more than 50 per cent of sales via the website, they remain classified in their appropriate ONS category. This makes it very difficult to establish the exact contribution of Internet-based retail sales in the UK market; however, taking this uncertainty into consideration, Mintel (2010) estimate that online sales account for between 6 per cent and 7 per cent of all retail sales, although in some sectors (books, music and home entertainment for example) the percentage is much higher.

Irrespective of the way we access the e-retailer, consumers expect retail organizations to be able to offer flexibility in terms of information gathering to supplement pre-sales shopping, purchase transaction, taking delivery of the product or service and accessing after-sales care. By using a number of different retail formats, retail business are better able to allow consumers this flexibility, and be able to satisfy customers irrespective of their shopping behaviour preference.

Generalist and specialist retailers

Another way in which a retailer might be viewed, whether they are store or non-store based, is according to their degree of specialism. Many retailers, such as supermarkets, are considered to be generalists who supply a relatively wide range of products to satisfy a large number of consumer requirements. Other retailers offer a range of products that satisfy a particular or narrowly defined consumer need, and these are considered to be specialist retailers.

Specialist retailers, whether they are a clothing specialist such as River Island or a computer specialist such as Apple, offer the consumer a limited number of product categories. However, the depth of product variation within those categories is great. A generalist retailer offers a large number of categories of merchandise, but a relatively limited product variation or brand choice within each product type. A neighbourhood supermarket, for example, will have a product range which is wide enough to satisfy the majority of basic consumer needs, but does not have the space to offer the brand and product variation in terms of flavour, colour and size that a superstore can. Superstores, like department stores, offer both depth and width in their product range and so cannot be easily classified as generalists or specialists. A small number of retailers successfully trade with a narrow and shallow product assortment; travel kiosks illustrate this type of approach.

The product orientation of a retail outlet has traditionally been the basis upon which trade and industry statistics are reported, with the sectors listed in Table 2.7 being the most important in the UK.

The largest sector is the mixed retail (non-specialist) sector, into which many of the largest retail organizations fall. This is because many of the more successful retail

Table 2.7 UK retail industry structure

Non-specialised food retailers (e.g. supermarkets)	Textile, clothing and footwear retailers	Other specialised retailers including: Computers and software, telecommunications equipment, carpets, books, newspapers and stationery, sprting equipment, games and toys, flowers and gardening, pets and petfood, watches and jewellery second-hand goods
Specialist food stores (e.g. fruit and vegetables, meat, fish, bread	Household goods retailers, including hardware, electrical appliances, furniture, audio and music	
Alcoholic drink, other beverages and tobacco stores	Pharmaceutical, medical, cosmetic and toiletries retailers	
Non-store retailing which includes mail order houses and market stalls	Automotive fuel retailers	

Source: Based on ONS statistics published January 2012.

players have reached their dominant position by extending their product ranges into more and more categories. All of the following retailers are classified as non-specialist, and therefore could be seen to be taking a generalist approach to their product offerings: Marks and Spencer, Argos and WHSmith.

A difficulty with the generalist/specialist approach to retail classification is that some retailers specialize in part of their product range, but adopt a generalist approach to others. Boots, for example, specializes in pharmacy, healthcare and beauty products, but adopts a more generalist approach in household goods. Petrol forecourt retailers specialize in products for the motor vehicle, complemented by a range of general groceries.

Non-store retailers can also take a generalist or a specialist approach. For example, the Great Universal catalogue would be considered a generalist retailer, given the higher number of product categories covered, but Boden would be considered as a specialist retail business, because it offers a limited number of product categories to a more narrowly targeted audience in a small catalogue format.

Lifestyle retailers

The term lifestyle retailer is becoming more widely used for retailers whose product range is specialized by consumer preference and related need rather than by more traditional product categorization. It relates to the increasing use of VALs (Values, Attitudes and Lifestyle) variables used in consumer segmentation (see Chapter 3 customers). Cath Kidston and Flight 001 (see Vignette 4.2) are examples of lifestyle retailers.

THE EVOLUTION OF RETAILING

Like the products that are sold by retailers, the formats used for retailing evolve over time. A retailing concept that appeared revolutionary when first introduced may become dated within a couple of decades, and so retail businesses must constantly evolve their own portfolio of retail formats to reflect the changing requirements and aspirations of the shopping public, whilst responding to constraints imposed by the political and legal framework in which they operate.

The ways in which retailers evolve have been the subject of academic debate for over half of a century. Many of the academic references use the term 'retail institutions' to describe a type of retail outlet. However, it is easy to confuse the term retail institution with a large retail business (stores like Marks and Spencer are often referred to as institutions), and so the term format will continue to be used in this discussion. The evolutionary theories attempt to provide some predictive suggestions relating to the likely pattern of development of retailer types rather than specific retail companies.

Cyclical theories

Industry observers and retail academics have been captivated by the cyclical nature of retail change for some time. This has resulted in the proposition of three key theories of cyclical development.

The generalist–specialist tendency – the accordion theory

The accordion theory (Hollander, 1966) concerns itself with the tendency that the retail industry has to alternate between periods of growth in specialist retail formats, offering narrow product assortments, followed by periods of growth in generalist retailing, when a greater product variety is on offer within the format (Figure 2.1).

While many examples of retailers who have succeeded outside of this general pattern can be found, retailers may need to consider product range extension and specialization as part of a long-term strategic response to a changing competitive environment. For example, most of the first purely Internet retailers, such as Figleaves, ASOS and Amazon Books, were specialists. As Internet retailing became more widely adopted, these retailers became more general (Amazon for example now has 12 major departments, each of which has further sections; ASOS has moved into mainstream fashion and houses hundreds of brands in different levels of the clothing market; and Figleaves.com offers a large range of clothing, home and giftware alongside the original lingerie specialism). Only time will tell how the specialist–generalist pattern will emerge in the online era. Certainly, clearer navigation and the use of sub-sites have been necessary within retailers' websites to help the consumer find their way around the 'online department store'.

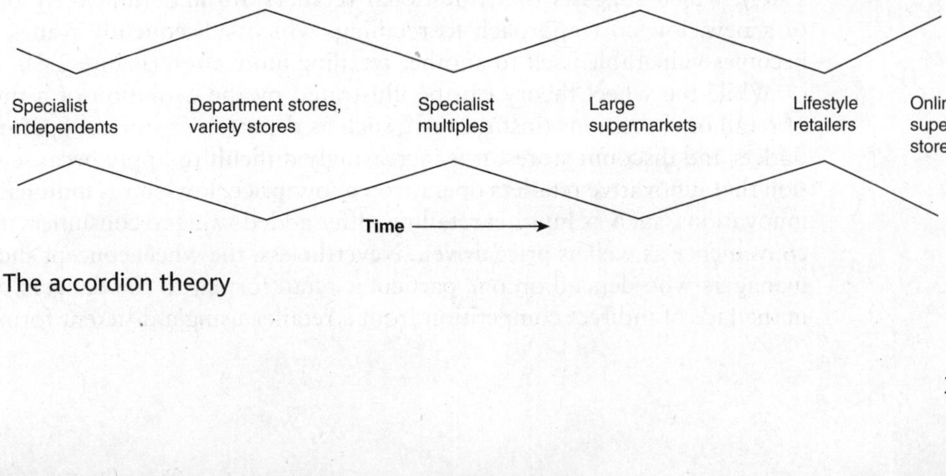

Figure 2.1 The accordion theory

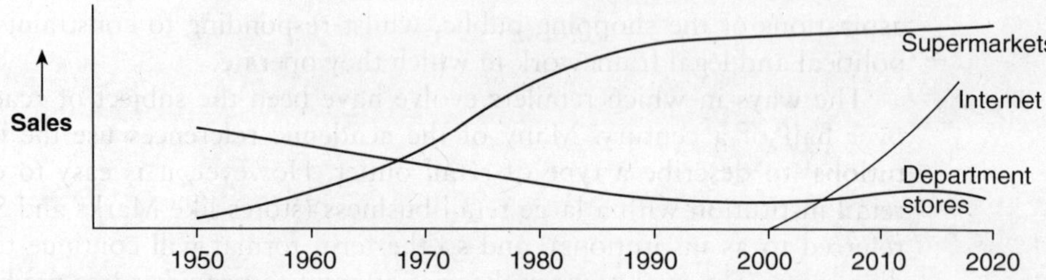

Figure 2.2 Retail life cycles

The retail life cycle

Like products, retail formats seem to have a life cycle that is influenced by fashion, technology and societal change, and that passes through introductory, growth, maturity and decline phases (Davidson et al., 1976) (Figure 2.2).

Introduction

- Mobile Internet shopping.

Growth

- PC Internet shopping (close to top).
- Lifestyle retailers.
- Pop-up stores.

Maturity

- Specialist catalogues.
- Department stores.
- Multiple specialists.
- Category specialists.

Decline

- Generalist catalogues.
- Independent specialists.
- Personal selling.

The wheel of retailing

In many cases the decline in popularity of an established retail format is triggered by entry into the retail market by an innovative method of retailing. This type of evolutionary development is explored in the theory of the wheel of retailing (Brown, 1987), which suggests that traditional retailers are undermined by the introduction of a new, low-cost approach to retailing, which subsequently trades up and finally becomes vulnerable itself to another retailing innovation (Figure 2.3).

While the wheel theory can be illustrated by the evolution of a number of types of retail organizations (institutions), such as department stores, supermarkets, factory outlets and discount stores, it is increasingly difficult to apply because of the assumption that innovative retailers operate on a low-price, low-status minimalist basis. Some innovations, such as Internet retailing, offer added value to consumers in ways that are convenience as well as price driven. Nevertheless, the wheel concept should alert retail managers who depend on one particular retail format to the dangers of vulnerability in the face of indirect competition from a retailer using a different format.

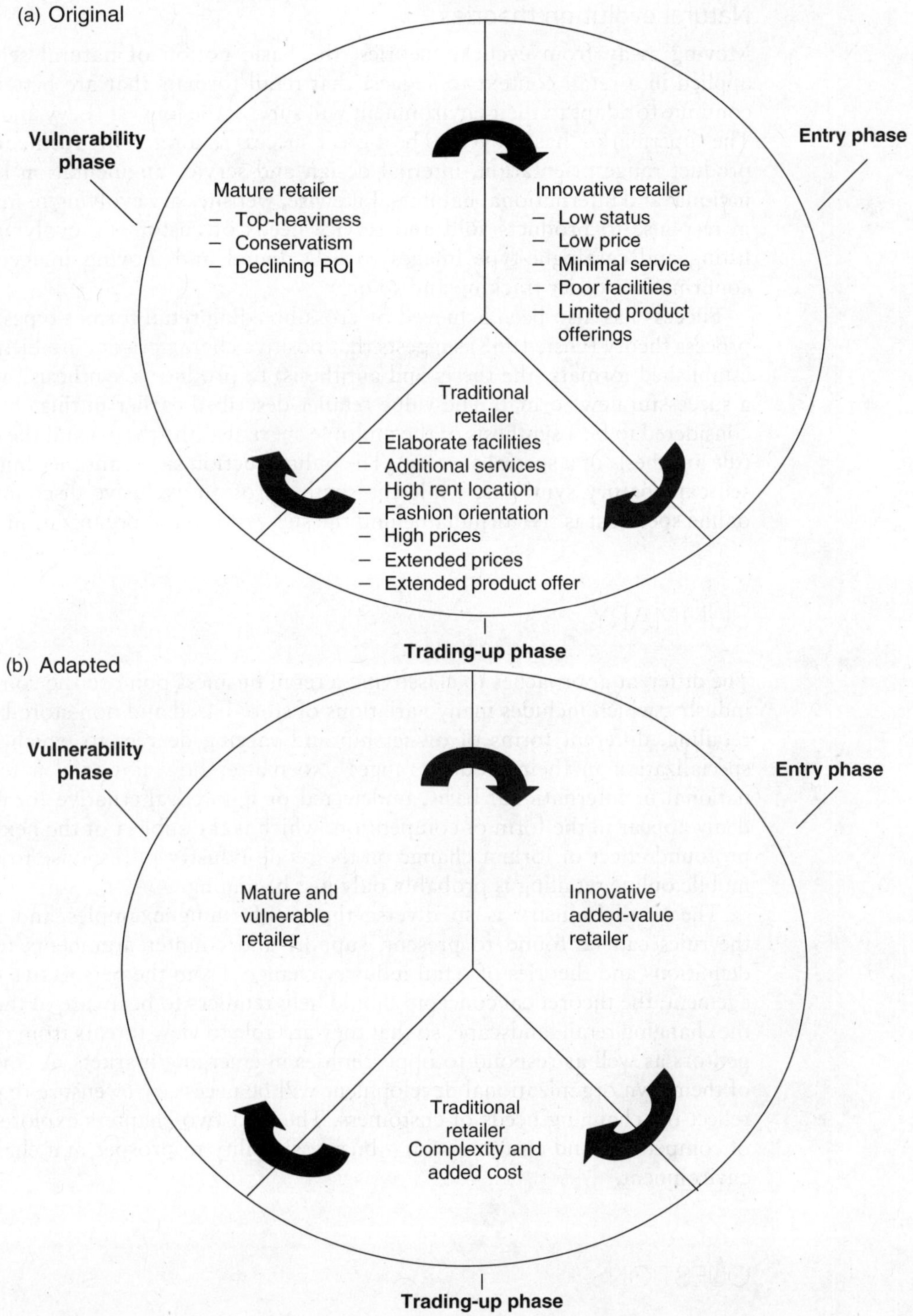

Figure 2.3 The wheel of retailing – original and adapted

Natural evolution theories

Moving away from cyclical theories, the basic notion of natural selection can be applied in a retail context to suggest that retail formats that are better adapted and continue to adapt to their environment will survive the longest (Levy and Weitz, 2001). The supermarket has proved to be a great success as a retail life form, adapted in size, product range orientation, internal design and service augmentation to a variety of national and international habitats. Likewise, websites are evolving in innovative ways in response to products sold and service needs of customers, evolving from online listing and catalogue-type images to 3-D digital and moving imagery, availability confirmation, order tracking and so on.

Success has also been achieved by cross-breeding retail format types. The dialectic process theory (Gist, 1968) suggests that positive characteristics are blended from two established formats (the thesis and antithesis) to produce a synthesis, which becomes a successful new format. The value retailer described earlier in this chapter could be considered to be a synthesis of the multiple specialist (the thesis) and the discount store (the antithesis of a specialist store). The online auction site is another hugely successful self-explanatory synthesis, while the synthesis of an exclusive discount club and an online specialist is the formula behind the successful retail organization vente-privee.

SUMMARY

The different approaches to classifying a retail business point to the complexity of the industry, which includes many variations of store-based and non-store-based forms of retailing, different forms of ownership and varying degrees to which retailers offer specialization in their product ranges. No matter how powerful a retailer is on a national or international basis, undetected or ignored alternative formats may suddenly appear in the form of competition, which is the subject of the next chapter. The profound effect of format change on the retail industry in response to the growth in mobile online retailing is probably only just beginning.

The retail industry is so diverse that conforming examples and exceptions to the rules can be found to present, support and counter arguments for established definitions and theories of retail industry change. From the perspective of retail management, the theoretical concepts should help retailers to be aware of their position in the changing retail landscape, so that they are able to view threats from emerging competitors as well as respond to opportunities in emerging markets. A continual review of their own organizational development will be necessary to ensure that adaptations reflect the changing needs of customers. The next two chapters explore the influence of competitors and customers on a business' ability to prosper in a challenging retail environment.

QUESTIONS

1. Classify the following retail organizations by means of ownership, product orientation and retail format:

Body Shop; Selfridges; Route One; Next; PC World; Waterstones; Boots Opticians; BHS; ASOS; White Stuff.

2. Discuss the reasons for the growth in online retailing. Suggest factors that may slow or halt the growth of online retailing.
3. Using a retail conglomerate or large retail group of your choice, discuss the various retail formats used by the different retail subsidiaries within the group, and the reasons for the format variation.
4. Attempt to predict the retail life cycle for a variety of retail formats over the next 20 years. Use a diagram to illustrate your answer and justify your predictions.
5. Referring to the dialectic theory, describe a retailer who is operating a synthesis of previously established retail formats to compete effectively in a competitive retail environment.

REFERENCES AND FURTHER READING

Broadridge, A. and Parsons, L. (2003) 'Still Serving the Community? The Professionalisation of the UK Charity Retail Sector', *International Journal of Retail & Distribution Management*, vol. 31, no. 8, pp. 418–27.

Brown, S. (1987) 'Institutional Change in Retailing: A Review and Synthesis', *European Journal of Marketing*, vol. 21, no, 6, pp. 5–36.

Davidson, W. R., Bates, A. D. and Bass, S. J. (1976) 'The Retail Life-Cycle', *Harvard Business Review*, vol. 54, no. 6, pp. 89–96.

Davies, K. (1998) 'Applying Evolutionary Models to the Retail Sector', *International Review of Retail, Distribution and Consumer Research*, vol. 8, no. 2, pp. 165–80.

Fernie, S. (1996) 'The Future for Factory Outlet Centres in the UK: The Impact of Changes in Planning Policy Guidance on the Growth of a New Retail Format', *International Journal of Retail and Distribution Management*, vol. 24, no. 6, pp. 11–21.

Gist, R. R. (1968) *Retailing: Concepts and Decisions* (New York: Wiley).

Hollander, S. C. (1966) 'Notes on the Retail Accordion', *Journal of Retailing*, vol. 42 (Summer), pp. 29–40.

Keh, H. T. and Park, S. Y. (1998) 'An Expanded Perspective on Power in Distribution Channels: Strategies and Implications', *International Review of Retail Distribution and Consumer Research*, vol. 8, no. 1. pp. 101–115

Kent T. and Brown R. (2009) *Flagship Marketing* (London: Routledge).

Key Note (2010) 'Automatic Vending Market Report 2010' http://www.keynote.co.uk/market-intelligence/view/product/2313/automatic-vending [accessed 25 August 2012].

Levy, M. and Weitz, B. A. (2001) *Retailing Management*, 4th Edition (New York: McGraw-Hill).

Markham, J. E. *The Future of Shopping* (Basingstoke: Palgrave Macmillan), http://academic.mintel.com/display/397473/

Mintel 2009 *Department Store Retailing January* http://academic.mintel.com/display/397473/ [accessed 25 September 2012]

Mintel (2010) *Clothing Retailing UK October* http://oxygen.mintel.com/display/479925/ [accessed 25 September 2012]

Morganosky, M. A. (1997) 'Retail Market Structure Change: Implications for Retailers and Consumers', *International Journal of Retail and Distribution Management*, vol. 25, no. 8, pp. 269–74.

Nielsen (2001) *Retail Pocket Book 2001* (Henley-on-Thames: NTC Publications).

Olins, R. (1997) 'Co-op at the Crossroads', *The Sunday Times*, 11 November.

Retail Intelligence (1999) Retail sans Frontiers: The Internationalization of European Retailing (London: Retail Intelligence).

Retail Intelligence (2000) *The Retail Rankings* (London: Retail Intelligence).

Ryan, J. (2009) 'Pop-Up Shops Are Here to Stay', *Drapers*, 12 December.

Trapp, R. (1995) 'Slot Machines That Pay Off', *Independent on Sunday*, 9 April.

Trendwatching.com (2009) http://www.trendwatching.com/trends/popup_retail.htm

Watson, A., Stanworth, J., Healeas, S., Purdy, D. and Stanworth, C. (2005). 'Retail Franchising: An Intellectual Capital Perspective', *Journal of Retailing and Consumer Services*, vol. 12, pp. 25–34.

SOURCES OF INFORMATION

www.riverisland.com

www.imrg.org IMRG Online Retail Association

www.brc.org British Retail Consortium

www, igd.com Institute of Grocery Distribution

www.bullring.co.uk Bullring Shopping Centre Information Site

www.ons.gov.uk Office for National Statistics

3 RETAILING AND THE COMPETITIVE ENVIRONMENT

LEARNING OBJECTIVES

- To understand the nature and dynamics of retail competition.
- To explore the various ways in which retail competition can be measured.
- To distinguish between different types of retail competition.
- To provide a framework for analysing retail competition at industry level.
- To understand the nature and role of strategic groups in retail competition.
- To appreciate the role of competition regulation in retailing.

INTRODUCTION

The way a retail firm operates, the demand for its products and the cost structures that it faces in the running of the business are all affected by the competitive behaviour of other retailers in the sector. It is therefore crucial that retailers understand their competitors and the competitive situation facing them. Retailing is increasingly characterized by intense competition. Evidence of this is provided, for instance, by the withdrawal of the American consumer electricals giant Best Buy from the UK market at the end of 2011, less than two years after first entering the UK. It is also mirrored in the fact that £5 billion (12 per cent) was wiped off the value of Tesco's shares when it issued a profit warning in January 2012, for the first time in over 20 years, that growth in its profits was going to be £450 million below expectations. The CEO of Tesco blamed the ferocious competition from its main rivals in the grocery sector. Competitive pressure was also the main reason behind the £3 billion takeover of Safeway by Morrisons in 2004; neither of the retailers by themselves was, at the time, large enough to compete with their larger rivals ASDA, Tesco and Sainsbury's in the grocery market.

The reasons for the intense competition include slow market growth and the increasingly mature nature of many retail sectors. Other reasons include the emergence of new retailing formats such as the Internet and changes in consumer expectations. Retailing competition has a number of unique features including intra-type and inter-type competition, the coexistence of large chains and small independents despite the increasing concentration and the importance of local competition.

With increasing internationalization of retailers, domestic competitors are not the only ones that retailers have to worry about. Whilst UK retailers are looking abroad for markets, foreign retailers have been entering UK markets. In the grocery market, the early 1990s saw the entry of European discounters Aldi, Netto and Lidl into the UK, and the end of the decade saw the entry of Wal-Mart via its acquisition of ASDA. Other significant entrants into the UK include IKEA and Toys 'R' Us. All of these retailers have taken a significant percentage of market share in their respective markets. In fact, since their arrival, IKEA and Toys 'R' Us have become market leaders in their respective markets in the UK. The entry of foreign retailers leads to intensification of competition in the sectors that they enter. Verdict, the retail research company, estimates that in 2009, 16 per cent of retail spend (that is £1 in every £6 spent in UK shops) went to international retailers operating in the UK. However, around half of that is accounted for by Wal-Mart's subsidiary ASDA.

The purpose of this chapter is to facilitate the analysis and understanding of the nature and dynamics of retail competition.

MEASURES OF RETAIL COMPETITION

A frequently used measure of the degree of competitiveness of a market is the degree of concentration in the market. Retail concentration can be measured in a number of ways, but the one that is used most often is the percentage of the total market that is controlled by the largest four to five retailers in a particular sector. An alternative measure of concentration is the Hirschman–Herfindahl index (HHI), which is the sum of the squares of the percentage market shares of all the competitors. The HHI ranges from approximately 0, depicting perfect competition (large number of firms, each with a miniscule market share), to 10,000, indicating a monopoly situation. This measure has the advantage of giving more weight to retailers with the highest market share. However, it has the disadvantage of being a little more difficult to interpret. The trend in most of the developed countries is one of increasing concentration or dominance of the market by a small number of players.

The increase in concentration, in the main, is a result of organic growth by the multiples, that is, by the addition of extra branches rather than by mergers and acquisitions. This is particularly true of food retailing, where rapid expansion of store numbers and size of stores in the 1980s and 1990s and mergers in the 2000s by the leading supermarket chains has led to a situation where the top five retailers have a market share of over 80 per cent (Table 3.1). More recently, the relatively slow growth of retail markets has also helped to increase the degree of concentration. For instance, grocery sales in the UK between 2000 and 2007 grew by around 3.0 per cent per annum, barely keeping up with the rate of inflation. However, between 2008 and 2012, the sales growth has only averaged around 1.1 per cent per annum. One of the main reasons for the slow growth is the fact that retailing expenditure is declining as a proportion of total income. In the UK the proportion of expenditure on retailing declined from an estimated 40.4 per cent in 1984 to 35.6 per cent in 1999 (Nielsen, 2001). As a result, both intra-type and inter-type competition has intensified in the retailing sector. More recently, the recession following the credit crunch of 2008 has further reduced growth in the sector and increased competition even further.

Table 3.1 Multiple grocers' market share, 2003–2011

Rank	Company	Market share %					
		2003	2005	2007	2009	2010	2011
1	Tesco	24.7	30.7	31.5	30.6	30.5	30.4
2	J Sainsbury	14.2	15.9	16.4	16.3	16.4	16.3
3	ASDA	13.3	16.4	16.7	16.5	17.6	17.4
4	Wm Morrison Group	13.1	11.7	11.4	11.5	11.8	11.9
5	Co-operative Group	3.2	–	–	–	5.8	6.8
6	Waitrose	2.5	3.7	3.9	3.8	4.1	4.3
7	Marks and Spencer	–	3.5	3.8	–	3.9	3.8
8	Aldi	–	1.3	1.5	–	3.0	3.3
9	Lidl	–	1.1	1.3	–	2.3	2.6
10	Iceland	1.5	–	1.8	–	1.8	1.9

Source: Various, including Competition Commission report (2008) and companies' annual reports.

A feature of retail concentration is that it tends to be much higher at the local than at the national level. This has led to some discussion of local monopolies, that is local retailing being dominated by one or two retailers. The variation in local competition can lead to different levels of intensity of competition, and hence retailers will tend to vary their competitive strategies depending on the local competition.

Whilst measures of retail concentration and market shares are good indicators of the intensity of competition, the data required for these measures are not always available. An alternative measure is the number of retail outlets of a particular type per thousand of population. The higher this ratio is, the higher the competitive intensity. When the ratio of stores to the population gets too high, the market is described as over-stored. That is, the size of the population is insufficient for all the stores to operate profitably, leading to intense competition as competing retailers try to improve their sales and profit performance. Conversely, if the ratio of stores to population is relatively small, the market is said be under-stored. In this situation there is unsatisfied demand and existing retailers will enjoy high profits. This leads to existing retailers expanding their operations and also attracts other retailers into the market. The above discussion assumes that all competing stores are of the same size. A more accurate measure is the total amount of retail space occupied by a particular type of retailer per thousand of population (or per head of population).

TYPES OF COMPETITION

In retailing, measures of concentration are usually likely to understate the level of competition faced by retailers because such measures usually only include direct competitors, that is intra-type competition. Intra-type competition is direct competition between similar types of retail formats or trading styles. The more similar the stores in terms of format, the more intense the competition. To reduce the impact of competition from similar retail formats, retailers must differentiate themselves from intra-type competitors. However, retailers also face inter-type competition.

Inter-type competition is competition between different types of retail formats selling the same type of merchandise. For instance, music retailers such as HMV face competition not only from other specialists but also from supermarkets such as Tesco and ASDA. Hence, when developing competitive strategies, retailers have to take into account inter-type competition as well as the direct competition from direct competitors.

Competition can also occur between different parts of the distribution channel. Vertical competition is competition between retailer and a producer, or a wholesaler selling products to the retailer's customers. For instance, if a retailer stocked a merchandise line that the producer was also offering through the Internet, the retailer and the producer would be engaging in vertical competition.

Another type of competitive strategy in retailing is corporate systems competition. This is where the manufacturing, distribution and retailing are controlled by single management. Examples include Thorntons and IKEA. Corporate systems can be formed by either backward or forward integration. Forward integration occurs where a manufacturer sets up its own distribution and retailing network, an example being Benetton, which began as a manufacturer and then set up company-owned retail outlets as well as an international franchise network. Backward integration involves retailers becoming involved in the distribution and manufacturing of products.

However, major retailers attempt to achieve the same control without total ownership of the systems. For instance, Marks and Spencer is famous for its control over its suppliers; they and other large retailers are able to achieve this control because the suppliers may have few (if any) alternative customers, and may be solely concerned with retailer-branded products. Another method of exercising control is by franchising parts of the system; for instance, the vast majority of car dealerships are operated as franchises by the major car manufacturers.

A FRAMEWORK FOR ANALYSING COMPETITION

A useful model for analysing the forces driving competition is Porter's (1980) five forces model of competitive structure. According to Porter, the forces that drive competition within an industry are threats of potential entrants, the threat of substitute products or services, the bargaining power of suppliers and the bargaining power of buyers (Figure 3.1). The different aspects of the model are discussed below.

The threat of new entrants

A major force driving competition within retailing is the threat of potential new entrants into the industry. The degree to which potential entrants find a particular sector of retailing attractive to enter depends upon the level of profitability of the sector and the barriers to entry. Generally speaking, the higher the profitability of a retail sector, the more attractive it is to potential entrants. Similarly, the lower the barriers to entry, the greater the likelihood of new entrants.

Assuming that there are sufficiently high levels of profits within a retail sector, the threat of new competitors entering the industry depends on the height of entry barriers to the industry including capital requirements, economies of scale, access to

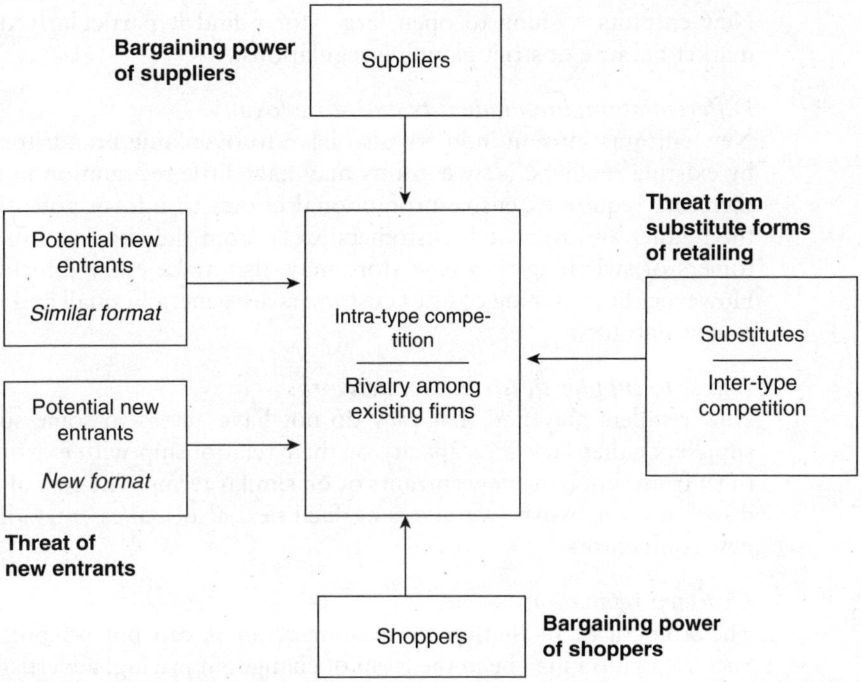

Figure 3.1 Forces driving retail competition

Source: Based on Porter (1980).

customers, access to suppliers or distribution networks, the degree of differentiation, brand identity and store loyalty and expected retaliation.

Capital requirements

The amount of capital required to enter into retailing is relatively small compared with other industries. For instance, the capital required to set up a bookshop is minimal compared with the cost of entering capital-intensive car manufacturing or aircraft manufacturing industries. However, to be competitive against national retailers requires far more capital. This is because greater investment will be required in stock, stores, promotion, IT and other management systems.

Economies of scale

The ability to achieve a reduction in costs through efficient large-scale operations can prevent the entry of new competitors. In retailing, major scale economies can arise in the areas of buying, distribution and promotion.

Access to customers or availability of sites

In order to get access to customers, the main problem for new entrants is to find suitable sites/locations for their stores. New entrants will normally find that the best sites are already occupied by existing retailers. It also takes time for new retailers to acquire suitable sites and open new stores, which gives existing retailers plenty of time to formulate their competitive strategies to combat the threat posed by new entrants.

New entrants wishing to open large stores find it particularly difficult to enter the market because of strict planning regulations.

Differentiation, brand identity and store loyalty

New entrants into an industry also have to overcome brand/store loyalty developed by existing retailers. New entrants may have little recognition in the market and will therefore require extensive promotional efforts to inform potential customers about the retailer and to switch customers away from the existing stores. The cost to customers of switching to a new store may also make entry difficult for new entrants. However, the switching costs of customers are generally small and not a major obstacle to new entrants.

Access to suppliers/distribution networks

New retailers may find that they do not have access to some suppliers because the suppliers either lack the capacity or their relationship with existing retailers prevents them from supplying new entrants or on similar terms. The cost of building an efficient distribution network (warehousing facilities) also makes entry difficult for potential new competitors.

Expected retaliation

The strength of retaliation by existing retailers can put off potential new entrants. Such retaliation may be in the form of changes in pricing, advertising and promotions, merchandising and service depending on the strength or perceived strength of the new entrant.

Figure 3.2 illustrates the fact that there are two types of potential entrant. One type uses a similar strategy and similar format to that already existing to enter a particular sector: for example, Wal-Mart's entry into the UK market via the acquisition of ASDA. Another type of entrant is one that uses a new type of retail format to enter the market. Examples include the German retailer Aldi, which entered the UK market using the hard discount format. New format entrants are potentially more difficult to deal with, as their basis of competition (or competitive advantage) is different from existing retailers. In the case of Aldi (and other hard discounters), for example, it is able to offer prices 20–30 per cent lower than those of large supermarkets on a limited number of lines.

Bargaining power of suppliers

The dominance of the majority of the retail sectors by large retailers has transformed the power relations between retailers and suppliers. In the past, big brand manufacturers could virtually dictate to retailers the shelf price, product range, shelving and promotion of products within stores. However, the abolition of resale price maintenance in 1964 in the UK loosened the grip of suppliers on pricing. The development of own brands and the increase in size of retailers (and their resulting concentration) have further eroded the power of suppliers. An indication of the power of retailers is that large supermarkets can nowadays demand slotting allowances (or fees) from suppliers for stocking their merchandise in the stores. In the grocery sector, where concentration is the highest, concern over the buying power of retailers led to referral to the Monopolies and Mergers Commission in 1977 on retailers' abilities to obtain discounts and other special terms. The commission eventually published its report in 1981, concluding that whilst larger retailers had been able to obtain discounts and special terms equivalent to around 7 per cent of sales, these practices were not against the public interest. The concern over retailer power has continued since, and further reports have been published by the Competition Commission, the most recent one in October 2008 (see Chapter 13).

The influence of suppliers on retailers depends on the relative size of the suppliers to the retailers. Some of the larger manufacturers such as Nestlé, Unilever, Procter & Gamble and Pedigree Petfoods have market shares far in excess of retailers in their respective markets and are in a position to negotiate terms of trade. These suppliers derive their power from the strengths of their brands and the loyalty of customers to them.

Smaller retailers, on the other hand, are particularly vulnerable to pressure. They can be forced by suppliers to carry products they do not particularly want in return for the right to sell the products that they do want from the suppliers. Suppliers may also apply pressure on retailers to sell products within an acceptable price range. Franchisees are particularly prone to such pressures because of the contractual basis of the franchise relationship.

Bargaining power of shoppers

Shoppers as individuals have little impact on retailers' competitive strategies. The main reason for this is the fact that shoppers' purchases are normally small in comparison to the retailer's total sales. Shoppers are also relatively immobile and uninformed: immobile in the sense that they are not willing (or unable) to travel long distances to find the right products, and less informed than retailers about product prices, availability and quality and so forth. However, the emergence of the Internet has reduced the mobility and information barriers to some extent, as customers can easily find product and price information online. This is further facilitated by price comparison websites such as Kelkoo and PriceRunner.

On the other hand, the relative smallness of shoppers' transactions means that the cost of switching from one retailer to another is also relatively small; hence, retailers can find that shoppers are quick to switch when more competitive offers are available from another retailer. Retailers also have to be careful not to exploit their advantage in the market too much as they are likely to see their activities regulated and circumscribed by legislation and regulatory authorities. The Competition Commission reports are examples of regulatory authorities responding to consumers' and suppliers' concerns.

Threat of substitutes

All retailers are likely to face some form of inter-type competition. For instance, the majority of clothes sales are through clothes specialists and variety stores (such as Next and Marks and Spencer). However, clothes are also sold through department stores and mail order. The Internet also now provides an alternative to virtually all forms of retailing. Most large clothing retailers now also have online presence in addition to online-only retailers such as ASOS.

Retailers can also face threats from outside of the retailing industry. For instance, eating out in restaurants competes directly with expenditure in grocery stores. The supermarkets have responded by providing increased quality and choice of convenience meals. Retail expenditure also competes with other forms of expenditure such as holidays and entertainment.

Intensity of rivalry

The intensity of the rivalry between retailers in a particular sector depends on a number of general market-related factors, and factors related to the firms competing in the market. For instance, slow market growth, high concentration, maturity of markets, low differentiation and high exit costs of leaving the market are likely to lead to intense competition between retailers. The relative balance between competing retailers and their competitive retail marketing strategies also influences the intensity of competition. For instance, competition is likely to be fiercer where there are a number of roughly similar-sized competitors pursuing a similar strategy.

STRATEGIC GROUPS

A group of stores (competing in similar ways) with similar target markets and similar marketing strategies is referred to as a strategic group. The aim of strategic group concept is to simplify analysis of competitive strategies and make predictions about competitive behaviour within and between strategic groups. For example, because of the relative homogeneity of the groups, members within them are affected similarly by changes in the environment.

The dimension(s) chosen to define strategic groups relate to shoppers' choice of store – price of goods, merchandise assortment (range), location of store, and service. The actual variables chosen depend on the retail sector concerned. In the clothing sector, for instance, quality, fashion orientation and selection could be used to identify strategic groups in the sector. These dimensions can then be used to map the competitors within the industry/sectoral competitive space (see Figure 3.2).

The intensity of competition between firms in different strategic groups depends on the 'distance' between the strategic groups in the competitive space. Competition between neighbouring groups is likely to be most intense as there is likely to be some overlap between their respective target markets. Conversely, competition is least intense between firms belonging to strategic groups furthest apart. Also, where a strategic group is placed between two other groups, it will face competition from both.

Although the strategic groups are relatively stable due to mobility barriers that limit the degree of movement between groups, they are constantly evolving because of rivalry and the emergence of new types of retailing. In fashion retailing for instance, mid-market retailers such as Marks and Spencer have lost market share both to specialists (such as Next and Gap) and the discount retailers such as Matalan, New Look and TK Maxx, as well as fast-fashion retailers such as Zara. Marks and Spencer has found

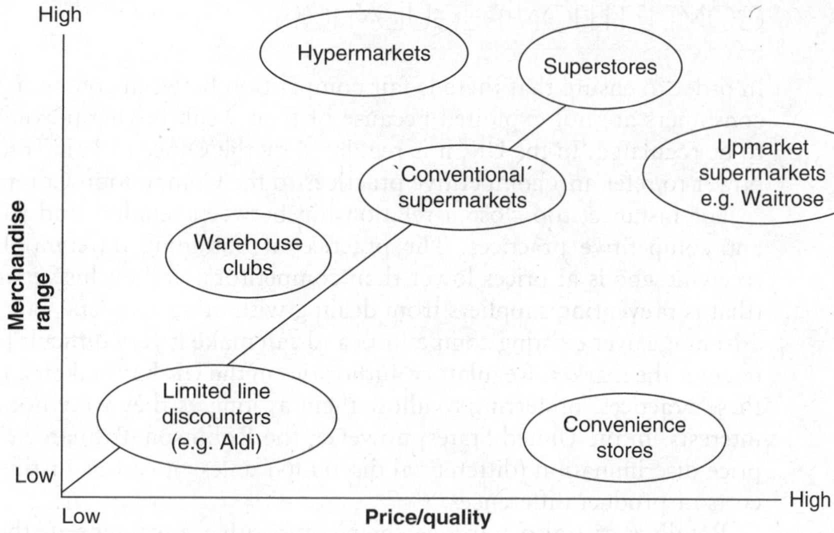

Figure 3.2 Strategic groups in the UK grocery market

it difficult to compete in these circumstances as its cost base is too high to compete with the discounters and its merchandise is not sufficiently fashion oriented to compete with the specialists. As a result, Marks and Spencer's market share declined from 14.0 per cent in 1997 to 11.3 per cent in 2000. Since then, it has lost further ground, with its market share down to 10.4 per cent in 2012 despite significant improvements to its supply chain.

Competition is most intense within a strategic group because members pursue similar strategies on the relevant competitive variables such as target markets, merchandise assortment, pricing, location and so forth. These similarities lead to consumers not being able to distinguish between retailers and making decisions based on price. For example, in petrol retailing, consumers cannot distinguish between the quality of petrol offered by different retailers and will therefore tend to purchase petrol from the cheapest retailer. Hence, where petrol stations are located near to each other, prices tend to be the same to prevent loss of business to the neighbouring retailer. Also, when prices are changed by one retailer, there is an immediate reaction from competing retailers.

In order to gain competitive advantage, therefore, retailers need to differentiate themselves from other members of the strategic group. The major methods of differentiation in retailing in addition to price are location, sales promotions, store atmospherics, merchandise assortment and service. However, once a store is built, the location of the store is fixed and can only be changed in the long term (see Vignette 3.1). As price is easily imitated and has direct impact on profitability, retailers are more likely to rely on merchandise assortment, promotions, store atmospherics and service to differentiate themselves from competitors. Nevertheless, discount retailers use price as their main differentiating feature.

COMPETITION REGULATION

In order to ensure that there is fair competition between competing retailers, and that consumers are not exploited because of their weak buying power, competition needs to be regulated. In the UK, it is regulated by the Office of Fair Trading, which has the power to refer anti-competitive practices to the Competition Commission for a ruling.

For instance, too close a relationship between retailers and suppliers can lead to anti-competitive practices. The practice of obtaining differential discounts (that is receiving goods at prices lower than competitors) and exclusive supply arrangements (that is preventing suppliers from dealing with other retailers) can give a retailer a big advantage over existing competitors and can make it very difficult for new competitors to enter the market. Regulatory authorities in the UK have taken a fairly lax attitude to these practices, preferring to allow them as long as they were not against consumers' interests. In the United States, however, the Robinson–Patman Act actually prohibits price discrimination (differential discounts) unless it can be justified by differences in costs or product differences.

Retailers can also improve their competitive advantage in the market by mergers or acquisition of competing retailers. For instance, ASDA's acquisition in 2010 of the 147 Netto stores allowed it to consolidate its second position behind Tesco's in the grocery market. Similarly, Tesco has built up its presence in the convenience market with an acquisition of 1,000 T&S stores, and more recently in 2010, it acquired 77 Mills Group's convenience stores based in North East England to increase its presence in that area. Acquisitions and mergers have the advantage of not only increasing market share, but also improving buying power and other economies of scale. Where a merger or acquisition is likely to significantly affect the competitive balance (or have a negative impact on consumer interest), the regulatory authorities can prevent such mergers or impose conditions on the merger before it can proceed.

VIGNETTE 3.1 MAJOR SUPERMARKETS TURN AGAINST SUPER-SIZED HYPERMARKETS AS INTERNET COMPETITION HEATS UP

Major supermarkets are switching strategy as customers begin to prefer online shopping over massive out-of-town hypermarkets. In January 2012, Tesco's Chief Executive, Phil Clarke, signalled that the days of the large hypermarkets were over. He questioned the need to build large hypermarkets when the Internet was taking so much of the market share in electricals, clothing and general merchandise. Tesco gained its position of market leader in the UK grocery market by opening ever-larger stores. That strategy began to be questioned when its profits fell in 2012, for first time in nearly 20 years.

As Internet shopping becomes increasingly popular, big hypermarkets (grocery stores with a sales area in excess of 60,000 sq. ft. and selling a substantial proportion of non-food merchandise) are beginning to look out of place in the grocery market. When customers can order online for delivery to their homes, or to collect at their nearest store, they do not need to spend money on driving to massive stores in search of items that may not be in stock. Offering a 'click and collect' service also means that retailers do not need larger stores to stock their entire merchandise ranges on site as customers' needs for non-stocked items can be serviced from smaller stores via the retailers' websites.

Some retail industry observers are even suggesting that it is probably ill advised for any supermarket to open stores over 60,000–70,000 sq. ft., as it is difficult to fill them with enticing merchandise. Also, supermarkets, in general, do not provide a particularly exciting shopping experience or customer service. Their main strengths are in convenience, reliability and price. The Internet is becoming ever more competitive on all these fronts, particularly in non-grocery area such as music, electrical goods, books and clothing. ASDA, Tesco's main competitor, has also recognized these trends, and its Chief Executive announced in February 2012 that ASDA was shelving plans to open any more supercentres (stores sized between 80,000 sq. ft. and 120,000 sq. ft.). ASDA had 32 supercentres at the time but the last one opened in Ellesmere Port in August 2006. Instead, it was planning to open more small local stores that offered convenience.

Source: Butler (2012), Thompson (2012)

SUMMARY

Retailers are facing an increasingly competitive environment due to the relatively slow growth of the retailing sector, increasing maturity and concentration of many retailing sectors, the emergence of new retailing formats such as the Internet, changes in consumer expectations and expenditure and competition from international retailers. Retail competition can take the form of intra-type, inter-type, vertical and systems competition. In addition, local competition can add to the complexity of decisions regarding competitive action.

The major drivers of competition within the industry are the threat of new entrants, the threat from substitute forms of retailing (that is inter-type competition), the bargaining power of producers, the bargaining power of shoppers and the intensity of rivalry between firms. The relative balance between competing retailers and their competitive retail marketing strategies also influences the intensity of competition. For instance, competition is likely to be fiercer where there are a number of roughly similar-sized competitors pursuing a similar strategy. Such a group of firms is referred to as a strategic group. Strategic group analysis is used to simplify analysis of competitive strategies and make predictions about competitive behaviour within and between strategic groups. For instance, it predicts that competition between neighbouring groups is likely to be most intense as there is likely to be some overlap between their respective target markets. Conversely, competition is least intense between firms belonging to the strategic groups furthest apart.

In order to gain competitive advantage, retailers need to differentiate themselves from their competitors. The methods that are likely to be most successful are likely to rely on merchandise assortment, promotions, store atmospherics and service. Competition is regulated by government bodies to ensure that it is fair, and to prevent the exploitation of consumers.

QUESTIONS

1. Describe the main methods used for measuring retail competition and discuss their relative advantages and disadvantages.
2. Outline the differences between intra-type and inter-type competition.
3. Outline the differences between vertical and systems competition.
4. What major barriers are potential entrants likely to face when entering a retailing sector such as the grocery market?
5. How far do you agree that shoppers are relatively powerless in relation to retailers?
6. What is a strategic group? How useful is this concept for analysing retail competition?
7. How can retailers best achieve competitive advantage in an increasingly competitive environment?

REFERENCES AND FURTHER READING

Anonymous (2002) 'Foreign-Owned Retailers Now Account for £1 in Every £8 Spent in the UK's Shops – And the Proportion Will Keep Rising', *International Journal of Retail & Distribution Management*, vol. 30, no. 3.

Burt, S. L. and Sparks, L. (2003) 'Power and Competition in the UK Retail Grocery Market', *British Journal of Management*, vol. 14, no. 3, pp. 237–54.

Butler, Sarah (2012) 'Tesco and Rivals Turn against Huge Stores as Internet Shopping Takes Over', *The Observer*, Sunday, 4 March.

Competition Commission (2000) *Supermarkets: A Report on the Supply of Groceries from Multiple Stores in the United Kingdom*, Cm 4842 (London: The Stationery Office).

Competition Commission (2008) *The Supply of Groceries in the UK Market Investigation* (London: Competition Commission).Lewison, D. M. and Delozier, W. M. (1986) *Retailing*, 2nd Edition (Columbus, OH: Merrill Publishing).

London Economics (1997) *Competition in Retailing*, Research paper no. 13 (London: Office of Fair Trading).

Monopolies and Mergers Commission (1981) *Discounts to Retailers: A Report on the General Effect on the Public Interest of the Practice of Charging Some Retailers Lower Prices than Others or Providing Special Benefits to Some Retailers Where the Difference Cannot Be Attributed to Savings in the Supplier's Costs, Select Committee Report to the House of Commons*, HC 311 (London: HMSO).

Nielsen (2001) *Retail Pocket Book 2001* (Henley-on-Thames: NTC Publications).

Office of Fair Trading (1985) *Competition and Retailing* (London: OFT).

Ogbonna, E. and Wilkinson, B. (1996) 'Inter-Organizational Power Relations in the UK Grocery Industry: Contradictions and Developments', *International Review of Retail, Distribution and Consumer Research*, vol. 6, no. 4, pp. 395–414.

Porter, M. (1980) *Competitive Advantage* (New York: The Free Press).

Robins, T. (2000) 'Shoppers Pay Extra in Store Monopolies', *The Sunday Times*, 27 February.

Thompson, J. (2012) 'Asda Is Cooling on Hypermarkets as Festive Sales Tick Up', *The Independent*, 22 February.

4 CUSTOMERS

LEARNING OBJECTIVES

- To define the role of retailing within the general arena of personal consumption.
- To explore the nature of changes in consumers and reflect on their likely effect on retailing activity.
- To appreciate the various levels of impact that changing consumer profiles can have on retailers.
- To understand the complexity of retailing as a socio-economic activity, and the way consumers interact with retailing activity including online.
- To appreciate that consumers have different motivations for shopping.
- To understand the role a retailer plays in the consumer decision-making process.
- To understand the different factors used by consumers when making choices between retail outlets.

INTRODUCTION

As discussed in Chapter 1, retailing is defined as selling goods and services to final consumers for their personal, or their family's, consumption. It is therefore in the interest of any retailer to gather as much information about the final consumer as they can in order to be confident that the goods and services offered remain relevant to customers. All consumers could be considered as potential customers of a retail business; however, it is more appropriate for retail managers to identify a group of people who are likely to become actual purchasers within an outlet. Viable customer groups may be defined in terms of their geographical location for example, or they might be more conveniently grouped according to product need or preferred way to shop. Information about customers that could be relevant to retailers in gaining a better understanding of their customers includes residential or work location; lifestyles and associated needs; age and family situation; brand preferences; disposable income; shopping behaviour and format preference; and media preferences and sources of information that are trusted.

There may also be relevant information about the relationship a customer has with other retailers in the sector (see also Chapter 3 on retail competitors). Examples are the extent of loyalty to different retailers, and how easy it would be persuade customers to switch; customer trends within the retail sector; and the identification of customers who have poor retail provision. Retailers who are in touch with their customers and their needs and wants are more likely to find retail formulas that are relevant to consumers. This chapter gives an overview of the various aspects of consumer characteristics and behaviour that are important when converting consumers to customers.

RETAILING AND CONSUMPTION

A retailer's role in the arena of personal consumption is that of distributor and facilitator, as outlined in Chapter 1. A retailer provides a convenient point for a consumer to obtain goods and services, either by being in a location that is closer than that of the producer and by selling in quantities appropriate to the needs of the consumer, or by providing added value in the offer, such as range assortment or additional services. In a developed society, retailers play a greater role than the distribution viewpoint would imply. They provide an information service and they provide an environment in which new products can be discovered, new fashions followed and lifestyle patterns endorsed. Retailers have the benefit of a direct interface with the final consumer; therefore, they should have an advantage over producers when it comes to gathering information about customers in terms of who they are and how and what they buy. However, all too often retailers make too many assumptions about their customers and do not have a thorough and researched awareness of how their customers' needs, wants and preferences can change over time.

THE CHANGING CONSUMER

It is claimed that modern societies are increasingly organized around consumption (Abercrombie, Hill and Turner, 1994, Outlook, 2011) and so the trends in the patterns of consumption that emerge over time are very important for retailers to observe and understand. Consumer trends describe how potential retail customers change over time and make predictions about how those people will consume in the future. A retailer can therefore build up a customer profile (sometimes referred to as a 'pen portrait') that gives an indication of who might 'typically' use their outlet. A retail customer profile is affected by the macro (general) business environment; for example the macro-economic policies a government pursues in relation to taxation and interest rates affect the spending power of retail customers, and the extent of broadband coverage will affect our propensity to use Internet-based retail formats to undertake shopping transactions.

A retailer's customer profile is also influenced by the micro environment, the specific business arena in which the individual retailer operates. For example, the entry of Amazon.com into the book retailing market gave traditional retailers like Waterstones and Borders new competition, in the form of not only a new company, but also a whole new way of shopping (see Chapter 3). Subsequently, store-based book retailers put more effort into creating a pleasant store environment, conducive to browsing and sampling a book over a cup of coffee, something that Internet retailers are unable to offer. Nevertheless, this was not enough to prevent the terminal demise of Borders, who went into administration in 2009. Some of the most radical changes in consumers are those that emanate from the changes in society itself: the changing nature of a population's age profile, the changes in the numbers and type of activity of the working population and the way in which lifestyles themselves are changing. The resulting manifestations of alterations in shopping behaviour and product preference are of interest to the retailer, as they may require some adaptation to the retailer's business in order to maintain an adequate customer flow. China, Russia and India for example have become key growth markets for luxury products, with sales growth in Europe and the United States being comparatively slow.

DEMOGRAPHICS

Demographics is the study of populations in terms of measurable aspects such as birth rate, age profiles, working patterns and occupations, family and household structures, education levels and total income and expenditure levels (Brassington and Pettitt, 2000). These changes are generally out of a retailer's control, depending very much on the social and economic development of a given population, and they are usually relatively slow-moving changes. However, retailers must be aware of the implications of such changes, so that they can be accommodated in a retailer's long-term strategic planning. Some of the demographic changes that are likely to have an impact on retailers are now explored in more detail.

Age Profile

The age profile of the consumer market can be extremely relevant to a retail business. Although out of a retailer's control, the death rate and birth rate influence the 'bulges' in generation cohorts, which may have positive or negative effects on the potential customer base. Retailers of young fashion may struggle due to a falling population of teenagers, at the same time as children's-wear retailers are thriving due to an upturn in the birth rate. Clearly, some retailers are more directly influenced by changing age patterns than others, when their product range is directly linked to the age of the consumer. For example, baby equipment retailers like Mamas & Papas (www.mamasandpapas.com) cease to be relevant once children get to school age. However, the market for laptops is much wider, with income, occupation and life stage rather than age being more relevant criteria for the identification of customers and their preferences.

One key challenge for UK retailers is how to adapt to the ageing population. Figure 4.1 shows the significance of the shift towards older age groups in the population. Although the younger end of the 'grey market' is relatively time and cash rich and healthy, elderly customers over time become less affluent and more demanding in terms of customer service. Levy and Weitz (2008) suggest a number of ways in which retailers can provide better service for this market. These include training staff to recognize the needs of senior people, and respond to them with clarity and respect; designing the store environment with the older customer in mind (good lighting, consistent layouts, rest areas); providing information in large print and in forms that customers can take away to study; and finally to employ older people who may be better able to empathize with the customer base.

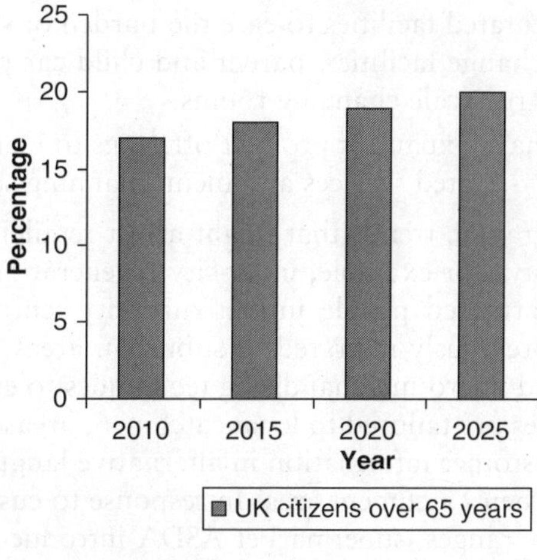

Figure 4.1 UK's growing elderly population
Source: UK Office of National Statistics:
http://www.statistics.gov.uk/statbase/Product.asp?vlnk=8519
http://www.statistics.gov.uk/downloads/theme_population/NPP-2006/wuk065y.xls

Working Patterns

The trend for more women to enter the workplace is continuing in Europe, and occupations have moved from the traditional manufacturing industries to the service sector. This type of employment, characterized by part-time and flexible working hours and 'lighter' work (such as call centre operation, catering and shop work), has generally suited female employees, and with the growth of communication and information technology, many job roles have adapted to the 'home-office' (Fernie, 1999). At the same time, the proportion of time spent by individuals in the workplace has increased. The trend for more women to work in both part-time and full-time occupations has had a number of very important influences on the way the retail industry has developed. Some of these are highlighted below:

1. The growth of convenience products in the grocery market, for example ready-prepared meals, was a product category initially pioneered by Marks and Spencer, and now most supermarkets have takeaway food bars.
2. The increased offer of products and services under one roof – the one-stop shop, or perhaps more accurately the one-stop household service. Many superstores offer pharmacies, dry cleaning, photograph processing, shoe repair and post office services, alongside the extensive food and non-food household product range.
3. The increased choice of retailers offering a 'working wardrobe' in the clothing sector. UK clothing retailer Next has been particularly successful in this market, and the re-positioning of 'casual' Chelsea Girl to 'smarter' River Island in the mid-1980s (Lea-Greenwood, 1993) was a response to the opportunity to sell young women their work attire alongside more fashionable items.

4. Child-orientated facilities to ease the burden of shopping with children, for example baby change facilities, parent and child car parking places, trolleys with baby carriers, large-scale changing rooms.
5. Retailers have expanded product offerings to include more services, such as health and beauty-related services and menu-planning services.

Other demographic trends that might affect retailers include geographical shifts and ethnic diversity. For example, inner-city regeneration schemes are attracting childless single and partnered people into luxury city-centre residential developments, who might have previously migrated to suburban areas. Large multiple retailers use geo-marketing and micro-merchandising techniques to ensure that their store formats and product ranges are tailored to local catchment areas. It may be important for retailers to provide customer information in alternative languages in order to reflect the ethnic character of their catchment area. In response to customer requests and the success of Asian grocery ranges, supermarket ASDA introduced a range of clothing specifically for Asian customers in 2009. The collection featured salwar kameezes (traditional suits), kurtas (tunics), *dupatta*s (scarves) and *churidar*s (slim leg trousers) and was launched into 23 stores (ASDA).

Income and Expenditure

Although the feeling of being better off is more likely to be influenced by our level of wealth relative to those we come into contact with, rather than our actual income level, the majority of consumers in Europe and the United States have, over a long time frame, enjoyed an increasing level of personal disposable income since the Second World War. More recently, disposable income in many areas of China and India too has increased, which has prompted economists to note that the balance of power is shifting from West to East (Outlook, 2011). UK consumers now spend a smaller proportion of their income on what might be termed 'the essentials' of life, such as housing and food, whereas the proportion of income spent on discretionary purchases such as fashion goods, household appliances, eating out, holidays and entertainment has increased. This means that retailers and manufacturers have been able to benefit by encouraging consumers to 'trade up' in their essential purchases, and make discretionary purchases appear to be 'essential'. During the global recession in the later part of the first decade of the twenty-first century, however, retailers revisited the idea of 'value' and 'essential' ranges as disposable income levels dropped.

Demographics are the measurable outcomes of societal change. For example, the UK has experienced a fall in the size of families and households over the last two decades as the result of a number of variables, many of which are interrelated: an increased number of women having a 'career' and so starting a family later or deciding not to have a family; an increase in the divorce rate, resulting in more households and 'irregular' family groups (for example a couple may live on their own in the week, with an influx of children from two previous marriages at the weekends); and more elderly people living independently, often single, for longer periods of time. Retailers need to be aware of these changes in terms of how they affect the number of consumers in different demographic categories, but equally important is to be able to have an understanding of how the changes influence the lifestyles of groups of people in the various demographic categories.

LIFESTYLE CHANGES

A complete and thorough exploration of societal influences on consumption is beyond the scope of this text. However, some of the lifestyle changes that have occurred in the recent past and have had a significant effect on retailers are the following:

1. Time poverty and therefore a resulting convenience orientation, particularly for working families (see earlier section on working patterns).
2. Car dependency, resulting in a growth of edge-of-town and out-of-town shopping centres.
3. Cellular families, resulting in a growth of spending on personal appliances; households with teenage children are likely to have multiple television sets, telephones, music players and computers.
4. Informality, as a result of the weakening influence of traditional bodies of authority such as the Church, the police, the state and the family. In particular, clothing retailers have been challenged by this trend, but it has also had its effect on home furnishings. IKEA, for example, has used informality and fun as a theme in its customer communications, with traditional and formal styles being portrayed as old-fashioned.
5. Use of technology, with mobile Internet access allowing consumers to shop on the move at any time. This is one of many factors that has encouraged the uptake of online retailing (Vignette 4.1).
6. More opportunity to travel and take more than one holiday in a year, encouraging fashion retailers to offer beachwear throughout the year and some retailers to offer a tailored solution service for the global commuter increased focus on leisure time (Vignette 4.2).

Longer working hours put a brighter spotlight on the quality of leisure time, and consumers are prepared to purchase items and services that will enhance their precious free time. Labour-saving appliances like dishwashers and microwaves have a high penetration in UK households, but retailers in general have to respond to the fact that shopping is increasingly regarded as a leisure pursuit which should be enjoyable, entertaining, interesting and hassle-free, with service offerings such as restaurants, bars and coffee shops, sporting facilities, beauty, spa and entertainment venues in close proximity.

VIGNETTE 4.1 THE INFORMED SHOPPER

Consumers do not just shop online: they incorporate a variety of technologies to facilitate their shopping activities. This includes retailers' web pages, in-store kiosks and tablets and interactive TV. They are also often shopping with technologies which allow them to shop with friends or others (for those who are too old or too young to easily shop for themselves). Communication via social media empowers shoppers with information about product and retail experience; friends and family are likely to be the first source of information (in particular via Facebook) and then they may move onto formal review sites, blogs and Twitter, which are all sources of knowledge that consumers tend to trust before retailers themselves. This gathering of information prior to purchase can be more like a series of shopping moments rather than a linear process, which the shopping process used to be. For example at one time the purchasing process for a washing machine was likely to be as follows: washing machine breaks down; go to local electrical category specialist; talk to sales assistant about needs and budget; buy; take delivery. Now the shopping process is more likely to be as follows: washing machine is getting old; have a conversation with family and friends about washing machines; spend a long time researching on the Internet about washing machines and their features, using both brand and retailer websites; look at a couple of blogs; have another conversation via a forum about washing machine performances; email a retailer's customer service email address about a particular feature; study scores and rating on a review site; visit a store to check a shortlisted selection to see what they look like in real life; trawl retailer websites to get best price and check availability; purchase online; track order on mobile phone; take delivery.

Retailers therefore must be prepared for this new type of consumer who wants to be served but not sold to. The customer may already know as they walk into a shop exactly which products and/or brands they want to buy and they only need the retailer to add ease and convenience to their shopping activity rather than advice. Nevertheless, this customer will also want to have a personalized, respectful service, tailored to their shopping context. Not only the skills of the retail sales personnel therefore need to be those of a product expert (but only to impart that information when requested), but also the salespeople need to be highly skilled in reading and listening to customers, recognizing how they want to shop. Sales associates therefore need customer training rather than sales training and need to be able to quickly tune into what a customer needs and not be pressurized by a retailer's aims. It is particularly important for store management to appreciate the positive influence a shop-based experience can make to an online purchase. Persuading customers to make impulse purchases is also a less likely scenario because the gathering of information by consumers has also included time for reflection. Social media use by brands is encouraging online engagement, which includes commentary and loyalty. By listening to the online voice of consumers and acting on their suggestions, retailers may be able to increase consumer expenditure, as many customers are prepared to pay a premium for what they really, really want.

Source: Based on IBM Global Business Services (2011)

VIGNETTE 4.2 FLIGHT 001

Flight 001 (pronounced Flight One) has taken advantage of a lifestyle-based consumer segment to build a successful niche retail business. The idea was conceived by two executives who felt the task of preparing for a business trip by visiting a number of different retailers for various items too time consuming and lacking in choice. They therefore opened a store that provides a tightly edited range of functional and fun products for the frequent traveller. The main categories are luggage, bags, protective bags (for example those for cameras and tablets), chargers and adapters, in-flight comfort, ID covers and luggage tags, maps and guides. The have also developed their own products such as the 'space pack', which allows the traveller to hold clean clothes in one side of the pack and then move them to a flexible dirty section as the trip goes forward.

Located in six cities in the United States and with one store each in Singapore and Sydney, this highly targeted retailer provides a useful shopping solution for the growing number of consumers whose lifestyles include the need or want to travel often and be organized for it. The store itself is shaped like an aircraft fuselage, which adds to the character and atmosphere of the store and makes a connection between the retailer and the relevant consumer segment.

There have also been changes in attitudes and values within the general body of consumers, which again has influenced the way they shop and the products they choose. These would include the weakening influence of traditional authority indicated above, environmental awareness and consciousness, health consciousness and cost orientation. There is much debate about the rise of the ethical consumer in terms of its growth and viability as a consumer market (Varley, 2009); however, a number of ethically differentiated retailers have emerged on the retail scene (see Timberland Vignette 10.1). There is some evidence of consumers becoming less trusting of large retail corporations, preferring to support local retailers and community-based enterprises (World Future Society, 2010).

Within this general appreciation of the nature of consumers as a living, changing, adapting and thriving body of potential customers, retailers need to audit the consuming population in order to establish the rate and impact of change on their own individual businesses.

THE CONSUMER BUYING PROCESS

As well as understanding the retail consumer from the point of view of the masses, or total potential market viewpoint, the study of consumer behaviour is also very much concerned with how we consume as individuals. Established theory suggests that each time we purchase something, we go through a process composed of a number of key stages as indicated in Figure 4.2.

It has also been suggested that consumer buying behaviour is influenced at least as much by retailers as by manufacturers (Knox and Denison, 2000), and so a retailer needs to be aware of the extent to which they can contribute to the purchase decision-making process. Each of the factors of Figure 4.2 is considered below.

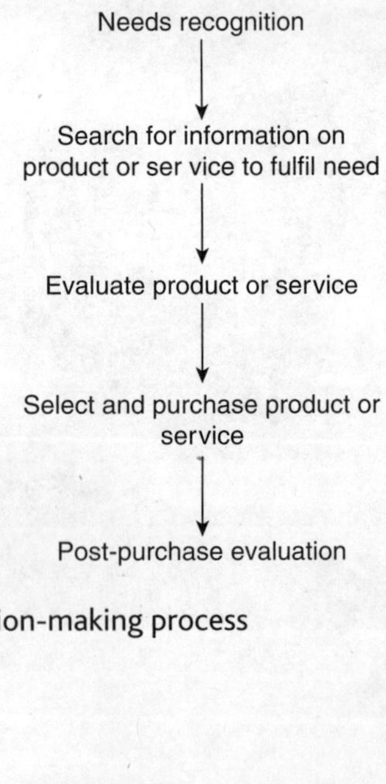

Figure 4.2 The consumer purchase decision-making process

Needs Recognition

To begin with, the retail environment itself can be used to draw attention to products and stimulate impulse purchases (see Chapter 10). In this case the need is generated during the shopping process rather than prior to it. In other instances, the recognition of need may be closely associated with the retail outlet that has become strongly connected to particular items. For example, an empty refrigerator is more likely to prompt the thought 'I must visit the supermarket' than the specific product-related thought 'I must buy a box of eggs'. Likewise, an invitation to a wedding is likely to prompt a swift wardrobe review followed by a visit to a major fashion shopping destination.

Information Search

In the second stage, consumers use retail outlets extensively for information about goods and services. Retailers provide information in many forms, including point-of-sale information, leaflets and catalogues, websites, interactive product trials such as food tasting, trying on garments or listening to music, and in the one-to-one advice given to customers about their intended purchase by sales personnel. In particular, a salesperson can help to move a customer from the stage where they are searching for information about products to the point at which they start to evaluate the alternatives on offer and make a choice.

The growth of Internet retailing has transformed consumers into multi-channel shoppers, who blend virtual and physical retailers in different ways throughout the purchase decision-making process. Browsing and purchasing may be conducted in different formats of the same retail brand (for example, a website, a catalogue and a store) and may involve a number of different visits to each format. A browsing shopper who does not purchase in store must therefore be valued as a customer as much as one who does. This has implications for determining profitability (see Chapter 13 on pricing).

Evaluation

Evaluation is the part of the purchase decision process where the consumer is comparing and analysing the alternative offers. During the search and evaluation stages, the retailer itself rather than simply the product may become the focus of a consumer's evaluation. Customer loyalty and the value of the retailer's corporate brand may encourage a consumer to restrict their search and evaluation activity. It is in the retailer's interest to progress a consumer to the purchasing stage efficiently in order to prevent them taking their business to a competitor's outlet. In a saturated retail market, ensuring that customers keep returning to your store or website is a vital ingredient of a retailer's strategy, and as European markets have matured, increasing focus has been placed on customer loyalty. Defining loyalty in retailing is not straightforward because it can be measured in more than one way; frequency of visit, extent of switching and expenditure levels all contribute to the extent to which a customer can be considered to be loyal (Knox and Denison, 2000). Irrespective of the way loyalty is measured, loyal customers are more profitable to retailers than other types of customers, and therefore every effort should be made to maximize their satisfaction. This is a growing challenge: as consumers face increasing choice through their own mobility and gain experience as shoppers, their loyalty levels are likely to fall.

Select and Purchase

The extent to which a retailer can influence this stage of the process is closely linked to the type of product being purchased. In low-involvement products, the consumer may be influenced by some in-store promotional activity, whereas in medium-involvement products, such as beauty products, the matching of product benefits to customer needs by sales associates will play an important role. In high-involvement purchase decisions, such as a carpet, the shopper may revisit alternative retailers a number of times to gather information on product attributes such as price, quality, colour, payment methods and delivery before making a final decision.

Post-Purchase Evaluation

Again, the extent to which the product or the retailer is judged after the sale will depend on the type of purchase. For high-involvement purchases, high levels of post-purchase customer service can help to alleviate any worries about installation and use, whilst clear and generous return and exchange policies can help to reassure the customer in the purchase of all types of product. This is particularly important for personal technology retailing. Apple have provided an exemplar in this sector in the form of their Apple stores, both online and in the physical 'emporiums', where group and one-to-one tutorials are carried out alongside very high levels of general customer service. John Lewis also use customer service to reassure customers after complex purchase decisions (see Vignette 13.2).

SHOPPING BEHAVIOUR

The model of the consumer purchase decision-making process assumes that the consumer is a rational and economic person, whose evaluation is strictly geared to physical benefits of the product bought. In fact the activity of shopping is tied up with a whole host of human emotions and behaviour, involving benefits sought to satisfy myriad psychological needs. Product needs vary from the functional (for example a vacuum cleaner's ability to clean floors) to the psychological (the boost to the user of a Rolex timepiece for example); however, most products offer both functional and psychological benefits. For example, the Dyson vacuum cleaner is designed with a transparent dust collection cylinder, providing the user with the psychologically satisfying view of all the trapped dirt! Shopping also fulfils functional and psychological needs, and the process of shopping itself can vary from being a chore to the most favoured leisure pursuit. A retail outlet can be designed to make the functional shopping easier and less of a chore by the following:

1. Locating the outlet in the most convenient situation, considering travel time, congestion, ease of parking and accessibility.
2. Providing a logical layout (applies to both store and virtual outlets).
3. Ensuring POS and pricing information is clear and easily understood.

4. Providing good accessibility, in particular considering the needs of families and the elderly.
5. Ensuring good stock availability.
6. Providing fast and flexible payment facilities.
7. Providing the opportunity for home delivery and online ordering.

A retail outlet can also be designed to encourage customers to view shopping as a pleasurable leisure pursuit by augmenting the opportunities for fulfilment, relaxation and fun:

1. Ensure customer service levels are high. Staff/customer interactions should be pleasant, cheerful and courteous. Staff should appear interested in and knowledgeable about the products(s) that they are selling.
2. Provide eating places. It is said that a way to keep customers happy is to keep them comfortable and well fed. The provision of restaurants, cafes and tasting bars all helps to keep the customer relaxed, and encourages prolonged shopping activity.
3. Entertain the customer. There are various ways in which customer can be entertained. For example some supermarkets have introduced 'live chef' sessions, and many clothing stores arrange fashion shows (on video if the store is too small). The store environment itself can be designed to provide entertaining features; for example customers are welcomed into Hamleys toy emporium by characters in costume, while innovative interactive toys are demonstrated across the store.
4. Make the store environment enthralling. An inspiring store is likely to encourage customers to browse, whereas one that is dull and badly laid out will do the opposite! The store design and the displays, together with music, lighting and even aromas can create an atmosphere that makes shopping 'an experience'.
5. Choose an outlet location that combines retail and leisure activities. Many modern shopping centres combine retail outlets with other leisure destinations, such as cinemas, sport facilities, cafes and bars, and tourist attractions. This encourages customers to view the shopping activity as part of a 'day out'. The proximity to other retailers in a centre can also be important in terms of generating high footfall (see Chapter 9 on location).

Shopping Missions

Another limitation of the consumer purchase decision-making model is that the way we shop can be influenced by the shopping mission. The following accounts of shopping for essentially what could be described as square sheets of absorbent paper illustrate how different missions have implications for the way a consumer shops, and for the retailer concerned with the purchase:

1. *Emergency situation.* Suffering from hay fever, Ms. X is in need of a packet of tissues fast! She will buy them from the nearest outlet that has product availability, and product attributes such as price, brand, quality and design are not relevant in this situation. Convenience stores are therefore able to apply high profit margins to this type of product.
2. *Routine buying.* On a visit to a supermarket to do the weekly household shop, Ms. X purchases a family pack of tissues. She assumes the current pack at home

will not last much longer. She may be influenced by promotional offers (such as 2 for 1) and may use other product criteria such as colour and use of recycled materials in her purchase decision. However, her overall involvement in the purchase is low, and she is likely to be influenced by price, resulting in a low margin for the retailer.

3. *Destination shopping*. Ms. X is organizing a dinner party. She needs to buy some table napkins and she wants to ensure that the quality of the napkins reflects her excellent cookery skills, and that the design complements the decor in her dining room. She heads for a department store located within a nearby regional shopping centre where she knows she will find a wide selection of designs to choose from. She is not price sensitive in her purchase, although she believes this reputable retailer provides good value for money. Colour, style and quality will lead her decision making, so the retailer can command a better profit margin.
4. *Browsing*. Later in the year Ms. X is doing her Christmas shopping. Whilst browsing through a variety store, she notices some novelty tissues with cartoon characters printed on them. She decides that these would make a good stocking-filler present for her 9-year-old daughter. Her product choice is influenced by the season, so the retailer can command good margins at this time. However, stock control is important, because after the seasonal event demand will fall and the product may need to be marked down and cleared (see Chapter 13 on pricing).

Shopping Motivations

Tauber (1972) was one of the first researchers to ask the question 'why do people shop?', appreciating that there were reasons other than the simple necessity to purchase physical products. He found that consumers' motivations for shopping are derived from many factors, some of which are less related to the buying of products, and more related to personal and social motivations of individuals. He went on to suggest that retailers need to consider the satisfaction that a consumer gets from the shopping activity itself, as well as the utility obtained from the product bought if they are to fully understand consumers' motivations for shopping.

Further consumer research has uncovered other psychological motivations for shopping, and Table 4.1 provides a summary of reasons why people go shopping other than to purchase a product for satisfying a physical need, such as running out of an item or something wearing out.

As a generalization, the shopping process can be broken down into two separate categories. The first is sometimes referred to as 'chore shopping', and is a reflection of how many people feel about, for example, grocery shopping. It is the kind of shopping that has to be performed in order to replenish food and household goods, or to replace worn-out items. Although many people love shopping for clothes, there is a significant section of the population (many of whom are mature males) who would consider clothes shopping to be a chore. However, a key feature of chore shopping is the low-involvement, routine nature of the task, and therefore it can be separated from clothes shopping. The main objective with chore shopping, for most people, is to perform the task as efficiently as possible.

The second general category of shopping activity is the one that usually involves high-involvement or 'one-off' purchases, and for these the consumer will go through

Table 4.1 Shopping motivations

Personal stimulation	The need for 'an experience'; the enjoyment of being in an interesting or different environment
Social experiences	The need to be with people; to go shopping with friends, to talk to people with similar interests, to have contact with a peer group
Learning	The need to acquire new knowledge in order to become an 'educated shopper'; finding out about new products, following fashion trends, talking to 'experts' in stores
Status and power	The need to exert authority, to gain attention from retail personnel, to have somebody 'serve' and show respect
Self-reward	The need to treat oneself, or to put oneself in a positive frame of mind
Diversion	The need to alleviate boredom, to provide a break in the daily routine, to get out and about
Exercise	The need to move about and get some fresh air
Role-play	The need to reinforce a role or to play a role to which one aspires; for example the role of the provider (in the gathering of the weekly family needs)
Bargain hunting	The need to show expertise in finding value in purchasing; the need to have 'beaten' the retailer by buying at discounted prices

all of the stages in the consumer purchasing process, and may spend a long period of time in the early stages gathering together information and trying out alternatives. The key difference in the two types of shopping from the retailer's point of view is that for low-involvement (chore) shopping it is in the consumer's interest to establish a routine in order to maximize efficiency, and one of the ways of doing this is to choose one store and buy as many things from that store as possible. When a consumer buys a high-involvement product they like to consider many alternatives, whereas in the routine process a customer will generally be happy with a smaller number of alternatives, and in many instances will have already decided amongst alternatives based on previous experience. How consumers choose between alternative stores is therefore as important to retailers as how consumers make decisions about what product to buy. As a consumer gains experience within a product classification, such as clothing or household appliances, decisions regarding store choice hold more weight than those regarding the products themselves. The choice of website from which to order is subject to a similar process of decision making.

RETAIL OUTLET CHOICE

There are many factors that influence how we as consumers feel about a retail outlet. Clearly in the light of the previous discussion, the product range offered is one of those factors. However, in a saturated retail market there may be a number of outlets offering very similar product ranges, and so other means of differentiation become important in the retail offer. The following factors were considered important by more than one quarter of respondents in a study of why customers chose one grocery store over another:

1. Attractive prices.
2. Location.
3. Quality of products.
4. Wide range of products.
5. Measures to reduce queues at checkout.
6. Fresh food service (delicatessen, fresh fish, etc.).
7. Longer opening hours.
8. Good own-label range.
9. Cashpoint facilities.
10. Express checkout.

(*Source*: Mintel, Food Retailing Report, Consumer Shopping, August 2000.)

Chaffey (2009) suggests that the following factors are important in the online customer experience and therefore will influence why one website might be used in preference to another: product range and price, interactivity in terms of the 'customer journey', flow and ease of data entry and service in terms of fulfilment of the order and support.

Attempts have been made to model the process of store-choice decision making, and these models can help retailers to carry out their own research in order to understand what is really important to customers (and potential customers) when choosing one outlet for their shopping over another. The multi-attribute model has been used widely in retail studies in order to measure the relevance of a retail outlet's attributes to the selection criteria used by shoppers (Gonzalez-Betino et al., 2000, McGoldrick and Collins, 2007), and the following hypothetical illustration shows how this type of store-choice modelling can be used.

The first stage of using the model is to identify stores that are in a customer's set of alternatives. The set may include outlets that compete on an inter-type or intra-type basis, and in this example we will use intra-type competition and consider the process of choosing between three different grocery superstores located within a 5 mile radius. Table 4.2 lists a number of store attributes (characteristics) and makes a qualitative assessment of each store according to their performance in relation to those attributes.

Table 4.2 Store attributes and individual store performances

Supermarket	X	Y	Z
Price level	Average	Above average	Average
Price offers	Few	Few	Many
Car parking	Unrestricted	Unrestricted	Sometimes difficult
Speed through checkout	Slow	Fast	Fast
General product assortment	Average	Wide	Below average
Organic produce	No	Yes	Very limited
Store environment	Average	Excellent	Average
Pharmacy	Yes	No	No

Customers can then be asked to score the three stores according to these characteristics, and these scores can be summarized under general attribute groupings as shown in Table 4.3.

The total scores indicate that all three stores are performing well, scoring between 26 and 30 out of a possible 40 points.

Even though different customers may rate these three stores similarly in terms of their general attributes, there may be particular characteristics that have a greater importance to different individuals, and therefore have a bearing on the store choice that they personally make. So, by asking individual customers to attach an importance weighting to the general attributes, we will gain a better insight into how different groups of customers choose stores. Table 4.4 shows the importance weights put onto the general attributes by two different customers. Customer A is 55, with grown-up children and a professional occupation. Customer B is a parent with three children and a low disposable income. By multiplying the importance weighting by the scores for the general attributes, we can see that different stores gain top scores for these two individual customers, and so they are likely to choose different superstores for their weekly shop (Table 4.5).

Although this model provides a useful framework for researching how customers make choices between alternative retail outlets using a multi-attribute scoring system, our decision making is not always transferable into numeric scoring. For example, the parent of young children (customer B) may need to use a pharmacy regularly, and so the presence of this single attribute might outweigh all others. Similarly, customer A may have made a decision to eat only organic foods, and so store Y would be the only acceptable choice for them, no matter how much stores X and Z improved other parts of their offer.

Table 4.3 Superstore scores according to attributes

	Superstore		
	X	Y	Z
Prices (level, offers)	7	5	9
Convenience (parking, checkout speed, pharmacy)	8	7	6
Product range (general assortment, organic produce)	6	9	6
Store environment	7	9	6
Totals	28	30	27

Table 4.4 Importance weightings given by two different customers

	A	B
Price	5	10
Convenience	9	6
Assortment	10	7
Shopping environment	7	2

Table 4.5 Weighted store attribute scores

	Customer weighting		Store attribute score		
	A	B	X	Y	Z
Price	5	10	7	5	9
Convenience	9	6	8	7	6
Assortment	10	7	6	9	6
Shopping environment	7	2	7	9	6
Total weighted scores			A 216 B 174	**A 241** B 174	A 196 **B 180**

RETAIL SEGMENTATION

The result of the type of research outlined above could indicate to retailers where loyalty might be generated within a specific customer group, and many retailers gear their offerings to particular groups of individuals who they have identified as being accessible enough and viable enough to support a business. For example, their level of need and willingness to be loyal provide a flow of income that maintains the operation. This process is known as segmentation and targeting: the retailer splits up the total population of the consumer market into a number of segments, into which individuals are placed according to their own physical or psychographic characteristics, and then the retail offer is aimed at the 'target' segment. A number of retailers have gained success by targeting a narrow segment, but for general retailers, the customer group served might be quite broad.

A deep understanding of the consumer is a prerequisite to successful segmentation. Some of the more common methods used by retailers to segment their markets are as follows:

1. Demographic: age, gender, family size, family life cycle, income, occupation.
2. Psychographic: social class, lifestyle, personality, attitudes.
3. Behavioural: benefits sought, loyalty status, usage rate.
4. Geographical.

The last type of variable (geographic) can be used either from the point of view of where the customer lives, or from the point of view of where the buying activity actually takes place. For example, some consumers can be geographically grouped according to their travel routes, or where they carry out their work. Boots, for example, target 'lunchtime' shoppers with their takeaway food range and lunchtime deals. Yet, two of those lunchtime shoppers may live in very different suburbs of the town in which Boots is located, and therefore be considered in a very different customer segment by a different retail company; indeed, to a convenience store, one of the customers may be a viable target, but the other who lives on the opposite side of town is completely irrelevant.

Some attempts have been made to group consumers on the basis of their shopping behaviour, which can generally be viewed as a combination of psychographic and behavioural segmentation. Categories have been developed such as the convenience shopper, the bargain-hunting or economic shopper, the environmental/socially concerned shopper, the personalizing or innovative opinion-leading shopper, the fashion follower, the traditional shopper, the creative shopper, the recreational shopper and even the apathetic or uninvolved shopper (Stone, 1954, Stevenson and Willett, 1969, Shim, Gehrt and Lotz, 2001). It has been suggested that online purchasers break down into six types of shoppers according to their attitude to shopping: realistic shoppers who are enthusiastic but like to see a product in real life; confident brand shoppers who are happy to use the Internet for well-known brands; carefree spenders who are happy to buy from unknown websites/brands on the Internet; cautious shoppers who are unlikely to buy from an online auction, and are concerned about quality and prefer to see the product; bargain hunters, driven by online price and not concerned about any other factor; and the unfulfilled, who find the process difficult and are not prepared to wait for delivery (BMRB research referred to in Chaffey, 2009, p. 202).

Segmentation has traditionally been very important to retail businesses. The viability of the segmentation process depends on the identification and ability to separate out accessible, measurable and viable groups of potential customers. If a target customer segment is no longer viable, or another segment looks more attractive, a retailer may need to use new criteria for segmentation and 're-position' the business. Primark for example targeted a more fashion-conscious customer and successfully re-positioned a family variety store into an emporium of fast fashion in the UK. Some larger retailers, however, will segment their customers within the outlet: for example New Look's 9–15 range for teenagers, or Marks and Spencer's designer-created Autograph range for customers with higher disposable incomes and fashion orientation.

SUMMARY

In this chapter we have outlined the importance to retailers of getting to know their customers, both as a group of people within a population, and as individuals. Having an in-depth knowledge about customers' product and shopping preferences allows retailers to gear their businesses towards the customer and make their product and service offerings more attractive than those of competitors. Customers exist within a society, and are subject to a whole host of influencing factors that shape the way they shop. Customers are complex human beings; they may act differently according to the type of shopping trip they are on, seeking value during one shopping mission, and then indulging themselves on another, wanting fast and convenient retail formats for everyday purchases yet prepared to spend time researching extensively online and seeking reassurance in store for high-involvement purchases. This gives rise to the notion of a hybrid customer, existing within a market of customers who seem to be increasingly less predictable as groups and seem to want customized products and services from retailers. At the same time, international retailing activity reflects an acceptance of global retail brands in a worldwide market in which needs and tastes converge.

QUESTIONS

1. For a retailer of your choice, discuss how elements in the product/service offer reflect the lifestyle of their customers.

2. Discuss the demographic changes that are taking place within your country. Identify retailers who stand to gain and those who may lose out because of these changes.
3. Review the buying process that you went through when you last purchased a high-involvement product. To what extent did the retail outlet (rather than the product itself) influence your choice? Can you think of anything further retailers could have done to get you to purchase within their outlet? What would definitely put you off buying this product in a particular retail outlet?
4. Review the different motivations for shopping. Give an example of a shopping incident that would illustrate each one.
5. Compare and contrast the concept of a shopping mission with that of a shopping motivation.
6. Referring to Vignette 4.2, describe how retailers can target consumers with particular lifestyles to create a niche offer to viable customer groups.

REFERENCES AND FURTHER READING

Abercrombie, N., Hill, S. and Turner, B. S. (1994) *Dictionary of Sociology* (London: Penguin).

ASDA (2009) Press release, available at http://your.asda.com/2009/9/14/george-launches-first-asian-clothing-range-on-high-street [accessed 15 September 2011].

Berman S. J and Bell R. (2011) *Digital Transformation: Creating new business models where digital meets physical*, IBM Institute for Business Value available https://www.academia.edu/5372612/IBM_Global_Business_Services_Executive_Report_IBM_Institute_for_Business_Value_Strategy_and_Transformation [accessed 20/09/2013]

Brassington, F. and Pettitt, S. (2000) *Principles of Marketing* (Harlow: Financial Times, Prentice Hall).

Chaffey, D. (2009) *E-Business and E-Commerce Management: Strategy, Implementation and Practice* (Harlow: Prentice Hall).

Fernie, J. (1999) *The Future for UK Retailing* (London: Financial Times Retail and Consumer Reports).

Gonzalez-Benito, O., Greatorex, M. and Munoz-Gallego, P. A. (2000) 'Assessment of Potential Retail Segmentation Variables. An Approach Based on a Subjective MCI Resource Allocation Model', *Journal of Retailing and Consumer Services*, no. 7, pp. 171–9.

Knox, S. D. and Denison, T. J. (2000) 'Store Loyalty: Its Impact on Retail Revenue. An Empirical Study of Purchasing Behaviour in the UK', *Journal of Retailing and Consumer Services*, no. 7, pp. 33–45.

Lea-Greenwood, G. (1993) 'River Island Clothing Co.: A Case Study on Changing an Image', *International Journal of Retail and Distribution Management*, vol. 21, no. 3, pp. 60–4.

Levy, M. and Weitz, B. A. (2008) *Retailing Management*, 7th Edition (New York: McGraw-Hill).

McGoldrick P. J. and Collins N. (2007) 'Multichannel Retailing: Profiling the Multichannel Shopper', *International Review of Retail, Distribution and Consumer Research*, vol. 17, no. 2, pp. 139–58.

Mintel (2000) *Food Retailing* (London: Mintel).

Shim, S., Gehrt, K. and Lotz, S. (2001) 'Export Implications for the Japanese Fruit Market: Fruit-Specific Lifestyle Segments', *International Journal of Retail and Distribution Management*, vol. 29, no. 6, pp. 298–314.

Stevenson, D. and Willett, R.P. (1969) 'Analysis of Consumers' Retail Patronage Strategies', in P. R. MacDonald (ed.), *Marketing Involvement in Society and Economy* (Chicago: AMA), pp. 316–22, cited in McGoldrick, P. J. (1990) *Retail Marketing* (Maidenhead: McGraw-Hill).

Stone, G. P. (1954) 'City Shoppers and Urban Identification: Observations on the Social Psychology of City Life', *American Journal of Sociology*, vol. 60, pp. 36–45.

Tauber, E. M. (1972) 'Why Do People Shop?', *Journal of Marketing*, vol. 36, no. 4, pp. 46–9.

Underhill, P. (2009) *Why We Buy: The Science of Shopping*, Second Edition (New York: Simon & Schuster).

Varley, R. (2009) 'Ethical Issues in Fashion Marketing' in Liz Parker and Marsha A Dickson (eds), *Sustainable Fashion: A Handbook for Educators* (Bristol: Labour behind the Label).

World Future Society (2010) 'Outlook 2011', available at https://www.wfs.org/Forecasts_From_The_Futurist_Magazine [accessed 20 September 2011].

5 FORMULATING RETAIL STRATEGY

LEARNING OBJECTIVES

- To understand what is meant by strategy.
- To appreciate the difference between corporate, business and functional strategies in retailing.
- To understand the strategic planning process and its components.
- To explore the alternative competitive strategies available to retailers and understand how retailers can use the value chain concept to implement those strategies.
- To understand and evaluate the various growth strategies available to retailers.
- To understand what is meant by a retail mix and its role in developing positioning strategies.

INTRODUCTION

Retailing strategy outlines the goals and objectives a retailer wants to achieve and a plan that determines how it will achieve them. It provides an overall framework for dealing with its operating environment, customers and competitors, given the retailer's resources and competences. Strategic management is relatively new to retailing and has emerged with the growth of large multiple chain stores and the resulting complexity of retail organizations. In the past, retailers tended to be largely reactive to changes in the business environment, but this is no longer viable as competition in all retail sectors is intense, and changes in consumer behaviour, technology and other environmental variables are happening very fast. Long-term analysis and planning are therefore required to ensure that growth opportunities are not missed and action is taken in good time to avoid the impact of negative trends in the retail business environment.

Strategy sets direction and scope of an organization over the long term, and creates sustainable competitive advantage through the configuration of its resources to meet customers' needs and expectations of stakeholders in a changing environment (Johnson and Scholes, 1997). This requires the development of a corporate mission that defines the scope of a retailer's activities, matching those activities to its business environment, building the organization's resource capability and competences and allocating or reallocating resources between business activities to achieve the retailer's organizational objectives.

LEVELS OF STRATEGIC PLANNING

Before discussing the nature of strategy it is necessary to discuss the levels at which strategic planning occurs in retail organizations. Many large retailers consist of a number of different business units. For instance, in addition to its supermarkets business in the UK, Tesco operates Tesco Direct (its online non-grocery business), Tesco Bank, Tesco Mobile (mobile phones) as well as supermarket businesses in a number of countries, including Poland, Slovakia, China and Thailand. Each of these businesses caters to a different set of customers, faces a different set of competitors and develops and executes its own marketing strategy. Such businesses are called strategic business units (SBUs). An SBU is a unit within the overall corporate entity for which there is an external market for its goods and services which is distinct from other SBUs; it is treated as a separate profit centre and is responsible for its own strategy. In multi-business organizations, such as Sainsbury's (see also Figure 5.1), there is a need to distinguish strategic planning at three levels, namely corporate strategy, business-unit strategy and functional or operational strategies.

In businesses consisting of two or more SBUs, corporate strategy is responsible for setting overall organizational objectives, and objectives for each of the SBUs such that they contribute to the achievement of overall organizational objectives. Corporate strategy is also responsible for allocating resources among the SBUs and coordinating their activities to maximize synergy between the SBUs.

A business-level strategy deals with how a particular SBU intends to achieve the objectives assigned to it in the corporate plan. This means, in effect, that business-unit strategy is concerned with how the SBU will compete in its particular market and create sustainable differential advantage. This necessitates decisions on the customers that the SBU intends to target, retailers that it intends to compete against and how it intends to deliver value to its customers. The distinction between corporate and business-level strategy is only relevant to multi-business organizations; for single-business retailers, such as the fashion retailer New Look, corporate and business-level strategies are the same.

Functional strategy specifies how each of the operational areas of the business (for example human resource management, finance, marketing, logistics and buying) contributes to implementation of the overall business-unit strategy.

It is also worth distinguishing between strategic and operational management. Operational management is routine, is limited to specific areas, deals with small-scale change and is resource led. Strategic management, on the other hand, deals with non-routine issues with long-term, fundamental, organization-wide implications

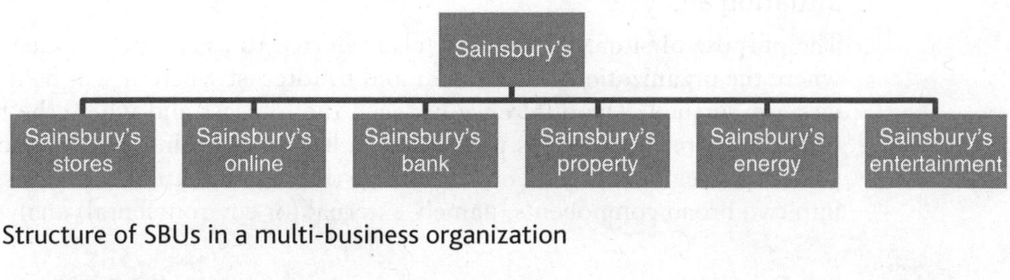

Figure 5.1 Structure of SBUs in a multi-business organization

and is driven by the environment or expectations rather than existing resources and competences.

THE STRATEGIC RETAIL PLANNING PROCESS

In order to develop retailing strategies, retailers need to follow a systematic procedure or planning process. The planning process describes analysis of the current state of the business, the formulation, choice and evaluation of alternative strategic directions and the implementation of the chosen strategies. Given the importance of strategic decisions for the future success of the business, a systematic approach is vital. The strategic planning process consists of the following major steps:

1. Defining the business philosophy and mission.
2. Setting corporate objectives.
3. Situation analysis.
4. Identification and evaluation of strategic opportunities.
5. Development of marketing and positioning strategies.
6. Development of suitable retailing mix strategies.
7. Implementation and control.

Defining the business philosophy and mission, and corporate objectives

The strategic planning process starts by identifying the firm's mission or purpose for its existence and hence the scope of the business. A mission statement needs to identify the products and services to be offered and the customers to be served. It also needs to indicate how the resources and capabilities of the firm will be used to create customer satisfaction and how the firm intends to compete in its chosen markets. An example of a mission statement is that of Tesco, whose mission is to 'create value for customers to earn their lifetime loyalty' (Tesco annual report and financial statement, 2012, p. 20). This is supported by Tesco's core values of 'No one tries harder for customers' and to 'treat people, how we like to be treated'. This reflects not only the way it intends to treat its customers, but also how it treats its employees and what it expects from them in return (see Figure 5.2).

Situation analysis

The purpose of situation analysis (also referred to as situation audit) is to determine where the organization is at present and to forecast where it will be if existing strategies are pursued. The difference between the forecast and where the firm is likely to be if the current strategy is pursued is called the planning or strategic gap. The purpose of strategic management is to bridge this gap. Situational analysis can be divided into two broad components, namely external (or environmental) analysis and internal

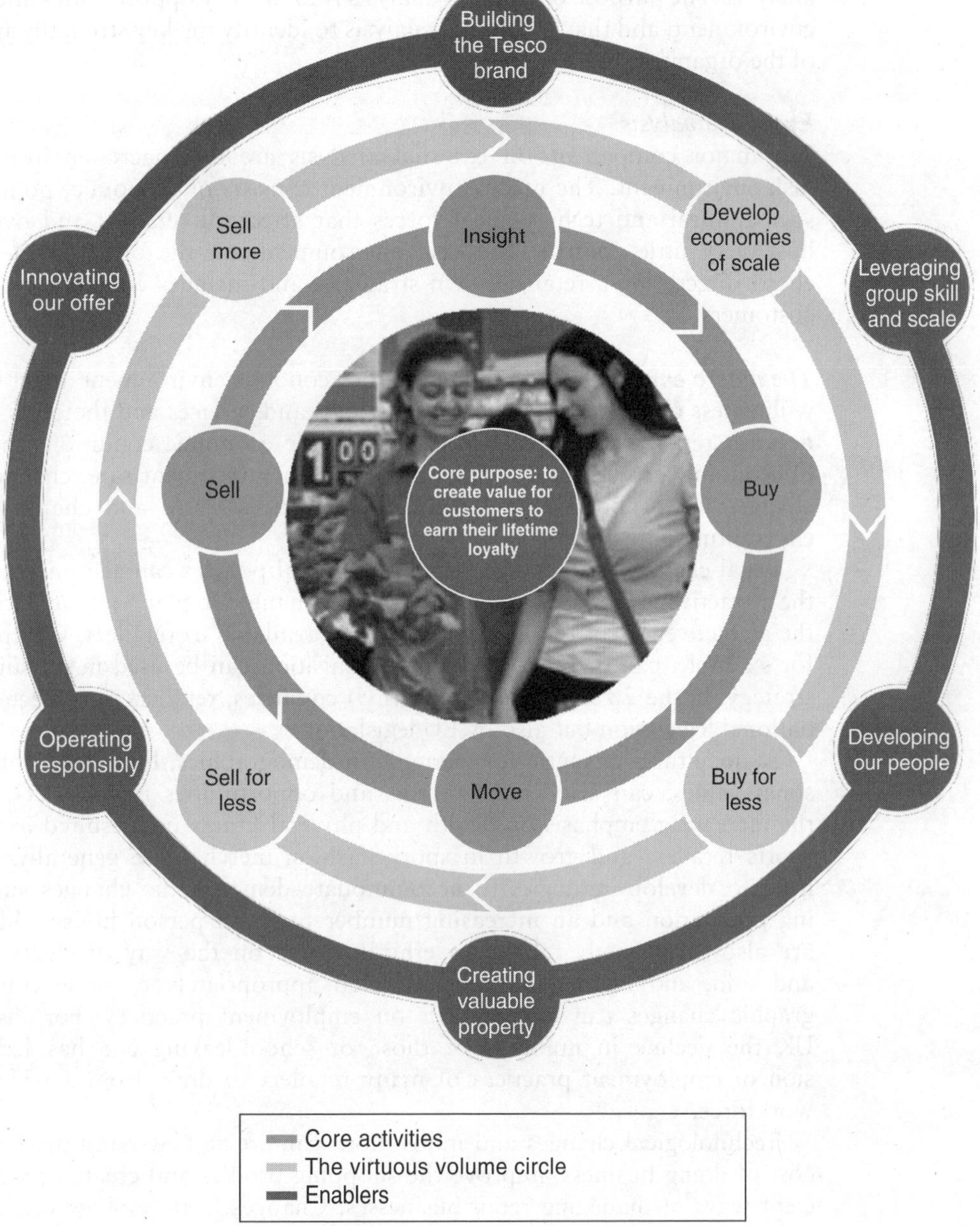

Figure 5.2 Tesco's Mission and Business Model

Source: Tesco Annual Report, 2012.

analysis. The purpose of external analysis is to identify opportunities and threats in the environment, and that of internal analysis to identify the key strengths and weaknesses of the organization.

External analysis

The major components of external analysis are the macro environment and the task environment. The macro environment consists of economic, political and legal, sociocultural and technological forces that affect all retailers and over which they have very little control. The task environment, on the other hand, can be influenced directly by a retailer's own strategies and includes competitors, suppliers and customers.

The macro environment Changes in the economic environment affect the ability and willingness of consumers to purchase goods and services and the costs of doing business for retailers. Important indicators of the economic conditions include the rate of economic growth, rates of inflation, the unemployment rate, changes in incomes, changes in corporate and personal debt, interest rates and changes in consumer expenditure patterns.

Legal changes and changes in governmental policies can also increase or decrease the attractiveness of a market. For instance, changes in planning regulations can affect the attractiveness of the locations that are available to retailers. Competition policy, for example, can determine whether acquisition can be used in pursuit of a growth strategy. In the 28 European Union (EU) countries, retailers are affected not only by national legislation but also by EU legislation.

Sociocultural changes, for example in demographics, lifestyles, attitudes and personal values, can also create threats and opportunities for retailers. For instance, the increasing emphasis on health and physical fitness has resulted in the growth of sports retailers and growth in sports fashion merchandise generally. Retailers also need to develop strategies to accommodate demographic changes such as an ageing population and an increasing number of single-person households. Consumers are also increasingly taking an ethical stance on the way products are produced and sold, and retailers need to respond appropriately to these concerns. Demographic changes can also impact on employment practices. For instance, in the UK the decline in numbers of those of school-leaving age has led to the revision of employment practices of many retailers to draw from a wider pool of the workforce.

Technological changes and innovations can create new retail markets, reduce the cost of doing business, improve the shopping process and create new and more efficient ways of managing retail businesses. Changes in technology can make retailers vulnerable to competition from new retailers, and existing competitors may be willing and able to exploit the new technology faster than them. In the past 20 years, information technology (IT) has transformed all aspects of retailing beyond recognition. The impact of IT can be seen in the now ubiquitous use of EPOS (electronic point of sale) and EFTPOS (electronic funds transfer at point of sale) terminals and loyalty cards, the use of EDI (electronic data interchange) to improve availability service to customers and improved communication between suppliers and retailers. The Internet is the latest IT innovation to transform retailing in all its aspects, creating new retailing channels, competitors and ways of cooperating and communicating with suppliers.

The task environment The task (or operating) environment has direct impact on the retailer but, unlike the macro environment, can also be influenced by the retailer's own strategies. Major factors in the task environment include competitors, suppliers and customers.

Competitive factors and the influence of suppliers have been discussed at length in Chapter 3; therefore, we concentrate here on market development and customer-related factors. Large markets are attractive to large retailers because they are more likely to generate the sales required to cover the large capital investments and the profitability required by these organizations. Growing markets are also more attractive than mature markets because competition is less intense and profitability is higher in growing markets. Hence, the strategies pursued by retailers need to be appropriate to the level of market development.

Many retail markets are seasonal, which requires accurate sales forecasting to ensure that most is made of the sales opportunities and that resources are used efficiently. For instance, fashion retailing is seasonal and requires an accurate knowledge of the latest fashion trends to ensure that the merchandise sells and that there are no stock-outs. Retailers can influence customers through their marketing strategies, but the ability to react quickly to changes in customer needs and competitors' marketing strategies is essential for survival in fast-moving retailing markets.

Internal analysis

The purpose of internal analysis (or an internal audit) is to assess the strategic capabilities of the retailer by examining the quality and quantity of resources available, how effectively they are used and the extent to which they are unique and difficult to imitate by competitors. Resources can be grouped into physical assets, human resources, financial resources and intangible resources. Intangible resources include goodwill embodied in the retailer's own brands and the retailer's image.

The following is an illustration of the type of questions that should be asked when conducting an internal audit of resources:

1. *Finance.* What is the cash flow from existing activities? What is the ability of the company to raise debt or equity financing? This will depend upon the financial standing of the company and the current levels of the debt-to-equity ratio (or gearing). What is the quality of financial management within the company?
2. *Merchandising.* How good are the knowledge and skills of buyers? How good is the company's relationship with its suppliers? How successful is the company at developing and managing own brands?
3. *Marketing.* What is the marketing capability within the company? To what extent is the firm market oriented? How good is the marketing research function? How good is the competitor intelligence system? How effective is marketing at generating new custom? How effective is marketing at maintaining customer loyalty?

4. *Management capabilities*. What is the capability of the company's management? Are the capabilities and experience of the top management team adequate? What are the capabilities of middle management? Is there sufficient depth? Is the management committed?
5. *Store management*. What are the capabilities of the store managers? What is the quality of sales assistants? Are the non-management-grade employees adequately trained and motivated? Is the staff turnover rate amongst employees at acceptable levels?
6. *Operations*. What is the overhead cost structure? What are the capabilities of the logistics/distribution system at delivering merchandise to stores? How good are the information systems? How effective are the stock control systems? How good are the loss prevention systems?

The effectiveness with which resources are used is often assessed by comparing present performance with historical performance, or with the industry norm. A problem with historical analysis is that the focus of analysis is internal and does not take into account the performance of competitors. This is rectified by comparison with industry norms. However, problems with industry analysis include lack of comparative information as well the fact that the industry as a whole could be performing poorly. For this reason there is increasingly a search for best practice and benchmarking relative to best practice. Best practice seeks to assess performance against 'best-in-class' performance wherever it is found, and not merely in the sector in which the retailer operates.

Differences in performance between retailers are usually due to more than just differences in resources deployed. Difference in performance also results from the way the resources are deployed to create competences within the organization. Certain competences created by the organization will be such that they enable the retailer to be more efficient than its competitors or provide its customers with better value. These core competences need to be difficult to emulate in order to provide long-term advantage.

Competitive advantage and competitive strategies

In order to survive over the long term, retailers need to build sustainable competitive advantage (SCA) over their rivals in the market. SCA can be built in many ways, and in essence any activity that a retailer undertakes can form the basis of competitive advantage. However, this competitive advantage must be such that it allows the retailer to fulfil customer's needs significantly better than its competitors and be sustainable over the long term (that is, difficult for the competitors to emulate). Major methods of creating SCA include opening stores at convenient locations, building customer loyalty, building close relationships with suppliers, efficient logistics and supply-chain management, creating good information systems (including customer database management), selling exclusive merchandise (including own brands), obtaining buying economies of scale, providing superior customer service and having a knowledgeable and motivated sales force.

SCA is most likely to be achieved through multiple approaches rather than any single approach. It is the specific combination of skills and competences of the organization that gives a retailer its specific advantage in the market. Essentially, however, there are two basic competitive strategies – differentiation and low cost. If these strategies are combined with the competitive scope of the firm (the width of the market targeted), this produces three generic strategies – cost leadership, differentiation and focus. The focus strategy can be further subdivided into differentiation focus and cost focus strategies. Each of the strategies requires specific skills, resources and business and organizational systems. A differentiation strategy, for instance, requires strong marketing capabilities, a reputation for quality and innovative products. This can take the form of exclusive or fashionable product ranges, convenient locations, store design and atmospherics and high levels of service. Cost leadership requires that all business systems and strategies are designed to control costs – requiring close supervision of labour, efficient store operation, low-cost distribution systems and strong buying (Vignette 5.1). A focus strategy attempts to achieve differentiation or low costs but is directed at a particular market segment (Porter, 1980) (see Figure 5.3).

VIGNETTE 5.1 IKEA: HIGH QUALITY AT LOW PRICES

The global furniture retailer IKEA's stated business mission is to offer a wide range of home furnishings with good design and function at prices so low that as many people as possible will be able to afford them. IKEA's offer can be summed up as 'affordable solutions for better living'. In other words, it offers differentiated products at low cost. IKEA's products are easily recognizable by their high-quality functional Scandinavian design. Consistency and clarity of design is achieved by centralizing the design function at its HQ in Älmhult, Sweden. Products are also designed to be low cost and easy to manufacture.

Prices and costs are kept low in a number of ways but mainly by producing furniture that can be flat-packed and transported and assembled by the customer at home. Costs are also kept low by working closely with manufacturers to reduce costs, and using global sourcing and bulk buying to purchase raw materials at the best prices. The product range of over 10,000 SKUs (stock-keeping units – product lines) is kept the same around the world, which helps IKEA to benefit from huge economies of scale. This is supported by an efficient supply chain that provides an effective system for ordering from its suppliers and integrating them with the stores. This has been accomplished by setting up a network of 28 distribution centres in strategic locations around the world, which has helped to reduce logistical costs, and minimized inventory holding costs.

Store location and operation are areas of further major cost savings. IKEA stores are located in out-of-town locations and provide little service in comparison with traditional furniture stores (except for a free supervised playroom for children). However, by use of coordinated displays (where products are displayed in room-like settings), product information on sales tags and a comprehensive product catalogue, customers are assisted in making their purchasing decisions. Adjacent to display areas is a warehouse or self-serve hall, where customers collect the merchandise themselves. The large store format (stores in the UK range from 170,000 sq. ft. to 300,000 sq. ft.) with a combined warehouse allows direct delivery to the store and avoids the need for centralized warehousing, enabling further efficiencies to be gained. The success of IKEA's business formula is evident in the fact that it had 175 stores in 31 countries, generating sales of 11 billion euros in 2003. By 2012 IKEA was trading from 338 stores in 40 countries. The IKEA group itself owns 298 stores, with the remaining 40 being franchised. Reported turnover for 2012 was 27.5 billion euros, and IKEA expects to nearly double its sales to 50 billion euros by 2020.

IKEA was slow in entering the online market, but claims to have a billion visitors to its site in 2012. Online presence extends its reach nationally, an improvement for those who do not live within easy reach of its 18 stores in the UK, for instance.

Source: Norman and Ramirez (1993), Lawson (2012), IKEA Website (http://www.ikea.com)

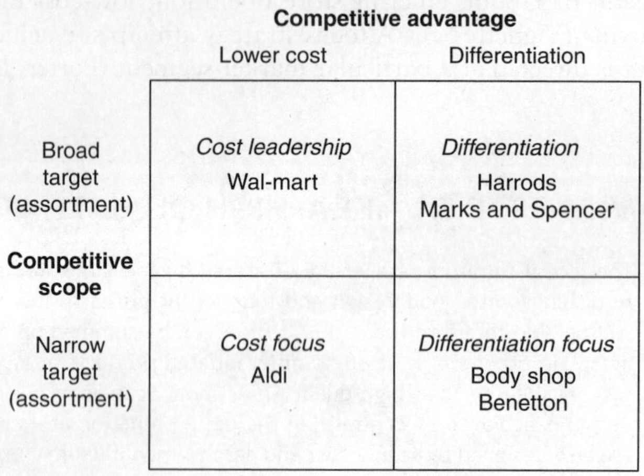

Figure 5.3 Generic competitive strategies

Porter (1980) suggests that a firm must pursue either a differentiation or a low-cost strategy; it cannot pursue both, or it will find itself 'stuck in the middle' and suffer from below-average profitability. However, evidence suggests that retailers following a hybrid strategy may be more profitable in the long run than those following pure differentiation or low-cost strategies. The reason for this appears to be the fact that firms following hybrid strategies are better able to cope with changes in the business environment. Furthermore, in an environment in which customers want good-value products without having to pay high prices for them, even retailers known for their differentiated offer cannot afford to ignore the cost side of the business. Also, some firms deliberately attempt to position themselves in the 'middle'. For instance, Sainsbury's have recently used the advertising message 'Living well for less'. Previously, Sainsbury's had also used the slogan 'Making life taste better, for less'. Sainsbury's advertising is clearly designed to indicate that high-quality products do not necessarily mean high prices.

The value chain and competitive strategies

The idea of a competitive strategy suggests that specific systems, or a value chain, need to be set up to achieve particular competitive objectives. A value chain consists of a set of activities ranging from design, production, marketing and distribution to support of the product that a firm markets. The activities in the value chain can be divided into what are called primary activities (operational activities) and support activities (or corporate functional activities). In retailing the primary activities consist of logistics and supply-chain management, merchandising, marketing, store operations and service. The support activities consist of human resource management, technology, buying and property management. It is the specific interrelationships between primary and support activities and the ways in which they are performed that give the firm its particular competitive advantage in the marketplace. Implementation of specific strategies requires consistency between the various elements of the value chain. For example a low-cost strategy would require that all elements of the value chain emphasize the reduction of costs.

Identification and evaluation of strategic opportunities

Having conducted internal and external analyses, the retailer should be able to identify its key strengths and weaknesses and the major opportunities and threats that it faces. This is often termed SWOT analysis – strengths, weaknesses, opportunities and threats. It is also sometimes referred as TOWS analysis, emphasizing that analysis of the external environment (threats and opportunities) should take place before internal analysis (strengths and weaknesses). Ranking of the issues in terms of importance helps to provide a focus for the strategic issues upon which the retailer should focus on.

After conducting the situation analysis, the retailer needs to decide on the strategic direction for the organization. The main strategies available are growth, consolidation and harvesting. For example, retailers in the mature or declining phase of the life cycle need to consider productivity improvements or even withdrawal from the market. In such a situation major injections of capital are difficult to justify; instead, the focus is on making as much profit as possible from the venture.

Productivity strategies aim to improve earnings and increase the efficiency of current resources through cost reductions, higher turnover and margins through an improved assortment and higher prices. Strategies for improving efficiency include increasing inventory turnover by utilizing store space more effectively, and reducing costs of labour, credit and logistics and other operating costs.

Consolidation means making specific changes in the way the company operates, although the merchandise assortment and the customers remain the same. It does not, however, mean doing nothing. In a growth market, the retailer may seek to maintain its market share as the market grows; a failure to do so may mean that it does not benefit from economies of scale to the same extent as its competitors and thus becomes uncompetitive. Recovering market share in a mature market is extremely difficult. In mature markets, retailers are likely to consolidate their position by increasing emphasis on building customer loyalty, improving service quality, increasing marketing activity and/or increasing emphasis on productivity improvements.

Strategies for growth

There are four main growth strategies that are available to retailers, namely market penetration, market development, assortment/format development and diversification. This is illustrated by the matrix in Figure 5.4, which suggests that growth can come

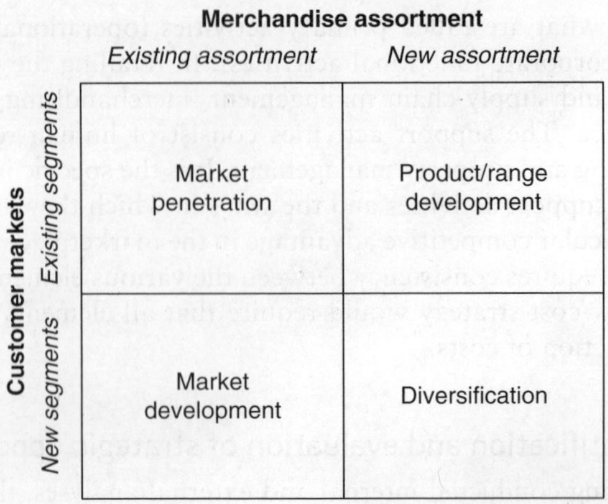

Figure 5.4 An assortment–market growth matrix

Source: Based on Ansoff (1965) and Kristenson (1983).

from either existing or new customer segments using either the existing merchandise assortment or a newly developed assortment package (Vignette 5.2).

VIGNETTE 5.2 GROWTH STRATEGY AT NEXT

The first Next store opened in February 1982 with an exclusive coordinated collection of stylish clothes, shoes and accessories for women. By the end of July 1982 there were 70 shops. This was followed by collections for men (1984), Next Interiors (1985) and children's wear (1987).

Next Directory, the mail-order catalogue shopping division, was launched in 1988 with 350 pages. The new larger format now has over 800 pages. Online shopping was introduced in 1999, and now the entire catalogue is available on the Internet – a first in home shopping in the UK. In September 2001 Next launched its own online flower retail service through http://www.nextflowers.co.uk. The site is also accessible from the Next Directory website. With sales of around £1,200 million, Next Directory now accounts for around a third of the company's total turnover, whereas it was around a quarter 10 years earlier. Next Directory has over 3 million active customers and websites serving around 60 countries.

At the start of 2003, Next was trading from over 330 stores in the UK and Ireland and 49 stores overseas. By 2013 the store numbers had increased to over 500 in the UK and Ireland, and Next International trading from nearly 200 mainly franchised stores in 60 countries. The company acquired the youth brand Lipsy in 2008. It designs and sells its own-branded younger women's fashion products.

In recent years Next has sought to achieve growth through the development of larger stores and expansion of product ranges, particularly in the home furnishings area. Since 2001, a number of larger format stores have opened in the UK, including at Bluewater Park, Middlesbrough, Bromley, Norwich, Belfast and Liverpool. Its largest store opened in 2011, with 57,000 sq. ft. of retail space selling its full range of products including all clothing departments, home, DIY and garden and leisure as well as Lipsy branded range. New store locations have tended to be in out-of-town retail parks.

Sources: Various Next annual reports and the Next Plc website (http://www.next.co.uk)

Market penetration involves targeting existing customers with the existing retail assortment/range of products, and increasing market share by attracting a larger proportion of the total sales generated within the trading areas of existing stores. This can be achieved either by getting existing customers to visit the store more often, or buying more on each trip, or attracting customers from competitors. Market penetration involves increasing retail marketing activities including the following:

1. Improved visual merchandising to increase impulse buys.
2. Store extensions/revamps.
3. Increasing customer loyalty.
4. Price reductions.
5. Increasing promotions.
6. Increasing convenience, for example by longer opening hours.

Market penetration strategies are most appropriate where the target market is still growing. In mature markets, consolidation via productivity gains may play a more important role. Market penetration strategies are most likely to succeed when they are based on the retailer's strengths that its competitors cannot match. For instance, price reductions can be easily copied by competitors and are unlikely to succeed in the long run unless they are based on low-cost structures.

Market development involves targeting new market segments using the existing merchandise assortment. This can take the form of either geographic expansion within the domestic environment, or targeting segments of the market not previously targeted by the retailer. Targeting new segments inevitably involves some re-positioning of the retail offer in order to appeal to the new segments. It involves the use of more capital and greater risk than the market penetration strategy.

Product/assortment development involves increasing sales from existing target markets by developing new products/service mixes to cater for the wider needs of customers. This can take the form of old lines being replaced by new ones, or the addition of new product lines and items, or both. This strategy has been used very effectively by the large grocery retailers who have added numerous non-food lines to their stores including stationery, books, CDs, clothes and electrical goods, amongst others.

Diversification involves targeting new markets with new products/retail formats. Diversification can be either related or unrelated to the current business. Related diversification involves undertaking activities that share some similarity with current business processes, marketing or technologies. The similarities might, for instance, involve using the same logistics/distribution system, or information systems. The

Arcadia Group, for example, has developed a diversified set of stores focusing at various segments of men's and women's fashion. The stores include Burton, Topman, Wallis, Miss Selfridge, Evans, Topshop and Dorothy Perkins. The group in essence constitutes a set of branded stores.

Vertical integration or the undertaking of activities further up the distribution chain, such as wholesaling or manufacturing, is a form of diversification as both activities involve different operational skills and competences compared with retailing. Examples of backward integration include retailers such as Benetton and IKEA, both of whom manufacture as well as retail their products.

Unrelated diversifications have no commonality with the existing retail business. For instance, Tesco and Sainsbury's have diversified into banking.

Range extension, market extension and internationalization

A more realistic view of product/assortment development and market development suggests that retailers do not move from current to new market segments in one step, nor do they move from existing merchandise assortments to new assortments in one leap. Such strategies would involve considerable risk. An intermediate strategy is to adapt current merchandise assortments and to extend market coverage by targeting closely related segments before targeting more difficult market segments and segments unrelated to the current ones. For instance, domestic geographical expansion would precede international expansion; this is illustrated in Figure 5.5.

Figure 5.5 suggests that in addition to market penetration, market development, product/range development and diversification, a further three growth strategies are available to retailers. These are range extension, market extension and

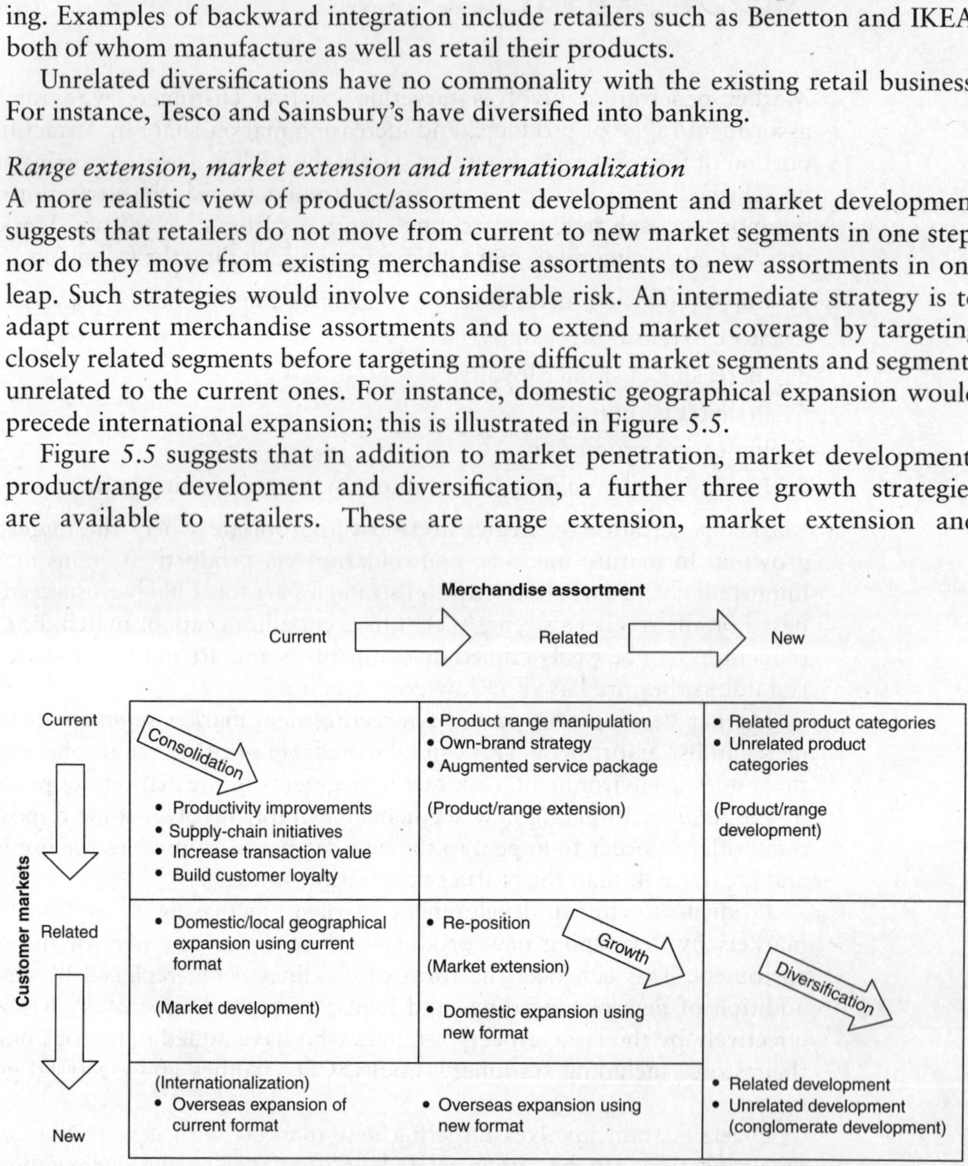

Figure 5.5 Retail strategy – merchandise assortment/market options

Source: Adapted from Knee and Walters (1985) and Omura (1986).

internationalization. Range extension involves the addition of some new lines not previously offered by the retailer. For instance, a clothes retailer may add shoes to its current lines, aimed at existing customers as a complementary purchase to clothes. It may also start offering own-branded products to its customers. Again, the own-branded products would offer more choice to customers without changing the overall merchandise offer.

Market extension involves development of related market segments with a modified but related product offer. Hence, market extension is more than just geographical expansion of the retail network An example is the development of convenience store formats by large supermarkets in the UK – for example Tesco's Express and Sainsbury's Local formats. In both cases the stores are smaller, sell a more focused set of lines aimed at the convenience shopper and are located in more convenient high-street locations or petrol forecourts for added convenience.

The introduction of the internationalization strategy allows us to distinguish market development in domestic markets from market development in foreign markets. This is necessary as international activities are much more risky than domestic activities, because the retailing environment is very different to the domestic one.

Evaluating alternative retailing strategies

Having delineated the strategic options available, the retailer needs to decide on a specific strategic action. This requires the evaluation of the strategies in terms of how they help to bridge the strategic gap, profitability, risk and the ability of the organization to undertake the particular strategy. One useful method of doing this is to compare the attractiveness of the market opportunities with the possible competitive advantages of the retailer. The technique suggests that the highest amount of resources should be invested in opportunities where the retailer has the strongest competitive advantage. For instance, a retailer targeting a new segment would evaluate the attractiveness of market opportunity in terms of

1. Market size.
2. Market growth rate.
3. Degree of competition and competitive structure.
4. Profitability of the segment.
5. Technology requirements.
6. Legal and regulatory issues.
7. Human resource requirements.
8. Environmental issues.

This information must be compared with the retailer's strengths relative to that of competition on factors such as

1. Current market share.
2. Merchandising skills.
3. Buying strength.
4. Supply-chain management and supplier relations.

5. New product development.
6. Own-label reputation.
7. Financial resources.
8. Sales force.
9. Managerial competence.
10. Fit with current retailer image in terms of breadth and depth of product lines, quality and reliability and customer service.

To operationalize the technique, the retailer rates each product area (or SBU) on each of the factors. The ratings are then combined into indexes of market attractiveness and retailer strength and plotted on a two-dimensional matrix. Each dimension is usually divided into three categories – high, medium and low. The position of the product reflects its attractiveness and suggests a course of action. For instance, where the market attractiveness and business position are strong, the retailer should invest aggressively and grow the opportunity. Where the market attractiveness and business position are weak, the recommended strategy is either to harvest or to divest unless the product category is to be vital to the overall success of the business. In the intermediate situation, where the opportunities are moderately strong on both dimensions, or moderately strong on one and weak on the other, firms are recommended to invest selectively.

Development of marketing and positioning strategies

By this stage the retailer has set general objectives and analysed a number of opportunities and decided on a specific direction for the organization and the opportunities it wishes to take advantage of. For each of the opportunities chosen, the retailer now needs to set specific objectives and allocate resources to achieve the objectives. In order to achieve the set objectives, marketing strategies have to be devised. These are normally developed for specific market segments rather than the market as a whole, as this makes more effective use of resources. After selecting the target markets, a positioning strategy must be developed.

A positioning strategy is a plan of action for how the retailer will compete in the targeted markets and how it will differentiate itself from competitors in those markets. Retail positioning is the process of creating and maintaining a distinctive and valued image of the retailer in the target customer's mind relative to its competitors. This emphasizes the fact that positioning is a relative concept and understanding consumers' perceptions is the key to effective positioning in the market. Positioning can be a deliberate attempt to differentiate from the rest of the market (for instance Harrods), or an attempt to be as close as possible to the average shopper's view of the attributes of an ideal retailer in a particular market segment.

Walters (1989) suggests that positioning should be either merchandise or service led. Wortzel (1987) suggests that another basis for positioning strategies is to distinguish between symbolic and functional merchandise, and whether it attracts high or low margins. The reason here is that people are motivated to buy the two categories and shop for them in different ways. Wortzel suggests three main positioning strategies, namely product differentiation, service and personality augmentation and price leadership.

1. Product differentiation is achieved through unique or exclusive products or brands, own-branded products and unusually broad or deep merchandise assortments.
2. Service and personality augmentation can be achieved in many different ways, including high levels of personal service, convenient locations, long opening hours, generous returns policy, home delivery and so forth.
3. Price leadership can be established through offering low or discounted pricing, and good value or price promotions on key items.

Positioning is not a once-and-for-all decision. Because of changes in the market (consumers and the competitors), the positioning may need to be adjusted. Re-positioning needs to be considered where there is a big discrepancy between consumers' perceptions and management perceptions. This is usually reflected in poor performance and declining market share. Re-positioning can also be used to target a new set of customers.

The retail mix

The retail marketing and positioning strategy is put into effect by the retail mix – the set of controllable variables that the retailer can use to satisfy customers' needs and to influence their buying behaviour and compete effectively in the market. To implement a specific retailing strategy, managers must decide the best combination of retail-mix variables and coordinate the activities of the different elements of the mix such as

1. Merchandise assortment.
2. Location.
3. Price.
4. Visual merchandising.
5. Store atmosphere.
6. Customer service.
7. Advertising.
8. Promotions.
9. Personal selling.

Walters (1989) suggests that positioning is the result of interaction between the four main areas of the retailing marketing mix: trading style/format strategy, merchandise strategy, customer service and customer communications strategy.

Implementation and control

Without effective implementation, strategies are nothing. Effective implementation requires that appropriate resources be allocated to required tasks, which requires budgeting in respect of specific elements of the retailing mix, personnel and so forth. Effective implementation also requires scheduling and coordination of retailing activities. It requires the translation of retailing strategies into tactics. Functional strategies lead to the establishment of long-term objectives that must be translated into day-to-day operational decisions. For instance, when to advertise, what media to use and the length of promotion campaigns are tactical decisions influenced by the competitive environment and the communication strategy.

The implementation of new retailing strategies inevitably requires changes in working methods and responsibilities, which can lead to resistance from employees, and organizations need to develop strategies to reduce this resistance to a minimum and to actively sell the new strategies to their employees.

In order to assess how effectively strategies are being implemented and how far the strategic objectives are being achieved, control procedures need to be established to determine whether the objectives set are being achieved in the specified time periods. Such procedures allow unsatisfactory performance to be identified at an early stage, and remedial action or the re-evaluation of retailing strategies and objectives to be instigated (see Chapter 6 for further discussion).

EMERGENT STRATEGY VERSUS PLANNED STRATEGY

The discussion of the strategic management process above has emphasized a systematic top-down planning approach that suggests that strategy formulation precedes strategy implementation. This suggests that organizations systematically create strategies that they pursue, but some strategy writers reject this view and argue that rather than strategies being deliberately created by organizations, strategies can emerge without formal planning. Mintzberg (1990), for instance, is particularly critical of the rational planning approach to strategic management. He argues that strategies can emerge without the explicit intention of managers as a result of the cumulative effect of operational, day-to-day decision making, and only in retrospect is the strategy identified from the pattern of actions taken. In practice, it is more than likely that the realized strategies are some combination of planned and emergent (or unplanned) strategies. However, the planning approach has the advantage that it suggests that senior retail mangers should be proactive in formulating retailing strategies rather than waiting for strategies to emerge. In the fast-moving retailing environment, proactive strategic management is indispensable for long-term survival.

SUMMARY

This chapter has explained the nature of retail strategy and the strategic management planning process. In broad terms, strategy determines the long-term direction and scope of the organization. Developing retailing strategy involves defining the company's mission, setting objectives, situation analysis, identifying and evaluating strategic opportunities, developing marketing strategies to take advantage of the opportunities, developing a retail mix to meet customer needs and compete effectively in the market and effective implementation and control. Situation analysis (or SWOT analysis) identifies the strengths, weaknesses, opportunities and threats facing the organization. It determines where the organization is at present and where it will be if it continues with its current strategies. The difference between where it wants to be and where it is forecast to be is the strategic gap. The chapter has also discussed the generic strategies (differentiation, cost leadership and focus) available to retailers. The concept of the value chain as an essential prerequisite for implementing competitive strategies has also been discussed. Strategies available to the retailer to close the strategic gap include growth, consolidation and harvesting, and a framework for analysing the major growth strategies has been presented. Those discussed include market penetration, market development, product/assortment development, diversification, range extension, market extension and internationalization. For each of the opportunities selected, marketing strategies have to be devised to target specific markets and to position the retail offer relative to the competition. The retail marketing strategies are implemented using a suitable combination of the retail-mix variables. Strategic analysis and strategy formulation can be undermined by poor implementation, and hence it is essential that mechanisms are in place to ensure effective implementation and control so that timely remedial action can be taken, if necessary.

QUESTIONS

1. Explain the distinction between corporate strategy, business-unit strategy and functional strategy.
2. What is meant by 'strategic gap'?
3. What are the major growth strategies available to a retailer? Give examples of retailers that have used each of the strategies.
4. Explain the value chain concept using a major fashion retailer as an example.
5. How far do you agree that 'stuck in the middle' is not viable as a long-term competitive strategy?
6. Explain what is meant by the retail mix and how it can be used for retail positioning purposes.

REFERENCES AND FURTHER READING

Ansoff, H. I. (1965) *Corporate Strategy* (New York: McGraw-Hill).

Johnson, G. and Scholes, K. (1997) *Exploring Corporate Strategy: Text and Cases*, 4th Edition (London: Prentice Hall).

Knee, D. and Walters, D. (1985) *Strategy in Retailing: Theory and Application* (Oxford: Philip Allan).

Kristenson, L. (1983) 'Strategic Planning in Retailing', *European Journal of Marketing*, vol. 17, no. 2, pp. 43–59.

Lawson, Alexa, (2012), 'Ikea Eyes 50bn Turnover', *Retail Week*, 23 October.

McGee, J. (1987) 'Retailer Strategies in the UK', in G. Johnson (ed.), *Business Strategy and Retailing* (Chichester: John Wiley & Sons), pp. 89–106.

Mintzberg, H. (1990) 'The Design School: Reconsidering the Basic Premises of Strategic Management', *Strategic Management Journal*, vol. 11, no. 6, pp. 171–95.

Norman, R. and Ramirez, R. (1993) 'From Value Chain to Value Constellation: Designing Interactive Strategy', *Harvard Business Review*, vol. 71, no. 4, pp. 65–77.

Omura, G. S. (1986) 'Developing Retailing Strategy', *International Journal of Retailing*, vol. 1, no. 3, pp. 17–32.

Porter, M. E. (1980) *Competitive Strategy: Techniques for Analyzing Industries and Competitors* (New York and London: The Free Press).

Porter, M. E. (1985) *Competitive Advantage: Creating and Sustaining Superior Performance* (New York and London: The Free Press).

Prahalad, C. K. and Hamel, G. (1990) 'The Core Competence of the Corporation', *Harvard Business Review*, vol 68, no. 3, May/June, pp. 79–91.

Robinson, T. M. and Clarke-Hill, C. M. (1990) 'Directional Growth by European Retailers', *International Journal of Retail and Distribution Management*, vol. 18, no. 5, pp. 3–14.

Sands, S. and Ferraro, C. (2010), 'Retailers' Strategic Responses to Economic Downturn: Insights from Down Under', *International Journal of Retail & Distribution Management*, vol. 38, no. 8, pp. 567–77.

Tesco (2012) Annual Report and Financial Statements http://www.tescoplc.com/files/pdf/reports/tesco_annual_report_2012.pdf [accessed 15 September 2013]

Walters, D. (1989) *Strategic Retailing Management – A Case Study Approach* (London: Prentice Hall).

Walters, D. and White, D. (1987) *Retail Marketing Management* (London: Palgrave Macmillan).

Wortzel, L. H. (1987) 'Retailing Strategies for Today's Mature Marketplace', *Journal of Business Strategy*, vol. 7, no. 4, pp. 45–56.

6 IMPLEMENTING RETAIL STRATEGY

LEARNING OBJECTIVES

- To understand the structural organization of a retail business and how this supports the implementation of a retail strategy.
- To appreciate the responsibilities of the outlet manager within a multiple retail organization, and the key role that they play in the implementation of a strategy at the customer interface.
- To gain an overview of the various departments that are likely to be found in a centralized multiple retailer, and an appreciation of the functions that they perform within the business.
- To understand the concept of taking an integrated approach towards monitoring and controlling the strategic plan.

INTRODUCTION

In the previous chapter we looked at the way in which 'the retailer' should go about formulating retail strategy. Formulating a retail strategy is a planning process; it is about establishing where a company is going to go in the future and allocating resources in order to reach the company objectives within that plan. The strategic plan must find a balance between the risk associated with the goals pursued, and the resources deployed in the attainment of those goals. Implementation of the strategy requires an orchestration of human resources, financial resources and assets, which includes tangible assets like outlets, distribution centres, information technology systems, web pages, head offices and stock, as well as intangible assets such as brand values, reputation and the image of the retailer.

Within a small retailer, the planning and operation of a retail strategy may be carried out by a single person or small number of people who have broadly defined roles. However, as organizations get larger, tasks become divided, so that the use of individuals' talents and experience can be maximized. This chapter considers the various ways in which tasks can be divided and how roles can be allocated so that the retail business runs as effectively as possible. It also explores how retailers go about introducing mechanisms for monitoring and controlling the activities of the various parts of the business, to ensure that the strategy is 'on track'.

MANAGING A RETAIL OUTLET

We have emphasized the need to be customer focused in the formulation of a retail strategy, and it therefore makes sense to start at the customer interface when considering how a retail business might be managed in order to achieve the objectives it sets for the strategic plan. Whether a retailer uses a store or non-store format, the way customers are dealt with is a real priority in the management of any retail business. In Chapter 15 we consider all aspects of retail service, and it is those members of the business who are employed as 'sales advisers, sales associates, sales consultants or customer services operators' who take on the task of implementing the customer-service strategy. Whether the general level of personal service is low, for example within a supermarket, or more involved as in a speciality store, the contribution of service to the overall strategy is supported at the outlet level. Customer-focused retailers will ensure that support is given to the teams of customer-sales employees in order that they can concentrate on the task of maximizing sales. This support might come in the form of a sales supervisor who organizes the sales team to ensure that the availability of sales staff is matched to the rate of customer flow, and to provide advice on any problems team members may have. The supervisor is likely to be a more experienced sales employee, who is prepared to take on the extra responsibility of leading the team. In a small retailer, the supervisory role may be taken on by the store or outlet manager, as one of many tasks in a multifaceted role.

Multi-channel retailing provides challenges for retailers in terms of implementing a consistent strategy across all shopping modes; however, the store remains central to that purpose and sets a standard for the rest of the retail organization. Even though sales may be made via a different customer route, the store remains the face of a business for the majority of large retailers. This chapter is therefore focused mainly on the implementation of strategy within a physical store, with a section at the end which considers how other retail formats in a multi-channel retailer complement the store in terms of strategy implementation. Many major multi-channel retailers are finding that their website has grown to be the most lucrative 'store' in their outlet portfolio.

THE OUTLET MANAGER

The main objective for the outlet manager is to meet the targets set for the successful running of that outlet. These targets are often instigated in the form of financial aims, based on sales turnover and/or profitability. However, other targets that could be set include the number of customers or the number of transactions. In addition, more specific targets such as the number of customers recruited for a store card, or sales of a particular type or brand of product, might be used during a marketing campaign.

The larger the store, the more likely it is for the responsibility of the store manager to increase, as numbers of staff and complexity of product range normally grow relative to store size. The diversity in a store manager's role will depend on the extent to which a central organization such as a head office or company headquarters takes on specific tasks, but the list below shows areas of responsibility that are common in the store manager's remit.

1. *Managing staffing levels.* This includes the general management of sales personnel and support or auxiliary staff (cleaners, maintenance, financial clerks and so on). It includes scheduling, recruiting, developing and, if necessary, disciplining employees. Staffing in the retail industry is complex and problematic because of the need for flexibility (multi-skilling) and the need to balance customer flow patterns with the availability of both part-time and full-time employees (Fraser and Zarkada-Fraser, 2000, Grugulis and Bozkurt, 2011).
2. *Organizing the sales environment.* This involves implementing store layout plans, managing the allocation and replenishment of stock and overseeing the implementation of visual merchandising (display) plans. A certain degree of interpretation of plans communicated from a central department may be necessary in the light of specific store characteristics. However, the outlet manager is ultimately responsible for the way the store appears to customers, and therefore supports the corporate brand image of the retailer.
3. *Supporting marketing initiatives.* This requires the implementation of the marketing tactics devised in order to pursue strategic marketing aims: for example organization of point-of-sale display materials and window displays, allocating space to promoted items, overseeing price amendments and raising awareness of marketing campaigns with the sales team.
4. *Staff development.* It is the outlet manager's responsibility to ensure that the training needs of the outlet staff team are met, by using either in-house or external training provision, and to identify potential candidates for promotion.
5. *Health and safety.* Implementing the company's health and safety policies, providing risk assessments and undertaking induction training for new staff are part of this process. Monitoring and updating those policies and ensuring procedures are followed is an increasingly important role in a litigious society.
6. *Monitoring performance.* This involves analysing sales and profit reports – these might be orientated towards product performance (at department or item level), or towards the performance of members of the sales staff (employee productivity). The outlet manager needs to accommodate detailed knowledge about how the outlet is performing in order to identify any problem areas for further investigation.
7. *Minimizing costs.* In order to maximize outlet profitability, the store manager needs to keep the costs of running the outlet as low as possible. This involves the elimination of waste, including overstaffing and the reduction of shrinkage (such as theft and damages). This aspect of a retail manager's job is especially important when a low-cost strategy is being pursued (Reynolds et al., 2005).
8. *Forecasting and budgeting.* The outlet manager is best placed to predict future performance by estimating sales through the outlet, estimating future costs and setting budgets. Agreeing forecasts with line managers (typically a regional retail operations manager, or a central retail operations department) and setting performance targets for the outlet based on forecasts are part of this process. Retail managers also need to provide feedback to and communicate with centralized

departments, such as the buying department about quality problems with stock or the human resource management department regarding a staff disciplinary action.

9. Team leadership. The outlet manager has the responsibility for motivating a team of colleagues and reducing any resistance to change in working methods that may be required when new strategic directions are set. They may be involved in setting targets and will be responsible for reviewing and appraising of team members' activities in accordance with the strategic objectives of the organization.

In a large retail store, such as a multi-department superstore, a team of deputy managers and/or department managers will support the store manager. These subordinates will have partial store management responsibilities, and in this instance the amount of time the store manager spends collating information and liaising with the management team will increase and the tasks of managing staffing levels and organizing the sales environment will be delegated.

THE CENTRALIZED RETAILER

The notion of a centralized retail structure was introduced in Chapter 2. In essence, any retailer that has more than one outlet but carries out functions on behalf of the outlets collectively as opposed to individually is operating a centralized structure. The term 'multiple retailer' is generally acknowledged to refer to a retailer that runs ten or more outlets, and one with less that ten outlets is considered, somewhat confusingly when the number is closer to ten than one, to be an 'independent retailer'. As a retail organization grows, the more specialized aspects of retail management tend to become the responsibility of individuals and then of dedicated departments, which are often then transferred to a separate, usually lower-cost, location. The benefits a retailer derives from centralization are essentially based on economies of scale and specialization. Many retail decisions that need to be made for one outlet need to be made for all outlets, and so a central body of employees becomes responsible for decision making for all outlets.

Figure 6.1 illustrates the relationship between a retailer's central head office, the stores network, the distribution centre, the call centre and suppliers in terms of product flow and information flow. The majority of employees at the head office work in departments dedicated to a particular aspect of retail management. Effectively, they are the departments that carry out the first stages of the strategic plan, while the personnel located within the outlets continue the implementation at the customer interface. Most central retail organizations will include the following departments:

1. Buying and merchandising (product/category management).
2. Marketing (may be separated into corporate marketing and store marketing). Public relations/publicity departments may operate separately to, or be incorporated with, the marketing department.
3. Logistics (distribution) – concerned with deliveries to store and/or customers and also deliveries from suppliers.

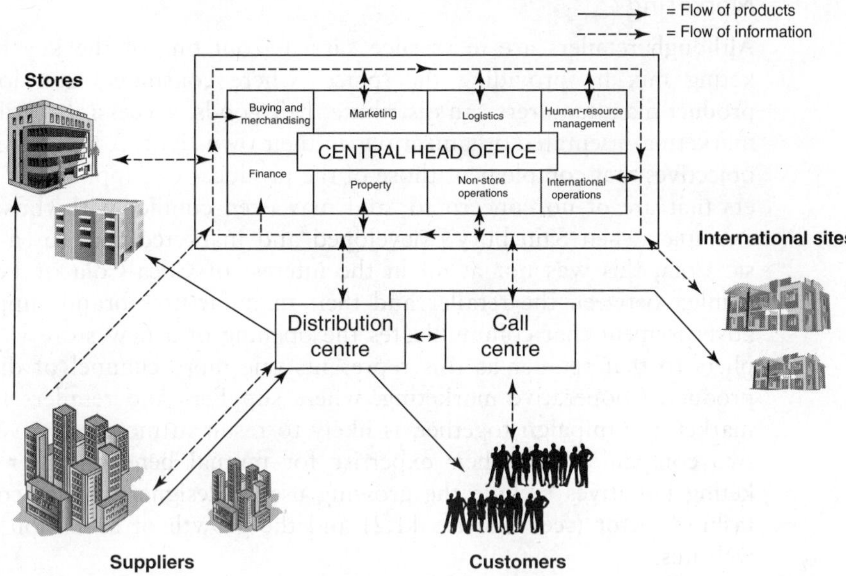

Figure 6.1 An international multichannel retailer

4. Human resource management (personnel).
5. Finance.
6. Property.
7. Non-store operations.
8. International operations.

An explanation of the operational responsibilities of each of these follows.

Buying and merchandising (product/category management)

The section of the central organization concerned with bringing the right products into the retail organization in order to satisfy the needs and desires of customers (often referred to as the buying office) is usually the largest section of a central organization in terms of number of employees. Teams of highly specialized experts with regard to particular product categories and their supply markets are responsible for allocating large sums of the retailer's money to products with the view to gaining an acceptable profit margin on those products when sold, which will be the lifeblood of the organization. Many of today's large multiples have been built on the back of talented 'traders' who developed a knack of buying the right thing and being able to sell it on well to consumers. Both Tesco and Marks and Spencer, for example, are retail empires founded by market traders. However, contemporary retail product management is a highly analytical task, involving the management of the movement of stock and the actions of the supply base in response to changes in consumer demand. A more detailed discussion of the buying and merchandising function can be found in Chapter 11.

Marketing

Although retailers are in essence carrying out one of the key functions of a marketing mix by providing the 'place' where consumers can locate products and product manufacturers can distribute their goods, successful retailers are often highly marketing-orientated organizations in their own right. A retailer may have marketing objectives that complement those of the producer or supplier, but they may have others that are of no concern to, and may even conflict with those of, suppliers. For example, when Sainsbury's developed and marketed their own-brand drink, Classic Cola, this was not at all in the interest of Coca-Cola or Pepsi, and it created conflict between the retailer and their manufacturer brand suppliers. However, an advertisement that communicates the opening of a new store is relevant to all suppliers to that retailer as this represents one more channel of distribution for their product. Cooperative marketing, where suppliers and retailers fund and develop a marketing campaign together, is likely to result in more effective campaigns, as the two companies pool their expertise for mutual benefit. Other collaborative marketing initiatives include the growing use of designer–retailer collaborations in the fashion sector (see Vignette 11.2) and the growth of affiliation marketing through websites.

Marketing has such a wide remit with regard to the implementation of a retailer's strategy that a number of more specialized departments may make up the marketing section. In particular, it makes sense to divide marketing communications into those that are corporate in nature (such as improving the overall image of the store, changing the retailer's market positioning or reinforcing the retail brand values), and those that are more specific in nature (such as store opening information, or product/price offers). Another way of organizing for retail marketing communications is to have one section devoted to the marketing needs of the individual outlets (store marketing), and another that deals with communications that are store-wide in nature. The advantage of this approach is that the relationship between the central marketing organization and the marketing initiatives that use local marketing service providers (such as the local press) is strengthened. In some retail organizations, individual outlets are responsible for their own local marketing. The drawback with this approach concerns control and consistency of the message across the retail organization.

Historically, it had been traditional for marketing departments and buying departments to operate separately within the central organization. Often the buying department had little or no responsibility for a product once initial orders had been placed. However, new buying approaches like category management (see Chapter 11) force the two functions together in order to achieve product-orientated objectives. Within the category, product developments and introductions have to be managed alongside established products and promotions so that the performance of the entire range is maximized. The buyer or product manager must therefore use marketing as a way of supporting the objectives set for the product category and the individual product items within it. The growth of online retailing and the parallel growth in online marketing opportunities have resulted in a converging of selling outlet and communication tool, especially when mobile devices are the facilitating technological device for retailer–consumer communications, and so multi-channel and multimedia marketing activity can be effectively integrated. See Chapter 14 for a deeper discussion of marketing communications for retailers.

The debate about whether or not public relations (PR) activities come under the umbrella of marketing continues and is reflected in the place of PR within the retail organizational structure. However, in an era when access to and immediacy of information is more actively sought, a department that manages external communications is very useful. Large retail organizations are under increasing scrutiny, particularly in relation to ethical issues, and corporate social responsibility is not a very familiar concept within the retail industry. Press releases as a means of disseminating good news through the media, or as a way to counteract negative publicity continue to be an important part of external communications in an era of increasingly fragmented, media channels.

Supply-chain management/logistics/distribution

Supply-chain management includes operations that move resources from raw material state to the consumer's carrier bag (Hines, 2004) and is ultimately responsible for providing the service of delivering stock to the retail outlet or, in the case of home shopping, to and from the customer. The department manages arrangements for deliveries from suppliers through the retail supply chain (involving transportation, warehousing and sorting) to the customer. It also includes the management of stock returns (reverse logistics). The supply-chain department liaises closely with both the buying and merchandising and the marketing departments to ensure that supply-chain operations support the product and marketing strategy of the organization. In some retail organizations, the departments are merged, for example in the case of fresh produce, because the logistics of food supply are so vital to the success of the product offer (Gustafsson et al., 2009). A more detailed discussion of the contribution that supply-chain management makes to the running of a retail business can be found in Chapter 7.

Human resource management

In spite of the growth of online retailing, the contribution of Internet-based analytical tools for deciphering online consumer behaviour and the growth of the informed customer, real people are still often best at fully understanding the needs and desires of customers, which can involve irrational, non-economically driven and emotional decision influences. Even though information systems provide a plethora of data on sales and consumer purchasing patterns, those data are only useful when interpreted by the retail buyer, stock manager or sales consultant and used to match customer needs and desires to product solutions, and so retailing operations still rely on the human resource for the implementation of strategy. In addition, retailers provide a social arena; the local post office, for example, may provide a focus for exchange of information in a community and indeed might provide a therapeutic service for the offloading of a moan or piece of gossip! Personnel employed for the many tasks within a retail business have to be 'people orientated'. No matter what powers of analysis an individual manager may have, unless they have the personal communication skills to convince others of their viewpoint, then the retail organization will be unable to benefit.

Human resource management may be decentralized or controlled by a head office, but it may make more sense to recruit for the outlets locally, operating within strict company guidelines. For example, wages for retail staff may vary across the country; unless a retailer is offering a competitive rewards package, they will not be able to recruit the best-calibre staff. Like the marketing department, the human resource department may be divided up, with one section dealing with managerial and head-office personnel, whilst another oversees the management of the sales teams within the outlets. Many large multiple retailers operate a system of regional human resource managers who monitor staffing levels and offer support and advice to store management on human resource issues. Where a retail outlet is large and employs a greater number of sales staff, then a personnel manager may be dedicated to and based at that outlet. In a competitive retail industry, good people are a source of competitive advantage, whether at head-office level or outlet level, where sales personnel become 'brand ambassadors', and so the management of human resources is central to implementing a retail brand strategy.

Employee motivation and development

Although many retail managers are highly regulated in terms of implementing and complying with decisions made centrally, 'leadership' in the areas of motivation and staff development is what most consider being central to their role as managers (Grugulis et al., 2011). These aspects of 'people management' are critical to ensure that teams understand and 'buy into' strategic objectives. According to Collins (2010) retailers are likely to improve staff retention if they offer professional development tailored to specific requirements and their own brand values. Development also needs to be held in esteem by all levels of management to demonstrate the crucial link between goals set out in a strategy and training given to help people to achieve them. High levels of motivation also improve employee retention and help to implement strategic objectives. Transparency regarding business performance and targets encourages people to feel part of a company and its strategy, and while money is the key motivator, family-friendly flexibility and acknowledgement of employees' commitments and responsibilities outside work can be more effective ways of letting staff know that they are valued. A thoughtful and detailed approach towards staff development and motivation can be cost-effective; for example a small retailer may be able to offer unique opportunities like taking sales associates on buying trips.

Career paths

The retail industry offers dynamic and lucrative careers. In a fast-moving and competitive business environment, only high-quality management can survive. Retail outlets are getting bigger, and with increased space the diversity of product offered has also expanded, and so the responsibility placed with store managers has also increased in size and complexity. Opportunities in specialist departments such as buying, merchandising, marketing and logistics have grown as retailers have become more sophisticated in their operations and approaches to the fundamental business functions associated with buying, distribution and selling. Many large retailers are now global players, with a network of stores across continents, and so retail management can provide the opportunity to work in familiar organizations overseas. Sourcing is another retail operation that is global in its outlook for many retailers, so this can also provide opportunities to work with supplying organizations in different countries, or in a role within a retailer's own overseas buying office networks.

In response to the growing demand for more appropriate retail skills and knowledge, training and development within the UK retail industry has improved and is supported by a number of key organizations such as the British Retailing Consortium (BRC Training Academy), the National Skills Academy (see Vignette 6.1), British Independent Retailer Association (BIRA) and the Fashion Retail Academy (FRA). There is a wide choice of retailing courses offered at higher-education institutions in the UK and a growing number of universities worldwide.

VIGNETTE 6.1 THE NATIONAL SKILLS ACADEMY

The National Skills Academy is a UK government-supported body whose vision is that of improved productivity in retail businesses and of their staff through training and development. The NSA provides a consistent national approach for training and development by operating a network of retail skills shops in partnership with national and local retailers, developers and training providers. The academy operates through a network of 'skills shops' which are supported by large national retail companies such as Tesco, Sainsbury's, House of Fraser, John Lewis/Waitrose and Boots and are adapted to the specific needs of local business areas. The shops provide services to both employees and retailers. Existing or potential retail workers can access training and coaching, careers and employment advice, pre-employment training, work experience opportunities and related vocational education. For retailers, initiatives include the following: masterclasses and learning and development qualifications, apprenticeships, business forums, development programmes specifically for independent retailers, management and leadership programmes and skills development programmes in specific areas such as customer service and selling or merchandising and replenishment. By working in partnership with employers, the National Skills Academy provides a consistent, sustainable yet responsive training approach to training and skills development in the largest private sector industry in the UK.

Source: http://www.nsaforretail.com/about-us/Pages/Services.aspx [accessed 15 August 2013]

As well as the development of retail managers, human resource management encompasses the 'personnel' function, which specifically deals with issues relating to people as employees of the retail organization, such as employment terms, wages and salaries, job descriptions, incentives and promotions. It also needs to be concerned that the retailer meets (or exceeds) its legal and moral obligations concerning health and safety, employee welfare, grievance procedures and so on.

Financial organization

As a retailer's business revolves around buying and selling, it is evident that financial management is a fundamental operational function, and its success enables the implementation of strategies such as geographical expansion or marketing development.

Funding the products entering the business and receiving income from sales are a perpetual aspect of the financial management of a retail business, and essentially determine the cash flow of the company. However, financial management is also concerned with the deployment of resources: making decisions about the spending of the profit generated on sales after the incoming stock has been paid for. In order to monitor the deployment of resources, spending needs to be managed at the outlet level, and centrally. At the outlet (store) level, the costs of running the outlet need to be balanced against the income generated by the store, and so sales targets, ordering forecasts, staffing budgets and running cost allowances can be used in the process of maintaining the balance sheet of the outlet. The extent to which the financial management is centralized varies. Some retailers may give their store managers financial autonomy and responsibility, whilst others may require stores to defer all decisions regarding spending to a head-office department.

At the central level, the performances of stores and product departments are reviewed on a regular (at least annual) basis, in order to identify trends that may require specific management attention. Any decision to change the outlet (for example to extend it, refurbish it or close it) is strategic in nature. For example, a particular store may currently be performing relatively poorly, but new retail developments in the town centre in which that outlet is located point to a better future for that store in years to come; therefore the outlet is kept within the portfolio with the view to improving performance in the future. As online retailing gains importance, many multiple retailers are reviewing their store portfolio. Smaller stores in particular cannot stock a full range of products, where the Internet has no limitation, and so may not be considered good representation of a retail brand. The costs of running a small outlet may outweigh the benefit of the level of sales generated, especially as more customers do multi-channel shopping, using larger stores as their reference points for browsing and trial and the Internet as the way to acquire the product. Changes to product ranges within the store are strategic decisions, taking into consideration the needs of the local catchment area, the presence of competitors (which may include different retailers according to product area) and the characteristics of the store itself. For example Primark may be considered to be competition to Marks and Spencer in the women's and children's clothing categories, but not in food or furniture. The multichannel shopping activity of local people may also influence which ranges are the best to hold in store.

Decisions regarding the funding of assets within the organization, for example building a new distribution centre or purchasing a new information management system, are also strategic decisions, concerning the deployment of considerable company resources from which the retailer hopes to generate a good return on their investment. This kind of investment therefore has to be sanctioned by the highest authorities, and monitored centrally.

The extent to which an organization puts pressure on individual departments and outlets to constrain costs is also strategic in nature. If a retailer is pursuing a cost-leadership strategy, then all decisions about running the organization have to be taken in the light of this strategic aim; spending at outlet and department level is likely to be severely restricted and heavily scrutinized.

The relationship between the money flowing out of the business to pay for stock and the money flowing in from the sale of products is usually managed by merchandisers (or stock controllers) who work with the buyers. They will schedule deliveries so that enough stock is ordered to meet anticipated sales, but they will also try to ensure that the retailer does not have too much stock. Slow-moving stock ties up company capital and runs the risk of the products becoming obsolete (especially fresh produce and high-fashion goods). Many recent supply-chain initiatives have reduced the levels of stock kept within a retail business, and this has helped retailers to improve their operational efficiency (see Chapter 7).

Managing performance in retailing

Economic downturns put a spotlight on cost reduction, performance management and productivity. According to Reynolds et al. (2005) retailers define productivity as the achievement of integrated targets in the following areas: sales, product range, service levels, availability, customer satisfaction, employee contribution and operating and financial performance. In terms of financial performance, achievement of profit is essential to survival, and the level of profit is usually an indicator of the success and health of an organization. In order to explore the management of profitability at store level, the case of a single-outlet retailer will be considered.

Given that profit is the surplus after deducting the cost of goods sold and running costs, profits can be increased by raising the gross margin on products (by increasing prices or reducing the cost of the goods from suppliers), increasing the quantities of goods sold to customers or reducing the costs of running the outlet.

The opportunities for increasing prices or increasing sales volumes may be limited by the competitive arena and the geographic location of the retailer, and while all the elements of the retail mix should be explored in order to improve sales (see Chapter 5), it may be more appropriate to consider reducing the costs of running the business (the operating costs) as a means of increasing profits.

The most significant everyday costs at store level for a retailer are wages/salaries, accommodation costs (rent, rates, maintenance, heating and lighting) and the costs of products sold. The opportunities to reduce product costs will depend on the relationships between retailers and their suppliers (see Chapter 11 on buying) and the negotiating skills of the retailer; however, the opportunities are unlikely to be great, especially in the case of the single-outlet retailer. It can therefore be concluded that control of labour, accommodation and administration costs is extremely important.

One way of managing the operation of a business is through budgetary control, which involves three essential stages. The first stage is to forecast the retailer's activity (such as sales and costs); the second stage is to monitor that activity, and make a comparison with the forecast; and the third stage is to investigate why the actual performance varied from that forecasted, and to undertake managerial action to put the company back on track.

Having put the budgeting and monitoring procedures in place, the task of the retail manager is to investigate any variance between planned and actual performance. Even if performance is better than the level planned, it is important to find out why this has happened so that opportunities are exploited as efficiently as possible. Part of the reviewing process into variances between planned and actual figures takes the form of 'ratio analysis', which is essentially a study of relationships between certain values within the financial make-up of the business (which are indicated in financial accounting summaries). The most useful ratios for retailers are as follows:

1. *Return on capital employed (ROCE)*. This compares the amount of profit (for example pre-tax net profit) made with the amount of money being invested to make that profit (for example the issued shareholding together with company reserves). The economic value added (EVA) of a company is a related concept, calculated by deducting the cost of capital from its operating profit.
2. *Liquidity*. This compares the amount of current assets that a retailer has with their current liabilities. It provides an indication of how easily the retailer would be able to meet their current financial obligations, should they need to.
3. *Stock turn rate*. This compares the amount of sales revenue to the amount of stock held to create those sales (using an average stockholding figure).

Whilst these measures indicate the overall health of the retail business, a deeper analysis of a retailer's performance as part of the management process may require the use of additional quantitative information. For example a commonly used performance measure in the retail industry is sales per square metre, often referred to as sales density. In some instances it might be appropriate to measure employee performance, for example by using sales per employee or sales per checkout as indicators.

In addition to the day-to-day operating costs associated with running a retail outlet, from time to time significant additional expenditure may be required in order to maintain or improve the overall level of business activity. Equipment such as tills and fixtures may need to be updated, or the whole shop may need to be redecorated, and so it makes sense to put some financial resources aside for this type of exceptional expenditure and build it into the budget for operational costs. The overall financial situation of the retail business can be summarized in the usual financial statements, such as the periodic profit and loss summaries and the balance sheet (see Figure 6.2).

In a multi-outlet retailer the costs of running a central organization will need to be built into the budget for operating costs and be subject to its own budgetary control. Given that a central organization does not earn sales income, it can only be considered as a cost, which then needs to be allocated to the income-earning sections of the business. This might take the form of a flat rate charged per store, for example, or it might be a small percentage allocation covered by the profit margins attached to each individual product. The detailed financial planning involved in running a multi-product, multi-outlet retailer is extremely complex and is not within the scope of this text. Significant additional complexities are arising because of the different costing model that applies to online retailing, where the location of the costs of making a sale may be different to where the transaction actually takes place. Nevertheless, it is important for an outlet manager to understand the accounting principles that are used within their businesses so that they understand the financial implications of their own decision making.

Profit and loss account for the 52 weeks to 31 March 2013		
Sales		840,000
Cost of sales		490,000
Gross profit		350,000
Expenses (salaries, advertising, running costs etc.)		266,000
Operating profit		84,000
Interest charges		21,000
Profit before tax		63,000
Taxation		5,000
Profit after tax		58,000
Profit retained		58,000
Balance sheet as at 31 March 2013		
Fixed assets		238,000
Current assets	140,000	
Creditors	80,000	
Net current assets		60,000
Total assets		298,000
Capital and reserves:		
share capital		240,000
Unappropriated profits		58,000
Total liabilities		298,000

Figure 6.2 Profit and loss account and balance sheet for V&R stores

Reynolds et al. (2005) identified 21 key performance indicators (KPIs) important to retailers, and split them down into three groups: labour KPIs, space KPIs and capital KPIs:

1. Labour KPIs: Labour costs per store; overall labour costs; sales/profit per employee; sales/profit per hour worked; gross margin return on labour; units sold per hour worked; till throughput (items per hour); efficiency ratio (comparing hours required to run a store efficiently according to a model with the actual hours used); staff turnover; customer satisfaction (for example number of complaints).
2. Space KPIs: Sales/profit density (for example sales, profit or units sold per square metre); stock availability; ratio of selling to non-selling space; linear density (most appropriate for retailers that use long shelving); trading density (comparing customer traffic to store space).
3. Capital KPIs: Return on capital employed (ROCE – see above); economic profit/economic value added (EVA); capital loan payback period; discounted cash flow measures; cost of maintaining capital (for example stores); depreciation as a percentage of sales.

The scope of this text does not allow for a detailed description of these indicators, many of which are essentially accountancy measures. Readers are advised to consult reliable accountancy sources such as Drury (2012) or Weetman (2010) for further information. However, what the list demonstrates is the wide range of indicators used by retailers to measure performance, which is appropriate in a business context that has such a wide number of variables. This variety is likely to make benchmarking and comparisons more difficult to achieve.

Property

As a retail organization grows, it may become necessary to devote an individual or a team of people to the task of finding suitable locations for new outlets. Over the years, a retailer may become increasingly involved in property management and development as a way of supporting their other areas of operational management. In fact many large retail organizations are asset rich when it comes to the ownership of retail property. This may make them less efficient in other operational functions, simply because they can be, as they are not having to pay back the investment put into a new site or pay an expensive lease.

Some retailers become heavily involved in the development, ownership and management of retail centres, and this can supplement the revenue that they receive from their trading operations. Alshaya, for example, employs 28,000 people in their retail division and have been a major player in international retailing since the 1980s, especially the Middle Eastern region, building on their regional market knowledge and business partnering expertise. The company is also involved in property development through its real estate division (Alshaya.com 2012). The importance of a retailer's location to its overall success is highlighted in Chapter 9, and so having a team of specialists who have the expertise to evaluate new sites, manage the site acquisition process (through architectural design, planning applications, tendering for leasehold, construction, refurbishment and so on), as well as liaise with property developers and local authorities and monitor the performance of the outlet within the overall property portfolio is a valuable resource to a growing retailer. As a retailer organization expands overseas, expert local knowledge about retail development in international locations becomes an additional requirement.

Non-store operations

Online retailing and multi-channel shopping have now firmly established themselves as central components in a retail strategy. The idea of a 'seamless' customer shopping experience across channels has been pursued by retailers for over a decade, but more and more retailers are achieving this goal by addressing the implementation of retail strategy in an operationally blended approach. Most large retailers now see their transactional website as their biggest and best-performing shop; the space is unlimited, the costs of running the outlet are comparatively low and it provides a customer experience that many enjoy. So, whilst consumers have always expressed the wish for 'one retail brand, many ways to shop', a multi-channel strategy that provides anything less is now unacceptable; a retailer that does not offer total flexibility in terms of how customers buy, take delivery and return goods continues at their peril.

Online shopping cannot replicate the store experience, but it complements it by offering convenience and depth of product information. Consumers are now often highly informed about a retailer's product offering before they step into a shop, and may be visiting the store to make a final decision about a purchase based on the aesthetics and 'feel' of a product, where online shopping remains at a disadvantage. Store personnel therefore need to be ready to recognize the informed shopper and provide an appropriate customer service and sales approach (Schaefer, 2011).

Online retailing also provides the opportunity for a higher level of two-way engagement and communication. This is a great opportunity for raising and personalizing customer service; however, it also exposes a retailer to criticism and complaint, which other customers will see. Any inconsistencies in pricing, availability and service will be uncovered by consumers and require transparent responses from retailers.

Implementation of a multi-channel strategy therefore follows the old adage 'retail is detail'. It is an opportunity retailers cannot afford to miss, but unless implementation is scrutinized through the lens of the customer, there is a danger that dissatisfaction with both online and store outlets will appear. Multi-channel operations such as 'click and collect' in particular require consistency in service standard across the retail chain; otherwise the objective of raising service levels can backfire by not delivering in accordance with raised expectations. Chapter 17 explores the multi-channel aspect of a retail strategy in more depth.

International operations

Due to the complexity of running retail outlets in non-domestic markets, international operations are usually supported by a dedicated team that works in close communication with other sections within the head office. For an in-depth discussion of retail internationalization, please refer to Chapter 16.

AN INTEGRATED APPROACH

Today's rapidly changing business environment necessitates a retail management approach that integrates the efforts of the different sections of a business, whether they are broken down into separate departments or not. Only by taking a holistic approach to tackle the challenges and opportunities that are faced can a retailer optimize the efforts of the total organization. According to Walters and Hanrahan (2000, p. 117) 'effective strategic planning relies upon a planning and control approach which embraces all interests of the business'. One such approach is the so-called balanced scorecard, which is a framework that takes the strategic objectives that a retailer sets itself and translates them into operational objectives that can be measured. The concept of the balanced scorecard was devised by Kaplan and Norton (1996) and has been interpreted in a retailing context by Walters and Hanrahan (2000). Figure 6.3 shows the relationship between the strategic direction and operational implementation from various perspectives of a retail business, and suggests how these retail operations can be measured.

The balanced-scorecard approach is important because it includes the consideration of qualitative (non-financial measures) as well as quantitative measures. It considers, for example, the way customers evaluate a retailer's strategy (such as number of repeat

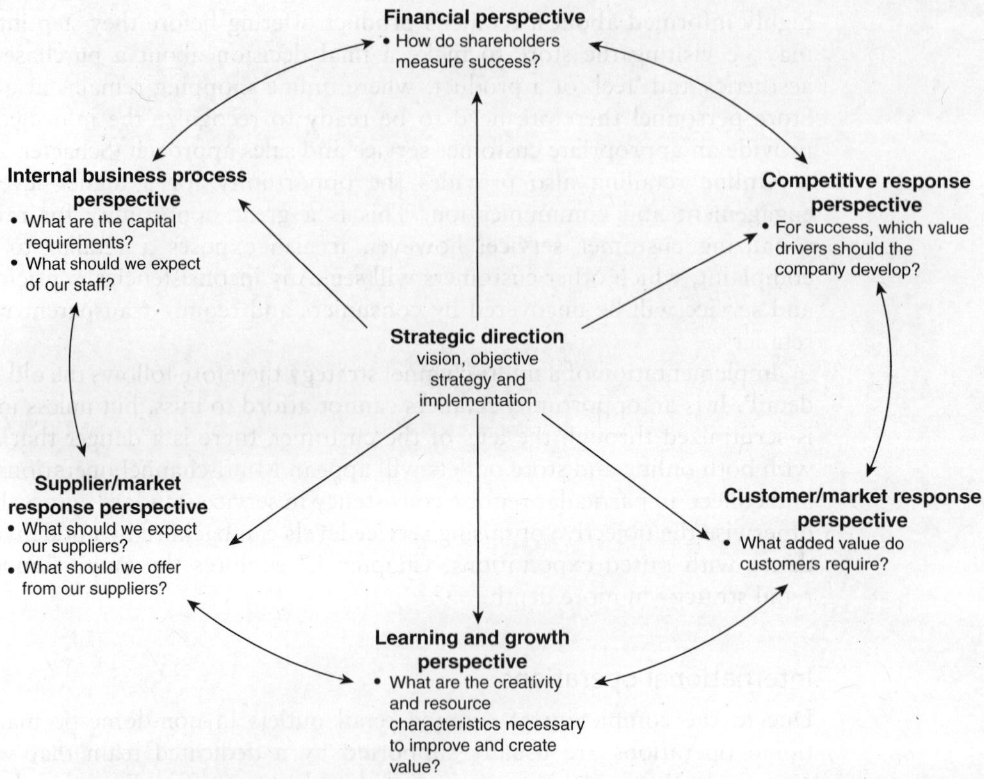

Figure 6.3 The balanced scorecard

Source: Walters and Hanrahan (2000), p. 117.

visits, or image perception), which cannot be measured unless customer research is carried out. This can be set against the financial evaluation that a shareholder may make, based on the performance of company shares. Even though shareholders and customers take different perspectives in terms of their evaluations of the retailer's performance, both are useful measures when it comes to monitoring the effectiveness of a strategy. By using such a broad range of performance indicators, the balanced scorecard integrates the goals set at board executive level and the activities carried out at outlet level and within the centralized specialized departments. It also helps to communicate those goals to the people who are ultimately depended upon for their attainment (Fraser and Zarkada-Fraser, 2000).

While the balanced-scorecard approach is still valid in principle, Lawson et al. (2005) suggest that strategy maps that are more fluid and adaptable can be more useful, by visualizing a chain of relationships which link various performance indicators, showing the dependence on each perspective (for example financial, customer, internal operations, training and development), and highlighting the need for a holistic approach towards measuring the success of strategy implementation. For example, effective staff training (training and development perspective) leads to high levels of complementary sales (operational perspective), which leads to customer satisfaction (customer perspective) and higher transaction values (financial perspective).

SUMMARY

Managing a retail business is a complex task, requiring a blend of diverse knowledge and skills to meet the challenges presented by customers, products, employees and financial resources. This chapter has moved from the strategic retail planning stage to the implementation of that plan at the organizational level. In particular, the roles and responsibilities of the outlet manager and the centralized departments have been examined in order to give an understanding of the relationships between the departments, and how they support the directional development of the retail corporate strategy.

Having gained an appreciation of how retail companies are organized to operate, we now move on to explore how supply-chain management and information management, two specific areas of retail operations, underpin the smooth running of a retail business. The latter part of the text will concentrate on the various elements of the 'retail mix' that contribute to a retailer's overall strategic market positioning; it is in this section of the book that a detailed analysis of the activities attributed to the specialized departments of marketing, property and buying and merchandising can be found.

QUESTIONS

1. Explain how the organizational structure of a retailer supports the implementation of a retail strategy.
2. Suggest personal characteristics that a retailer would look for when recruiting retail outlet managers.
3. Briefly describe the functions performed in the following centralized departments within a retail organization:
   (a) buying and merchandising
   (b) marketing
   (c) logistics
4. Although the notion of a multiple retailer is one of a centralized structure, there are instances when decentralized decision making in the areas of human resource management and financial management are more appropriate. Explain, using examples to illustrate your answer.

REFERENCES AND FURTHER READING

Alshaya (2012) Company website, available at http://www.alshaya.com/retail.jsp [accessed 15 August 2012].

Collins, J. (2010) 'Turn Your Staff into Top-Flight Talent', *Drapers*, 17 September.

Drury, C. (2012) *Management and Cost Accounting*, 8th Edition (Andover: Cengage Learning EMEA).

Fraser, C. and Zarkada-Fraser, A. (2000) 'Measuring the Performance of Retail Managers in Australia and Singapore', *International Journal of Retail and Distribution Management*, vol. 28, no. 6, pp. 228–42.

Grugulis, I., Bozkurt, Ö. and Clegg, J. (2011) 'No Place to Hide'? The Realities of Leadership in UK Supermarkets', chapter 10 in Grungulis, I. and Bozkurt, Ö. (eds) *Retail Work* (Basingstoke: Palgrave Macmillan).

Gustafsson K., Jonson, G., Smith, D. and Sparks, L. (2009) *Retailing Logistics & Fresh Food Packaging: Managing Change in the Supply Chain* (London: Kogan Page).

Hines, T. (2004) *Supply Chain Strategies: Customer Driven and Customer Focused* (Oxford: Elsevier).

Kaplan, R. S. and Norton, D. P. (1996) *Translating Strategy into Action: The Balanced Scorecard* (Boston, MA: Harvard Business School Press).

Lawson, R., Stratton, W. and Hatch, T. (2005) 'Achieving Strategy with Scorecarding', *Journal of Corporate Accounting and Finance*, vol. 16, no. 3 March–April, 62–68.

Oldfield, B. M., Schmidt, R. A., Clarke, I., Hart, C. and Kirkup, M. H. (2000) *Contemporary Cases in Retail Operations Management* (Basingstoke: Palgrave Macmillan).

Reynolds, J., Howard, E., Dragun, D., Rosewell, B. and Ormerod, P. (2005) 'Assessing Productivity of the UK Retail Sector', *International Review of Retail, Distribution and Consumer Research*, vol. 15, no. 3, 237–80.

Schaefer, M. (2011) 'Capitalizing on the Smarter Consumer', *IBM Global Business Services Executive Report* (New York: IBM Corporation).

Walters, D. and Hanrahan, J. (2000) *Retail Strategy: Planning and Control* (Basingstoke: Palgrave Macmillan).

Weetman, P. (2010) *Financial and Management Accounting: An Introduction*, 5th Edition (Harlow: Financial Times/Prentice Hall).

7 MANAGING THE RETAIL SUPPLY CHAIN

LEARNING OBJECTIVES

- A familiarization with the structure of 'typical' retail supply chains, and the roles of the components of that chain.
- To understand the way in which logistics support the objectives of retail activity.
- To understand the importance of controlling supply-chain costs.
- To appreciate the importance of achieving logistical efficiency.
- To understand the enabling role of information technology in retail supply chains.

INTRODUCTION

As sellers of merchandise to the final consumer, retailers are dependent on the supply of that merchandise in order to provide a high level of service to their customers. In some instances manufacturers may deliver goods that they produce directly to a retail outlet, or in the case of direct retailing to the final consumer, but in many cases a product item will travel through a complex route encompassing transportation, warehousing and various handling systems in order to get from the production location to the consumer's home. Some products, such as fresh grocery, have the complication of specific requirements needing to be met during this process, such as a chilled environment, and so the whole organization of what is commonly called 'the supply chain' needs to be integrated with the requirements of the retailer, and ultimately the consumer. The range of activities involved in the physical distribution of products through the supply chain is often referred to as retail logistics, and the management of those activities is referred to as supply-chain management.

Supply-chain management is a key support area for any retail operation, and at most large multiple retailers its importance is reflected in the organizational structure of the company. Logistics has not always had such a central role in the eyes of the retailer (Fernie and Sparks, 2009); however, more and more retailers have turned to supply-chain management as a potential opportunity for making 'efficiencies' that simultaneously save costs and improve the stock service to the outlet and/or the final customer. Many of the efficiencies that have been introduced, however, have only been possible because of advancements in information technology systems upon which logistical arrangements depend, and so the development of supply-chain management has gone hand in hand with development in technological applications. Integrating the logistical demands of a home-shopping arm of the business and maintaining high customer-service standards across a multi-channel retailing business have been important supply-chain challenges for retailers in recent years.

RETAIL SUPPLY CHAINS

Figure 7.1 illustrates different supply chains that can be found within the retail industry, and shows how products move through various stages between the supplier's factory and the customer. Many large retailers have a global supply base, in which case extra stages in transportation that incorporate sea freight or airfreight will be required to bring the product into a distribution centre. Retail logistics are further complicated with issues concerning the ownership of goods and the supply of the logistics service. In some situations, the goods may be made exclusively for a particular retailer, and from the point at which they leave the factory gates they are owned by the retailer and taken through a logistical set-up that is run by the retailers themselves. On the other hand, in some retail supply chains the ownership of the goods may pass from the manufacturer to a broker or agent, and then to a wholesaler, before reaching the retailer. Even when there are no other intermediaries in the supply chain, the logistical operations may be contracted out to a 'third-party' logistical service supplier, for example Christian Salvesen, or Exel, which provides transportation, warehousing and distribution management facilities for their retailer clients.

The actual product involved has a great bearing on the way a retail supply chain is run. For example, for fresh produce and other short-shelf-life articles, it is vital that the supply chain is geared up to very fast transportation, to ensure that the retailer's customers receive the product in good condition. Fragile products have extra requirements in terms of packaging and handling arrangements, so that the risk of damage is reduced. Frozen and chilled produce requires very specific handling, warehousing and transportation throughout the supply chain, in order to ensure that the

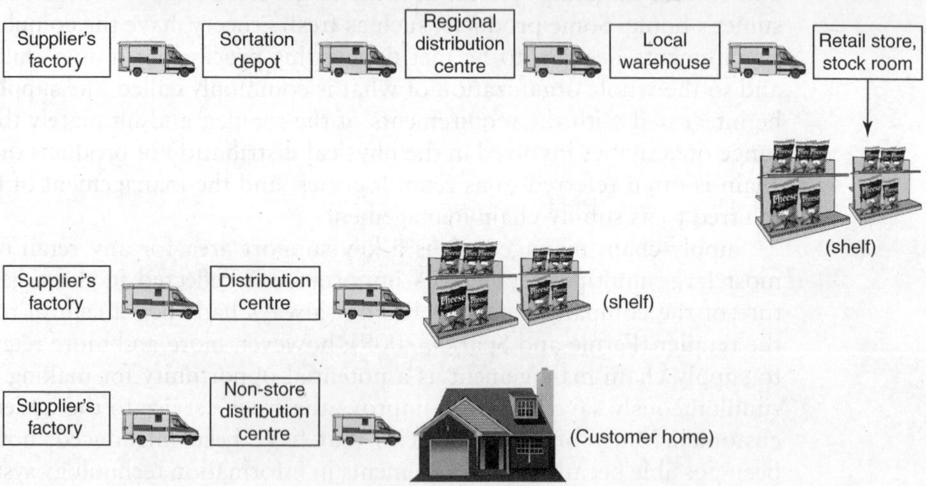

Figure 7.1 Retail supply chains

stringent food safety legislation is complied with and that the produce is at its best for the consumer. Clothing products are often taken through their supply chain on hangers, rather than in boxes, which means the stock is ready to put straight onto the shop floor without further 'pre-retailing' processes to make the product look its best.

The role of the distribution centre

The distribution centre plays a key part in the retail supply chain of all large multiple retailers, and so a deeper insight into the role that it plays in support of the overall retail strategy is necessary. Its main functions can be broken down into breaking bulk and storing products, providing a vital link in the distribution channel, amalgamating and preparing stock for stores and providing the base from which to fulfil website orders.

Successful online retailing essentially depends on the operational effectiveness of two main elements: the web pages for attracting customers and taking orders, and the logistical infrastructure to fulfil those orders. The development of Internet retailing has seen many successful online store fronts let down by ineffective logistical arrangements that result in lower than expected levels of customer service. Retailers now accept that customer expectation is built by brand, rather than by method of shopping, and that a fully integrated shopping service is vital to success in the multi-channel era, but this was not always the case with many stores not being able to accept returns of Internet purchases for example. The distribution centre is therefore the epicentre of an online retail business.

Breaking bulk and storing supplies

One of the benefits of large-scale multiple retailing is the scale economies derived from collating store orders and placing large-quantity orders with suppliers. However, this gives retailers the challenge of breaking those 'bulk' orders down again so that they can be fed in manageable quantities to the retail stores. The distribution centre therefore provides the facility to receive stock in bulk, provide some temporary storage space for large quantities of product and then collate assortments of products that are appropriate in quantity and characteristics for individual stores. In the case of online retailing, where deliveries are made to individual customers, the distribution centre is the tangible infrastructure that results in order fulfilment and therefore customer satisfaction.

Distribution

Having suppliers deliver in bulk to one or a number of regional distribution centres means that the distribution of produce is more efficient. Figure 7.2 is an extended version of the earlier Figure 1.2 and shows how distribution centres provide an intermediary service in the distribution channel between producers and consumers, saving on transportation costs and refining assortments in the light of regional or specific locational demand.

Amalgamation of product assortments for stores

The stock requirements of individual stores will differ according to their size and the demand patterns generated by their own customer sales. The distribution centre can

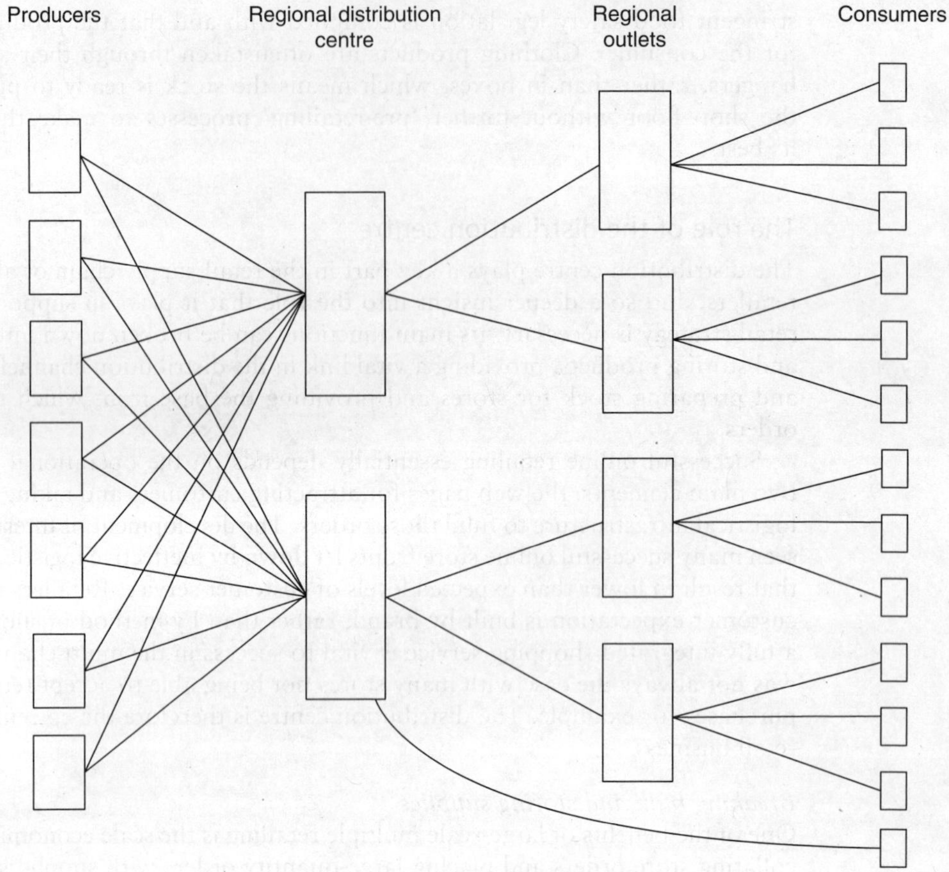

Figure 7.2 The role of the distribution centre within a multiple retailer

therefore prepare an assortment of products from all the different suppliers tailored to the needs of the store, which can be delivered, in some cases a number of times daily, to the stores. The stock service level to stores is therefore extremely high, in terms of both getting the right products and getting them delivered quickly.

Preparation of merchandise

In addition to the collation of store deliveries and the fulfilment of website orders, distribution centres often carry out processes that are involved with the preparation of stock, so that products can go straight from the delivery lorry onto the shop floor to replenish shelves. Merchandise preparation can include the following activities:

1. Removing all packaging.
2. Putting price tickets on the products.
3. Cleaning and dusting the products, and hanging and pressing garments.
4. Collating products by department and organizing according to a store's requirements (according to store or stockroom layout for example).

Other elements within the supply chain

Sortation depot

In the supply chains of large retailers, which require vast quantities of products from their suppliers, it is sometimes necessary to introduce another link between suppliers and distribution centres. This is effectively a large-scale warehousing operation which breaks down supplies into appropriate quantities for the regional distribution centres.

Regional warehouse

Sometimes a link is introduced between the distribution centre and the retail store. For example, where a retail outlet is limited for space, and yet the distribution centre is located a long distance from the outlet, a warehouse near to the outlet can store supplies and provide a more efficient replenishment service. Effectively, it is providing additional storeroom space for the retailer, located at a lower-cost site.

Transportation

In any supply-chain operation, goods have to travel from one location to another. Supplies may be carried from different sides of the globe, and then transferred from air- or sea freight to a land-based transport system (rail or road) for onward delivery to a distribution centre or store. An extensive discussion of transportation issues is not within the scope of this text (see for example Christopher, 2010, for an extensive discussion); however, one issue that is high up on the strategic agenda is the environmental impact of retail logistics (see Vignette 7.1).

VIGNETTE 7.1 GREEN SUPPLY CHAINS

Since the early 1990s, retailers and their supply-chain partners have been under increasing pressure to become more responsible towards the environment. The objective of providing a better service to the customer can directly conflict with a corporate objective to reduce the impact of retail logistics on the environment in areas like vehicle emissions and congestion, vibration and accidents, fuel usage, packaging and waste, land use for warehousing and climate change. Retailers are facing pressure from a number of sources: international and local legislation, industry peer groups, local authorities, green campaign groups and the media. Customers are also demanding that companies take social and environmental responsibility. Many retail companies have initiated environmental policies including Body Shop, J Sainsbury's, Marks and Spencer, Waitrose and H&M. The companies that set trends and anticipate legislative pressure could well have a competitive advantage in the future over those companies that ignore the environmental issue, as they run the risk of causing customer unease and have to be reactive in their compliance with environmental legislation.

Source: Worsford (2001) and McKinnon et al. (2010)

Suppliers

Any supply-chain system starts with suppliers, whether they are the immediate producer or whether they are acting in the capacity of agent for a producer. Suppliers can play a passive role in the supply chain, with their involvement restricted to waiting for orders, packing the goods up and handing them over to a carrier, or they may become highly involved in logistical arrangements in partnership with their retail customers. The benefits of taking a partnership approach to logistics are explained in more detail later in the chapter.

Hubs

A hub is a term used for a multifunctional link in a supply chain. A hub may, for example, combine sourcing activities with distribution activities in an international market. For global retail players, intermediaries such as hubs will play an increasingly important operational and strategic role in ensuring a reliable and cost-effective flow of merchandise from supply markets to outlets without having to send goods from one side of the globe to another and back again (Fernie et al., 2009).

COSTS IN THE SUPPLY CHAIN

The importance of containing costs at the retail outlet level cannot be overstated. However, an outlet manager at a multiple retailer has no control over the costs involved with getting produce into the outlet. These are essentially incurred and controlled centrally, but can be analysed further according to the activities involved with the procurement of goods. Each link in the supply chain incurs its own individual costs, and it is the detailed analysis of these costs that is the basis of much of the work on logistics efficiency. Figure 7.3 gives a breakdown of logistics operations, the likely costs involved and the factors that directly affect costs, which can be viewed as a starting point for a supply-chain cost analysis.

Although cost analysis is fundamental to achieving efficiency, decisions about logistics are not made on costing information alone. Other factors that have to be considered are the ability to move products very fast through the supply chain, the ability to provide a reliable service and flexibility. Any stock that is in the supply chain is, as far as the retailer is concerned, tying up capital that is only released when the goods are sold. Therefore, the less time a product spends in the supply chain, the lower the costs of financing 'pipeline' stock. A supply chain should ideally be without

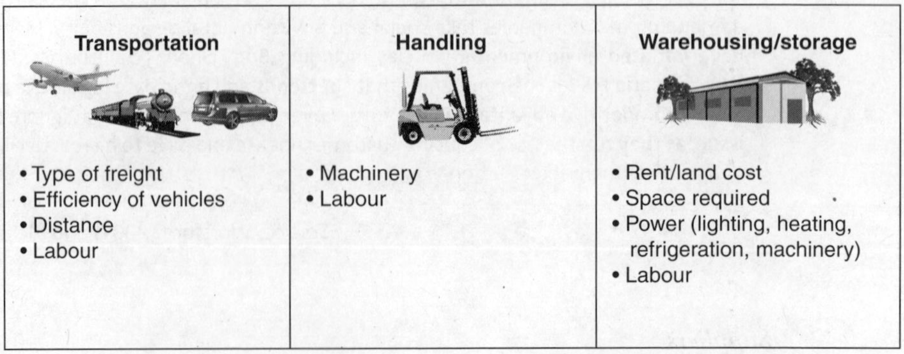

Figure 7.3 Logistics operations

any forms of inaccuracy that can hold up the flow of stock. Defects can originate in many ways:

1. *Damage to stock.* This can require returning stock to manufactures for reprocessing, or rectification in a distribution centre, causing delay.
2. *Shortages.* For example the actual quantity does not comply with the stated number on an invoice, causing delay to payments and the possibility of a breakdown in supply relationships.
3. *Assortment inaccuracy.* Incorrect quantities in terms of product variation such as colour, flavour, size and so on.
4. *Information inaccuracy.* For example wrong barcode or inconsistent product descriptions can cause difficulties in identifying stock accurately, resulting in a delay to acceptance of stock.
5. *Non-conformance with packaging specification.* For example a wrong-size carton may mean the goods cannot be automatically received onto a conveyor belt in the distribution centre. On a larger scale, inaccurate case weights can cause problems with transportation loading.

Retailers and their supply chains should ideally be able to react quickly and easily to any changes in consumer purchasing patterns that switch demand from one product to another, or result in surges or downfalls in demand. The inability to use resources flexibly can result in additional costs in the long term and a lowering of service efficiency in the short term. Vignette 7.2 discusses the logistical challenges of dealing with the upsurge in demand created by consumer spending associated with Christmas celebrations.

VIGNETTE 7.2 PRE-CHRISTMAS LOGISTICAL PLANNING

The success of pre-celebration trading can mean make or break for retailers anywhere in the world, and the ability to respond to the Christmas seasonal demand in the UK must be planned carefully, whilst allowing response to opportunities as they arise. For different retail sectors, demand peaks at different times: clothing generally earlier, electrical and electronic midway and fresh food latest of all. Flexibility is required at all levels. Increased staffing levels in store is essential to ensure shelves are quickly replenished; extra transportation services are required for home delivery; temporary additional warehousing capacity and extra picking capability are needed at distribution centres; and every inch of stockroom space is needed at the store. Christmas is not just about responding to demand; it is also a great opportunity to drive sales with effective marketing communication and maximize those opportunities by collaborating with suppliers on sales forecasting and replenishment plans. Clear communication of delivery options and services at this time also helps to achieve customer satisfaction. There is nothing a retailer can do more to raise negative emotions than deliver a Christmas present late.

Source: Jack (2009)

In the pursuit of cost and service efficiency in the supply chain, it becomes apparent that scrutinizing the retailer's own internal costs is often not enough. Suppliers and logistics service suppliers also need to be considered. Many of the initiatives that have saved costs in the supply chain, which can eventually be passed on to the consumer in the form of lower product prices, have been the result of extensive collaboration between retailers and their suppliers. Sharing sales and stock data, consolidating deliveries and joint forecasting are collaborative practices used across different retail sectors. By working together on supply-chain management issues, cost and waste have been reduced and leaner stock levels achieved across business organizational boundaries.

Supply-chain cost reduction is also achieved via sourcing from the lowest-cost producers. China has been the country of choice for much of the non-food importation by retailers across the rest of the world in the last decade. Labour costs and modern production methods suggest good value; however, using the analogy of an iceberg, Hines (2004) warns of the extent of hidden costs which are not immediately apparent when sourcing from further afield. These costs include additional freight costs, particularly airfreight if an order is needed quickly, the need to purchase high quantities with every order, the inability to reorder quickly in response to fast sales and the added complexity and expense associated with developing products with suppliers based overseas.

LOGISTICS AND INFORMATION TECHNOLOGY

As in the case of many technological innovations, retail logistics systems were revolutionized on the basis of a relatively simple application – the barcode. By converting product codes to a system of monochrome bars, which could then be read by an infrared scanning device, the capture of information about products sold within a retail business became both fast and accurate. Feeding barcode data into computers provided the means by which retailers could count electronically, rather than manually, how many products had been sold and how many had been taken into the business, and therefore the level of stockholding (and if required, the level of stockholding in the various parts of the retail supply chain) could be quickly established. As computer systems grew in sophistication, their ability to read, analyse and transmit data increased, and so the quality of information fed to retail decision-makers improved. In terms of retail logistics, the systems highlighted areas of inefficiency, such as goods waiting to be processed, or unsold stock being held in various locations in the supply chain.

Another technological innovation that underpinned retail logistics information systems development is electronic data interchange (EDI) via internal company networks. This provided the means to link stores, head offices, distribution centres and suppliers electronically and enabled the immediacy of electronically transmitted information. This cut out the need for hours of manual sales reporting over the telephone, or in a written format; with EDI it became possible to transmit sales data directly from the electronic point of sale (EPOS) in real time, allowing immediate reaction to those sales to be made. The Internet has enabled much of the paperwork associated with logistics systems to become redundant, and virtual documents are now the norm in a retail business. The vast quantities of data exchanged on a real-time basis have allowed further fine-tuning of cost analysis and the raising of logistics service standards.

PRODUCT-PUSH AND CUSTOMER-PULL-BASED SUPPLY CHAINS

The product-push system is based on the concept of a quantity of goods being brought in according to a level forecast in advance, and then placed on the shelf to wait for a customer to buy. Suppliers make goods according to orders placed by the retailer, but after sending the goods into the retailer supply chain, they have no further involvement in the process. If the goods sell well, the retailer reorders when stocks are diminishing; if they do not, the retailer has to lower the price to shift the unwanted stock.

The customer-pull system is based on the concept of responding to each customer's purchase, where the recording of the sale of a product triggers a sequence of events in the supply chain. First, the sales data are sent electronically to all members of the supply chain. The distribution centre responds by automatically replenishing the item sold. The lowering of the stock level at the distribution centre may then trigger an order suggestion to the buying office to call more product in from suppliers. In the meantime, the buying office will have received sales notification, and will have already started to consider their response to those sales, either by calling in more product from suppliers or (if the product is seasonal, for example) to let the stock run down. The supplier, which also obtains the sales information in real time, can get ready to make more of the product in anticipation of another call from the retailer. The customer-pull system is therefore centred around responding to customer purchasing, unlike the product-push system, which is based on the notion of holding stock and waiting (or hoping) for sales.

Although both approaches to logistics have the same aim, which is to provide a good service to customers, there are a number of factors that have encouraged more and more retailers to adopt a responsive retail supply chain.

1. The system of automatic replenishment allows a retailer to maintain low stock levels at the store, and this has enabled retailers to reduce the number of products on the shelf, and to increase product variety. It has also allowed retailers to convert stockroom space to sales space, as there is no need to hold stock in a storeroom at the outlet.
2. The sharing of sales information with suppliers allows them to see sales patterns emerging, so they can gear their production up for the fast-selling lines, and cut back on slow-selling items. This has the effect of reducing the number of products needing to be marked down to sell, and helps to maximize the sales of good sellers by keeping them in stock, leading to more profits for both retailer and supplier.
3. The elimination of slow-selling stock from the supply chain means that less money is invested in stock, stock turnover improves and so the return on capital employed is raised.

The success of responsive retail supply chains led to the development of a new philosophy within retail organizations: efficient consumer response (ECR). In addition to the key benefits of a responsive system outlined above, combined with the use of increasingly detailed information systems, retailers have found that they have been able to take a very close, analytical view of their supply-chain and logistical operations in order to cut out unnecessary costs. This has led to a business philosophy that not only aligns all logistical operations to customer response, but also runs through all aspects of the product management process.

EFFICIENT CONSUMER RESPONSE

Figure 7.4 outlines the scope of ECR. The outer circle represents activities that are concerned with the management of supply within a retail organization, whilst the inner circle represents activities that are concerned with the management of consumer demand and the initial response to it. The management of supply relates to activities that often fall within the remit of logistics and buying and merchandising departments, whilst the activities concerned with demand management are generally more marketing and outlet orientated. However, ECR makes this kind of departmental boundary somewhat redundant, because of the totally integrated approach that the ECR system requires. The critical success factor in an ECR system is the satisfaction of the final consumer, and this becomes the driver for all retail activities (shown in the central position in Figure 7.4).

Collaboration with suppliers

In addition to the integration of activities within the retail organization, ECR is also dependent on an integrated approach to the business right through the supply chain, and into supplier organizations. In order to achieve maximum efficiencies, all parties need to work together to identify problems, and agree on initiatives to overcome them. Only then can the necessary seamless interface from consumers' purchasing patterns to suppliers' production schedules be achieved and the benefits of ECR derived (Lowson et al., 1999, Christopher, 2010). Figure 7.5 illustrates how both retailers and their suppliers benefit from ECR initiatives.

Limitations of efficient consumer response

The principle of efficient consumer response appears to be so logical that the reader may be surprised to learn that not all retailers are able or willing to organize their supply chains in this way. However, there are a number of reasons why ECR may not be applicable.

Logistics and the small retailer

Small retailers do not have the resources to get heavily involved in supply-chain management, nor would it be cost-effective for them to do so. In addition, the opportunities

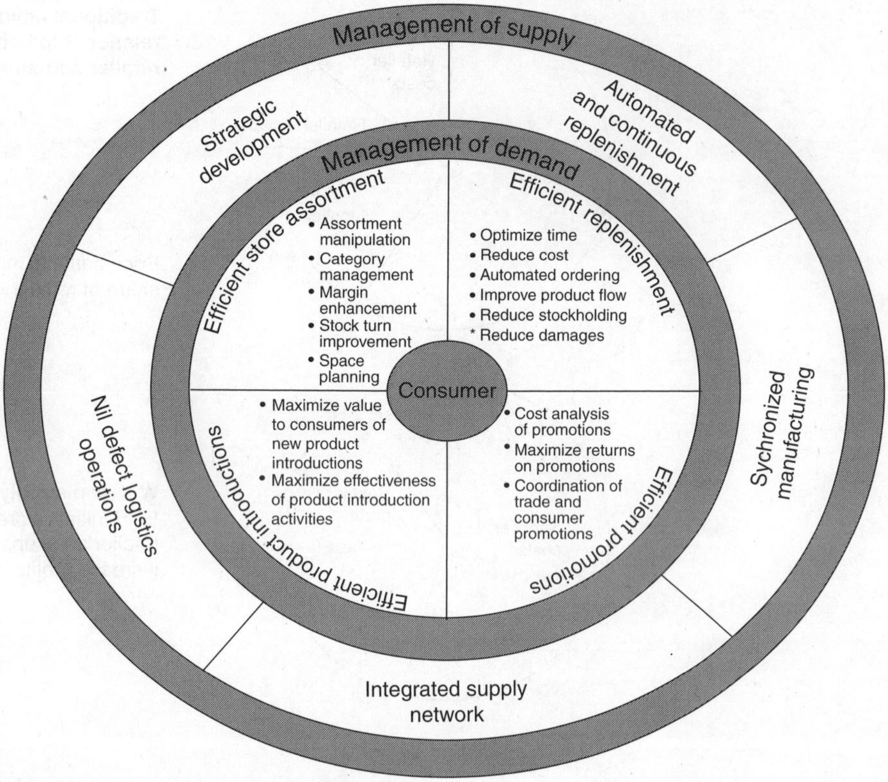

Figure 7.4 The scope of efficient consumer response

for them to collaborate with suppliers may be severely limited. However, they still need to make decisions regarding logistics arrangements on a small scale. For example, is it more cost-effective to collect orders from suppliers, or have them delivered? How often do they need to visit a wholesaler, and to what extent can they risk running down stock levels between visits? In a competitive and saturated retail market, customers are intolerant of stock-outs; therefore, small retailers must manage their stock to the best of their ability. Periodic review (Figure 7.6) is a simple but effective stock control system appropriate for small and medium-sized retailers, where items sold have a relatively predictable demand pattern. The essence of this system is that the stock position in a retail outlet is reviewed on a regular basis. When stock falls to a predetermined minimum level, a replenishment order is placed. Between the time of order placement and delivery (called the 'lead time'), demand for the item is met by an amount of 'safety stock'. Safety (or reserve stock) is a safety cushion to ensure that the retailer does not run out of merchandise before the next order arrives due to an unexpected increase in demand. The order point in the periodic review system is defined as

$$\text{Order point} = [(\text{Demand/day}) \times (\text{Review time} + \text{Lead time})] + \text{Safety stock}$$

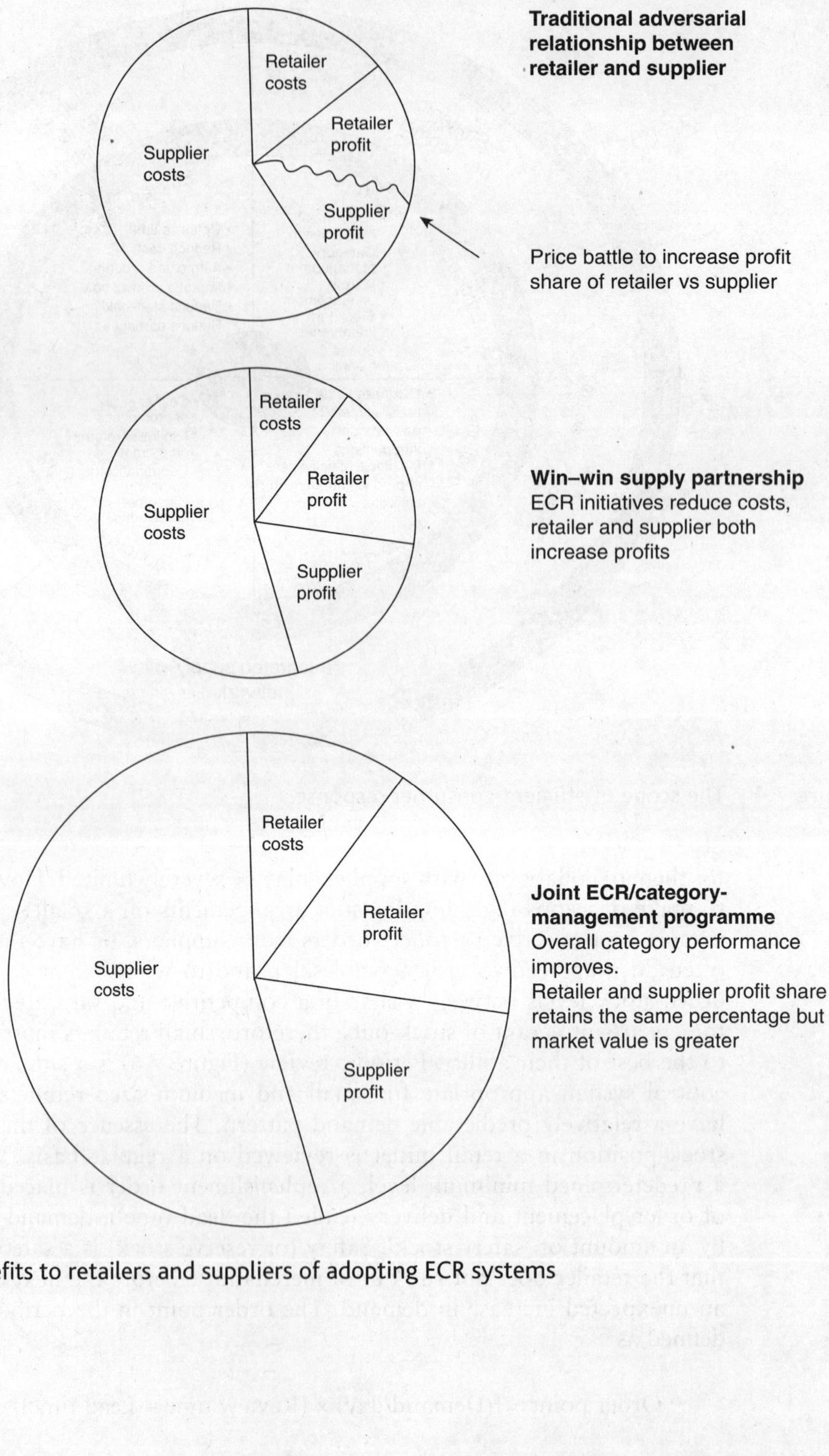

Figure 7.5 Benefits to retailers and suppliers of adopting ECR systems

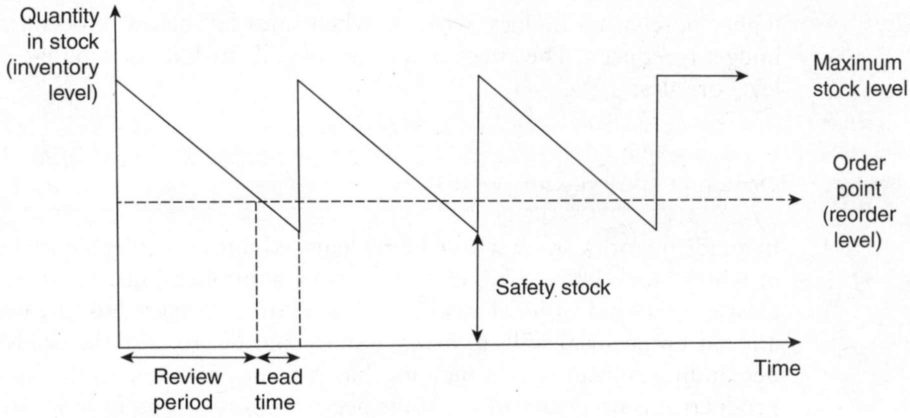

Figure 7.6 The periodic review system

Illustration. Assume that a small pharmacist sells 10 units of a headache remedy per day. The stock is reviewed fortnightly and the lead time is one week. The safety stock is 20 units. The order point can be calculated using the formula above.

$$\text{The order point is } [10 \times (14+7)] + 20 = 230 \text{ units}$$

The question still remains as to how much the retailer should order (the order quantity) when the available stock is less than the order point. The order quantity should be enough so that the cycle stock (or the stock required to meet the forecast demand) is not depleted and sales do not eat into the safety stock. For instance, in the example above, if the available stock is 180 units, then the order quantity is 50 units because the order point is 230 (i.e. 230 – 180 = 50). The actual quantity may be higher than this if, for instance, the headache remedies come in boxes of 20. Then the retailer would have to order three boxes of 20, or 60 units.

The periodic review system helps the small retailer to ensure that their product range is maintained with an adequate stock service. However, it may be necessary for the retailer to make further decisions based on the trade-off between the feasibility and costs associated with holding larger amounts of stock and ordering (or collecting) less frequently, and the feasibility and costs associated with taking in less stock on a more frequent basis.

Seasonal products

One of the problems concerned with both periodic review systems and automatic replenishment systems is that they are geared to a situation where the demand for a product item is relatively consistent. However, many products are seasonal and therefore have a demand pattern consisting of rises, peaks and falls. A stock control system that goes some way to helping retailers cope with fluctuating sales patterns is the open-to-buy (OTB) system. The basis of the OTB system is a sales forecast, which is based on the previous year's sales, taking into consideration any relevant external variations. The sales forecast then determines the stock-level requirement for those sales to be made. As the season progresses, a sales level that exceeds the forecasted level allows a higher purchasing budget, whereas when sales fall below expectation the purchasing budget is reduced. The effect is that the overall stock level is managed according to the level of sales.

SALES FORECASTING

In an ideal world, stock would be replenished into a retailer's outlet exactly at the rate at which stock left the store in customers' shopping bags. However, retailers do not exist in this kind of ideal world, and so retail managers have to use their experience and entrepreneurial skills to manage stock in order to fulfil the needs and desires of the demanding consumer in a manner that is most profitable in the long term. For many products it is necessary to use some degree of forecasting in order to ensure that stock levels are high enough to cope with customer demand. Most forecasting techniques use previous sales figures as a base from which future sales are estimated; however, simply looking to the past is a rather narrow way of anticipating future performance. More sophisticated forecasting methods take into consideration external factors that are likely to have a negative or positive impact on sales. By allocating numerical values to these factors, which are then applied to the basic 'past-sale indication', a more accurate forecast emerges. Factors that might be quantified include weather patterns, promotional activities, competitors' marketing activity, market or seasonal growth in a particular product category and so on. It is particularly difficult to match supply and demand for seasonal products; for example it would not be in a retailer's interest to replenish the stock of Christmas wrapping paper at the rate it was sold in the week commencing 18 December in the following week, whilst a shortage of this item in the week prior to Christmas would lead to considerable customer frustration. It is therefore necessary to build stock levels of seasonal items high enough to allow customer demand to be fulfilled at the peak of the season. For some products, like gifts, or dresses, customers like to have a wide choice from which to make a purchase, which again pushes up the stock requirement.

Many fashion products combine a situation of a short shelf life (before becoming outdated) and long chains involved in their manufacture and supply (for example, for a pair of trousers, yarn has to be spun out of fibres that have to be produced, cloth has to be woven from yarn, garments have to be cut out, sewn and pressed). This situation has led fashion retailers and their suppliers to investigate ways of aligning fluctuating customer sales as closely as possible to manufacturing and supply systems, an approach termed quick response (QR). Fashion retailers such as Benetton, Oasis, Gap, Zara and Mango are all known for the use of QR systems in order to respond faster to sales of fashion items; for example Benetton have a system of dyeing ready-knitted sweaters to the fashion colours that are selling well, instead of knitting up pre-coloured yarn. This means that the introduction of the fashion element (colour) happens at a later stage of the process. Other companies have also found ways of introducing flexibility in their design and manufacturing systems that allow production to quickly switch from slow-selling styles to 'hot items'. A common method is to source the base fabric for garments ahead and then send it to manufacturers who convert the cloth into styled garments at the very last moment, so that the latest styling details can be incorporated.

The expression 'fast fashion' is now well known and refers to the ability to take ideas from the designer fashion catwalks and incorporate them into low-priced fashion garments within a very short time. Quick-response methods have undoubtedly helped fast-fashion retailers to achieve their aims, but unfortunately the fashion industry is often accused of using unfair labour practices in sweatshop factory conditions in the pursuit of getting inexpensive products delivered within short lead times. Fast-fashion or quick-response systems rely on powerful information systems to analyse sales trends and plan stock intake, as well as efficient and flexible logistics in order to move product fast from the production to selling point.

LOGISTICS AND THE NON-STORE RETAILER

Most non-store retailers have a simpler logistics requirement than store retailers. Orders for goods are taken remotely, and the goods sent directly to the customer from a distribution centre. In the case of direct online retailing, goods do not need to move down a supply chain at all but move in a customer-specific delivery system, from producer to consumer. However, a major drawback of non-store retailing is the high level of returned goods. When a product is represented rather than real, and the customer is unable to test or try the product in store, there is a higher risk of product dissatisfaction. The distribution centre for a non-store retailer therefore acts as a two-way receiving station, with bulk orders arriving from suppliers, and individual returns from customers. The returned products have to be checked and reprocessed before being returned to saleable stock, and any faulty goods have to be returned to suppliers or scrapped. In non-store retailing, the condition in which a package arrives at a customer's home is likely to impact upon their perception of the product and the retailer, and so the quality level of the packaging and delivery service must be in line with the overall retail image. Many clothing retailers use attractive tissue and customized boxes, so taking delivery of the package is more like receiving a gift.

Reverse logistics

In an era where retailers have generous and flexible returns policies across sales channels, the disposal of unwanted merchandise is a growing, costly and complex problem. This has given rise to the concept of 'reverse logistics', which is concerned with managing returns in the most efficient way. For example third-party service providers can set up a dedicated system that captures data on customers' returns that are ready to be collected from stores, and arranges for them to be collected and taken to a 'reverse logistics' site where the goods are assessed for damage. The goods are then categorized by type and/or supplier, and then collated for redistribution either back to suppliers for repair, back to stores for resale, or to be disposed of through non-conflicting retail channels (for example factory outlets or market stalls) or, if all else fails, to landfill sites. The use of online shopping features such as detailed size charts, zoom-in facilities and even virtual try-on facilities not only enhance the consumer shopping process, but also help to reduce the number of returned goods.

The advantages of non-store retailing

E-retailing avoids a whole layer of operational costs; the costs of running a store are removed, and the order fulfilment operation can be positioned in a low-cost location. In order to achieve a good delivery service to customers, however, non-store retailers have to hold stock from which to fulfil customer orders. Next, for example, offer a next-day delivery service (subject to availability) from the receipt of a customer's order. As a way of helping to keep fashion products in stock, most home-shopping retailers issue a preview catalogue ahead of the season to a group of loyal customers, whose purchasing helps the company to forecast the demand for products in the main catalogue. In a similar way, multi-channel retailers use sales reaction online to plan product availability in stores. Retailers who trade exclusively on the Internet, in theory, do not need to hold stock but do need a highly developed information system in order to keep track of customer orders and deliveries, and supplier stock positions and order fulfilment in order to ensure that their customer stock availability service is operating at an acceptable level (see Vignette 7.2). Many retailer websites now allow customers to see stock availability prior to order so as to cut out the frustration of only finding out something is out of stock at the point of order confirmation.

The final stage in the retail supply chain is receiving much attention, as the online retail sector gets more competitive. By their nature online shoppers are often time-poor, and chances are they will not be at home when their purchased item arrives. Retailers are therefore trying to improve their home delivery services by offering increasingly precise and accurately timed delivery. Some, like ASOS.com, are also absorbing the cost of a standard delivery so that they can maintain a competitive price advantage. Multi-channel retailers are also adding more flexibility in terms of responding to how the customer prefers to shop. Marks and Spencer, for example, offer a service called 'Shop Your Way', which introduces flexibility in the online shopping process by allowing customers to order either online or in store and then collect in store or have goods delivered, whatever is the most convenient to shoppers at any particular time (Clements, 2010). The popularity of similar so-called click and collect systems is growing; by ordering online and collecting in store, the customer avoids delivery charges and the inconvenience of not being able to receive deliveries while at work, and for the retailer having customers visit stores means an opportunity for complementary or impulse purchases.

SUMMARY

Supply-chain management plays a central role in the implementation of a retail strategy. Today's customer is intolerant of stock-outs of basic products, yet happy to respond to time-limited offers of a desirable product. Without the support systems that move products efficiently into outlets and/or customers' homes, a retailing strategy is pointless. If a retailer is unable to deliver or make available adequate supplies in good condition of what customers want, when they want it, they will find that a competitor soon will! Poor logistics can therefore place a retailer at a significant competitive disadvantage. The enormity of supply-chain arrangements for large multiple retailers means that any change to its operations can have a major cost implication, and so customer-service levels, total logistics costs and total benefits to the retailer have to be finely balanced. In a competitive and saturated retail market like the UK, the approaches that have made supply chains more efficient are moving forward into the management of customer demand and the so-called last mile of retail logistics. The integration of marketing operations and logistical operations therefore support a customer-responsive retailer in the pursuit of its strategic objectives. In response to more diverse and less predictable demand patterns, retailers need lean and agile supply chains to prevent valuable retail space being cluttered with unwanted and loss-making stock.

QUESTIONS

1. Provide an analysis of the role of the distribution centre within a multiple retail organization.
2. Multi-channel retailing provides some additional logistics challenges to retailers. Discuss the nature of these challenges.
3. Lowering costs is one, but not the only, objective of efficiency in the supply chain. Discuss other objectives that retailers may seek to achieve with their logistics systems.
4. Explain the benefits that a retailer might accrue from a customer-pull distribution system.
5. ECR involves taking on not only a new operational alignment in logistics, but also a new company philosophy. Discuss.
6. Identify specific products that might present particular challenges for retail supply chains, and discuss ways in which these challenges might be tackled.

REFERENCES AND FURTHER READING

Christopher, M. (2010) *Logistics and Supply Chain Management* (Harlow: Financial Times/Prentice Hall).

Clements, A. (2002) 'Return Ticket', *Retail Week*, 1 November.

Clements, A. (2010) 'Signed, Sealed, Delivered', *Drapers*, 17 April, p. 41.

Collins, A., Henchion, M. and O'Reilly, P. (2001) 'Logistics Customer Service: Performance of Irish Food Exporters', *International Journal of Retail and Distribution Management*, vol. 29, no. 1, pp. 6–15.

Fernie, J., Maniatakis, P. A. and Moore, C. M. (2009) 'The Role of International Hubs in a Fashion Retailer's Sourcing Strategy', *International Review of Retail, Distribution and Consumer Research*, vol. 19, no. 4, pp. 421–36.

Fernie, J. and Sparks, L. (2009) *Logistics and Retail Management* (London: Kogan Page).

Fiorito, S. S., May, E. G. and Straughn, K. (1995) 'Quick Response in Retailing: Components and Implementation', *International Journal of Retailing and Distribution Management*, vol. 23, no. 5, pp. 12–21.

Gattorna, J. L. and Walters, D. W. (1996) *Managing the Supply Chain* (London: Macmillan).

Gustafsson, K., Jonson, G., Smith, D. and Sparks, L. (2009) *Retailing Logistics and Fresh Food Packaging* (London: Kogan Page).

Hines, T. (2004) *Supply Chain Strategies: Customer Driven and Customer Focused* (Oxford: Elsevier).

Jack, S. (2009) 'Coping with Christmas', *Drapers*, 29 August, p. 90.

Lowson, B., King, R. and Hunter, A. (1999) *Quick Response: Managing the Supply Chain to Meet Consumer Demand* (Chichester: John Wiley).

McKinnon, A., Cullinane, S., Browne, M. and Whiteing, A. (2010) *Green Logistics: Improving the Environmental Sustainability of Logistics* (London: Kogan Page).

New Look (1999) Company report (Weymouth: New Look).

Whitehead, D. (1998) 'The DIY Man Gives Fashion a New Look', *Draper's Record*, 5 September.

Worsford, F. (2001) *The Green Logistics Company* (Kingston upon Thames: Croner CCH).

8 MANAGING INFORMATION

LEARNING OBJECTIVES

- To understand how EPOS, EFTPOS and EDI can be used to improve customer service and retailer efficiency.
- To explore how loyalty cards can be used to improve store performance.
- To appreciate the role of IT in improving marketing and merchandising.
- To understand data-warehousing and data-mining concepts.
- To explore the different types of information systems used by retailers and their role within retailing organizations.

INTRODUCTION

Information is a key resource that retailers need to manage effectively in order to satisfy their customers' needs and to remain competitive in the industry. The number of products carried by a retailer and the large number of customers and suppliers means that retailers generate huge amounts of information. The advent of information technology (IT) has given retailers the means to harness it and enabled them to improve the efficiency of their businesses and the service that they provide to customers. Information technology is ubiquitous in retailing today, with its most obvious manifestation in the electronic point of scale (EPOS) cash register and the laser scanner used at checkouts by the vast majority of retailers. EFTPOS (electronic funds transfer at point of sale) systems also allow customers to pay by either credit or debit cards at checkouts without cash. Many retailers also use electronic loyalty cards to add incentives. In the background, store retailers use the information provided by the EPOS system and direct communication with their suppliers through electronic data interchange (EDI) to allow automatic reordering and replenishment. The Internet has also changed how retailers communicate with their suppliers, and retailers use information technology in general to improve their marketing and merchandising performance. The Internet also allows retailers to interact with customers and with shoppers whilst they are in the store through Internet-enabled smartphones.

Despite the above, retailers were relatively slow to adopt information technology. Although computer technology has been used by retailers since the 1960s, it was not until the early 1980s when computer technology became relatively cheap that retailers began to seriously consider its widespread use within stores. One study estimated that in 1991 the expenditure on IT by major European food retailers, the lead sector in terms of IT use, amounted to only around 0.5 per cent of sales. And more recently it has been estimated that the expenditure of US retailers amounts to only around 1 per cent of sales compared with 5 per cent of sales for the industry as a whole. Nevertheless, information technology is now integral to the operation of retail stores.

IT has been used by retailers for three main purposes: item identification, improvement of communication internally and externally and information processing and analysis. EPOS systems are a direct outcome of item identification. The development of internal networks, intranets and EDI and the Internet represents attempts to improve communications internally and externally. Retailers have gone beyond simply using information technology to collect information; increasingly, they are using it to analyse and better understand the needs of their customers and to improve retail business processes.

This chapter examines the use of information technology and its impact at store level. Internet retailing, which is revolutionizing retailing and shopping, is discussed separately in Chapter 17.

ELECTRONIC POINT OF SCALE (EPOS) SYSTEMS

An EPOS system consists of a laser scanner capable of reading a universal product code (the black and white stripes or barcode found on most merchandise today), attached to a computer that can recognize the product, with, in addition, a price look-up table of all products sold in the store. The EPOS terminal is itself connected to the company computer, which collates information from all stores in the chain. On scanning a product, the computer records the sale and displays the price for the customer to check, and at the end of the transaction an itemized receipt is produced for the customers. An alternative system for product identification is RFID (or radio frequency identification). In this system, products are tagged with electromagnetic tags (consisting of an integrated circuit) which employ radio frequencies to transfer electronically stored information about the product to a reading device. Unlike the barcode, RFID tags can carry much more information than a simple product code and can be used to track the movement of the product through the whole supply chain. A key advantage of RFID tags is that unlike barcodes they do not require line of sight for reading. Also, a whole basket can be scanned in one go rather than having to scan each item individually. However, RFID tags are considerably more expensive than barcodes and have been mainly used for tracking cases of merchandise through the supply chain rather than individually tagging products.

However, as the costs of RFID tags has declined, a number of retailers have begun to use item-level tagging, particularly for more expensive items. The clothing sector in particular has seen a growth of RFID item tagging, with Wal-Mart and Marks and Spencer leading the way. The main reasons for the adoption of RFID in the clothing sector is a big reduction in the time and labour required for inventory taking, inventory accuracy, reduced shrinkage and a big reduction in out-of-stocks, leading (as a result of the improved accuracy) to increased sales.

EPOS systems provide retailers with up-to-date information on how fast goods are moving and hence when stocks need replenishing. A major saving to retailers, such as supermarkets, in adopting EPOS systems is that items do not need to be priced individually, with resulting savings in labour costs. Also, by monitoring changes over time retailers are in a position to detect changes in customer behaviour to which they can respond more quickly than non-EPOS-based systems. In fact, the availability of this information has given retailers extra bargaining power as they frequently have more information about the popularity of goods than the manufacturers.

EPOS systems are particularly useful in the fast-moving consumer goods (FMCG) area both from the customer's and the retailer's perspective. From the customer's perspective, the major benefit is that checkout time is reduced, and hence there is less queuing, and an itemized list also gives them the opportunity to check their receipts in detail. Another major benefit to both customers and the retailer is that stock-outs are less frequent, and the increased efficiencies help to maintain low costs or allow the provision of extra services for customers. For instance, many supermarkets now provide help with packing. To increase benefits to consumers even further, some retailers have introduced self-scanning into their stores. The UK food retailer Tesco makes the most extensive use of self-scanning in its stores (see Vignette 8.1), although others, such as Sainsbury's, are also experimenting with the system. With self-scanning, the shopper scans the merchandise that they want to purchase as they move around the store. This is done by using either a hand-held scanner provided by the store or a scanner fitted to the shopping trolley. At the till the shopper simply pays the bill without having to unload the shopping and wait for it to be scanned, thus considerably reducing the time spent queuing, which is the most disliked aspect of food shopping.

VIGNETTE 8.1 SCAN AS YOU SHOP

Improving customer service is a key issue for grocery retailers and their time-pressed customers. One of the pet hates in grocery shopping is the time spent queuing at checkouts, and anything that reduces it would be welcomed by customers. One system that helps with this is Scan as You Shop developed by Tesco. The system involves customers using a hand-held scanner to scan their own shopping as they go around the store. The scanner is obtained from a dispenser using the Tesco's Clubcard. The scanner displays a running total of the products that are in the shopping trolley. Products can be easily deleted if the customer makes a mistake or decides to change their mind using the 'minus' button on the scanner. Once the shopping is completed, the customers take their bagged shopping to a separate payment area, where they have to scan the 'end of trip' barcode, pay and go but without loading and unloading, thereby considerably reducing the queuing and checkout time. However, re-scanning is carried out randomly to ensure that the system is accurate and to prevent theft. This involves scanning a small number of items (rather than the whole shopping) and means that the process is still quicker than the manned checkouts. The system has quickly gained popularity with Tesco shoppers, who like its convenience, reduced shopping time, not having to queue and being able to track their expenditure as they shop. For the retailer, it helps reduce costs as well as allows a more tailored use of Clubcard vouchers suited to the needs of the individual customers.

Tesco carried out initial trials of the system in its Romford store in 2010 but has since rolled it out to 100 of its stores after learning from the trials that 15 per cent of the sales were going through the system. Mobile scanning is not a new concept to UK retailing as it was first introduced in 1995 by Safeway and had been introduced into 150 stores by 2003 before the company was acquired by Morrisons. Waitrose has been offering a service called Quick Check since 1996, which is now available in over 170 of its stores. Sainsbury's is currently trialling a different system based on customers using their smartphones called Mobile Scan & Go. This involves customers downloading the Mobile Scan & Go on their phone, which then allows them to scan their shopping on their smartphone, pack their purchases as they go and keep a running total of exactly how much is being spent and how much they have saved. When they have finished shopping, customers can pay at any checkout and they do not have to unload their items from their trolley or basket. They just need to scan the QR code at the checkout and pay as normal. Sainsbury's is currently trialling Mobile Scan & Go in four of its stores, namely Bethnal Green Local, Clerkenwell Road Local, London Colney and Tadley.

Source: Quinn (2012) and various other sources including company websites

ELECTRONIC FUNDS TRANSFER AT POINT OF SALE (EFTPOS)

An EFTPOS system is basically designed to facilitate cashless payment by customers. An EFTPOS terminal connected to the sales till is connected not only to the retailer's central computer, but also to the computers of participating high-street banks, building societies and credit card companies. The system allows customers to pay for their shopping using debit or credit cards swiped through a scanner on the till. The details of the transaction are instantly transmitted to the customer's bank or credit card company, which checks to see if there is enough money in the customer's account to pay the bill, and authorizes the retailer to proceed with the transaction and debits the customer's account within three days of the transaction. At the same time, the retailer's account is credited. For the customer, EFTPOS is convenient; for the retailer, it is quicker and less open to fraud than cheque card-based systems and there are savings to be gained from the reduced handling of cash. An emerging area in electronic funds is mobile payments, that is payments made via the use of a mobile phone rather than cash, debit or credit cards. The development of mobile payment systems in the UK and other western countries is currently in its infancy and will require cooperation between banks, mobile phone operators and retailers to make mobile payments widely acceptable. In some developing countries, such as Nigeria, it is already being used more widely.

ELECTRONIC DATA INTERCHANGE (EDI)

Electronic data interchange is the electronic exchange of information between the retailer's computer and that of its supplier. The exchange can consist of orders, delivery notices, invoices, returns and even sales data. Retailers have found that EDI links with suppliers considerably reduce the lead times required for deliveries, and hence large savings can be made by the consequent reduction in inventory required. Additional benefits include a huge reduction in paperwork and consequently an increase in productivity. The constant exchange of information between the retailer and its suppliers also helps retailers assess more accurately suppliers' performance, accuracy and quality of service. This information can also be used in price and contract negotiations.

Initially, EDI systems were proprietary, that is owned by either the retailer, the supplier or an independent third-party provider known as a value-added network (VAN). The proprietary systems were very expensive to develop and needed considerable investment by both retailers and suppliers to develop communication and business protocols, and thus could only be afforded by larger retailers and suppliers. Small suppliers were particularly vulnerable to exclusion as retailers began to insist on EDI compatibility. One advantage of using VAN networks is that retailers and suppliers with different EDI protocols can communicate with each other through the VAN provider translating the data from each party before transmitting them to the other.

With the development of the Internet, however, data are now being transmitted either directly to suppliers/retailers or via an extranet. An extranet is an Internet-based collaborative network linking suppliers and their customers. An advantage of such systems is that the cheap and uniform Internet communications platform means that small suppliers are not excluded from the network and the networks are potentially global in scope. Sainsbury's, for instance, uses an Internet-based extranet, Touchpoint, to communicate a variety of information other than orders with its supply-chain partners.

A rapidly emerging application of extranets is reverse auctions. This is where a retailer specifies merchandise details on the extranet and invites interested suppliers to submit proposals/bids within a specified time period. Reverse auctions mean that the retailer is not limited to existing suppliers for merchandise, and receives a number of competitive quotes for specified merchandise at little extra cost, hence enabling them to reduce their costs further.

QUICK-RESPONSE (QR) REPLENISHMENT SYSTEMS

When EPOS systems are combined with EDI, retailers are in effect adopting just-in-time replenishment or quick-response (QR) replenishment methods (Figure 8.1). Ordering of merchandise is thus based on current rather than historical sales. Sales-based ordering systems are now commonplace. The lead time (the time between placing an order and its arrival in the store) and the speed of response of suppliers can be further enhanced if retailers agree with their suppliers the level of sales at which orders are automatically triggered; that is an automatic reordering system. A big advantage of QR systems is in reducing stock-outs and the amount of inventory carried, hence improving the service to customers and reducing costs to the retailer.

Collaborative efforts between retailers and their suppliers to reduce inventory costs and improve responsiveness to consumer demand are more generally known as efficient consumer response (ECR), and are particularly popular in the grocery industry. One technique that extends the use of EDI to a higher level is collaboration, planning, forecasting and replenishment (CPFR). CPFR is an inventory management system designed to improve store-level sales and provide forecasts based on the previous sales history and forthcoming merchandising and marketing activities of the retailer and suppliers. CPFR requires the retailer to send information in real time to a supplier who uses the data to forecast the required inventory and replenishment schedule. The supplier shares the forecast with the retailer before acting on it.

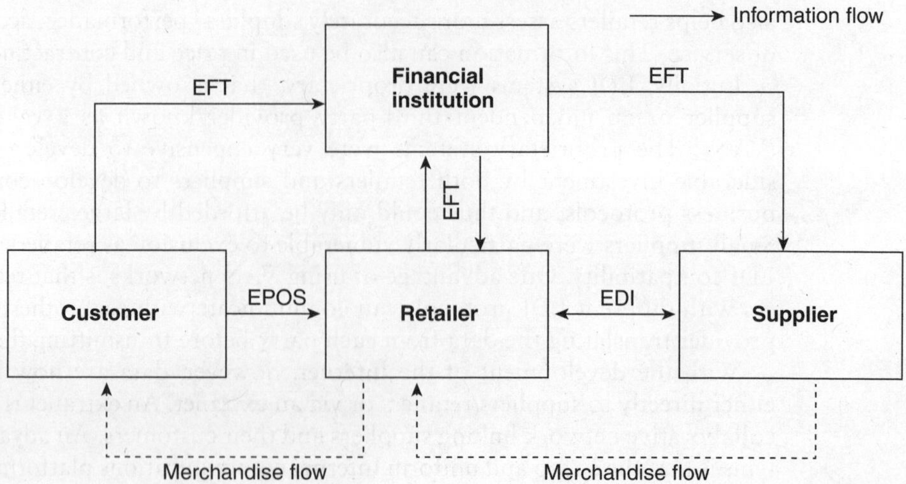

Figure 8.1 A simplified quick-response replenishment system

In an increasingly competitive retail market, a major function of retail marketing is to maintain customer loyalty. Loyalty can be developed by providing customers with incentives to shop at a store, and by ensuring that a store's merchandise is tailored to the needs of its customers. Information technology may help retailers achieve the first aim by the use of electronic loyalty schemes which reward customers based on their store expenditure. The second aim is being facilitated by the ability to analyse information at the local and individual level, which has enabled retailers to develop micro-marketing strategies or customized marketing and merchandising programmes for each store based on local preferences.

ELECTRONIC LOYALTY SCHEMES

A major problem with EPOS data is that they do not carry any information about the customer. Hence, whilst the data are useful for monitoring sales and the impact of sales promotions and so forth, they provide little information as to who is buying the merchandise. Retailers have overcome this problem by setting up EPOS-based loyalty schemes. In order to become members of the loyalty scheme, customers are asked to fill in a form with their personal demographic information (name, address, occupation, marital status, income and so on) and some questions regarding product preferences. Customers are given a personalized electronically readable magnetic card. When a purchase is made, it is recorded by scanning the card. Customers earn a number of loyalty points (based on the size of their purchase), and these are added to their account and also printed on their till receipt for checking. The points collected are redeemable against either their next shopping bill, promotional gifts or other promotional offers such as air miles.

The basic rationale behind loyalty schemes is to increase profits by developing long-term relationships with customers, particularly loyal customers. An important underlying reason for targeting existing customers is that it is easier to sell more to existing customers than to recruit new ones. Loyal customers also tend to spend more than the average customer per visit, and hence the loss of loyal customers can have a highly detrimental effect on store profitability. It is widely recognized that Tesco's Clubcard helped it to wrest market leadership, in terms of market share, from Sainsbury's.

A major driver of the current wave of loyalty schemes (see Table 8.1) is that they enable retailers to build up, relatively cheaply, a database of their customers who can be encouraged to remain or become the store's most loyal customers. With electronic loyalty schemes it is also possible to gather data on the shopping habits of customers and to use this information to target specific groups with customized incentives and offers. The data can also be used to define trade areas for stores and to target current and potential customers with marketing promotions. Of course, an essential prerequisite of electronic loyalty schemes is the existence of an adequate IT network.

Loyalty cards are, however, expensive to operate, and as a consequence a number of schemes have been disbanded (for example WHSmith's Clubcard was closed down in 2007). Other retailers prefer not to have them (for example ASDA and Morrisons), and instead focus on offering lower prices and better promotions to their customers. There is also evidence that loyalty cards may be becoming less effective as most shoppers now possess more than one and in recessionary times shoppers are more interested in lower prices and promotions than loyalty points. Despite this, retailers operating loyalty schemes feel that the value of the information provided by the schemes outweighs the costs. One loyalty scheme that addresses some of these concerns is the Nectar loyalty card launched by Sainsbury's, Debenhams, Barclaycard and BP in September 2002, replacing their individual schemes with a single multiparty one. From the retailer's perspective, a multiparty scheme has the advantage that the costs of running the scheme are shared between scheme members and it potentially allows retailers to form a more rounded picture of their customers. It also has the advantage that customers can collect loyalty points faster, thus making it more attractive to them. The disadvantage from the retailer's point is that it makes it much more complicated to tailor and personalize the scheme specifically to the retailer's needs and that of its customer. It may also be difficult to disentangle store and card loyalty. As result of some of these issues, two of its founder members, Barclaycard and Debenhams, withdrew from the scheme in 2005 and 2008, respectively. Nevertheless, the Nectar card has proved to be popular as 6 months after the launch of the Nectar scheme, it already had 11 million active cardholders, and by 2013 it rivalled Tesco's Clubcard in popularity with around 17 million active members.

Table 8.1 Examples of loyalty schemes in the UK

Retailer	Loyalty programme	Year launched	Rate of return on money spent	Estimated number of members
Sainsbury's	Nectar card	2002	1%	17 million
Tesco	Clubcard	1995	1%	17 million
Boots	Advantage card	1997	4%	18 million

CUSTOMER RELATIONSHIP MANAGEMENT (CRM)

A more general term for programmes designed to build and manage customer loyalty and to increase sales and profitability from existing customers is customer relationship management (CRM). CRM programmes require the collection and analysis of customer data. Such data can be acquired in a number of ways, including loyalty cards, credit cards, customer guarantee forms, invoices and so forth. For mail-order and Internet shoppers, information identifying customers is less of a problem as it is provided by the customer when purchasing products. The purpose of analysis is to identify patterns and trends in customer shopping habits in order to meet customer needs more precisely. The information is used to develop marketing, customer services and customized merchandise programmes for targeted groups or individuals. The power of CRM programmes is most evident in the area of Internet retailing, where the technology is available to personalize web pages and to tailor offers to each customer.

DATA WAREHOUSING AND MICRO-MARKETING

A data warehouse consists of a collection of various internal retailing databases such as EPOS data, loyalty card data, customer payment data and external data such as geodemographic profiles, competitor data and market research information from third parties. The idea behind constructing such data warehouses (or stores of data) is so that the relationships within and between the databases constituting the warehouse can be analysed for useful patterns and structures for marketing and other purposes. These patterns are identified by using various statistical, database and artificial intelligence data-mining techniques, amongst others. An important facet of data warehousing is that it allows information to be shared with different parts of an organization in the required format, whilst separating analysis from operational activities.

The data warehouses can be used for any number of purposes ranging from forecasting sales trends, pricing and measuring effectiveness of displays and promotions, to tracking customer profitability. One particular use of data mining is that of micro-marketing. Micro-marketing is the identification of the needs of store-specific markets and tailoring marketing and merchandising efforts to satisfy those needs. A corollary of micro-marketing is micro-merchandising or the development of the store-specific product mix required to satisfy the needs of the target market. Wal-Mart is one retailer that has adopted the micro-marketing and micro-merchandising approach by using data mining to help each of its stores to adjust its merchandise mix to local preferences, ensuring that the range and prices are in line with local spending patterns. There is no real reason why this approach cannot be extended to one-to-one marketing. Internet retailers in particular have information on individuals and the ability to target them individually. However, the benefits of one-to-one marketing must be weighed against the costs.

For large retailers, in particular, the data collected can take up vast amounts of computer memory. For instance, the world's biggest retailer, Wal-Mart, has a data warehouse considered second in size only to the Pentagon. Given the size of the investment in terms of time and money, data warehouses need to be actively managed to obtain the best information from them.

RETAIL MANAGEMENT INFORMATION SYSTEMS

Given the quantity of information generated by retailers, it needs to be organized so that management can use it effectively for decision-making purposes. A retail information system systematically collects, processes, stores and distributes information to the relevant decision-makers for the purposes of planning, controlling and monitoring business processes. An information system has four basic components: information inputs, information-processing capability, outputs and information storage capacity. Information systems also require feedback, which is output that is returned to those dealing with information input so that they can evaluate or modify the data entered at the input stage.

Information inputs are essentially either internal or external to the retailer. Internal inputs are either information routinely collected, or information collected on an ad hoc basis such as market research. Routinely collected information includes EPOS sales data, loyalty card data, store card data, returns, customer complaints, coupon redemptions and so on. Other information inputs include costs of merchandise, costs of operations and financial budgets, merchandise plans, product information, inventory, orders, deliveries, pricing, promotions and so forth.

External information is information from external organizations such as market research companies, government sources, suppliers and so on. For instance, Nielsen's Homescan Consumer Panel provides panel data on consumer shopping behaviour across all types of retailers and products. The Mosaic and ACORN lifestyle and geodemographic databases are available from the market research companies Experian and CACI, respectively. Much of this information is available in electronic format and can therefore be easily integrated into retailers' information systems. External information performs an important function in that it provides an external view of the market and fills in gaps in retailers' knowledge of the market.

The type of information input into a system depends upon the purpose for which it is required. For instance, if the retailer wants to estimate the profit that each individual product contributes (direct product profit, DPP) to the overall profitability of a department, information on the revenue generated by each product and the costs associated with selling it will be required. On the revenue side, the sale price, any promotional support from the supplier and invoice cost are required to calculate the gross profit. On the costs side, transport direct costs, warehousing direct costs, store direct costs (space, labour and so on), promotional costs and pre-warehousing costs (for example ordering costs) would be required as inputs to calculate the costs associated with each product (see Figure 8.2).

Database management

In order to maximize the value of the information that the organization collects, it needs to ensure that the information from different databases is effectively integrated and actively managed. For instance, a retailer may collect information on customers using its store card, from responses to promotional campaigns and from third-party lists, and maintain separate databases for each. However, to maximize the value of these databases, they need to be integrated into a master customer database. Direct marketing campaigns based on such a database are much more likely to be

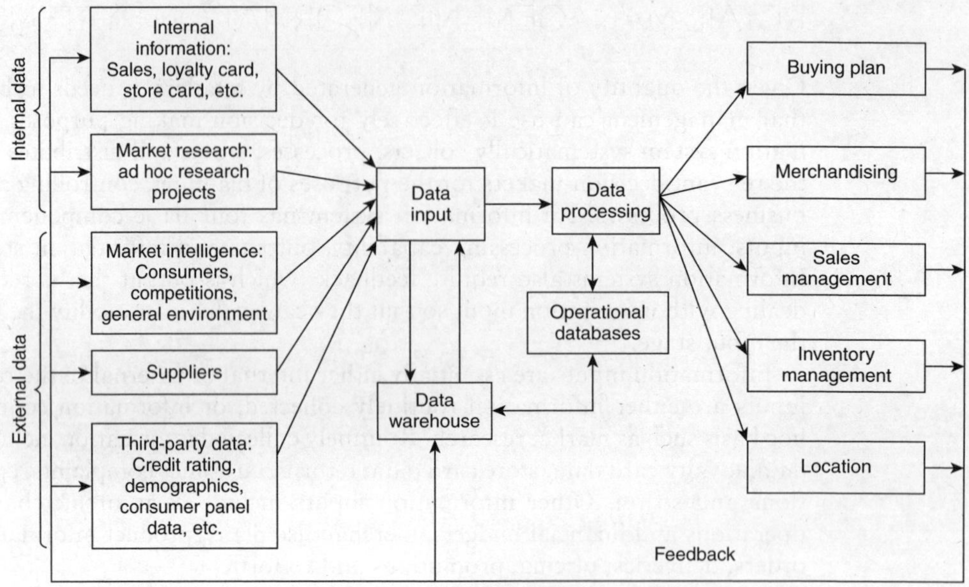

Figure 8.2 A hypothetical retailing information management system

comprehensive and effective than those based on the individual databases. Active management of such a customer database also means that the data are used to analyse the recency, frequency, average spend of customers and lifetime value of the customer to the organization, so that the most valuable customers can be identified and targeted for direct marketing campaigns.

Types of information systems

Retail information systems can be divided into four basic types, as follows:

1. transaction processing systems (TPSs),
2. management information systems (MISs),
3. decision support systems (DSSs) and
4. executive support systems (ESSs).

Transaction processing systems (TPSs) are used to facilitate customer transactions and other routine business processes necessary for the conduct of business on a day-to-day basis. Examples include sales recording by EPOS systems, payroll and employee record keeping. A breakdown in TPSs is likely to have a severe impact on the operation of the business and thus requires regular monitoring by managers. The information collected by TPSs forms a major input into other systems.

The purpose of management information systems (MISs) is to assist middle managers in their monitoring, controlling and decision-making activities. MISs normally provide routine summary or exception reports in the form of either a report or online access. The reports are usually summaries of transaction data from TPSs indicating the firm's current performance. The reports provide answers to questions that are pre-specified and usually only contain simple summaries and comparison rather than sophisticated analysis of the data. An MIS report for a store manager, for instance, might consist of a report on weekly sales by each department of a store.

A decision support system (DSS) is an information system designed to assist managers in making non-routine semi-structured or unstructured decisions. A DSS combines use of models with data from various sources including both internal and external data (where relevant). A DSS typically allows the user to conduct 'what if' analyses by changing the assumptions underlying various components of the decision. In retailing, a DSS may be employed in assisting store location decisions, for instance. Such a system would require internal data on existing locations and criteria that the new store must satisfy. External information, for instance on the demographics of the trading area of the proposed store, would also be required. In addition, the DSS would also incorporate a model (either theoretical or one proposed by management) as to how this information should be combined to arrive at a location decision.

An executive support system (ESS) is designed to support senior managers responsible for making strategic decisions in the company. As strategic decisions are non-routine and require information about trends in the external environment as well as internally, an ESS incorporates information from both MISs and DSSs and external data about competitors' activities, the regulatory environment, the economic environment and so forth.

SUMMARY

IT is now integral to all aspects of retail management. The use of EPOS, EFTPOS and EDI has increased store productivity and improved customer service. The combination of EPOS and EDI has allowed retailers to develop quick-response systems which gives them more flexibility, reduces inventory costs and improves customer service. The use of loyalty cards has not only given retailers a way of offering incentives to customers, but the data provided by the schemes gives retailers more precise insight into customer behaviour. Retailers have been able to use this internally generated information and external databases to develop new micro-marketing techniques to target customers more precisely with more tailored merchandise. Retailers are also beginning to use sophisticated information systems designed for specific types of management decisions ranging from transaction processing systems for routine decisions, to executive support systems for strategic decisions. In order to make the most effective use of the information available, retailers need to integrate their various information systems to give them an edge in a rapidly changing environment.

QUESTIONS

1. What are the benefits of using EPOS systems for retailers?
2. How have shoppers benefited from the use of information technology by retailers?
3. Explain how a QR system can reduce inventory investment and improve customer service.

4. What are the benefits of electronic loyalty schemes for retailers? Why do many retailers not have loyalty schemes?
5. Discuss how retailers can exploit various databases at their disposal.
6. Describe the key elements of a retail information system.
7. Explain the functions of the different types of information systems used by retailers.

REFERENCES AND FURTHER READING

Burden, R. and Proctor, T. (1997) 'Information Systems Development in Retailing', *Marketing Intelligence and Planning*, vol. 15, no. 2, pp. 106–11.

Clarke, I. and Rowley, J. (1995) 'A Case for Spatial Decision-Support Systems in Retail Location Planning', *International Journal of Retail and Distribution Management*, vol. 23, no. 3, pp. 4–10.

Cohen, B. (1992) 'How Micromerchandising Can Work for Big Chains', *Chain Store Age Executive with Shopping Center Age*, vol. 68, no. 2 (February), p. 58.

Dawson, J. A. (1994) 'Applications of Information Management in European Retailing', *International Review of Retail, Distribution and Consumer Research*, vol. 4, no. 2, pp. 219–38.

Fisher, M. L., Raman, A. and McClelland, A. S. (2000) 'Rocket Science Retailing Is Almost Here: Are You Ready?', *Harvard Business Review*, vol. 78, no. 4 (July/August), pp. 115–24.

Larson, P. D. and Lusch, R. F. (1990) 'Quick Response Retail Technology: Integration and Performance Measurement', *International Review of Retail, Distribution and Consumer Research*, vol. 1, no. 1, pp. 17–35.

Laudon, K. C. and Laudon, J. P. (2013), *Management Information Systems: Managing the Digital Firm*, 13th Edition (London: Prentice Hall).

Levy, M. and Grewal, D. (2000) 'Supply Chain Management in a Networked Economy', *Journal of Retailing*, vol. 76, no. 4, pp. 415–29.

O'Brien, L. and Jones, C. (1995) 'Do Rewards Really Create Loyalty?', *Harvard Business Review*, vol. 73, no. 3, pp. 74–82.

Pearce, M. R. (1997) 'Succeeding with Micromarketing', *Ivey Business Quarterly*, London, vol. 62, no. 1, pp. 69–72.

Quinn, I. (2012) 'Scan-as-You-Shop Technology to Roll Out across Tesco', *Grocer*, 29 September.

Rafiq, M. (1997) 'Developing Customer Loyalty: The Savercard Experience', in C. Hart, M. Kirkup, D. Preston, M. Rafiq and P. Walley (eds), *Cases in Retailing: Operational Perspectives* (Oxford: Blackwell Business), pp. 43–61.

Rafiq, M., Fulford, H. and Lu, X. (2013), 'Building Customer Loyalty in Online Retailing: The Role of Relationship Quality', *Journal of Marketing Management*, vol. 29, no. 3–4, pp. 494–517.

Rowley, J. (1995) 'Multimedia Kiosks in Retailing', *International Journal of Retail and Distribution Management*, vol. 23, no. 5, pp. 32–40.

Steidtmann, C. (1999) 'The New Retail Technology', *Discount Merchandiser*, vol. 39, no. 11, pp. 23–24.

Sweeney, T. (2001) 'Web Kiosks Spur Spending in Stores', *Information Week*, 12 March, no. 828, pp. 126–28.

Wasserman, T., Khermouch, G. and Green, J. (2000) 'Mining Everyone's Business', *Brandweek*, New York, vol. 41, no. 9 (28 February), pp. 32–6.

Wright, C. and Sparks, L. (1999) 'Loyalty Saturation in Retailing: Exploring the End of Retail Loyalty Cards?', *International Journal of Retail and Distribution Management*, vol. 27, no. 10, pp. 429–40.

9 RETAIL LOCATION

LEARNING OBJECTIVES

- To understand the importance of retail location decision making.
- To distinguish between different types of available retail locations.
- To explore patterns of retail development.
- To appreciate the importance of defining and estimating a trade area and selecting the best sites.
- To explore the use of geo-demographics in location decision making.
- To understand the various methods of assessing the potential of retail sites.
- To appreciate the impact of planning regulations and online retailing on the evolution of retail development.
- To introduce key principles associated with locating a retail business online.

INTRODUCTION

Location has long been recognized as one of the prime determinants of success in retailing. It is for this reason that, in spite of online retailing being ubiquitous, it is still often said that the three determinants of retailing success are 'location, location and location'. Whilst other aspects of the retail mix can be changed relatively quickly, many location decisions are long term in nature and difficult to change in the short term. The costs of wrong decisions can be high, and paybacks are considered over a long time frame. With online retailing changing consumer shopping habits, the decision to invest in physical stores is even more crucial than ever. Many large retailers have property departments that work with this specialist area of retail management, which not only manage the store portfolio and new store development but will also be involved in refurbishment projects.

Location decisions are complex, as stores need to satisfy consumer needs for convenience, accessibility and quality. A chosen location must take into account other operational needs such as adequate access for deliveries and availability of labour. Also, the choice of retail locations provides a variation in suitability for different types of retailers. For example whilst clothing retailers benefit from trading in a critical mass, grocery retailers prefer to be located apart from direct competitors. Some of the alternative locations include traditional town centres or 'high streets' and major regional centres; out-of-town centres; speciality centres such as historical districts, waterfronts, factory outlets and old industry sites; free-standing locations such as greenfield sites;

retail warehouse parks; petrol station forecourts; and motorway service stations, airports and other transport terminals. At the same time the choice of location in many retail markets is becoming increasingly difficult because of increasing competition and the shortage of large sites due to strict planning regulations. For many retailers, location decision making now has an international dimension.

TYPES OF RETAIL LOCATION

Solus or free-standing site

A solus site is a stand-alone site away from other shopping centres. Such stores are usually purpose built. Generally, retailers that select free-standing sites are seeking either to benefit from spatial monopoly or are there for reasons of operational efficiency. Typical examples of free-standing stores are grocery superstores and non-grocery stores such as DIY and furniture stores. For grocery stores, it is essential that the store location is convenient for customers and that the trading area is not shared with other direct competitors. For a furniture retailer such as IKEA the availability of a low-cost, large, flat site for an extensive display showroom, a warehouse area and a large car park is essential. A major disadvantage of a solus site is that the retailer cannot rely on a 'centre' to attract customers and has to undertake its own promotional activity to generate footfall. Another problem with solus sites is that new sites are likely to require planning permission, which may be difficult to obtain.

Unplanned shopping centre

An unplanned shopping centre is one that has evolved in a gradual, piecemeal manner. Typical unplanned centres include the 'high street' or central business districts (CBDs) in well-established town centres. Suburban centres also tend to be unplanned. This type of centre relies on customer traffic generated by other attractions as well as retailing, including business and leisure attractions. A major attraction of such centres is the variety of retailers, which facilitates comparison shopping for customers. A distinctive feature of unplanned locations is that ownership of the centre is fragmented and therefore consensus decision making for the benefit of all retailers may be difficult to organize, and with the retail composition of unplanned centres being unregulated there are no quotas on particular types of retailers within the centre, unlike planned centres.

Planned shopping centre

A planned shopping centre is one that has been deliberately designed and developed for retail use. This may be a single building with a number of stores, for example a shopping mall, or a group of physically separate stores with common access and car parking (such as a retail park). Planned centres are designed to serve a specific, geo-demographic segment of customers, are normally under single ownership and are actively promoted by their managers as a single entity. As a result they have the advantage of a consistent image for the centre whereas this is much more difficult for unplanned centres. In order to maintain this image, planned centres will restrict retailers' activities, such as the type of store design, and the tenant mix will be carefully coordinated.

The choice between planned and unplanned centres depends on the amount and type of customer traffic a centre generates, and the quality and suitability of the site for specific retailers and the retail activity.

PATTERNS OF RETAIL DEVELOPMENT

A number of theories exist to explain the pattern of retailing locations and the interrelationships between them. These include the central-place theory, which attempts to explain the existence of shopping districts, their size, composition and spacing and the hierarchical relation between them; the bid-rent theory, which provides an explanation of internal spatial organization in unplanned shopping districts; and the agglomeration theory, which provides explanations for the clustering of similar types of retailers.

Central-place theory

The central-place theory is a model that explains the economic forces that lead to a hierarchical supply of shopping facilities in urban areas. It was first proposed by Christaller in the 1930s and further developed by Losch (1954) and others. The theory is based on the premise that as the distance to a retail centre/district increases, demand for a product will decrease due to increased cost of travel. The maximum distance that a customer will travel to obtain a product is known as the market area or range of the good. The threshold is defined as the minimum population required to make the supply of a good worthwhile. In order to be viable, the range of the good needs to exceed the threshold for the product. Using this framework the theory predicts that low-order (frequently purchased, low priced, convenience) products will require low threshold and low range to be successful, whereas high-order products (infrequently purchased, expensive products) such as comparison goods require larger ranges (market areas) and thresholds to be successful. For these products the shopper is willing to travel a greater distance in order to make comparisons and to buy. This suggests that high-order goods are supplied only from large populous 'central' places and lower-order goods are supplied locally, leading to a hierarchy of shopping centres at different levels, such as regional shopping centres, district shopping centres and neighbourhood shopping centres. Furthermore, as the model assumes identical sellers (that is they sell a single line of merchandise, and overheads and buying costs are the same for all retailers selling similar goods) and no barriers to entry, it follows that the retailers of each item are equally spaced in a triangular fashion and have non-overlapping hexagonal trade areas, the size of which depends upon the order of the good sold.

This model came to be seen as an ideal arrangement or hierarchy for shopping centres by UK planners (particularly in the 1950s and 1960s) and is one major reason for the comparatively late emergence of free-standing hypermarkets/superstores, and out-of-town and retail parks in the UK.

The central-place theory has come under severe criticism for some of the assumptions that underpin it. For instance, the assumption that consumers have identical needs and undertake single-purpose (product) shopping trips to the nearest centre that supplies the merchandise is no longer tenable; whilst single-purpose shopping visits may have accurately described a situation in the past when grocery shopping involved buying meat from the butcher, bread from the bakery and vegetables from the greengrocer, in the era of the superstore and hypermarket such a description is not realistic where all grocery shopping needs are supplied in one location. The central-place theory also implies that the only factor that differentiates one store from another is location, which ignores other factors such as quality and image, which also play an important role in store choice.

The relevance of the theory in developed countries today has been almost completely undermined by the transformation of shopping and retailing in the emergence of mass car ownership. One of the major effects has been to turn the accessibility of town centres (or central places) on its head, as they have changed from being the most accessible to the most congested. As a consequence, there has been a huge shift of retailing from town centres to out-of-town locations in the last 30 years in what has been called 'waves of decentralization' by Schiller (1986). This began with the development of grocery superstores in the early 1970s, followed in the mid-1970s by space-hungry specialists such as electrical, carpet and furniture stores. The vast majority of comparison shopping still remained in town centres until the early 1980s, when the first retail parks started to emerge. The 1990s saw the emergence of out-of-town regional shopping centres which are large enough by themselves to compete directly with town centres. These developments have fundamentally altered the traditional retailing hierarchies, which led Dawson (1979) to comment that central-place theory can no longer be used as a basis either for the explanation of present retail development patterns or for the planning of future retail locations. Despite the criticism, central-place theory is useful for drawing attention to the fundamental importance of the distance-decay effect: that is, the attraction of a retail centre/location to consumers declines as the distance to it increases. It is also useful in that it highlights the fact that suitability of location (central place or not) depends upon the type of merchandise that is being offered.

Bid-rent theory

Whilst in planned centres the location of actual stores is largely determined by centre management, in unplanned centres the location of retailers is determined by competition for the sites between different potential users. The bid-rent (or land-use) theory attempts to explain the spatial arrangement of retailers within centres. The theory is based on the premise that accessibility is of paramount importance for explaining patterns of urban land use. In urban settings, the city centre is the focal point of transportation networks and is, therefore, the most accessible and offers the maximum potential and optimum access to customers and labour. Competition is highest for a central location, and land goes to the highest bidders, those that can derive the greatest utility from the location. Hence, rents are highest in the centre and decline with distance from the core. Access to consumers is of paramount importance to retailers, and they are therefore prepared to pay the high rents that city-centre locations demand.

However, only some retailers are able to afford the cost of these prime sites. Invariably prime-pitch locations (those with the highest customer traffic) are more likely to be occupied by department stores, variety stores or speciality fashion stores. Grocery and furniture stores are more likely to be located towards the edge of the centre because of their need for cheaper sites with large amounts of surface area and car parking spaces.

Explanations of retail clustering

Bid-rent theory does not explain agglomeration, which is the tendency of similar retailers to cluster together. Early explanations of this phenomenon are based on Hotelling's (1929) principle of minimum differentiation, which suggests that a retailer would be able to maximize profits by locating or relocating closer to a competitor in order to gain a larger market area. Using the example of two similar profit-maximizing firms operating in a linear market (for example two ice-cream vendors on a beach), Hotelling argued that if one vendor were free to relocate, he would maximize his 'hinterland' or market (and hence his profit) by setting up shop adjacent to the other on the 'long' side of the market. If both sellers are footloose, a process of leapfrogging to the 'longer side' of the market develops, resulting in eventual clustering in the centre of the market (see Figure 9.1).

More recent explanations of agglomeration are based on the existence of positive externalities (benefits) for retailers locating together to attract a higher flow of customers. For instance, clustering could lead to improved infrastructure, or reduction in costs due to shared car parking, and hence improved access for customers of all the retailers. Agglomeration also makes sense where retailers can take advantage of traffic generated by destination stores (such as department stores) by intercepting customers on their way to and from the store. Department and other destination stores are aware of the customer pull that they are generating and in planned shopping centres are able to negotiate considerable reductions in their rents. Landlords in these centres recoup these costs by charging higher rents to retailers located near the

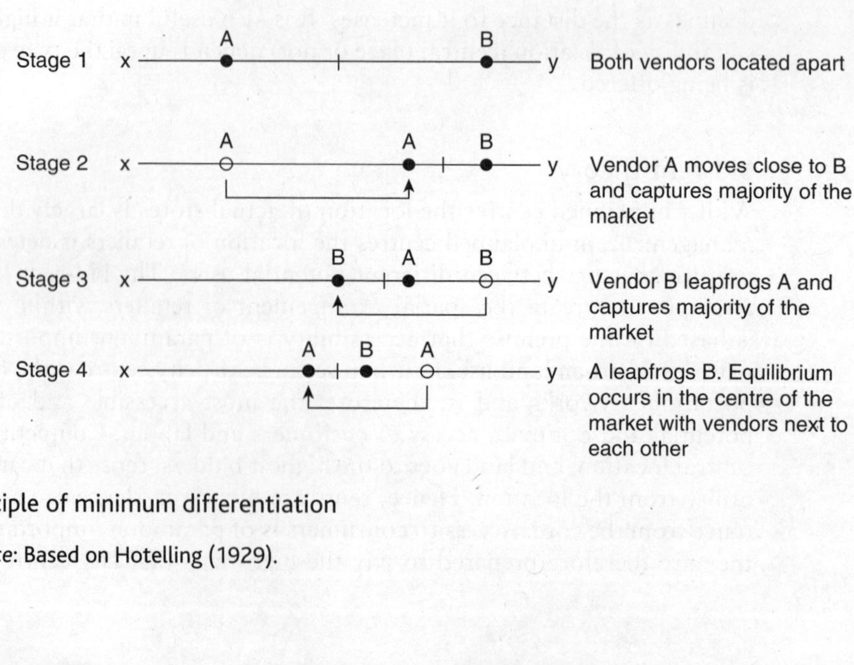

Figure 9.1 Principle of minimum differentiation

Source: Based on Hotelling (1929).

destination stores. The benefit of clustering of similar stores also suggests an increase in the total sales of all retailers unlike the arguments supporting the principle of minimum differentiation. Consumers attempt to reduce search and uncertainty costs by undertaking multi-purpose, multi-stop and comparison shopping and therefore prefer shopping where retailers are conveniently clustered. These explanations are better able to explain why, for instance, motor car dealers tend to cluster together outside of central locations.

THE RETAIL LOCATION DECISION PROCESS

Retail location decision making is a stepwise process, and it begins with the identification of the most attractive market areas or regions. The regions in this context can be towns, cities, metropolitan conurbations or even geographic regions. Such analysis is necessary as there can be a great deal of variation in demand and competitive conditions between regions. The next step is to identify suitable sites within a viable trading area (or catchment). The trade area is the geographical area that contains the potential customers for a particular retailer. The third step is the selection of the best site taking into account not just the potential revenue that the site can generate, but also the costs of locating at the site.

Region/market-area decision

Most retailers expand organically, that is by adding additional branches to their existing networks. This usually means that they will expand in a stepwise fashion from their original area of location or region and will only consider other regions when they have saturated the original region. Expansion is hereafter usually into neighbouring regions and not distant ones, as this minimizes the need to set up new distribution and logistical centres to support the new stores. However, in later stages of growth, retailers may consider regions more distant from their original location and infill intervening regions at a later stage – a strategy that was employed for instance by Kwik Save (Sparks, 1990). More recent examples include Aldi, IKEA and Toys 'R' Us.

Decisions on which regions to locate will depend on a number of factors including demography, economy, competition and infrastructure. For instance, Aldi entered the UK market by opening its first store in the West Midlands region of the UK because the region's socio-demographic profile matched the customer profile of the Aldi customer; that is households that are likely to be on a tight budget or interested in a value-for-money proposition when shopping for groceries. Even within regions there is a considerable amount of diversity, and decisions have to be made regarding which trade area(s) within the regions to target. For upmarket retailers like designer clothing outlets, a region may represent a whole country, because the only viable location for their particular customer profile may be in capital cities.

Trade-area decision

The trade area (or catchment) is defined as the geographic area from which a particular store or shopping centre draws its customers, and essentially determines the potential sales for a store. The extent of the trade area is determined by the type of store (and consequently the type of merchandise and the total size of the assortment sold by the retailer) and the degree of mobility of the customer and relative location of competitors. For instance, the trade area of a convenience store is likely to be less than a mile, whereas that for an IKEA store may extend to more than 20 miles. The difference is due to the fact that customers are not willing to travel long distances for convenience items such as bread and milk, but will travel much longer distances to stores that offer speciality and comparison goods and large assortments. Other major influences on trade-area size are

1. Population density/distribution.
2. Socio-economic status of consumers.
3. Distance and time to travel (actual and perceived).
4. Transport/communication networks.
5. Level of car ownership.
6. Business attractions of the centre where the store is located.
7. Social attractions of the centre where the store is located.
8. Competition from neighbouring stores/centres.
9. Presence of complementary retailers.
10. Geographical barriers (for example a river).

The exact shape and size of the trade area will be determined by the interaction of all these factors. A consequence of this is that stores do not draw trade from all areas of their catchments in equal proportions. In fact, trade areas can be divided into primary, secondary or tertiary zones. The primary trade area is designated as the area from which the store attracts 60–65 per cent of its customers and is the area closest to the store. This area has the highest density of customers and generates the highest expenditure per head. The secondary trade area generates around 20–30 per cent of the store's sales, and the remainder of the sales come from the tertiary trade area. Its customers may shop at the store when they are in the vicinity, for example on their way to or from work. It also includes shoppers who lack adequate retailing facilities closer to where they live if the site is served by excellent transport connections.

Figure 9.2 shows the trade areas of supermarkets in the UK. Research by the Competition Commission (2000) showed that for large supermarket operators such as Sainsbury's, on average 73 per cent of customers come from within a radius of 3 miles (designated as primary trade in Figure 9.2), a further 15 per cent travel come from a distance of 4–5 miles from the store (secondary trade area) and the remaining 12 per cent from more than 5 miles away (the tertiary trade area). The research further showed that shoppers living in highly urbanized areas (for example London) tended to travel shorter distances than the average, and that those living in rural areas tended to travel further than the average.

The question arises whether it is more appropriate to describe trade areas using the distance travelled, or the travel time to a store. Given that the majority of shoppers are car-borne (particularly in the case of grocery shopping), it is common practice to use drive-time isochrones to delineate trade areas. Isochrones are contours on a map representing equal travel time (usually drive time) from the store. An advantage of

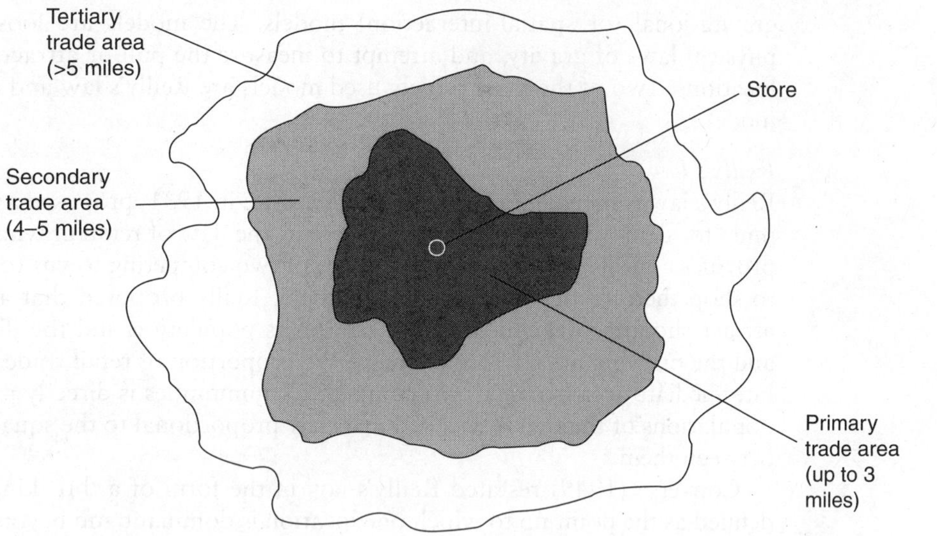

Figure 9.2 Trade areas for a large supermarket

drive-time isochrones is that they take account of traffic conditions as well as distance. The Competition Commission research found that 66 per cent of food shoppers travelled 10 minutes or less to a supermarket, a further 25 per cent travelled between 11 and 20 minutes and 7 per cent between 21 and 30 minutes. Therefore, when considering potential sites for new stores, the majority of UK food multiples use a 15–20-minute drive-time-based measure as the main factor in determining the size of a store's trade area, as 80–90 per cent of customers are likely to come from this area. Local demographics and the presence of competitors and own stores are then used to refine the initial estimate.

Recent indications suggest that shoppers are tending to use a more diverse range of retailers including local and online businesses when they can, partly in response to rising petrol costs; therefore trade area analysis is likely to shift to more qualitative judgement based on shopping behaviour and lifestyle variables, in addition to quantitative variables such as driving time and distance.

Determining trade areas

There are two main techniques for determining trade areas: 'spotting' techniques and mathematical models. The first technique is used by retailers to determine the extent of trading areas for existing stores, whilst quantitative techniques are used with new stores. Essentially, 'spotting' attempts to spot the customer's origin on a map. The technique allows retailers to determine the extent of trading area as well as the major areas within the trading area from which customers originate. Some common spotting techniques include customer surveys, customer records (for example customer credit, service and delivery records), loyalty schemes and sales promotion techniques such as contests and sweepstakes. The most commonly used mathematical models for determining the catchment areas of a store are the so-called gravitational (or spatial-interaction) models. The models are loosely based on the physical laws of gravity, and attempt to measure the pull or attraction of each of the locations. Two of the more widely used models are Reilly's law and Huff's probability model.

Reilly's law

Reilly's law is named after William Reilly, who, in 1931, proposed a mathematical formula for determining a trade area known as the 'law of retail gravitation'. Reilly's law provides a measure of the relative power of two competing towns to attract customers to shop there from the area between them. Reilly proposed that a town's ability to attract shoppers depended on the size of its population and the distance between it and the outlying area. More formally, the proportion of retail trade attracted from an intermediate area between two competing communities is directly proportional to the populations of the two towns and inversely proportional to the square of the distances between them.

Converse (1949) restated Reilly's law in the form of a 'breaking point', which is defined as the point up to which one location is dominant and beyond which the other is dominant. In other words, the breaking point defines the point between competing centres where the probability of a consumer visiting either centre is the same. The relationship is stated in the form of a formula as follows:

$$BPa = Dab \prod (1 + \text{œ}Pb \prod Pa)$$

where BPa is the distance of the breaking point from town A (that is the catchment of town A), Dab is the distance from A to B, Pb is the population of town B and Pa is the population of town A.

As an illustration consider the case of two small towns located 8 miles apart. Town A has a population of 10,000 and town B a population of 40,000. Substituting into the formula gives the boundary between the two towns as follows:

$$\text{Distance from breaking point to town B} = 8/(1 + \surd 10{,}000/40{,}000)$$
$$= 8/(1 + 0.5) = 5.3\,\text{miles}$$

Thus the breaking point in this example is 5.3 miles from town B and 2.7 miles from town A. The model can be easily modified to measure the breaking point between shopping centres by replacing the town populations by the size of the shopping centres. A trading area can be determined by computing the breaking point between one retail centre and all competing centres. The formula assumes that the attractiveness of a centre can be represented by the size of the population and that shoppers are deterred by distance. Specifically, it is assumed that the further away a retail centre is, the more likely the shopper will be deterred from visiting it. This is mainly due to increasing travel costs. Gravitational models assume that competing centres are equally accessible and that retailers in both areas are equally effective and do not have any significant competitive advantage over each other. The model can be modified to measure the breaking point between shopping centres by the replacement of distance by travel time as consumers are more likely to perceive distance in terms of time due to the widespread availability of personal transport and given that consumers are time-poor. The size of the population of a destination can also be replaced by the total retail floor space of a centre, which is more likely to reflect the attractiveness of the centre to potential customers.

According to Huff (1964), a major weakness of the gravity models is that they do not provide interval estimates of the likelihood of attracting customers above or below the breaking point between two centres. This is particularly important, as the form of the breaking point equation will vary according to the type of shopping trip. For instance, shoppers are likely to travel furthest for speciality goods, least for convenience goods and moderate distances for comparison (shopping) goods. As discussed above, from the retailer's perspective a given store will have primary, secondary and tertiary (or fringe) trading areas:

1. Primary trading area – closest to the store, attracts 60–65 per cent of sales; within this area the store has the best competitive advantage.
2. Secondary trading area – attracts around 20–30 per cent of sales; in this area the store has to compete with other stores to attract customers.
3. Tertiary trading area/fringe area – area from which the store occasionally attracts customers (5–10 per cent); the competitive position in this area is the weakest as competing stores are more accessible.

The physical extent of the zones depends on the type of store, accessibility, competition and the mobility and willingness of customers to travel, and can be defined in terms of physical distance or drive time. The shape of the trading area is determined by transportation networks, the physical geography of the area and the location of competitors. The store may also attract transient customers who patronize the store because they either are in the vicinity, are variety seekers or are very loyal to the store.

Huff's probability model

To overcome the difficulties of Reilly's model, Huff proposed a model to predict the trade area of individual stores rather than towns. Huff proposed that the trade area of a store is determined by its relative attraction: relative, that is, to all other similar stores in the area. Hence, to estimate the trade area of a DIY store, its attraction relative to all other DIY stores in the area must be assessed. Huff further proposed that the value or the attraction of a store to a customer depends on its size and the distance the customer has to travel to shop there. In the model the attraction of a store to a customer is given as:

$$A_{ij} = S_j a / D_{ij} b$$

where A_{ij} is the attraction of store j to customer i, S_j is the size of store j, D_{ij} is the distance or travel time of customer i from store j, a is a parameter reflecting the sensitivity of the customer to store size and b is a parameter reflecting the sensitivity of the customer to distance.

Given the above, the probability that a customer is attracted to a particular store, P_{ij}, can be expressed as a ratio of the attractiveness of a given store to the sum of the attraction of all competing stores:

$$P_{ij} = \frac{\text{Value of store } j}{\text{Sum of the values of all stores}}$$

Given the number of competing stores, n, the above formula can be restated as:

$$P_{ij} = \frac{S_j a}{D_{ij} b} / \sum_{j=1}^{n} \left(\frac{S_j a}{D_{ij} b} \right)$$

The values of the parameters can be used to reflect the relative importance of store size, a, and distance, b, in a given shopping situation. For instance, a high value for b can be used to reflect the deterrent effect of distance in the case of convenience shopping. In the case of comparison shopping, the distance parameter is likely to be lower and the size parameter higher. Hence, accurate estimates of the parameter values are an important determinant of the accuracy of the predicted trade areas. The parameter values are usually determined by surveys of shopping patterns for the particular type of store. Alternatively, estimates based on similar locations may be used.

Example 9.1: An illustration using the Huff model

Consider an individual who has the choice of shopping at two supermarkets in a town. The distances from the customer's home and the sizes of the two supermarkets are as follows:

Store	Distance (miles)	Size (square feet)
A	3	20,000
B	4	40,000

If the parameter $a = 1$ and parameter $b = 2$, the relative attraction of each of the three stores to this individual can be calculated as follows:

$$\text{Attraction of store A} = 20,000/3^2 = 2,222$$

$$\text{Attraction of store B} = 40,000/4^2 = 2,500$$

The probability of this individual visiting store A is

$$\frac{\text{Attraction of store A}}{\text{Sum of attractions of all stores in the area}}$$
$$= 2,222/(2,222 + 2,500) = 0.47 \text{ or } 47 \text{ per cent}$$

Similarly, the probability of the consumer shopping at the store B is

$$2,500/(2,222 + 2,500) = 0.53 \text{ or } 53 \text{ per cent}$$

Index of retail saturation

The attractiveness of an area to a retailer depends not only on the potential demand within an area but also on the degree of competition. An area with high demand may not be suitable because of high levels of competition. The index of retail saturation (IRS) measures demand relative to the supply of retail floor space within a specified area. IRS is the demand for a product category divided by the total retail floor space for that product category:

$$IRS_i = \frac{C_i \times RE_i}{RF_i}$$

where C_i is the number of customers in area i for the product category, RE_i is the average customer spend in area i for the product category and RF_i is the total retail square footage in area i allocated to the product (including the proposed store).

A low value of IRS indicates over-storing in the area, for the specified category of store, and a high value indicates under-storing. The relative attractiveness of different areas can be obtained by ranking different areas by their IRS scores. However, the IRS figures need to be compared with a retailer's organizational norm to ensure that a proposed store meets minimum sales expectations. The IRS figure provides an average sales per square foot figure across all retailers. The actual sales per square foot achieved by a particular retailer will differ from that depending on the retailer's competitive advantages in the marketplace including size of store, location, pricing strategies and so forth. Also, IRS reflects existing demand and supply in an area. However, a new retailer coming into a market may expand demand due to its marketing activities. Demand may also expand due to agglomeration effects; that is demand expands due to more retailers being located near to each other (see Vignette 9.1).

VIGNETTE 9.1 ASDA'S UNRESTRICTED ENTRY AND EXPANSION SCENARIO IN BIRMINGHAM

An application of the index of retail saturation is illustrated by ASDA. In its submission to the Competition Commission (2000), ASDA estimated that there were an average of 671 people for about every 90 sq. m. (1,000 sq. ft.) of supermarket floor space. It then used this average as a benchmark to assess whether different areas of the country were under- or over-stored in terms of grocery provision. For instance, in the Birmingham postal area it estimated that there were an average of 857 people for about every 90 sq. m. (1,000 sq. ft.) with a total supermarket floor space of 0.2 million sq. m. (2.1 million sq. ft.). Given the population of Birmingham, ASDA estimated that the floor space necessary for the Birmingham postal area to have average levels of provision was 0.25 million sq. m. (2.7 million sq. ft.). The difference between the actual provision (0.2 million sq. m.) and that necessary to achieve average national levels of provision (0.25 million sq. m.), that of +0.05 million sq. m. (+0.6 million sq. ft.), gives the relative under-provision of grocery facilities in Birmingham. This is equivalent to 12 superstores of around 50,000 sq. ft., roughly the average size of an ASDA store. The analysis is somewhat crude but gives an indication of the number of new superstores that might appear if there were no barriers to entry. However, new entry not only is affected by the ability to obtain planning permission (likely to be difficult in out-of-town locations in the current climate), but also depends on the availability of suitable sites at reasonable cost. The analysis also assumed that the 'average' level of provision was the correct level of provision; however, it may be that the average is not the right benchmark for determining which areas need more food retailing provision.

Most of the traditional models of location work on the understanding premise that the shopper is a rational, economically driven operator and that the sole purpose of an outlet for a retail business is to generate maximum sales volumes. In fact, modern retailing is about creating value in the shopping process, and consumers are able and willing to make trade-offs between the benefits of shopping in a particular place with costs to themselves. An important non-monetary cost is time, but also physical and emotional stress, the risk to personal safety and the psychological cost of shopping at a particular retailer or centre; therefore, the extent to which these costs can be reduced may encourage a shopper to expend more money or time travelling to a particular location if the shopper believes they will have a more pleasant and time-efficient shopping experience once they get there. Centre management, including town centres that provide additional quality and value in the retail mix, other attractions and services to reduce non-monetary costs are likely to keep attracting shoppers (see Vignette 9.2).

VIGNETTE 9.2 WESTFIELD CONCIERGE SERVICES LIGHTEN THE LOAD

In September 2011 the largest urban shopping centre opened in Stratford, in East London, in a location next to the main site where the 2012 Olympic Games took place. The shopping-centre development cost £1.45 billion and provides sites for 300 shops, 70 restaurants, a cinema, three hotels and a bowling and casino. The opening ceremony included pop star performances and Olympian athletes' book signing.

Although the site was 95 per cent let at the time of opening and the customer footfall on the opening weekend healthy, this area of London was one of the most deprived and underdeveloped in terms of retail provision, and in its early life Westfield appeared to be struggling to play the key regeneration role that it had planned to be. The combination of a hugely successful Olympic games, however, combined with excellent new transport links to Central and Greater London, and an attractive mix of retailers across all sectors and levels has meant that Westfield is now popular and successful. To encourage spending by shoppers who are now used to ordering online and not have the burden of bag carrying, Westfield offers an extensive list of concierge services including hands-free shopping and bag storage, home delivery (to local, hotel, airport or international destinations), cloakroom check-in, shop mobility and kiddy car rental.

Source: BBC News (2011) and uk.westfield.com (2013) [accessed 15 August 2013]

Geo-demographic information systems

In order to ensure the success of stores, retailers need to know not only the size of the trade area but more precise information on the location and demographics of potential customers. This is provided by geo-demographics, which is a system of classifying customers by linking demographic data (for example age, income) to geographic areas of residence using postcodes or census enumeration districts. Postcodes are more precise for location purposes as they represent on average 14–15 households, compared with census enumeration districts which average 148 households, and therefore they are used more frequently these days. This information enables location analysts to visualize the information on a digital map which can also provide additional information on road networks and traffic flows and hence facilitate the accurate calculation and depiction of trade areas.

The demographic data are based on a combination of census and market research data, and this information is used to classify individuals into meaningful socio-economic groups using clustering statistical techniques. A number of commercially available systems exist on the market. The earliest system, A Classification of Residential Neighbourhoods (ACORN), was developed by CACI and consists of 64 groups (www.acorn.caci.co.uk) based on demographic data, social factors, population and consumer behaviour. Another consumer classification system widely used in retail planning research is Experian's Mosaic system (www.uk.experian.com). All geo-demographic classification systems are based on the assumption that people living in similar neighbourhoods are likely to have similar behavioural and lifestyle patterns and hence purchasing patterns. Each system divides neighbourhoods into groups based on similarities in income, education, household type and other available data (such as attitudes and product preferences). Retailers can enhance the geo-demographic information with their own information (such as that derived from loyalty cards or store credit cards) to develop a geo-demographic information system (GIS) to help target markets more accurately.

SITE ASSESSMENT TECHNIQUES

There are a number of techniques that retailers can use to help them assess the potential of new sites and to select the best specific site for their business. This section discusses techniques that are frequently used by retailers, namely checklists, ratio-of-space method, analogue method and multiple regression.

Checklists

A checklist is most commonly used to assess the potential of retail sites. It attempts to identify the most important locational factors for the success of a store, and is usually based on previous experience and/or judgement of retail managers. It is a relatively straightforward and fast technique, based on specific factors, which makes it an inexpensive and effective way of initially assessing a site. A typical list of factors will include demographics, accessibility, competition and costs (see Table 9.1). More sophisticated methods use a weighted checklist, where each identified factor is rated in terms of its quality, and according to its overall importance in the location decision, with a weighted rating obtained for each identified factor by multiplying the rating by its importance factor. An overall rating or index is obtained by summing all the

Table 9.1 Site selection factors

Site selection factor	Explanation
Strength of interception	The ability to intercept customers as they move from place to place within the centres. Shops located on routes popular with shoppers (for example routes between car parks, bus or railway stations and the shopping centre) will have stronger ability to intercept shoppers than other locations. Shops located between anchor stores will also benefit from additional traffic as shoppers move between them.
Cumulative attraction	The degree of pull that results from similar and/or complementary retailers locating together. The existence of leisure, social, business and other attractors is also important as they have the ability to generate additional impulse trade for stores.
Compatibility	The degree to which stores in close proximity are likely to interchange customers. This is more likely to occur where the merchandise mix of the stores is complementary, as in the case of a clothes store, shoe shop and jewellery outlet. The degree of compatibility is enhanced if the stores also have similar pricing strategies. Competing stores may also be considered compatible where they satisfy the need for comparison shopping for customers.
Competition	Not all competition is benign, and therefore it is important to take into account the size, number and type (inter- or intra-type) of competing stores and their relative locations to a proposed store, as they are likely to directly impact on the sales potential of the store.
Accessibility	A key determinant of customer patronage, and hence new sites need to be evaluated in terms of their closeness to (and size of) car parks, transport terminals and traffic arteries. Customer safety and security are also important considerations, as close proximity of road traffic and lack of pedestrian crossings may deter many potential customers.
Suitability	For the purpose of business. As mentioned above, the cost of sites within centres varies depending on their distance from the centre. Whilst high customer traffic may increase sales, high-rent leasing, high purchasing price or high building costs may make the store unprofitable. Retailers need to take into account the acquisition, operating and fitting costs of any site. Planning restrictions on the use of the property or any architectural changes may also impact suitability.

weighted ratings. Alternative sites may then be ranked according to the weighted rating. The retail organization may also set a minimum overall score before considering a location. Checklists have the advantage of simplicity and require little expertise. Their major disadvantage is that the relationship between different factors is not usually known (or articulated), and it is therefore difficult to estimate their precise effect on the location decision. For example competitors can have varying degrees of impact from detrimental to beneficial and this may not be possible to determine accurately. Checklists are therefore used as a starting point for store location and evaluation decisions.

Ratio-of-space method

Here, sales are allocated to a proposed store in proportion to its share of competing space in the trade area. This is a fairly crude method and can be used in the absence of reliable data. The method assumes equal productivity amongst retailers, which is not a tenable assumption given the different market positioning of different retailers.

Analogue method

The analogue method for estimating the sales potential of a new store was pioneered by Applebaum (1966) and involves measuring the market share of the trade area of one or more existing stores that are similar to the proposed store, and then using the data as 'analogues' to extrapolate turnover estimates for new sites. The procedure for using the analogue method is as follows:

1. Identify stores within the current network that are similar to the proposed store in terms of store size, the size of the trade, demographics, competition, merchandising policies, pricing and so forth.
2. Divide the trade area into drive-time zones.
3. Estimate the sales generated from each drive-time zone using either internal store data or customer surveys.
4. Use the sales estimates from each zone to calculate the per capita expenditure for each zone by dividing the sales generated by the population in the zone.
5. Use the per capita expenditure estimates for each zone of the analogue store to estimate the sales forecast for the proposed store by multiplying it with the total population of each zone of the proposed store.
6. Adjust the estimate up or down to take into account factors specific to the new location.

A major advantage of the analogue method is that it is based on actual shopping patterns and it is relatively easy to implement. However, the choice of the analogue store is critical in the accuracy of the forecast, but, inevitably, a certain amount of subjectivity is involved in the selection of analogue stores. However, the degree of subjectivity can be reduced by using more than one analogue store and taking the average of the estimates as a sales forecast. A further problem with the analogue approach is that forecasting becomes more difficult as the number of stores grows and more complex patterns of relationships are identified. At this stage it is more appropriate and viable to use multiple regression techniques.

Multiple regression

Unlike the analogue procedure, multiple regression uses data from a large number of existing stores to forecast the sales of a new store. Regression is a statistical technique for establishing the relationship between a dependent variable (such as turnover) and a set of independent variables that affect it (for instance catchment population, competition, store size and so on). The technique estimates the line of 'best fit' that minimizes the variance between individual data points, that is the stores being analysed. Multiple regression requires a minimum of 30–40 cases (stores) and at least 15–20 cases (or stores) per variable used in the regression. Regression models are, therefore, mainly used by large multiple/chain retailers with large number of branches.

When using this technique, it is first necessary to identify all variables that influence store sales. In order to be able to use a variable within the regression equation it must be independent of other variables in the equation (that is it must not be highly correlated with other variables as, for example, is the case with car ownership and income). If a number of variables are correlated with each other, one solution is to use factor analysis to identify a common factor underlying the variables. The key variables are then used in the regression model to forecast, for example, expected sales. The general form of the regression model is:

$$Y = a + b_1X_1 + b_2X_2 + b_3X_3 + \cdots + b_nX_n + E$$

where Y is a dependent variable (for example sales); $X_1, X_2, \ldots, X_n$ are various independent (explanatory) variables (for example competition, size of store); a is a constant (or intercept term estimated by regression procedure); $b_1, b_2, \ldots, b_n$ are regression coefficients that measure the impact of the independent variables on the dependent variable; and E is an error term.

The regression coefficients represent the degree of impact of the independent variables on the dependent variable. The signs of the coefficients indicate the direction of influence (positive or negative). The explanatory variables will differ by the type of store. For instance, for a convenience store the main determinants of sales performance are likely to be the trade-area population and the number of competitors in the area. For a DIY store, on the other hand, home ownership and household income are likely to be more important variables. Although the precise variables differ between retailers and store types, most regression models used for predicting sales performance include store attributes, location factors (shopping-centre characteristics), demographics and competition variables.

Whilst regression models are relatively complex to develop, once developed they are easy to use. Their use simply involves entering values for a new site on the relevant predictor variables, multiplying them by their associated regression coefficients and then adding the resulting values to arrive at the forecast for store sales. However, in order for the forecast to be accurate and meaningful, the model should be built using a sample of similar stores to the proposed store. For example, it would be inappropriate for Sainsbury's to forecast sales of a new 'Local' store (usually located in town centres and measuring less than 10,000 sq. ft.) using a model that is built on a sample of Sainsbury's edge-of-town stores averaging over 40,000 sq. ft. This also highlights the necessity of developing a number of different models where a retailer operates a number of different types of stores aimed at different market positions and different target segments.

The advantage of regression models is that they allow a large number of factors that influence store performance to be considered together. The models indicate which factors are most important in predicting sales and hence allow managers to focus their efforts. Analysis of residuals (the difference between forecast and actual sales) allows retail managers to assess the performance of their current portfolio of stores by identifying underperforming or overperforming stores and the factors behind their performance. The major problem with regression models is that they are costly and complex to develop, and the need for statistical and practical retail know-how for the proper specification of the model. The models need to be regularly re-estimated to take account of changes in the retailing environment; the accuracy of regression is critically dependent on the quality of data. Advantages and disadvantages are summarized in Table 9.2.

The techniques discussed above are usually used in conjunction with each other rather than in isolation. In fact, the location techniques employed by major UK supermarket operators suggest a combination of approaches, which reduces the risk involved in store location assessment by comparing the different predictions; recently, large supermarket companies have been accused of acquiring land on what appears to be a speculative and offensive strategy, to 'get in first' and then release the site later if the location does not demonstrate a good predicted return. The use of checklists reduces the cost and time required to assess a large number of stores before using the analogue approach and regression modelling. Whilst these techniques provide more accurate estimates, they are more expensive. There is no single 'best' technique for assessing a retail location. The techniques employed will depend upon the amount of information available, costs in terms of time and money and the sophistication of the retailer.

Selecting the specific site

The exact location of a store within a shopping centre/district is extremely important, as a few yards either way can be the difference between success and failure. This is because customer flows vary greatly within centres; for example customer traffic can be very different on the two sides of the same shopping street.

Within any centre, one specific location will have the highest level of customer traffic. This will usually be where destination or anchor stores (so called because they secure a retail development) are located, where accessibility is easy due to close proximity of transport terminals and where other attractions are located nearby. This area is known as prime pitch and is given a 100 per cent rating. The remaining locations are rated in relation to the prime pitch. Hence a site rated as 60 per cent pitch would have 60 per cent of the customer traffic of the prime-pitch location.

Factors that need to be considered when assessing specific sites are shown in Table 9.1.

Table 9.2 Advantages and disadvantages of regression models for forecasting store sales

Advantages	Disadvantages
• Systematic framework/objective discipline • Quantitative measure • Purpose built • Allows what-if scenarios to be constructed • Can identify underperforming/ overperforming stores	• Complex and costly to develop • Minimum number of observations (>30) required for statistical validity • Needs to be redeveloped for changed circumstances • Not suitable for diverse portfolios of stores • Can only predict within range

VIGNETTE 9.3 LEASING IN RETAILING

Although some retailers own the freehold of their properties, most retailers are more likely to lease a property than to buy it. This frees up capital and gives the retailer more flexibility to respond to the changing environment. In many cases it is not possible to purchase a property, particularly in the case of shopping malls. Leasing retail properties is a fairly complex business, and retailers need to make sure that the type of retailing agreement that they undertake is suitable for their needs. Relevant factors and terminology include the following:

- Straight lease – an agreed sum paid over life of lease.
- Percentage/turnover lease – rent is linked to sales.
- Net lease – retailer is responsible for maintenance and utility charges.
- Prohibited-use clause – prohibits the landlord from leasing to tenants who may affect image of the business.
- Exclusive-use clause – prohibits landlords from leasing to direct competitors.
- 'Zone A' rental – rent paid per sq. ft. on the first 20 feet back from the storefront.
- Upward-only reviews – rents can only rise in periodic reviews.

Leases normally run for long periods, such as 5 or 10 years, and if a business fails before a lease runs out, a landlord can be left with an empty outlet and a short time left on the lease that may not be attractive to another retailer. Short leases however can provide useful opportunities for 'pop-up' retailing, where a business trades for a short period of time, possibly with an advantageous rent. Fashion brands in particular have taken advantage of short-term availability of good-quality retail space to showcase special ranges, trial new concepts, test reactions in international markets and raise awareness by doing something innovative and experiential that could be risky on a long-term basis.

PLANNING REGULATIONS AND LOCATION

In addition to market-related factors, retail location is greatly influenced in most countries by government regulation and planning policies. In fact, planning policies can be so influential that Davies and Bennison (1978) complained that in the UK the spatial organization of shopping districts was more the result of planning polices than of market forces. In the UK, local authorities are responsible for administering requests for planning permission, with appeals being administered by the central government. Local authorities consider planning applications in the context of the Unitary Plan for the district, which they are required to produce by the Town and Country Planning Act 1990. These plans incorporate national planning guidelines and indicate major areas of action such as development, redevelopment and improvements in retailing over the long term. Hence it is essential for retailers to understand these plans when they are proposing new developments, as they are likely to be rejected if they do not fit the structure plans for the district. Refusal of planning permission usually relates to issues of suitability of land use for retailing, traffic-related issues, impact on existing centres and design quality.

Until about 1970, the maintenance of existing retailing hierarchies was the prime concern of planning authorities in the UK, with comparison shopping being clustered in large shopping centres and convenience shopping more widely spread out. This policy was relaxed a little in the 1970s and saw the spread of stores in the UK, although comparison shopping remained in city centres. However, further relaxation of the regulatory framework in the 1980s led to a rapid development of out-of-town retailing in the form of retail parks and regional shopping centres, with many comparison retailers moving out of city centres and undermining the traditional retail hierarchies. In the late 1990s the government issued stricter guidelines (PPG6 and PPG13) for out-of-town retail developments to prevent the further erosion of high-street retailing. This has necessitated retailers to reconsider their location policies. Retailers such as Tesco responded by developing specific high-street concepts (for example Metro stores) to comply with the new regulatory framework. A new National Planning Policy Framework was published in 2012 by the Department for Communities and Local Government which consolidated these guidelines and other planning policy statements and guidance notes.

Many UK retailers who are faced with saturated market sectors and little growth prospect due to demographic and economic factors are looking to international markets to expand. However, the need to analyse locations at both macro and micro levels is vital if growth opportunities are to be realized, and gaining access to information for systematic location decision may be difficult. Competitor comparisons and analysis can be helpful, and all the usual variables can be considered; nevertheless, the lack of success in international markets of a retailer even with the resources of Tesco suggests that this highly strategic aspect of retail management is very challenging (*Guardian*, 2013).

LOCATING ON THE INTERNET

Clearly, many of the location principles discussed in this chapter can also be adapted to the analysis involved in aspects of online retailing such as where to locate delivery hubs or warehouses and how much to charge for delivery. However, when it comes to online retailing in terms of having a presence on the World Wide Web, location takes on an entirely different meaning. As location of the retail itself is virtual, it is the presence of a retailer's name or brand in cyberspace that needs to be managed in a way that encourages shoppers to find the retailer's website. This text does not have the scope to explore this topic in a high degree of detail, and there are a plethora of excellent texts on the subject; however, it is important to mention some important aspects of what is often referred to as e-marketing to introduce the key principles of locating an online retail outlet.

The principles of locating a retail outlet online can be divided into those concerning a potential customer who is looking (searching) for a retailer and those concerning how a browsing customer can be guided to a retailer. Chaffey and Smith (2013) refer to these activities as traffic building, demonstrating the link between offline and online locations as having the importance of high customer traffic, or footfall as we might say in the physical world. An Internet search for a retailer involves the complex world of the search engine (such as Google, Bing or Yahoo), and it is the experience and expertise of these organizations that has informed the way online retailers have responded to them.

The activity that ensures a consumer finds the retailer they are looking for quickly and accurately is search engine optimization (SEO). SEO allows a retailer to achieve the highest possible position in the listing on a search engine results page in response to particular words (keywords or combinations of words that form a 'key phrase': Chaffey and Smith, 2013). Although in what are termed 'natural or organic listings' there is no charge, optimization requires a detailed knowledge of how search engines are programmed in order to maintain a good ranking, and this expertise may need to be paid for or brought in. As well as appearing on the natural listings, companies can pay to appear (at the top or on the right-hand side typically) on listings pages which are linked to particular key phrases. However, unlike traditional media advertising where the space is paid for irrespective of resulting consumer action, search engine advertising works on the basis of paying per click (PPC), so the search engine only gets paid by the advertiser when the shopper ends up visiting the retailer's website. Search engine advertising and optimization are therefore highly targeted and effective methods of gaining relevant online customer footfall. SEO not only is important for helping online shoppers to find online retailers, but is also useful for retailers to use it for shoppers wanting to find a retail business in the real world; so adding a geographical location into a key phrase can draw customers to physical retail stores in a particular vicinity.

Not all customers or potential customers will be actively searching for a particular retailer of even a particular product or service. The term browsing has been associated with consumer's Internet activity since its inception and so the more places a retailer's name (or other content such as brand or images that associates with a retailer) is located (positively) in other websites, the more likely shoppers will end up drawn to the retailer's own site. Such locations include portals, blogs, other business websites (for example affiliates), emails, online media (magazines and news sites) and viral marketing. These can combine with more traditional marketing communications to raise awareness of online retail businesses or information about a retail business online.

ONLINE RETAILING AND LOCATION STRATEGY

The continuing popularity of online retailing has had fundamental implications for location strategy, and currently it is common in the UK to read headlines concerning the effect of online retailing on bricks-and-mortar retailers and the changes to the location strategies of multi-channel retailers. In 2013 the Centre for Retail Research (www.retailresearch.org) published a report which gave predictions about what would happen to the UK retail industry in the next 5 years. They forecasted that store numbers would fall by 22 per cent and that total online retail sales would rise from 12.7 per cent (2012) to 21.5 in 2018. For many, the 'online flagship' is the outlet which has the highest sales. For some retailers who have a small number of stores, the online shop can provide access to customers from long distances (nationally and internationally potentially), which completely changes the notion of a catchment area based on travel time or distance. The precise implications of the introduction of an online shop and how to manage the financial performance of it depend on the characteristics of individual retailers including the type of merchandise, the number of stores currently in the chain, the location and size of those stores and so on. Some retail locations are more likely to be affected than others. Locations with a wide mix of retailers and social attractions that provide more than shopping are likely to remain strong destinations for shopping and prime locations for retailers. Secondary locations are likely to come under even more severe pressure.

Managing the online outlet at a multi-channel retailer seems to work best when fully integrated with store-based retailing with performance and productivity linked to stores. For example linking online sales in regions close to physical stores demonstrates a managerial view that good experience in stores is likely to lead customers to multi-channel shopping with the same retailer online. Returns to stores by online customers can be demoralizing if those refund values are deducted from physical store sales, whereas from a customer viewpoint the fully integrated multi-channel customer experience is important. Another implication of online retailing is that the customer gets used to seeing the full range of merchandise a retailer offers on a website, which may only be available in larger stores in city centres. Customers who live a long distance from these stores may feel frustrated with the restricted offer in the smaller stores they have access to locally. Retailers may take the view that these smaller outlets do not contribute enough to the overall business and close them; the Centre for Retail Research (2013) for example suggests that retailers with a strong Web offering only need 70 stores to create a national presence compared to 250 in the mid-2000s. A more enlightened approach is to turn smaller stores into a kind of multi-channel hub where customers can pick up, return, receive advice and engage in conversations about the retailer's offer, focusing on brand experience and customer service rather than viewing the store as a sales-generating box. This is a more appropriate strategy for retailers of specialist goods rather than FMCGs; however, the success of the 'top-up and convenience' version of major FMCG retailers demonstrates the importance of location decision making based on lifestyle and shopping behaviour rather than on sales volumes only. For less well known retailers who have smaller store portfolios, the online shop can complement the physical stores well, providing an alternative route to customer markets. Many specialist and international retailers are finding that the 'online/offline flagship strategy works well' (Knobs et al., 2013), integrating the retail brand experience in a seamless and interactive way.

VIGNETTE 9.4 THE HIGH STREET AS THE HEART OF THE COMMUNITY?

In March 2012 the UK government Department for Communities and Local Government issued a report which responded to a review of British high streets undertaken by Mary Portas, who is widely acknowledged as the UK's retail guru. As a TV presenter, retail consultant, retailer brand and lingerie manufacturer, Mary Portas is also a high-profile celebrity having been there and done that in many areas of consumer marketing. It was therefore bound to make headlines when her report was published. For the retail industry, however, it was the government's response to her report that would really earn Mary Portas her legacy. In the Prime Minister's foreword to the report, David Cameron grasped the nettle straight away: 'Internet shopping and out-of-town shopping centres are not going to go away – they offer the convenience and choice that customers welcome. So for our high streets to thrive they must offer something different.' The response document then went on to detail the 28 recommendations Mary Portas made and how the government would respond to them. Overall the government welcomed most of the recommendations and started to put measures in place to support some of them straight away.

A key recommendation was the setting up of Town Teams to work within communities so as to pilot creative plans for regenerating struggling high-street retail centres. This initiative was accepted and made possible by funding through local government. A High Street Innovation Fund of £10 million was set aside for particular areas blighted by empty shops and those recovering from inner-city riots, which took place in 2011. The Town Team remit includes making the town accessible, attractive, safe and somewhere that both retailers and shoppers would benefit from and enjoy.

Mary Portas made recommendations concerning powers of Business Improvement Districts, encouraging involvement from the local communities, neighbourhood plans, adjustments to business rates, high-street use deregulation, car parking schemes, schemes such as National Market Day to encourage more entrepreneurs to try small retail business ideas out, mentoring of local and independent retailers by larger ones and leasing and arrangements regarding empty retail space. Crucial recommendations for retail planning were to make an explicit presumption in favour of town-centre development in the wording of the National Planning Policy Framework: an 'exceptional sign off by the Secretary of State for all new out-of-town developments, and for all large new developments to have an "affordable shops" quota'.

Telford (2013) agrees that Portas' report has the correct emphasis on broadening the high streets' use from retail to hubs for social, commercial and cultural enterprises with housing and medical centres all part of the mix, but goes even further to suggest that small urban production units and agriculture could be part of the high street of the future.

Source: Department for Communities and Local Government (2012), Telford (2013)

SUMMARY

This chapter has emphasized the importance of location decisions given that they are long term in nature and therefore difficult to change quickly and consequently the costs of wrong decisions can be high. Location decisions are also complex, as they not only need to satisfy consumer needs for convenience, accessibility and quality but must also provide a competitive advantage for the retailer.

Retail location decision making is a stepwise process beginning with the identification of the most attractive market areas or regions and followed by the identification of suitable sites with a viable trading area. The most commonly used models for determining the trade areas of a store are the so-called gravitational (or spatial interaction) models, namely Reilly's law and Huff's probability model of retail attraction. The final step is the selection of the best site taking into account not just the potential revenue that the site can generate but also the costs of locating at the site.

Retailers need precise information on the location and demographics of potential customers. This is provided by geo-demographics information systems (GISs), which enable location analysts to visualize the information on a digital map. Techniques that are frequently used by retailers to estimate the potential of a specific site include checklists, the ratio-of-sales-to-space method, the analogue method and multiple regression. In addition to market-related factors, retail location is greatly influenced by government regulation, retail planning policies and the evolution of the industry in response to changing shopping behaviour brought on by the use of the Internet. Managers in retail property departments will be working with internal and external data sources and agencies, to support property management, location decision making and location strategy formation. They will therefore need to be analytical, methodical, accurate and collaborative. They may also need to have specialist knowledge, such as estate management or surveying skills, and be prepared to be trained on specialist information management systems.

QUESTIONS

1. Distinguish between the main types of retail locations available to retailers. What advantages do planned locations have over unplanned locations?
2. Discuss why some retailers prefer to cluster together and others do not.
3. Discuss the main factors that influence the size of a store's trade area.
4. How can GIS assist retailers in their location decisions?
5. Explain the circumstances under which the analogue approach may be used to estimate the potential demand for a new store. Outline the steps involved in using this method.
6. Explain the multiple regression approach to estimating demand for a new store. What variables might be included to predict the demand for a supermarket? A DIY store?
7. Explain how planning regulations influence store location decisions.
8. Discuss the implications of the growth of online retailing on location strategy.
9. Compare and contrast the managerial skills and attributes needed for location decision making for physical stores and online retailers.

REFERENCES AND FURTHER READING

Applebaum, W. (1966) 'Methods for Determining Store Trade Areas, Market Penetration and Potential Sales', *Journal of Marketing Research*, vol. 3, no. 2, pp. 127–41.

BBC News (unattributed) (2011) Westfield Stratford City shopping centre opens, http://www.bbc.co.uk/news/uk-england-london-14022954 [accessed 15 August 2013].

Birkin, M., Clarke, G. P., Clarke, M. and Wilson, A. (2002) *Retail Geography and Intelligent Network Planning* (Chichester: John Wiley).

Brown, S. (1993) 'Retail Location Theory: Evolution and Evaluation', *International Review of Retail Distribution and Consumer Research*, vol. 3, no. 3, pp. 185–229.

Chaffey D. and Smith, P. R. (2013) *E-Marketing Excellence*, 4th Edition (Abingdon: Routledge).

Christaller, W. (1933) *Die zentralen Orte in Suddeutschland*, translated by C. Baskin (1966) as *Central Places in Southern Germany* (Englewood Cliffs, NJ: Prentice Hall).

Clarkson, R. M., Clarke-Hill, C. M. and Robinson, T. (1996) 'UK Supermarket Location Assessment', *International Journal of Retail and Distribution Management*, vol. 24, no. 6, pp. 22–33.

Competition Commission (2000) *Supermarkets: A Report on the Supply of Groceries from Multiple Stores in the United Kingdom*, Cm 4842 (London: The Stationery Office).

Converse, P. D. (1949), 'New Laws of Retail Gravitation', *Journal of Marketing*, vol. 14, no. 3, pp. 379–84.

Craig, C. S., Ghosh, A. and McLafferty, S. (1984) 'Models of the Retail Location Process: A Review', *Journal of Marketing*, vol. 60, no. 1, pp. 5–36.

Davies, R. L. and Bennison, D. J. (1978) *The Eldon Square Regional Shopping Centre – The First Eighteen Months* (Corbridge: Retailing and Planning Associates).

Dawson, J. A. (1979) *The Marketing Environment* (London: Croom Helm).

Department for Communities and Local Government (2012) *High Streets at the Heart of Our Communities: The Government's Response to the Mary Portas Review*, https://www.gov.uk/government/publications/high-streets-at-the-heart-of-our-communities-government-response-to-the-mary-portas-review [accessed 15 September 2013].

Ghosh, A. (1990) *Retail Management*, 1st Edition (Chicago: The Dryden Press).

Guardian (2013), 'Local Shops Set to Bear Brunt of Online Shopping Growth', Theguardian.com, 28 May 2013, available at www.theguardian.com/business/2013/may/28/local-shop-to-close-retail [accessed 15 August 2013].

Hotelling, H. (1929) 'Stability in Competition', *Economic Journal*, vol. 39, no. 3, pp. 41–57.

Huff, D. L. (1963) 'A Probabilistic Analysis of Shopping Centre Trade Areas', *Land Economics*, vol. 39, no. 1 pp. 81–90.

Huff, D. L. (1964) 'Defining and Estimating a Trading Area', *Journal of Marketing*, vol. 28, no. 3 pp. 34–8.

Jones, K. and Simmons, J. (1990) *The Retail Environment* (London: Routledge).

Knobs, K, Moore, C. and Kent, T. (2013) *The Digital Flagship Store as a Luxury Brand Icon, the Proceedings of the 15th Annual IFFTI Conference* (Los Angeles: FIDM).

Losch, A. (1954) *The Economics of Location* (New Haven: Yale University Press).

Morphet, C. S. (1991) 'Applying Multiple Regression Analysis to the Forecasting of Grocery Store Sales: An Application and Critical Appraisal', *International Review of Retail and Consumer Research*, vol. 1, no. 3, pp. 329–51.

National Planning Policy Framework (2012) 'Department for Communities and Local Government', https://www.gov.uk/government/organisations/department-for-communities-and-local-government [accessed 15 September 2013].

Observer (2013) 'Tesco on the Retreat as Overseas Expansion Turns in Rotten Returns', *The Observer Online*, 11 August 2013, http://www.theguardian.com/business/2013/aug/11/tesco-retreat-overseas-rotten-returns [accessed 15 August 2013].

O'Malley, L., Patterson, M. and Evans, M. (1997) 'Retailer Use of Geodemographic and Other Data Sources: An Empirical Investigation', *International Journal of Retail and Distribution Management*, vol. 25, no. 6, pp. 188–96.

Reilly, W. J. (1931) *The Law of Retail Gravitation* (New York: Knickerbocker Press).

Rogers, D. (1992) 'A Review of Sales Forecasting Models Most Commonly Applied in Retail Site Evaluation', *International Journal of Retail and Distribution Management*, vol. 20, no. 4, pp. 3–11.

Schiller, R. (1986), 'Retail Decentralisation – The Coming of the Third Wave', *Planner* (July), vol. 72, no 7, pp. 13–5.

Schiller, R. (2001), *The Dynamics of Property Location: Values and Factors Which Drive the Location of Shops, Offices and Other Land Uses* (London: Routledge).

Sparks, L. (1990) 'Spatial-Structural Relationships in Retail Corporate Growth: A Case Study of Kwik Save Group Plc', *Service Industries Journal*, vol. 10, no. 1, reprinted in Akehurst, G. and Alexander, N. (eds) (1995) *Retail Structure* (London: Frank Cass), 25–84.

Telford, C. (2013) 'To Rescue Britain's Dying High Streets We Need to Stop Obsessing over Shops', *City A.M.*, 6 June.

The Centre for Retail Research (2013) 'Retail Futures 2018', available at www.retailresearch.org/retail2018.php [accessed 15 August 2013].

uk.westfield.com, 2013 Westfield Information Site, available at http://uk.westfield.com/london/ [accessed 15 August 2013].

10 RETAIL DESIGN AND VISUAL MERCHANDISING

LEARNING OBJECTIVES

- To understand the role of design in retailing and how it can be used to differentiate a retail offer.
- To explore areas of the retail outlet where design can be used to contribute to an overall retail identity.
- To understand the scope of visual merchandising as a specialized area of retail management concerning layouts, displays and product presentation.
- To appreciate that different types of layouts, displays and fixturing are appropriate for different types of retailers.
- To gain an understanding of the need for retail space to be productive, and the various ways in which space productivity can be measured.
- To understand the key principles of planning and allocating space to the various product categories that make up a retailer's offer.

INTRODUCTION

In the multi-channel era a retail brand not only strives to attract shoppers over direct and indirect competitors, but it also has to consider the consistency of its own brand message at every customer contact point across the different types of outlet. The environment in which the retailer–customer interface takes place should be designed to make target customers feel comfortable, inspired and encouraged to purchase. Managing the selling environment is a two-stage interlinked process beginning with the design of the outlet itself, and then moving on to the presentation of the product-service offering within. Choosing a design for most types of retail outlet is a long-term decision; store development and refits are large investments with a long and indirect payback, and although website design can be more readily manipulated, it also requires a considerable input of time and expertise to manage the introduction of an entirely new website. Retail design is completely integral to a retailer's strategy, communicating strong messages about who that retailer is, the positioning they are seeking within the market and what their retail brand stands for. At the same time, a retailer needs to provide the type of space in which customers feel comfortable and find convenient for their shopping process. The way that products are displayed on fixtures or web pages and how product adjacencies are managed to create a logical customer journey are also key elements in the overall design of the selling environment. Those aspects of a retail environment that change according to variations in the merchandise assortment are often referred to as visual merchandising, and provide a strong link between the retail identity and the management of the product range.

DESIGN IN RETAILING

Design in retailing has always been important. An outlet that is aesthetically pleasing and logically laid out is appealing to customers, whilst the efficient use of space makes a major contribution to the running of a profitable retail business. In saturated and mature retail markets, innovative design is a way of keeping the retail offer fresh and providing differentiation from competitors. It is also a means by which the retail brand can be strengthened by forging links between the selling space, the corporate identity, product design and display. In a small business, retail managers may have to concern themselves with all of these aspects, as well as being responsible for the day-to-day running of the business. In large multiple retailers, design management may involve teams of specialists or retailers may recruit the services of a third party such as a retail design agency. Whether or not the retail management remit has any direct involvement in design or not, an appreciation of the role of design in retailing is a key part of a manager's personal development. Retail design input must reinforce and support the strategic aims of the retailer whilst facilitating the practicalities of strategy implementation. In addition, the design of a retail outlet can have a significant impact on staff morale, influencing how employees feel about working for a company, and the extent they feel to be brand ambassadors for it. Without good store designs the focus of retailing activity reverts back to price, and so good retail design adds value and can encourage retail brand loyalty.

THE RETAIL BRAND IDENTITY

The selling environment is a very useful vehicle for reinforcing a retailer's corporate identity. This begins with the initial impression the retailer makes with the exterior of the store or the home page of the website, and then moves on to the interior of the outlet or the navigation path around the site. The retail fascia, which includes external features above and around any windows and doors into the outlet, communicates the name of the business, and may also incorporate a logo that helps customers to recognize the retailer from afar.

Fascias usually use distinctive corporate lettering and colours, which can then be linked to other design elements within the outlet, such as in-store signage, point-of-purchase materials and carrier bags. The corporate identity may be extended further to own-label packaging, and product information sources like leaflets. It is easier to reinforce a corporate identity within a store environment, but that does not mean that non-store retailers should overlook this area. For example, the use of corporate colours and lettering within a website or a catalogue can be linked to the packaging and livery used in home delivery. Multi-channel retailers like NEXT frequently use the same or a similar corporate identity across all formats in order to transfer the positive associations built up in the traditional store environment to the virtual outlet. Although the corporate copycat approach to retail design strengthens brand identity and provides the opportunity to obtain economies of scale in the design process, there is a trend to move away from 'the cloning of the high street', with retailers designing stores that have more affinity to their catchment area and architectural surroundings. Urban Outfitters, White Stuff and Timberland (see Vignette 10.1) have all taken this non-corporate approach to store design.

VIGNETTE 10.1 TIMBERLAND

Timberland has a global spread of feel-good stores selling a range of casual, stylish and outdoor-orientated footwear and clothes for men, women and children. The company has its roots in New Hampshire, USA, but with 750 retail locations worldwide, Timberland is a global concern with a retail network covering North America, Europe, Asia, Latin America, South Africa and the Middle East.

Corporate social responsibility is at the heart of the company although Timberland is not predominantly viewed as an 'ethical clothing' company. This is probably because the company philosophy is so embedded that it has been reluctant to publicize on this issue, knowing how complex it is. Timberland is committed to the three Rs of environmental consciousness: reduce, reuse and recycle. The most visible pursuit is that associated with recycling products. In 2007 the company trialled the idea of taking back old boots, and whilst the 'built to last' boots proved to be a challenge to take apart, leather uppers were reused and the outsoles, liners and laces were replaced with components made from recycled materials and trim waste The product proved to be very popular and the Earthkeepers 2.0 boot range was launched in 2009, which is designed to 'close the loop' of corporate environmental responsibility, joining a broader collection of eco-conscious footwear.

Timberland's stores are designed to reflect the complementary themes of 'living' and 'environmental stewardship'. For example, the 2005 refurbishment of the Covent Garden store used reclaimed wood, stone, metal and leather, suggesting a journey through the outdoors, within the retail environment (Ryan, 2005). In 2005 the company also received press acclaim for the preservation of original features of the grade 2 listed fruit wholesale store in Spitalfields. The continued relationship with retail design company Checkland Kindleysides led to the striking design for the store in the recently opened Westfield shopping centre in West London, which opened in 2008 (see Figure 1). This store features a mix of reclaimed, reused and recycled materials and was constructed using processes and materials with the lowest environmental impact. The store features a 'nutritional label', an idea originally used on products, which shows the store 'ingredients' in terms of construction materials and energy consumption. Timberland extend this environmentally consciousness into their wholesale marketing, with a fashion trade show stand made from salvaged shipping containers which doubled up as shipment crates and exhibition stand. The stand (see Figure 2) also featured several 8-foot versions of the shoebox nutritional labels.

RETAIL DESIGN

The growth of online retailing has resulted in the need for retailers to consider the design aspects of a website very carefully. Technological advances and received wisdom regarding the effectiveness of various website design elements have encouraged retailers to manage virtual retail space with the same attention to detail as real space. This chapter will make an attempt to provide an analysis of retail design across different routes to market, highlighting similarities and differences in context.

A retail outlet can usually be considered as a combination of five key elements: the customer-facing exterior or initial landing page, the interior space whether physical or virtual, the method of merchandise presentation, the merchandise itself and the customer.

Given the need for change to accommodate product seasonality, changes in customer footfall and shopping behaviour, a degree of flexibility needs to be built into retail design. Mintel (2007) suggests that store refurbishments are becoming more frequent, but the spend on each refit tending to be lower and focused on the customer experience.

The exterior

The exterior of most stores includes the fascia, mentioned above, the store entrance, the architectural features of the building and windows. The contribution of these parts of a store's exterior to an overall design can vary in importance according to the type of store format and the products on offer. For example, superstores, hypermarkets and large retail specialist stores rarely use elaborate window displays, but have bold fascias and easy-to-access entrances. Stand-alone stores may have to conform to strict architectural guidelines imposed by government planning authorities, whilst the centre management team may control the exterior of stores in a planned regional shopping centre. Entrances can be designed to be open and welcoming, or closed and exclusive. A key consideration for retailers is the need to be accessible for all members of society.

The interior

The interior of a store can be viewed in a similar way to living space. It comprises ceiling, walls, flooring and lighting, but instead of furniture a retail outlet houses fixtures for the presentation of merchandise, and fittings for equipment such as tills. In choosing the materials used for the interior, retailers have to consider the type of product being sold, costs, store traffic and health and safety. For example, the store interior for a food retailer needs to be easy to clean and hygienic, but able to withstand high levels of customer footfall; high-quality materials are therefore likely to be a worthwhile investment. Alternatively, a high-fashion retailer like Topshop will place more emphasis on less expensive but fashionable furnishings and materials, in the knowledge that an updated refit is likely to be necessary in less than 5 years. All retailers have to conform to heath and safety trading standards such as those set out under the Health and Safety at Work Act 1974.

Atmospherics

There are many ways in which retailers can try to enhance the appeal of their stores by stimulating the senses. Creating an aura or an atmosphere in a store can include the use of different aromas, sounds, colours, lighting, textures and temperatures. Some examples of elements that can be used for atmospheric purposes are listed below. It is up to the retail designer to choose appropriate elements in order to create an effect that is suitable for the product being sold, and the type of customer. The use of sustainable materials is moving up the agenda in retail design, and this can provide an opportunity for differentiation as well as an expression of social responsibility (see Vignette 10.1).

Atmospheric elements in a retail outlet

1. Aromas: bread, coffee, chocolate, floral, spices.
2. Sounds: popular music, classical music, 'mood' music, voice (announcements, shop radio).
3. Colours: neutrals such as black, grey, white; natural materials, warm colours (reds, oranges, pinks, yellows), cool colours (blues, pale greens, white), earthy colours (browns, greens, oranges).
4. Lighting: cool lighting (blue, bright), warm lighting (orange, yellow, pink, subdued), spotlights (to pick out and highlight), ambient (general) lighting, sculptural light (in alcoves, behind panels and so on), illuminated panelling and signage, neon.
5. Texture: shiny and smooth (chrome, gilt, marble), metallic (brushed, galvanized, embossed), textile (carpet, fabric, fur, sacking), wood (polished, raw, smooth, knotted), stone/brick.

THE STRATEGIC ROLE OF STORE DESIGN

Most large retailers have a huge investment or asset tied up in their store portfolio. It is therefore in their interest to keep a high level of customer traffic moving through the store in order to maintain an adequate return on that investment. Good use of design in stores helps to keep customers interested in store-based shopping. When consumers have a high level of choice, they will visit places where they feel comfortable, inspired and even entertained. Customers are nowadays more design literate; consumers are not willing to tolerate badly designed and poorly decorated space. The increased tendency towards shopping online means that the store environment has to have something special to offer, and competition is forcing retailers to pay more attention to their selling environments. Spanish fashion retailers Mango and Zara, for example, use and have successfully penetrated international markets by offering inexpensive clothing in well-designed clean-cut store interiors more akin to designer fashion outlets, thus providing customer perception of added value in the total retail offer.

Store design has always been used to reinforce other elements of a retail strategy. For example, plush carpeting and marble used in a store denote high-quality merchandise and may suggest a high-price positioning. Strip lighting and dump bins for merchandise bring the word 'bargains' to mind. However, as retail markets mature, the design of retail space is increasingly being used as a means by which strategic aims are reached. Value retailer Primark has used retail design effectively in two ways: first, the use of clear large-scale signage helps the customer to orientate themselves in large busy stores, and second, the window displays are very fashion led, so that the brand is positioned with other fashion-forward clothing retailers rather than family variety stores, which was Primark's previous market positioning.

DESIGN IN NON-STORE RETAILING

Although non-store retail formats place some significant restrictions on the use of design in the selling environment, innovative approaches have often paid off as a source of competitive advantage. For example, when Boden launched their catalogue, it was unlike anything customers had previously encountered in the UK home-shopping market. The format was more like a photo album than a catalogue, with the models in homely settings and unconventional poses. The tone of the copy within the catalogue was an informal, chatty narrative, rather than impersonal and factual product detail. This 'lifestyle' type of approach to retail design has proved successful to other mid-market clothing retailers such as Anthropologie and Desigual.

RETAIL WEBSITE DESIGN

Although retail websites have been dismissed in the past as ubiquitous (Gerdes and Nachtwey, 2000), many retail entrepreneurs in the early days of Internet retailing attempted to use sophisticated design as a way of overcoming the shortcomings of virtual retailing. Getting the balance right between something that is familiar and usable and a selling environment that provides an opportunity for differentiation via visual interest has been a challenge for most e-retailers. Much of the attraction and competitive advantage of website shopping is based on convenience, and so reminding the customer of the frustrations incurred in store shopping such as not being able to locate items, or waiting (for downloads as opposed to in checkout queues) is bound to cause shopper dissatisfaction. Nevertheless, learning from successes and failures has resulted in a wealth of dissemination of good web-design practice and conceptual frameworks to manage the process. Chaffey (2009) for example suggests that website design and structure is based around three key elements – style, organization and navigation – while web-page design focuses down onto aspects such as consistency of style and copy, the ability to resize and interact with images, providing an option to print and the journey on to other web pages. The virtual world continues to push the boundaries in terms of new shopping environments. Three-dimensional virtual retail space is a reality, with the shopper personified as an imaginary avatar (Varley and Taylor, 2007), or more usefully for long-term retail strategy perhaps as a 3-D virtual version of consumers themselves (myvirtualmodel.com, 2012). However, given the high-profile negative reaction to some of these earlier 3-D virtual retail experiments, it appears that the technology needs to be developed further before this medium becomes more widespread.

VISUAL MERCHANDISING

Visual merchandising is concerned with presenting products to customers within the retail space. It is a term sometimes used as an alternative to merchandise display, but is generally understood to have a wider definition encompassing all activities concerned with the presentation of the product within the retail outlet, including the choice of store layout, the method of product presentation, the choice of fixture and fittings, the construction of window and in-store displays and the use of point-of-sale material. It also has a very close connection with the allocation of space within the outlet. Visual merchandising is more important in some retail sectors than others. For example, fashion and home-furnishing retailers have always devoted considerable resources to displaying products in a visually appealing way, whilst discount grocery retailers are much more concerned with space efficiency. However, the need to adapt to style-conscious twenty-first-century customers is as relevant to the way products are presented as the way a store environment is designed.

The implementation of a visual merchandising strategy within a retail business is not standardized across the industry. Lea-Greenwood (1998) found that visual merchandising could be the responsibility of directors of corporate communications, promotion or marketing, whilst some retailers gave the function the status of a specific directorship. Given the increased emphasis on the creation and management of the retail brand (see Chapter 12), the term visual retail is becoming more frequently used to cover all aspects of customer-facing retail design elements, and a 'creative director' may be employed to coordinate these activities. The high-profile role that window and in-store displays play within visual retail, however, means that visual merchandising remains the most important aspect of visual operations for most retailers, especially for those in the fashion sector. Often a multiple retailer will employ a team of regional visual merchandisers who rotate through a number of stores in a given area. The creative aspect of the visual merchandiser's role attracts people with a design training or background, although specific training for visual merchandising is becoming more common with more emphasis on commercial understanding. One of the advantages of using a centralized team is that the retail brand identity can be controlled across all outlets, and visual merchandising can tie in with other corporate communication themes and messages. There is, however, a danger that a centralized approach to visual retail may prevent a retailer from adapting to local environments, themes, preferences and competition.

Store layouts

There are a number of different types of layouts commonly found in retail stores (Figure 10.1). The layout used will be dependent on the width and depth of the product range, the nature of the product categories sold, the type of fixturing used and the constraints of the outlet in terms of size and shape. The objective of a store layout is to maximize the interface between customers and merchandise.

One of the most common store layouts is that of a grid. This layout is used with fixturing in a shelving format (the gondola), separated by aisles through which customers flow. The grid layout provides logic and space efficiency, but it is less flexible and standardized and therefore not useful for creating interesting product displays.

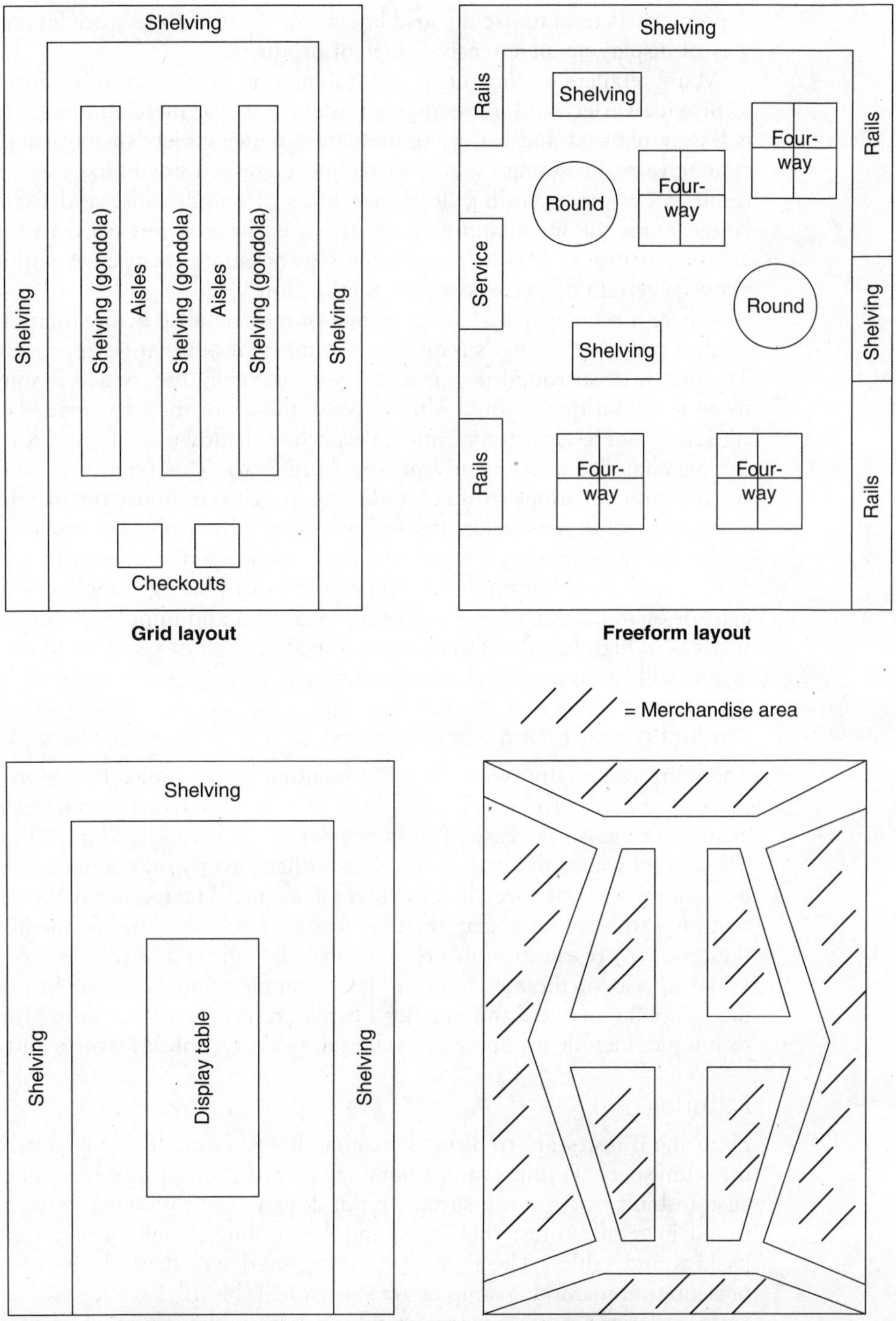

Figure 10.1 Alternative types of store layout

Supermarkets tend to use the grid layout for most of their store layout, as it is a good way of displaying an extensive range of products.

Many retailers use layouts that combine grid areas with other formations in order to provide variety and more appropriate layouts for merchandise. A free-form layout is less systemized and can accommodate a wider variety of fixturing. It is also more conducive to browsing. Whilst providing increased flexibility, free-form layouts can result in customers feeling 'lost' in a mass of merchandise and fixturing, and so in larger stores the merchandise areas are often broken down by a series of walkways and/or partitions. This helps customers to orientate themselves within the store and allows a certain degree of departmentalization.

Where a retailer has a limited range of merchandise or in situations where a high level of personal selling is required, a number of alternative approaches can be used. The first is to surround the customer with merchandise, which is sometimes referred to as the boutique layout. Alternatively, the store may be divided up into 'service stations', where a customer and salesperson sit down to discuss the purchase, with the merchandise conveniently nearby to refer to. This type of layout is used in personal communications stores. Another approach is to house the merchandise behind a counter, a technique used in high-value merchandise stores because of the security risk.

As well as exposing customers to as much merchandise as possible, layouts can also make a contribution to the selling process by placing complementary merchandise categories adjacent to one another, and seasonal and impulse product categories near to areas of high footfall. Decisions on the allocation of space within the general outlet layout will be discussed later in the chapter.

Product presentation

There are essentially two ways of presenting merchandise in a store. The first is to place or stack a product on some kind of fixture; stacked merchandise can be neatly arranged or, as in the case of promotional items, it can be 'dumped' into a container. The second way is to hang the product: either directly onto a hanger, or onto a prong, using some kind of specially designed packaging. Having decided on the type of presentation to be used, it may then be necessary to use a specific method of organizing the product presentation in order to provide logic in the offering, or to enhance the visual appeal of the merchandise. For example, clothes are often presented according to colour themes, and greetings cards are presented according to end use. Other techniques include grouping according to price, technical features and size.

Fixturing

Fixturing is necessary to display merchandise to customers, whilst making best use of the retail space. Fixtures can be obtained from a shopfitting wholesaler, or they may be custom-built to tie into a specific retail design. The following fixtures are commonly found in retail stores: shelving, gondolas, railings, four-ways, round fixtures, bins, baskets and tables. The type of fixturing used will depend on the product and its presentation method; examples are shown in Table 10.1.

In order to create a consistent look within the outlet, it is sensible to choose fixturing that is coordinated in terms of the type of material and style. An array of different types of fixturing may provide flexibility, but it can make a store appear

Table 10.1 Alternative fixture types

Fixture	Merchandise example	Presentation
Shelving	Home accessories	Stacked/placed
Gondola	Grocery products	Stacked
Railings	Clothing	Hanging (front or side view)
Four-ways	Clothing	Hanging (front and side view)
Round	Stationery	Bubble-packed
Bins/baskets	Small DIY products	Dumped
Tables	Gifts	Placed

cluttered and untidy. It is generally the merchandise rather than the fixturing that should be noticed, although some fashion stores do use unique designs for fixtures that help to reinforce a specific design-led retail brand image (Vernet and de Wit, 2007).

Displays

Fixturing is generally concerned with the housing of merchandise in what is sometimes termed 'on-shelf' displays. This is the routine display of goods from which customers are expected to make their selection. 'Off-shelf' or feature displays are used to create a visual impact with the merchandise, or to show how the product might be used. They might also be used to introduce and promote new products or to support supplier promotions or trade initiatives (such as fair trade). As they are not intended to be used in the routine selling of the products, they can be artistically arranged and situated in parts of the store that are not useful for selling purposes, such as in the window, high up on walls or within an alcove (although the closer to the selling stock the better, in order to encourage customers to respond to the display). Often, more than one product is used in an off-shelf display, for example to suggest complementary purchases or to show the depth of offer in a particular product category; mannequins are used for displaying complementary or coordinated clothing products in this way and are themselves often styled or chosen with characteristics that reflect the retailer's customer profile (see Vignette 10.2).

VIGNETTE 10.2 DEBENHAMS

In spring 2010, the international department store retailer Debenhams introduced size 16 mannequins into its window displays. Most fashion retailers, including Debenhams, use mannequins of a size 10, in spite of the fact that the majority of women in the UK are either size 14 or 16. The mannequins were used for the launch of one of Debenhams' many designer collaboration ranges, the Ben De Lisi for Principles collection, which was an attempt to breathe new life into the well-established retail brand Principles that was a victim of the recent recession. With a broad target market, Debenhams hopes that the more curvy mannequins will win the approval of their customers, but they are not making assumptions; signage next to the mannequins asked customers, 'I'm a size 16, do you want to see more of me?'

Source: *The Appointment* (2010)

Feature displays often follow a theme to add interest within the selling environment. Themes for displays include seasonal, colour and lifestyle orientations. Within the calendar year there are a number of seasonal opportunities over and above the general 'weather'-dictated seasons of Spring, Summer, Autumn/Fall and Winter: for example New Year (celebrations and resolutions), Valentine's Day, Mother's Day, Easter, Father's Day, Holidays, Back to School, Halloween and Christmas. Lifestyle themes can take an extensive variety of forms, and follow some kind of preference in terms of personal consumption or time expenditure. Lifestyle themes that retailers could use include sporting interest or participation, health interests, musical preference, home entertaining, hobbies, occupations and so on.

Another type of off-shelf display is the promotional display. This is a technique frequently used in grocery stores and features a display comprising a large amount of stock of one item, often housed on a dedicated fixture. This type of display is often found at the end of the gondola (on 'end caps'), where the sheer volume of one product item catches the shopper's attention.

For many retailers, the most important display space is their windows, as they are the means by which customers are attracted into the store. The window communicates the type of product the retailer sells and is also used to indicate market positioning. Window displays can be open, where the customer can see behind the merchandise into the store, or the window may have a closed back, which allows the retailer to create a more elaborate display. Destination stores like department stores often use closed window displays, but many retailers are of the opinion that the backed window can act as a barrier between customers and store, and therefore is less welcoming to customers. Diamond and Diamond (2007) suggest that effective displays follow one or more of the general principles of design, which are balance, emphasis, proportion, rhythm and harmony. Figure 10.2 gives a graphical illustration of these (Vignette 10.3).

SPACE ALLOCATION

The allocation of space to products within a retail outlet links the designed selling environment to the financial productivity of the retail space. Space management has to consider the long-term objectives concerning market positioning and customer loyalty, alongside short-term objectives concerning stockturn, sales and profits. A retail outlet that looks beautifully spacious will not stay that way if there are not enough products selling to sustain the business, yet if the store is full to bursting with merchandise some customers may choose not to enter it. Retail space is costly and increasingly scarce (see Chapter 9), and so whatever the visual merchandising strategy is, an adequate return must be made.

The usual method for measuring retail performance is according to the amount of sales (or profits) generated by a given amount of space. Sales per square metre is a commonly used method of assessing the value of retail space, but linear and cubic measures can also be appropriate. Space planning needs to take account of not only the amount of space allocated, but also the quality of space; for example the space nearest to the front of the store and the till areas are usually the most productive. Certain practicalities also have to be taken into consideration, such as the size and weight of merchandise.

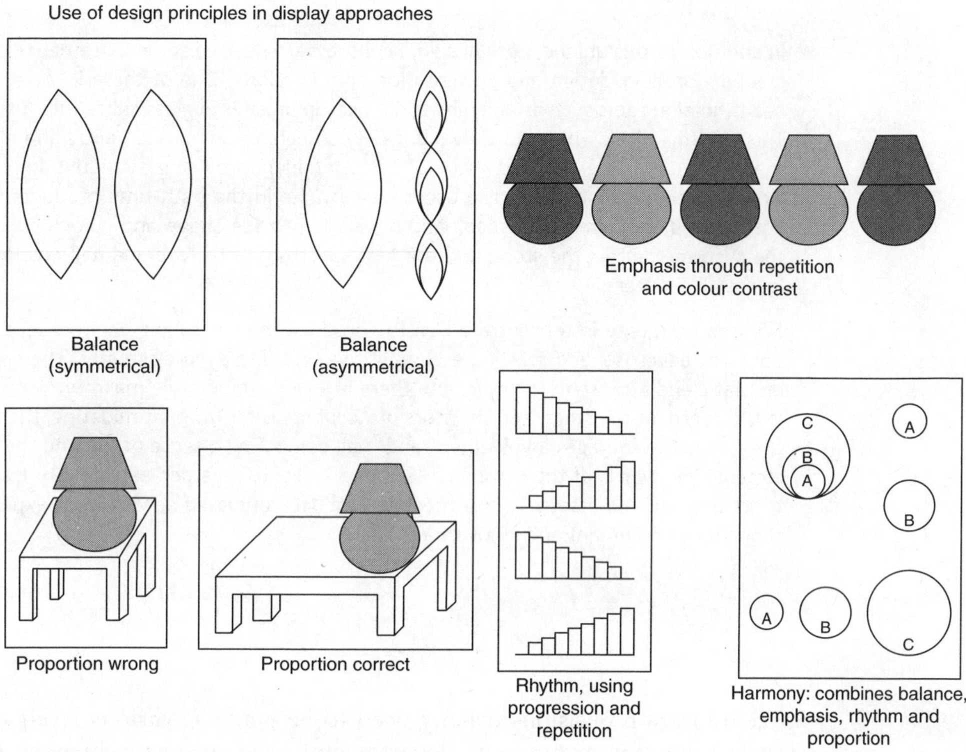

Figure 10.2 Principles of design within the context of retail display

VIGNETTE 10.3 SEPHORA

Sephora, the international beauty retailer owned by the LVHM luxury brand conglomerate, has used store design and visual merchandising in a bold and innovative way to carve out a distinctive positioning in a crowded marketplace. Sephora faces many strong direct and indirect competitors. The retail market for beauty products encompasses department stores, health and beauty specialists, fashion retailers that have extended their product ranges and even supermarkets. Traditionally, beauty-store environments have used polished materials like marble, glass, gilt and mirrors to create a luxurious and clean feel, with pale and cool colours such as white, cream, grey and pale green used to relax the customer and provide a neutral backdrop to the colourful merchandise. Sephora, however, have taken a very different stance, combining a bold and rich colour theme with distinctive design features in both the store's architectural design and the presentation of the products themselves.

Two prominent features of the store's interior design are a deep-red plush carpet, which covers an area of the floor, and the bold black-and-white tiling that is used on pillars to break up expanses of space within the store and on the floor to create a sharp edge around the red carpet. The black-and-white theme is reflected throughout in the fixturing, the signage, the carrier bags and the outfits that the sales associates wear.

In addition to this unique store design, Sephora have devised some extremely clever attention-grabbing product design and presentation combinations. One of these involves the display of beautification tools such as nail files and make-up brushes in glass cubes full of tiny metal balls. The resulting display method allows ungainly objects to be housed neatly and effectively, with the repetition in the size and shape of the containers providing a creative impact. The use of extensive colour blocking is also used: for example in the bath-time products, where circular bottles of bath foams, oils, soaps and novelties provide shape and colour impact as soon as the customer enters the store, and the vast spectrum of lip, eye and nail colours displayed on low-level counters.

Sephora's strategy is concentrated on the product and the selling environment. The company does not advertise, and prices are competitive and displayed discreetly. The stores play loud, dramatic and atmospheric music, and there is a Hollywood-style make-up demonstration area in the centre of the store. Yet, the store atmosphere is far from intimidating; the accessibility of the product encourages involvement and trial, combining a sense of fun and theatre within the store. In the words of the company: 'Sephora is highly regarded as a beauty trailblazer thanks to its unparalleled assortment of prestige products, unbiased service from experts, interactive shopping environment and innovation.'

Source: http://www.Sephora.com (2013)

Space allocation decisions usually need to be made at various levels of merchandise classification, for example at departmental level, product category level and SKU (stock-keeping unit) level. Retailers usually have some historical data that can act as guidance in the allocation of space, for example a similar store's performance, or historical department sales figures, but the need for maximization of financial objectives means that space planning and allocation is under constant review and refinement at individual store level. The allocation of space can be geared towards different objectives, for example achieving the highest sales turnover, maximizing product profitability or maximizing customer satisfaction, and a retailer may be faced with making trade-off decisions in order to achieve those objectives. Those products that generate the highest sales value may only achieve low profit margins, but concentrating on high-profit items may put unnecessary emphasis on products that are less of concern to customers, thereby decreasing their levels of satisfaction. The matrix in Figure 10.3 suggests alternative space allocations according to whether a product has high profitability or high sales.

Consideration of the financial implications of allocating amounts of space must be conducted within the framework of an outlet plan that is geared to making the shopping experience of the customer a satisfactory one. Too much emphasis on the retailer's financial objectives could result in a store being laid out illogically and make products difficult to find. Long-term profitability is dependent on customer satisfaction and loyalty, and so space planning must incorporate factors other than individual product sales and profitability. Aspects such as seasonal goods, the physical size and weight of the product, the type of fixturing required and the need to display complementary goods in close proximity should all have a bearing on the overall plan.

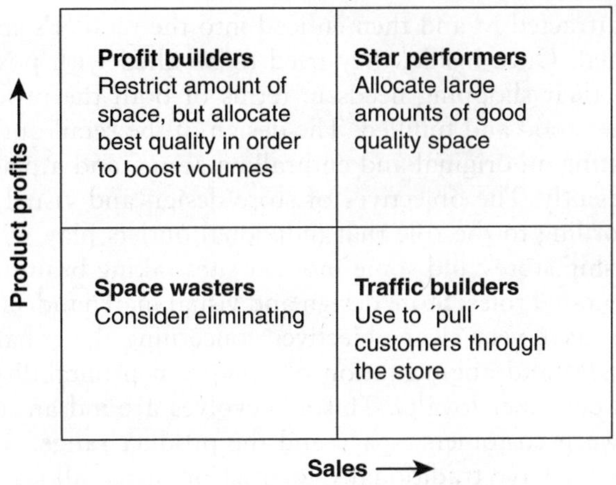

Figure 10.3 Space allocation alternatives

The complexity of space allocation decisions has encouraged the use of computer-based systems as a retail management aid. Modern space allocation systems such as those produced by JDA (jda.com) and Mockshop (visualretailing.com) are able to synthesize a plethora of quantitative and qualitative data such as product costs, sales forecasts, product sizes, complementary purchasing potential, store dimensions, fixturing details and so on. The output of these systems can be a 3-D or 2-D space allocation plan or planogram that shows exactly how the products should be displayed on the fixturing, including the number of facings of each product that the customer should see.

Although space allocation systems have resulted in retailers using space in a much more productive way, they do have limitations. Most large multiple retailers have a portfolio of stores that differ in size and shape, and so unless that retailer has access to individual store input data and the system is capable of producing customized plans for each store, the planogram will have to be subject to a certain degree of interpretation at store level. Many retailers have tackled this problem by grading their stores by size and producing a set of plans for the different store grades. However, grading by size is a very crude method of assessing different stores. Advances in micro-marketing have shown that the profile of a store's catchment area gives a better indication of the type and amount of merchandise required than the size of the outlet (Ziliani, 1999). As retail management information systems become increasingly sophisticated (see Chapter 8), this type of store performance analysis and customer-profile customization will become more widespread. Space allocation systems are expensive to implement, and so may be beyond the resources available to the smaller retail organization.

SUMMARY

In retail industry, where the consumer is growing increasingly style literate, the 'persona' of the retail outlet, whether it is a store, a catalogue or a web page, needs to connect with the customer, both functionally and psychologically. Customers must be attracted to and then enticed into the retailer's space whether space is physical or virtual. Once inside, they need to be filled with positive emotions and associations, and their shopping needs in terms of both the product and the process have to be understood and fulfilled. The design of the retail outlet has to find a balance between creating an original and enthralling arena, and a place where shopping is carried out efficiently. The objectives of store design and visual merchandising may be different according to the role that individual outlets play within the retailer's portfolio, with flagship stores and some Internet sites taking brand-building rather than profitability orientated roles. Store design and visual merchandising in most retail businesses, however, have very clear objectives concerning the enhancement of products, generation of sales and augmentation of long-term profitability through successful positioning and customer loyalty. This all revolves around an understanding of the relationship between customers, space and the product range. According to Webb (2006) retailers that have traditionally focused on space allocation and its impact on sales and profits are now widening their horizons to consider visual merchandising from the viewpoint of the total store environment, and its ability to interest, enthral and entertain. At the same time, fashion retailers that have been traditionally adept at using the store environment to encourage shopping as a leisure pursuit are now becoming more disciplined about making retail space more productive. The tendency for the customer to shop across retail channels means that the design of both physical and online store environments must be focused on the shopping process as much as on the product range in order to obtain optimum retail brand engagement and loyalty.

QUESTIONS

1. Explain why retail design is a strategic issue for organizations operating in mature retail markets.
2. Outline the aspects of retail management that come under the umbrella term 'visual merchandising'. Explain why certain aspects of visual merchandising may have a different emphasis in different product sectors, such as grocery retailing and fashion retailing for example.
3. By using observational research in your nearest shopping centre, make a critical analysis of the use of design at a retailer that you think has a pleasant shopping environment. Then find a shop you do not feel comfortable in and try to analyse why you feel that way.
4. Retail stores have been referred to as a form of free advertising. Discuss the extent to which you agree with this description.
5. Discuss the main considerations retailers would have when embarking on a space allocation exercise.
6. Using a large multi-channel retailer of your choice (one that you can visit), compare and contrast the design elements found in the various store and non-store outlets that are used. To what extent is the retail brand reinforced and supported by the different retail formats?

REFERENCES AND FURTHER READING

The Appointment (2010) 'Debenhams to Trial Size 16 Mannequins', 1 March.

Atkinson, K. (2001) 'Carlos's Way', *Retail Interiors*, no. 14, February.

Bouchard, N. P. (2009) 'Timberland Brings Sustainability to New Generation of Outdoor Users'. available at www.sportsonesource.com/news/article_printed.asp?ID=27919 [accessed 14 May 2009].

Chaffey, D. (2009) *E-Business and E-Commerce Management: Strategy, Implementation and Practice*, 4th Edition (Harlow: Pearson Education).

Clements, A. (2000) 'Scents and Sensibility', *Retail Week*, 12 May.

Diamond, J. and Diamond, E. (2007) *Contemporary Visual Merchandising*, 4th Edition (Englewood Cliffs, NJ: Prentice Hall).

Din, R. (2000) *New Retail* (London: Conran Octopus).

Doyle, S. and Broadbridge, A. (1999) 'Differentiation by Design: The Importance of Design in Retailer Repositioning and Differentiation', *International Journal of Retail and Distribution Management*, vol. 27, no. 2, pp. 72–82.

Exhibitoronline.com (2009) 'Eco-Friendly Exhibiting', available at http://www.exhibitoronline.com/exhibitormagazine/article.asp?ID=1186 [accessed 2 September 2009].

Gerdes, C. and Nachtwey, J. (2000) *Cybershops* (London: Thames & Hudson).

Kent, T. and Brown, R., (2009) *Flagship Marketing* (London: Routledge).

Lamacraft, J. (1998) *Retail Design: New Store Experiences* (FT Retail and Consumer Reports, London).

Lea-Greenwood, G. (1998) 'Visual Merchandising: A Neglected Area in UK Fashion Marketing?', *International Journal of Retail and Distribution Management*, vol. 26, no. 8, pp. 324–9.

Morgan, T. (2008) *Visual Merchandising: Window and In-Store Displays for Retail* (London: Lawrence King).

Morrell, L. (2000) 'The Flagship Enterprise', *Retail Week*, 15 December.

Sephora.com (2013), 'About Sephora' [accessed 10 May 2013].

SportsOneSource (2009), available at www.sportsonesource.com/news/article_printed.asp?ID=27919 [accessed 14 May 2009].

Timberland (2008) 'Timberland Opens New Store in London's Premier Retail Centre', Company press release (web-page reference and date accessed unknown).

Timberland (2009) Timberland Takes Sustainability One Giant Step Forward with its First Recyclable Footwear, Company Press Release, available at http://finance.yahoo.com/news/Timberland-Takes-bw-15616055.html [accessed 26 June 2009].

Vernet, D. and de Wit, L. (2007) *Boutiques and Other Retail Spaces: An Architecture of Seduction* (London: Routledge).

Webb, B. (2001) 'VM – Is It Working for You?', *Retail Interiors*, no. 21, September.

Ziliani, C. (1999) 'Retail Micromarketing: Strategic Advance or Gimmick?', in *Proceedings of the 10th International Conference on Research in the Distributive Trades*, Institute for Retail Studies, University of Stirling, August.

11 RETAIL BUYING

LEARNING OBJECTIVES

- To understand a retailer's objectives that guide the buying process.
- To appreciate the complexity of retail buying tasks, and the impact a buying situation has on the buying task.
- To explore retail buying organization structures.
- To understand product management approaches, including category management and lifestyle retailing.
- To appreciate the product and supplier selection factors involved in retail buying.
- To understand the different types of relationships between retailers and their suppliers, and how these relationships may affect the buying process.

INTRODUCTION

'Its all about the product' is a statement that most retailers would agree with. The outlet may be in reach of a viable population, the exterior of the store may look very inviting and the interior may look interesting and well appointed, but if the products are not what the customer wants to buy when they get inside the outlet, a retailer will not be able to implement other areas of strategy and will not meet its financial objectives in terms of sales and profits. Products are an important aspect of a retailer's corporate strategy, as discussed in Chapter 5, as they are a means by which a retailer is able to target a particular customer and differentiate itself from its competitors. The operations that are used to acquire a product range, and the ways in which retailers organize themselves to carry out these operations are key areas of retail planning and management and are the subject of this chapter.

THE BUYING TASK

Managing the product offer within retail businesses has traditionally been the task of retail 'buyers', who work from buying offices, usually located at the company's head office. It is the buyer's responsibility to select the right products as well as to negotiate with suppliers to obtain products for the entire retail organization, in sufficient quantities to meet consumer demand, and at the time of year, week or day that consumers wish to purchase. Buyers have to ensure that the deals they obtain from suppliers enable the retail organization to sell products at a suitable level of profit. They also have to be concerned with the logistical arrangements for the products that they buy. The larger the retail organization, the more complex the buying task becomes, and so buying is usually carried out by teams, or departments, rather than individuals, with their activity being supported by the supply-chain operations within the organization (see Chapter 7).

RETAIL BUYING OBJECTIVES

Like most other organizational purchasing tasks, the process of retail buying is guided by the need to meet the following objectives (Baily et al., 2008):

1. *The right product.* Retailers need to be sure that the product range includes the kind of products customers want to buy. This involves recognizing consumer needs, tracking consumer purchasing patterns, being aware of changes in fashion and tastes and introducing new products to customers. It also involves brand management, whether the brand strategy of the retailer is all own-brand (for example Body Shop) or a blend of producer and retailer brands (for example Boots). Chapter 12 provides an in-depth discussion about retailer branding and its implication for retail management.
2. *The right time.* Different products are needed and wanted at different times, and a retailer must manage their stock so that the product offer reflects the requirements of customers at any particular time. For example, a confectionery, tobacco and newspaper (CTN) retailer must make sure that the latest edition of a newspaper is available as soon as possible, as the shelf life of a daily newspaper is only a few hours. Other products such as Easter eggs and suncream have seasonal sales patterns, whilst staple products such as salt have a more constant demand pattern. Shelf life, season and fashion are key factors in the time aspect of retail buying, which is often referred to as 'stock control' (see Chapter 7).
3. *The right quantity.* Closely linked to the timing aspect, buyers must manage the quantities that are bought into the retail business. There is nothing a customer dislikes more than a retailer running out of stock of their favourite items, yet too much stock is problematic to a retailer for a number of reasons. Not only does excess stock tie up capital, but it also uses up space that would be better devoted to a faster-selling product. Too much stock inevitably means a price reduction to speed up the sell-through process, and this means a smaller profit margin for the retail business.
4. *The right place.* Large retail organizations such as J Sainsbury are not only selling ranges of products on a wide geographical spread, but they are also selling products in a variety of retail formats which have their own characteristics in terms of size, location and customer profile. The product range sold in each outlet should ideally reflect these characteristics, and so buyers have to consider where they will be selling products when buying for the retail business. Logistical concerns may also influence how a buyer orders from suppliers, for example whether store or warehouse delivery is required.

5. *The right price.* Much of the focus of a retail buyer's activity will be on negotiating the 'right' price for the product they wish to purchase from a supplier. A retail buyer needs to consider the role of the product in terms of its contribution to the overall profitability of the retail business. A retailer may be happy to make a very small profit margin on a frequently purchased item, but expect a higher level of profit from a less frequently purchased product. The different levels of profit will be determined by the price that the retailer sets and the cost price of the product that the retailer pays to suppliers, and the overall profitability will be determined by the rate of sales of the whole product range and the profit margins set within the product range as well as supply-chain costs, buying costs and financing costs. The rate of sales is influenced by the price level the consumer is willing to pay, and so the setting of prices becomes another area of complex decision making for retail buyers (see Chapter 13 on retail pricing).

RETAIL BUYING DECISIONS

The complexity of buying decisions varies enormously. On the one hand an owner-manager of a small convenience store may notice that there are only three tins of baked beans left on the shelf, and only two left in the box in the stockroom. He or she therefore adds beans to the list of items they are planning to pick up at the cash-and-carry wholesalers the next day. They know that the demand for beans is quite high but regular, and, from years of experience, that two boxes of 12 cans each will be enough until the next visit to the wholesalers. Consider on the other hand the kind of buying decisions that have to be made for a knitwear garment from a major retailer like Next. First of all the characteristics of the garment itself in terms of design will have to be considered far in advance of the season, as will the composition of the yarn it is knitted in, the style, the colour(s) and so on. Then a supplier has to be chosen who has the machinery and enough production capacity to make the product in the kind of quantities that Next would need. A price that enables both the supplier and the retailer to make satisfactory levels of profit has to be negotiated, and in order to reach a particular selling price, the buyer may need to make compromise decisions such as using cheaper raw materials, or simplifying the style. Then the stock control decisions have to be made. Will the garment be sold in all stores, or just some? How many of each colour should be ordered for the initial delivery? Should all the colours on offer be ordered in the same quantity? None of these questions can be answered without further considerations. Who is the intended customer for the product, and what are their purchasing habits? Will coordinating garments, such as trousers, be offered at the same time? Quickly, it becomes apparent that buying situations can vary from a simple restocking task to a much more complex range of new decisions.

Table 11.1 shows three different buying tasks involving different stages in the buying decision process. The table illustrates how in the case of the new task buying situation the buyer has to undertake all the stages in the buying decision process: that is determining customer needs, searching for a supplier or developing a specification to meet customer needs, sourcing a supplier to make or supply the product and supplier performance. In the case of straight re-buy, the task is a routine one (for

Table 11.1 Different buying situations and the effect on the buying process

Buy class stages	New task buy	Modified re-buy	Straight re-buy (reorder)
Recognition of retail customer need	Yes	No	No
Write specification of product to satisfy need	Yes	Maybe	No
Search for supplier to produce specified product	Yes	Maybe	No
Select supplier	Yes	Maybe	No
Specify order	Yes	Yes	Yes
Evaluate performance of product and supplier	Yes	Yes	Yes

Source: Adapted from Robinson, Faris and Wind (1967).

example restocking an existing product). The only stages that are involved are specifying the order details and monitoring delivery and sales. The modified re-buy task relates to a situation where some aspects of the product or supplier variables need to be changed. For instance, a supplier may not have performed to the standards required by the retailer and is replaced by a new supplier. In this situation some of the stages of the decision process have to be revisited but the whole process does not have to be undertaken again.

RETAIL BUYING ORGANIZATIONS

In large retail organizations the buying task is extremely complex, involving large teams of people and often several layers of management. In this section we describe the ways in which such larger organizations are structured for the buying process.

Centralization

Most multiple retailers carry out their buying operations through a central organization. Centralization has been a key feature of the evolution of the retail industry through the last half-century; smaller retailers have gradually been taken over by larger retailers and buying operations have been amalgamated, leaving central buyers in control of larger volumes of goods with increased financial responsibility. A centralized approach brings the advantages of scale economies and augmented buying power, as well as the opportunity to employ product specialists. It also allows the product offer to be centrally coordinated, supporting the corporate retail brand. Between 1960 and 1970, the number of buying 'points' controlling 80 per cent of the UK grocery market dropped from 1,621 to 647 (De Chernatony and McDonald, 1992, p. 190), and by 2001, over 70 per cent of the grocery market was controlled by seven retailers (Nielsen, 2001). By 2010 an even greater share was controlled by just four companies namely Tesco, ASDA, Sainsbury's and Morrisons (Grocerynews.org, 2013).

Buying departments and teams

The buying offices of multiple retailers are usually managed on the basis of splitting the total product range into manageable subsections and allocating a team of people to manage a part of it. In order to maximize the use of product expertise, the product range will be divided on the basis of similarity of product characteristics, so that for example in a department store the same buying team may be responsible for coats and dresses, but a separate team is likely to be used for stationary and gift wrapping. Some buying organizations allocate buying responsibility according to the turnover of the department, so that each department handles roughly the same proportion of the total buying budget. To some extent, the larger the retail organization, the more narrowly the buying areas will be defined, because of the larger volumes of product and cash flowing through the organization.

Rarely, in large retail organizations, are all the buying decisions for a product range left to an individual. The buying team may consist of a number of people carrying out different roles. The buyer/merchandiser buying-team structure is the basis of many buying-team formations. Within this arrangement the buying function is broken into a selecting role which is chiefly concerned with the 'right product and price' function and a merchandising or stock control role that is concerned with all the other factors (time, quantity, place). The people who carry out these tasks work interdependently, working together towards the same departmental goals. They are also likely to each have one or more assistants. The buying teams will be overseen by senior management whose titles may be merchandise manager, buying director or similar.

Buying committees

A highly complex buying decision, such as introducing a new product line, will have an impact on all areas of retail management. The buyers have to consider the supply side, the merchandisers have to consider the stock levels and space allocation for the product and the store management has to concern themselves with how the product should be displayed and how it should be sold to customers. Ultimately the most important person in this process is the consumer, in terms of the new product line's ability to meet unsatisfied needs or desires. Retailers therefore have to have some mechanism by which all the needs of the people involved with the product are considered in the buying decision-making process.

One way in which these various concerns can be considered is by using a group of people to make buying decisions. These groups are often referred to as buying committees; representatives from all the areas of the retail business get together on a regular basis to consider product ranges. The advantages of this system are that the committee represents a considerable wealth of product expertise, and whatever decision is made has the backing of all members. However, gathering a committee can take time and the group may not be able to reach a consensus view, which may result in some buying opportunities being lost.

Decentralized buying

Whilst most buying decisions and operations are carried out within the central buying organization within a multiple retailer, it may be more efficient to carry out some buying on a regional basis, or even at store level. Fresh produce, such as meat and vegetables, is sometimes bought by regional grocery buyers because of the geographically fragmented nature of supply. Likewise, it makes sense to manage regionally specific products such as newspapers or heritage-orientated gifts by store personnel. As catchment areas are increasingly saturated with retail provision, catering for regional preferences has been a way for retailers to attempt to achieve a differentiated product range. For example, supermarket retailer J Sainsbury plc initiated local sourcing when the company opened stores in Northern Ireland, where the retailer's own-brand name did not have the heritage and appeal that had been built over the years of the retailer's development in England. The move proved to be successful, and so local sourcing was replicated in Scotland, Wales and then South West England (Abdy, 2001). Local and regional suppliers sat well with Sainsbury's premium product 'Taste the Difference' range, and by 2008 supporting British and regional products became one of the four tenets of the company's 'sourcing with integrity' policy. The three other principles outlined in their *Corporate Responsibility Report* (J Sainsbury plc, 2008) are offering a wide range of organic products, supporting fair trade and undertaking ethical and sustainable sourcing.

Regional buying has been seen to be more appropriate when the catchment areas of stores show marked differences within a domestic market or where a retail chain has international coverage. However, most retailers' sales analysis is likely to show that a high percentage of goods can be bought centrally, giving the organization the benefits outlined earlier.

PERSONAL ATTRIBUTES OF BUYING PERSONNEL

Given the importance of the buying function within a retail organization, the people involved in these processes need to possess a unique set of attributes in order to cope with the constantly evolving and fast-moving aspects of their organizational role. It has been suggested that a retail buyer should be educated to graduate level, enthusiastic, analytical, articulate, numerate, product knowledgeable, creative, objective, organized, dedicated and flexible (Diamond and Pintel, 2007, Prospects, 2011). However, the buying function is so central to the organization's success that retailers should ensure that these innate personal characteristics should be combined with specific skills development, such as negotiation, leadership, team-working and communication skills. Buying personnel in large organizations will work on dedicated computerized support systems requiring computer literacy and in-house training.

PRODUCT-RANGE MANAGEMENT

Decisions about single product items have to be made within the context of the product range offered by a retailer. The decisions regarding the knitwear garment mentioned earlier on in the chapter will be taken within the framework of the knitwear product range, and ultimately the whole of the clothing product range. A retailer like Next has a wide product range, and so the number of knitwear styles will be relatively small compared to the whole number of product items of offer in the store. Product ranges can therefore be wide, covering a large number of product types (or categories), but usually with a more limited choice within those categories. At the other extreme, a very small number of categories or a single category may be stocked, but the choice within that category is seemingly endless. N.Peal of Burlington Arcade, London, is an upmarket specialist knitwear retailer, which offers cashmere sweaters in an array of colours and styles that cannot be matched by the mainstream clothing retailer. Product ranges have traditionally been determined by specific product area or category, so that customers know which retailer to visit for certain products. However, as retail choice increases, retailers are becoming more adept at tailoring their product ranges to a particular customer type; this is often referred to as lifestyle retailing (see Vignette 4.2). Another term for the total range of products on offer within a retail outlet is the product assortment, and we now describe strategies for managing that assortment.

PRODUCT ASSORTMENT STRATEGIES

Width and depth

Product assortment strategies tend to be determined by the store format used, so that for example a neighbourhood supermarket offers a wide assortment of many different product categories to fulfil the majority of basic grocery needs, but little choice is offered within each category. A specialist retailer like Accessorize, however, offers a deep assortment in a relatively narrow band of categories. Department stores generally offer both width and depth in their product assortment. The name 'category killer' is applied to larger specialist retailers such as IKEA and Toys 'R' Us, and is derived from their assortment strategy, which is to constrain the categories of merchandise on offer but to explode the depth of choice within those categories, effectively killing off any nearby competition in those categories. Figure 11.1 illustrates the concepts of product range width and depth (assortment).

Service level

Part of the assortment strategy must be the stock service level (or the degree of product availability at any particular time) a retailer wishes to offer, and then for each SKU (stock-keeping unit) within each category, a stockholding level must be decided. This level may vary according to whether a product item is considered to be a core line, which should have a service level close to the ideal of 100 per cent availability, or whether it is non-core. For the latter, a service level of 80 per cent availability may be sufficient, which means that most customers will be satisfied most of the time. The higher the service level, the higher the stock investment, so an appropriate service level is an important part of range planning.

Consistency and flexibility

Samli (1998) considers consistency and flexibility as further dimensions to range planning. Consistency relates to the level of compatibility between merchandise within

A wide assortment plan – giving category variety

Category	1	2	3	4	5	6	7	8
Brand A	◆		◆	◆	◆	◆	◆	◆
Brand B	◆	◆	◆	◆	◆	◆	◆	◆
Brand C		◆		◆				◆

Total number of SKUs is 18

A deep assortment plan – giving depth within categories

Category	1	2	3
Brand A Variation 1	◆	◆	◆
Brand A Variation 2		◆	
Brand B Variation 1	◆	◆	◆
Brand B Variation 2	◆		
Brand B Variation 3	◆	◆	
Brand C	◆		
Brand D		◆	◆
Brand E Variation 1		◆	◆
Brand E Variation 2	◆		
Brand F	◆		◆

Total number of SKUs is 18

Figure 11.1 Contrasting wide and deep assortment strategies

and across buying departments, in terms of product attributes such as quality and price level. The merchandise on offer in Harvey Nichols, for example, is consistent because the products on offer in all departments are high quality, stylish, directionally fashionable and premium priced. New Look, on the other hand, is consistent with its mainstream, value-orientated, reasonable-quality merchandise. Inconsistency within a product range is confusing for customers and damaging for the retail brand image. Consistency must also be considered in relation to the congruence between the merchandise and the store environment that surrounds it, an aspect of retail management discussed in Chapter 10. A clear merchandise strategy and good communication between departments are key requirements for a consistent approach. A good example of congruence between the store environment and merchandise is provided by the Apple Store, with an emphasis on aesthetics, tactile quality and interactive customer service.

Flexibility refers to the extent to which a product range reflects regional sales opportunities, buying opportunities and seasonal variation. Pumpkins, for example, are only stocked by supermarkets in October for the seasonal demand created by Halloween. Product categories such as gifts, chocolate, lingerie and slippers are offered in increased depth in the Christmas period. Flexibility allows retailers to improve cash flow by maximizing short-term sales opportunities, but it may conflict with the aim to be consistent.

Lifestyle retailing

Selecting products for a lifestyle retailer requires a detailed knowledge of a particular customer type, in terms of their attitudes and opinions and the activities they choose to identify with. In this way the retailer is able to offer a choice of products determined by a living pattern which is not easily described by more traditional segmentation variables such as age, income level or geographical location. Planet Organic (www.planetorganic.com) for example offers a wide range of organic products, appealing to the customer who would choose organic produce over other products irrespective of brand, price or product design. The Gadget Shop offers a product range which is geared towards people who readily adopt new ideas and gadgetry into their living patterns. A key concern of lifestyle consumers is if the product reflects the image that they want to portray to others. Does this help them feel complete? Lifestyle retailing is, in essence, aspirational. Lifestyle retailing has enabled some specialist retailers to extend their product ranges without losing sight of the core business. Victorinox (www.victorinox.com) for example has extended the product range from 'Swiss Army' multi-tool pocket knives to cutlery, timepieces, travel accessories, fashion and fragrance.

PRODUCT SELECTION

The task of selecting products for a product range can involve decision making at two main levels. First, the buyer has to decide whether there is a place for the product in the retailer's offer at all. This level of decision making is all about getting the product range right, and ensuring that whenever a customer enters the outlet the product offer is interesting and relevant to them. The second area of decision making concerns the detail of the product itself; the buyer has to be sure that the product reflects the image the retailer is trying to portray in every respect.

Product-range (assortment) decisions

Space is an expensive commodity in retailing. Retailers have to make sure that their outlet space is producing maximum benefits to the organization, and the products that occupy that space should therefore reflect the needs and desires of the customer at the moment they choose to enter the outlet. Retail buyers should be constantly reviewing the product range on offer. It may be time to delete a product item; it may be time to scale down the offer in a particular product category. On the other hand, customers may have requested a product item, or a buyer may have seen a new product when visiting a supplier and decide they would like to offer it to their customers. Ranging decisions should be made with the life cycle of the product category in mind. Figure 11.2 illustrates the product life cycle, and the related buying decisions are as follows:

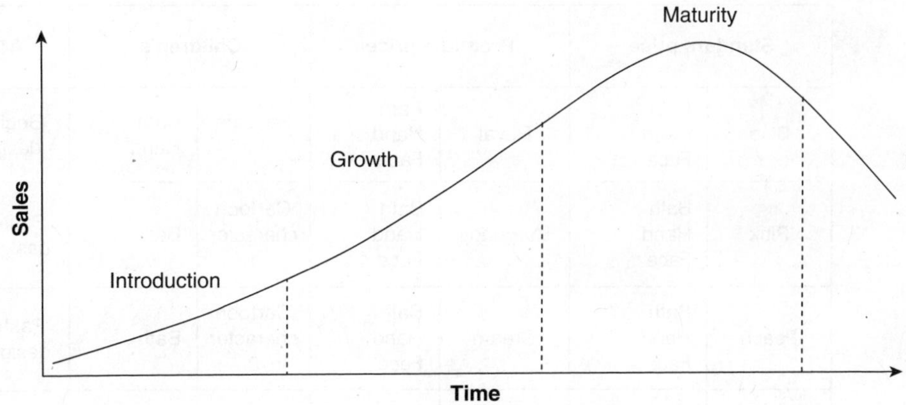

Figure 11.2 The category life cycle

1. Introduction phase – trial product; restricted offer in limited number of stores.
2. Growth phase – increase store distribution; increase product variation (colour, flavour, pack size, brand choice).
3. Maturity phase – all-store distribution; core product offer with additional variation according to store profile.
4. Decline phase – Reduce product variation to core lines; determine store distribution according to branch sales; phase out product category completely.

The product assortment plan (the model stock list)

The assortment plan is an aid to product management that considers the selection of products from a physical, rather than a financial, viewpoint. It therefore complements the stock-planning systems outlined in Chapter 7. It is a written representation of the ideal product selection that a customer should face at any one time, indicating the colours/style/flavour, size and price-level variations. The grid shown in Figure 11.3 illustrates the use of an assortment plan within the context of a towel range for a department store.

New assortment plans will be drawn up in line with seasonal changes, and to reflect the expansion or contraction of a product category.

Product selection criteria

Within the framework of the product range, selecting products is also concerned with getting the detail of the product correct. Products represent a blend of a number of features, all of which need to be considered by the buyer so that customers' needs are met most closely and satisfactorily. Table 11.2 presents a generic list of product features that may bear upon a product's ability to satisfy a consumer; see also Vignette 11.1

Standard price		Premium price		Children's		Adult patterned	
Blue	Bath Hand Face	Royal	Bath Hand Face	Seaside motif	Bath Hand	Brights design	Bath Hand
Pink	Bath Hand Face	Burgundy	Bath Hand Face	Cartoon character 1	Bath	Pastels design 1	Bath Hand
Peach	Bath Hand Face	Cream	Bath Hand Face	Cartoon character 2	Bath	Pastels design 2	Bath Hand
Aqua	Bath Hand Face	Fashion colour	Bath Hand Face				
White	Bath Hand Face						
Fashion colour	Bath Hand Face						

Figure 11.3 Assortment plan for towels

Table 11.2 Product features: a generic list

Feature	Indicators/considerations
Physical properties	Size, weight, volume, components, ingredients
Packaging	Aesthetic, protection, added value, promotional vehicle
Product quality	Raw materials, production processes, social and ethical issues, product standards
Brand	Trademark, certification, association approval, designer
Style	Design, taste, fashion, sensory factors
Utility	Functions, maintenance, durability, versatility, health and safety, environmental issues

VIGNETTE 11.1 BUYING FOR AN ONLINE FASHION RETAILER

Undertaking a buying role for an online fashion retailer is not so different to buying for a retailer with stores. Travelling to fashion capitals and trade shows to gain inspiration and source product, interpreting trends with the customer in mind and negotiating with suppliers to get the most appropriate range of brands and products at the best price is all part of the job. An additional consideration for the buyer for online retailers is how the product will look on a screen rather than on an in-store fixture. Often a buyer will help to style the product for a still photograph or on a 'catwalk' video to make sure the special features of a product are highlighted, such as a discrete pocket, a hood to a jacket or a print lining.

Online retailers have the opportunity to extend product ranges indefinitely, as there is no restriction on space; however, logic in categorization of product and navigation of ranges for customers is important to prevent products getting lost. In addition, the availability of product behind the visual representation is vital to achieve a good level of customer service, and so efficient stock management and close relationships with suppliers are equally important to online retail buyers. Web-based retailing offers the opportunity to trade across unrestricted geographic boundaries, which can mean a wider variation in customer sizes and tastes and different climates, all of which need to be taken on board in range planning.

Source: Drapers (2010)

Price/value as a product feature

The ability of a product (represented by the relevant features taken from the list in Table 11.2) to provide customer satisfaction will be determined in the light of the price tag. Price will be considered as one of the product features, and, like style or quality, different customers will perceive a price (or value represented by price) differently. When the retailer is making satisfactory profit margins and the collection of product features represents good value to the majority of customers, a buyer will have made good selection decisions, although a price that represents value will have some flexibility (see Chapter 13 on retail pricing).

Product development

When retail buyers select a product, they might be involved at a number of different levels. They may buy a product from a supplier exactly as it is shown to them; for example products that carry a manufacturer's brand (for instance Cadbury's chocolates) are bought in this way – a retail buyer simply decides the quantity of the product they wish to stock. Many retailers, however, offer products that are branded with a retailer's own label, and in this instance the retail buyer has more control over the way the product is made and presented. Some retailers get involved with the development of products at a very early stage, making choices about raw materials and components and methods of production. Marks and Spencer operate in this way and have been referred to as the manufacturer without factories (Tse, 1985). The main advantages for retailers in developing their own products are as follows:

1. A unique product range can be created and controlled.
2. Products can be developed according to the retailer's customer needs.
3. Repetition or gaps in the overall product range can be avoided.
4. Higher profit margins are generated.

An extensive discussion on retailer brands can be found in Chapter 12.

However, not all retailers have the resources to operate in this way. In order for a retail buyer to be competent in product development, they not only need the business skills of a keen negotiator, but they also need the specific technical product knowledge of their particular product area. The buying quantity also has to make it worthwhile for a retail supplier to enter into a product development arrangement with a retailer. In addition, access to a particular supplier may only be possible by buying supplier-branded products. Kellogg's (2010) cereal manufacturers, for example, make a clear statement regarding own-label supply: 'If it doesn't say Kellogg's on the box, it won't be Kellogg's in the box.' Collaborations are a way of blending expertise in product development (see Vignette 11.2).

VIGNETTE 11.2 COLLABORATION IN RETAIL PRODUCT STRATEGY

Collaboration is generally regarded as a business strategy involving the sharing of expertise for common organization goals and is seen in a plethora of forms at retailers. Collaboration is increasingly being viewed as a way of gaining specialist competencies in order to build competitive advantage. Vertical collaboration, involving retailers and their supply-chain partners in order to gain operational efficiency, is not uncommon, with the aligning of information and logistical systems being a widespread business practice at many large retailers.

Collaboration also occurs in buying and product development departments at retailers. Collaborations with celebrity experts is one example, such as chef Jamie Oliver and J Sainsbury plc collaborating on recipes and product development and the television stylist Gok Wan collaborating with Specsavers on eyewear ranges. Collaborations in the fashion retail sector commonly involving horizontal collaborations between a fashion house and a mainstream retailer to produce a time-limited collection are becoming more frequent (H&M and Lanvin in 2011 for example). Other design collaborations are ongoing and can give an injection of excitement and help to boost the image of the retailer. The department store group Debenhams has well-established ongoing designer collaborations at the heart of its product strategy with over 40 designer ranges spread over clothing, home ware, soft furnishings and other product categories.

BUYING CYCLES

In Chapter 7, various techniques to help retailers forecast demand for products were discussed. Forecasting demand for consumable, fast-moving consumer products with a relatively stable demand pattern is challenging, but with the use of sophisticated computer programmes the task has been greatly facilitated and fine-tuned. Managing product ranges that change with the seasons, or with fashion (often combined!) poses additional problems. Demand forecasting can only be based on a similar, rather than the same, product item. New products invariably have long lead times (the time between ordering and delivery) because the supply company has not had the benefit of experience, and set-up times need to be added to the normal production times. In order to achieve the five rights (see pp. 189–90) of buying for seasonal/fashion-orientated products, buyers need to adhere to a critical path within a buying cycle. A simplified buying cycle for fashion products is shown in Figure 11.4.

It must be noted that Figure 11.4 represents the cycle for one season. Fashion products have two main seasons and a number of additional 'sub-seasons' (such as 'party', 'cruise', 'high summer', 'transitional'), and so at any one time a buyer could be working on different sections of a number of cycles. For example, in September a footwear buyer will be concerned with current Autumn sales and deliveries, be in the process of finalizing the range of Spring/Summer styles and be starting to gather new styling ides for the next Autumn range. The concept of 'fast fashion' indicates a continuous introduction of new ranges throughout the year, and so buying is less cyclical and more responsive to demand and sales opportunities.

CATEGORY MANAGEMENT

In product areas that are fashion orientated, customers have a high expectation of change within the product range. They expect the product offer to change with the

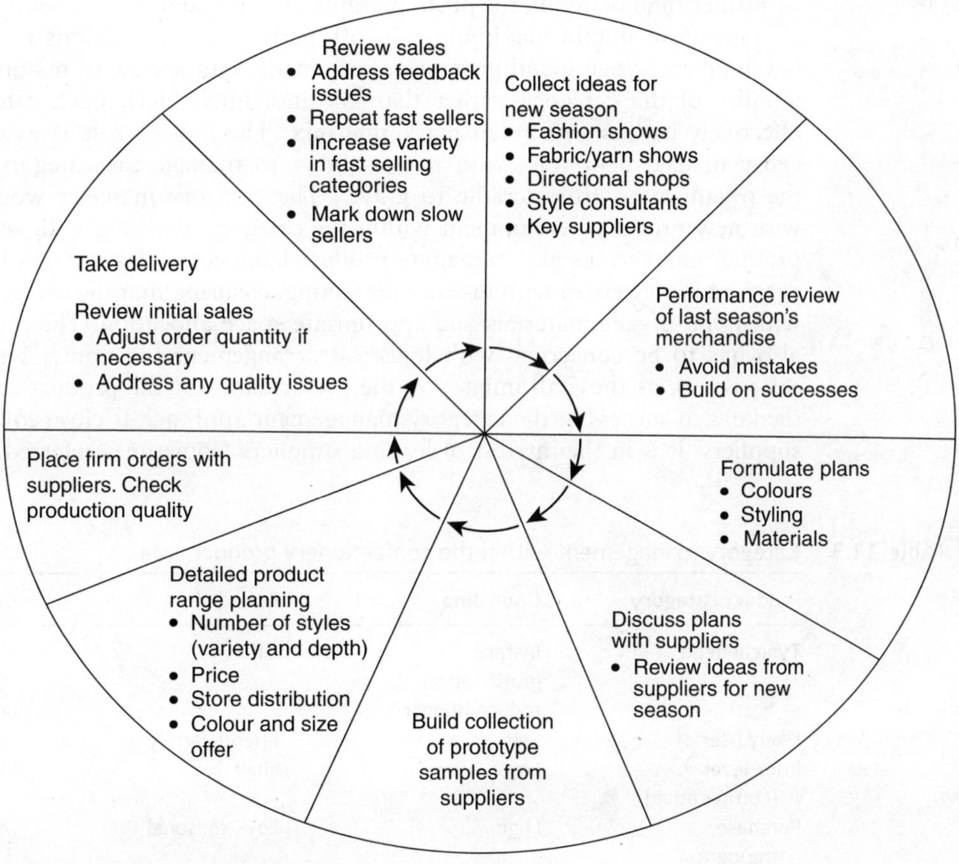

Figure 11.4 Buying cycle for fashion products

seasons, presenting them with a continuous array of new product ideas. In other product areas, for example grocery products, frequent changes to the product ranges would be confusing and irritating. Many products and brands have a loyal customer following and a constant demand, and should such a product not be available, customers are likely to show high levels of dissatisfaction. At the same time, however, customers of the twenty-first century like novelty and trying new product variations and new product ideas. Product ranges therefore have to be managed so that the popular items can always be found, but at the same time advantage can be taken of consumers' tendencies to seek variety.

An approach to the buying process that allows for this type of product-range management is category management. A merchandise category is the term used for an assortment of product items that a customer sees as reasonable substitutes for each other. Each product unit (SKU) is able to satisfy the same basic need, but the category would include a number of product variations which satisfy individual preferences. For example, the product area 'confectionery' can be broken down into three distinct categories: boxed, bagged and countlines (bars). A countline bar (such as a Snickers or Mars) fulfils a need which is different to products in the other two categories, as shown in Table 11.3.

Rather than planning the profit margins of individual items, products are managed as a group to obtain maximum category performance. Decisions regarding product development, pricing and promotions are made with a view to maximizing the profitability of the category, rather than the individual SKU. Each category therefore effectively has its own retail marketing mix. The buyer's role is extended to a category management role, with responsibility to manage the category right through the organization from 'cradle to grave'. The category manager would be involved with new product development within the category, working with suppliers on new product innovations and managing product launches. A large part of category management is concerned with in-store marketing, ensuring that the category is supported with point-of-sale materials and appropriate space allocation. The category manager also has to be concerned with logistical arrangements, customer service and after-sales issues, as these all impact on the performance of the product category. One of the keys to success in the category management approach is close collaboration with suppliers. It is in the interest of leading suppliers (sometimes referred to as 'category

Table 11.3 Category management within the confectionery product area

Product category	Countline	Boxed	Bagged
Typical need	Instant gratification, reduce hunger	Gift	Sharing, immediate and later consumption
Likely user	Self	Friend, family	Family, self
Price level (comparative)	Low	High	Medium
Purchase frequency	High	Low, seasonal	Low/medium

champions' or 'category captains') to work with a retailer to make a merchandise category as successful as possible, because the retailer's success will mean higher sales volumes for the supplier (Morgan et al., 2007). In some cases, for instance Wal-Mart, the retailer will appoint a leading manufacturer such as Proctor & Gamble as category captain to manage the category for the retailer. Category management is an integral part of the efficient consumer response (ECR) approach to retailing discussed in Chapter 7.

RETAIL SUPPLIERS

Throughout the retail industry, supply sources come in many different guises, from the individual craftsperson to the sprawling factory. Supplies can be purchased directly from a manufacturing unit (small or large), or the retailer may use another intermediary such as an agent, a wholesaler or a broker. Retailers will use supply sources that are appropriate to their needs. A supplier's ability to meet a retailer needs will be determined by the following factors:

1. Product range – design, quality and brand recognition.
2. Price level – negotiation opportunities, discounts and payment terms.
3. Capacity – volumes, lead times, available capacity.
4. Service – delivery service, sales service and after-sales service.
5. Flexibility – ability to manufacture different products and make fast changes to production planning.
6. Technology – use of technology in production, and information systems.
7. Approach – understanding of retailer's needs, partnership, being opportunistic.
8. Location – local, domestic or global.

Retailers will have a set of suppliers that they currently order from. Some suppliers might be used on an intermittent basis; others may be supplying on an ongoing basis. Either way, suppliers that are current are termed 'active' suppliers. Alongside the list of active suppliers will be a set of 'inactive' suppliers that a retail buyer will keep as their consideration set. This set of suppliers might include those who have recently made approaches to the buyer but offer a similar product proposition to an existing supplier, and it may include suppliers who have been used in the past. Buyers who work for large retail organizations very rarely have to search out suppliers, as they are frequently approached by producers who wish to increase their distribution coverage. However, if a retailer is planning to enter a new product area, or is keen to supply a new type of product, then a supplier search might be necessary. Smaller and specialist retailers may also need to search for suppliers.

Sources of information on suppliers include the following: trade journals and magazines, local and international trade associations, trade fairs and exhibitions, and catalogues. Although it is time consuming, buying teams should always be open-minded when reviewing suppliers who make approaches to the retailer, particularly in a changing supply situation. It is often the task of an assistant buyer to screen supplier representatives for the departmental buyer. New product ideas and new suppliers very often go hand in hand, but it is not uncommon for new product ideas to be quickly copied by retailers, using existing supply sources.

ETHICS IN SOURCING AND SUPPLY

The relationship between a retailer, the products it offers to customers and how they are made is an area of increasing public scrutiny, and ensuring acceptable standards in areas of ethical concern is an important part of retail management. Relevant areas of concern are as follows: are products safe and suitable for consumption, especially considering children; are the products damaging to the environment in the way they are manufactured, supplied or disposed of; are people who work in the supply chain for the product treated fairly and humanely; is the product sold in a way that is not misleading to customers? In long supply chains that take products from a point of manufacture at one side of the globe to a point of sale on the other, it is difficult to ensure that high ethical standards are achieved at every stage; however, a retailer must take the responsibility to assure acceptable standards for their customers, who demonstrate trust in a retail brand by being loyal. For a wider discussion on the ethics of sourcing and supply of retail products, readers are referred to Chapter 18.

GLOBAL SOURCING

As indicated in the previous section, it is common for retailers to source products from the global marketplace in order to achieve the availability of saleable products at acceptable prices to both the retailer in terms of profit margins achieved and the consumer in terms of competitive offerings. International trading was occurring well before the retailers we are familiar with today were established and brings the benefit of the wide variety of goods we are now used to; however, the pursuit of manufactured consumer goods using low-cost labour has been the chief motivation for global sourcing, in particular for products where a high labour content is inherent, such as clothing or electronic products. These industries have been fundamental to the growth of the so-called emerging economies such as China, India, Bangladesh and Vietnam, and many well-run factories in these countries produce high-quality goods and play key roles in retailers' supply chains. However, there are some inherent characteristics of global sourcing which can cause difficulties and additional costs to the retailer. Hines (2004) uses the concept of an iceberg to suggest that global sourcing can be affected by a variety of hidden costs that may not be immediately apparent to a retail buyer when they see an attractively small price for a product. These costs could include the cost of transportation to the retail market; the cost of having high minimum order quantities, which may incur storage or markdown costs if demand for the product is lower than the minimum order quantity; the cost of complexity, for example dealing with people who may not understand your instructions, resulting in less than perfect products which may need to be sold at a lower price; the cost of travelling to source; and the cost of assuring high standards of quality and ethical supply.

BUYING GROUPS AND BUYING ALLIANCES

Earlier in this chapter, the advantages of centralized buying were outlined. Some small retailers become members of a third-party buying organization in order to gain some of the advantages of centralization. In this situation, the orders of a large number of smaller retailers are amalgamated so that lower prices can be negotiated with suppliers, and a wider range of supply sources used. The Associated Independent Stores (AIS) buying group for example represents around 250 independent retailers. The organization acts like a retail head office, offering not only buying expertise and negotiating discounts with suppliers on behalf of members, but also training on merchandising, marketing, customer service and so on. Membership to buying groups may be at a flat rate, or it may be paid on a commission basis. Symbol groups (such as Nisa) operate in a similar way, although members may be bound by certain buying agreements, and they may be required to display the symbol group's trademark (for example on the shop fascia). Some larger retailers also collaborate in order to tap into each other's buying expertise. The Internet has led to the development of e-commerce trading networks, which offer the opportunity for retailers to combine their buying power. The WorldWide Retail Exchange (WWRE), for example, includes Tesco, Marks and Spencer, Casino, Ahold and Kmart within its membership, and as a Web-based marketplace facilitates commercial interactions between retailers and suppliers. This type of collaboration can be used for non-resale sourcing, for example for shopfitting or office equipment, as well as for stock for resale.

RETAILER–SUPPLIER RELATIONSHIPS

In a previous section of this chapter, the ideas of intermittent and ongoing supply sources were introduced. Some retailers have a relatively small number of suppliers who provide large quantities of products in many merchandise categories; others tend to 'shop around' between large numbers of suppliers. Over the last decade, however, many of the large multiple retailers have gone through a process of supply-base rationalization, resulting in smaller numbers of suppliers who are responsible for larger order quantities. This type of approach to buying is often termed the 'partnership approach', because the suppliers are considered to be partners in the success of the retailer, even though there is no financial ownership linking the two companies.

Partnerships

Partnerships are highly developed retailer–supplier relationships and are usually the result of a long-term association between the two companies. They are characterized by a 'corporate approach' to the relationship, where contacts are formed at all levels of the organization, not just at the point between retail buyer and supplier sales representative. Figure 11.5 illustrates how retailer–supplier partnerships involve the whole of the retail organization.

Figure 11.5 The retailer–supplier partnership

Source: Adapted from Davies (1993), p. 74.

Benefits of the partnership approach to supplier management include the following:

1. Suppliers gain a deep understanding of the retailer's operational organization. They are therefore able to offer a better-quality service to the retailer and meet stringent standards, for example in delivery requirements.
2. Suppliers gain a better appreciation of a retailer's strategic positioning and aims. They will understand the retailer's customer profile and the retailer's business objectives.
3. Corporate supplier management means that supplier contact is not 'lost' when, for example, a buyer leaves the retail organization.
4. Suppliers will be more willing to make adaptations to their own businesses to accommodate the needs of the retailer. This is particularly relevant to information technology. The use of certain systems such as a product life-cycle management (PLM) system may be a prerequisite to the formation of a trading relationship with some retailers. More effective systems facilitate faster reactions to market opportunities and can help to reduce administrative costs.

Although partnerships are very common in retail buying, there are dangers involved with this approach. Partners may become interdependent, which certainly encourages commitment, but it can also breed complacency, which is a dangerous state in a fast-moving environment like retailing. Concentrating on existing supply partners may also cause a buyer to overlook product opportunities offered by other supply sources. For this reason a buying department may be using a portfolio of different suppliers, with varying types of relationships amongst them (Figure 11.6).

Transactional buying

A partnership approach is not appropriate for all retail buying situations. Small retailers, and those who are not concerned with developing their own retail branded

Core suppliers	Supply partners
• Use on regular basis for specific skills • Increasing business according to competence	• Ongoing supply • Shared strategic objectives • Operational adaptations
New/intermittent suppliers	**Inactive suppliers**
• Emerging product markets • Occasional purchase requirement (seasonal) • Fads	• Dormant • De-listed • Emergency supply

Figure 11.6 A portfolio of supplier relationships

products, may find that a transactional approach is more profitable. In this situation the supplier that offers the best deal at the time of purchase is the supplier that is selected for the order. Here, suppliers do not expect continuity, but neither will they be willing to change the way they operate to accommodate a retail customer. This type of relationship is sometimes referred to as the 'arm's-length' relationship, and may demonstrate adversarial characteristics because of the focus on short-term gains for both parties.

SUMMARY

This chapter has been concerned with an area of retail management that is fundamental to both strategy and operations. The chapter introduced the main objectives associated with any retail buying task and then outlined how the complexity of a buying decision might vary according to the familiarity of the task. The way in which retail organizations tend to be structured for the buying process was explored followed by some approaches to product-range management. The crucial role that retail buying personnel play in this process was highlighted and their responsibilities outlined.

Whilst retail buying operations play an exceedingly important role in the implementation of a retail strategy, specific buying objectives are unique to each retail organization and will depend on its positioning strategy. This chapter has provided a discussion of the structures and decision-making processes which are likely to be included in one form or another in any retail business as they go about buying merchandise, but the interpretation of these generic approaches will be dependent on the individual internal organization and operation of each retailer. The relationship between the management of products and related aspects of retailing such as price setting, communicating and delivering the product to the customer are explored in the subsequent chapters.

QUESTIONS

1. Using a manufacturer-branded product and a retailer of your choice, outline the various buying process stages that would be necessary for the retailer to introduce an own-label version of the product, assuming the original manufacturer is not interested in supplying under a retail brand. Make a list of the product and supplier selection factors that would be important for the chosen product. Some suggestions are given below:

Product	Retailer
Gucci-style fashion bag	Marks and Spencer (variety store)
Oasis fruit drink	Cooperative retail stores (supermarket)
Kindle e-book reader	WHSmith (variety store)

2. Describe the assortment strategies that would be appropriate for the following retail organizations:
   - A general department store.
   - A convenience store in a small town.
   - An out-of-town home furnishings retailer.
   - An audio specialist retailer, operating from a secondary site within a town centre.
   - A lifestyle retailer.
3. Outline the principles of category management, and discuss why partnerships between retailers and suppliers are necessary for this approach to product retail management.
4. Explain why many buying decisions within multiple retailers are made by groups of people rather than individuals.
5. Outline the main benefits of a centralized approach to retail buying. Discuss instances when a decentralized approach would be more appropriate.

REFERENCES AND FURTHER READING

Abdy, M. (2001) 'Pros and Cons of Keeping It Local', *Retail Week*, 31 August.

Baily, P., Farmer, D., Crocker, B., Jessop, D. and Jones, D. (2008) *Purchasing Principles and Management*, 10th Edition (London: Financial Times/Prentice Hall).

Bowlby, S. R. and Foord, J. (1995) 'Relational Contracting between UK Retailers and Manufacturers', *International Review of Retail, Distribution and Consumer Research*, vol. 5, no. 3, pp. 333–60.

Cash, R. P., Wingate, J. and Friedlander, J. S. (1995) *Management of Retail Buying* (New York: John Wiley), p. 84.

Davis, G. (1993) *Trade Marketing Strategy* (London: Paul Chapman).

De Chernatony, L. and McDonald, M. (1992) *Creating Powerful Brands* (Oxford: Butterworth-Heinemann).

Diamond, J. and Pintel, G. (2007) *Retail Buying*, 8th Edition (Englewood Cliffs, NJ: Prentice Hall).

Drapers (2010) 'Just the Job', *Drapers*, 9 January, p. 44.

Faithfull, M. (2003) 'Market Trader', *Retail Interiors*, April.

Gowerek, H. (2007) *Fashion Buying*, 2nd Edition (Oxford: John Wiley/Blackwell).

Grocerynews.org (2013) UK Supermarkets Market Share 2013, http://grocerynews.org/2012-06-16-08-27-26/supermarkets-market-share/grocery-stores [accessed 25 July 2013].

Hart, C. and Rafiq, M. (2006) 'The Dimensions of Assortment: A Proposed Hierarchy of Assortment Decision Making', *International Review of Retail, Distribution and Consumer Research*, vol. 16, no. 3, pp. 333–51.

Hines, T. (2004) *Supply Chain Strategy* (London: Routledge).

Hogarth Scott, S. and Parkinson, S. T. (1993) 'Retailer–Supplier Relationships in the Food Channel: A Supplier Perspective', *International Journal of Retail and Distribution Management*, vol. 21, no. 8, pp. 11–18.

Jackson, T. and Shaw, D. (2001) *Mastering Fashion Buying and Merchandise Management* (Basingstoke: Macmillan).

Kellogg's (2010) Corporate website, http://www.kelloggs.co.uk/whatson/provenance/ [accessed 4 August 2011].

McGoldrick, P. J. (2002) *Retail Marketing* (Maidenhead: McGraw-Hill).

Miller, L. (1997) 'The Changing Role of Buyers', *Drapers Record Focus*, October.

Morgan, N. A., Kaleka, A. and Gooner, R. A. (2007). 'Focal Supplier Opportunism in Supermarket Retailer Category Management', *Journal of Operations Management*, vol. 25, no. 2, pp. 512–27.

Nielsen (2001) *Retail Pocket Book 2001* (Henley-on-Thames: NTC Publications).

Prospects (2011) Retail Buyer Entry Requirements, http://www.prospects.ac.uk/retail_buyer_entry_requirements.htm [accessed 25 July 2013].

Robinson, P. J., Faris, C. W. and Wind, Y. (1967) *Industrial Buying and Creative Marketing* (Boston, MA: Allyn & Bacon).

Samli, A. C., (1998) *Strategic Marketing for Success in Retailing* (Westport, CT: Quorum Books), p. 295.

J Sainsbury plc (2008) *Corporate Responsibility Report*, http://www.j-sainsbury.co.uk/investor-centre/reports/2008/corporate-responsibility-report-2008/ [accessed 15 August 2009]

Swindley, D. (1992) 'The Role of the Buyer in UK Multiple Retailing', *International Journal of Retail Distribution Management*, vol. 20, no. 2, pp. 3–15.

Tse, K. K. (1985) *Marks and Spencer: Anatomy of Britain's Most Efficiently Managed Company* (Oxford: Pergamon Press).

Varley, R. (2006) *Retail Product Management* (London: Routledge).

Wills, J. (1999) *Merchandising and Buying Strategies: New Roles for a Global Operation*, Financial Times Retail and Consumer Reports, London.

12 RETAIL BRANDS

LEARNING OBJECTIVES

- To understand the reasons for the emergence of retailer brands.
- To identify the different types of own brands used by retailers.
- To understand the brand development strategies employed by retailers.
- To explore the use of lookalike brands and their impact on brand manufacturers.
- To understand consumer perceptions of quality of retailer's product brands
- To understand how brands can be used in the overall retailer brand-building strategy.

INTRODUCTION

Retail branding has developed to such an extent that today retailers are perceived as being brands themselves rather than as distributors of manufacturer brands. Many retailers have developed such a strong consumer franchise that customers are more loyal to the retailer than they are to any manufacturer's brand. This shift is mainly due to the extensive development of own brands and a more marketing-orientated approach to retailing. Retailers have been rewarded for their focus on customer needs and aspirations by increased levels of loyalty and patronage from customers.

This chapter examines the branding strategies of retailers and the contribution of brand management to the overall retail positioning. It begins with a discussion about the scope of retail branding as a management issue and then moves on to consider retail branding under two main themes. The first is the theme of the retailer as a corporation or organization and what is generally considered to be the holistic understanding of a retail brand, and the second theme is the use of a brand name applied to a product sold within a retail outlet that is owned and controlled by the retailer themselves. This brand may or may not have the same name and/or symbol as the corporate brand, and thus the two themes combine in an appreciation of the benefits a retailer derives from the organizational brand and product brands working together. The chapter also includes an overview of the different types of retailer brands and own-branding strategies used by retailers, with particular emphasis on the controversy over copycat/lookalike own brands.

RETAILER BRANDING

The term 'retail-er branding' was used by Burt and Davies (2010), and their conceptualization consolidated the recognition that the power of the brands of retailers is not derived from a name or logo applied to storefronts, products or delivery trucks, but as a blend of all aspects of a retailer's business which work together and form a perception when a retailer's name is mentioned, read or considered. The numerous facets of retailer brands like Tesco's, Carrefour or Wal-Mart, whose complexity are influenced by all the different products, services and retail formats offered to consumers, are sometimes referred to a brand touchpoints. Notwithstanding this recognition, product branding by retailers is a huge aspect of retailing and involves retail managers in many different areas of a retail business including buying and sourcing, product development and presentation packaging; promotional activity and marketing communications, visual merchandising and sales training. The concept of a retail-er brand combines these aspects of branding and recognizes the retail brand as a wider concept than that of a brand applied to a product or a brand applied to a service provider.

The branding of the retail corporation

In the context of distributive service provision, retail brands are close to reaching the status of brand, such as Hoover which became synonymous with a type of product. UK consumers are more likely to say that they are going to Sainsbury's or Tesco rather than say they are 'going shopping at the supermarket'. Likewise, they will say they will visit Debenhams rather than 'the department store'. These retail brands represent certain values to consumers which are associated with the experience gained when using the particular outlet, which may not end in the purchase of anything or may involve the purchase of goods only labelled with manufacturer's or supplier's brands. It is the set of processes which a consumer encounters when dealing with a retailer in any of its formats and will include both tangible and intangible elements of that experience. Viewed passively from the organizational viewpoint, a retailer's corporate brand is composed of activities and interpretations undertaken by corporate marketing communications, such as implementing corporate colours into a store design, livery, website pages and so on. However, given that a customer's experience is active, searching, touching, reading, having conversations, taking in atmospheres and responding to stimuli (including product displays and store designs), all of these things contribute to formation of the retail brand image that the customer holds. Kent (2003) explored the relationship between brand identity, brand personality and brand image in the context of retailing and found that visual and other tangible cues which build a brand identity are interlinked with a retail brand's personality, which is an extension of the values and cultural meaning extolled and the creation of a brand image. Retailers as the embodiment of social culture is a theme that is becoming increasingly relevant as some of the larger companies become so dominant (El-Amir and Burt, 2010), and recognizes the interplay between retailers, customers, suppliers, shareholders and society in general and its affect on retailer brand image.

Product-based retail brands

It was not uncommon for a retailer-branded product to be dismissed in academic sources as an inferior-quality product with a specific price-orientated positioning (for example Dick et al., 1996, Myers, 2003). However, in the UK in particular, the notion that retailer branded ranges could be something different from low-price and watered-down versions of manufacturer brands was quickly adopted as they became popular in the 1990s. Helped by a number of retailers, especially Marks and Spencer, who have always traded on the basis of almost all own-brand merchandise, and other very successful non-food traders such as Next and IKEA, retailer-owned and -controlled branded ranges are now understood as a central aspect of strategic product management.

THE DEVELOPMENT OF RETAIL PRODUCT BRANDS

The development of brands owned and controlled by retailers, variously known as own brands, own labels, private labels, store brands and house brands (see the next section), has paralleled the growth of multiple retailers, particularly in the grocery sector. It was in the 1960s that the major multiples began to realize that they could increase their product profit margins significantly if they did not have to pay for manufacturers' branding overheads. The substantial costs associated with the task of branding mean that branded products are unable to compete on a level price basis with own-brand lines. A 1994 survey by the magazine *Which?* concluded that consumers could save more than 25 per cent of a weekly shopping bill if they purchased the own-brand equivalents of branded goods (Hobson, 1994), although this survey did not include budget own-brand lines, such as Tesco's 'Value' range. Given this price positioning, it is not surprising that own brands are popular with consumers, particularly during periods of economic downturn, when value for money is increasingly important to consumers. As mentioned above though, not all retail brands have a low-price positioning, and ranges such as Tesco's 'Finest' and Sainsbury's 'Taste the Difference' appeal to more affluent consumers who are prepared to choose grocery products on the basis of attributes other than price, such as quality, sophistication and convenience.

Retailer brands are now a dominant force in the grocery sector of the UK retailing industry. The share of grocery sales allocated to own-brand products has increased over time; Simmons and Meredith (1984) estimated an own-brand share of around 20 per cent in 1975 but this had grown to just over 40 per cent in 1998 (*Grocer*, 1998). As would be expected, the level of own-brand sales was even higher within the major multiple retailers, with Sainsbury's having the largest proportion of sales, own-branded products being at just below 49 per cent. However, by 2001 the own-brand share of packaged grocery sales had fallen to 38 per cent, according to TNS, and in 2011 the British own-brand market share of food and drink was just over 35 per cent (Mintel, 2011). This is partly explained by aggressive sales promotion activity by brand manufacturers. The total own-brand market, including all non-food categories, was deemed to be just under 30 per cent in 2010 (Mintel, 2011).

The size of the retail brand market in the UK is greater than anywhere else in the world; the United States, for example, has had an own-brand share of around 20 per cent for many years. Perhaps unsurprisingly, the product categories that are now dominated by retailer brands tend to be those where traditionally there have been few (if any) strong brands. As retailers have gained greater confidence in the sales potential of their own-branded lines, they have ventured into new product categories, including some where there has always been a strong manufacturer brand presence such as confectionery or hair care. The use of exclusive retailer brands made by leading manufacturers has helped to achieve this. Although in the past, own-brand products were positioned as cheap alternatives to manufacturers' brands, in recent years retailers have upgraded the quality of their own-branded goods. Hence, many shoppers now accept that own-brand products are of an equal quality to their branded rivals. One of the main reasons why such a strategy has been implemented is because multiple retailers are now competing head-on against other multiple retailers; the independent sector has been reduced to an insignificant size, and most future growth of a multiple retailer must be at the expense of other multiples. In the UK some of the most highly regarded and consistently successful retailers have a high-percentage own-brand strategy, including Marks and Spencer, Next and Primark.

A TYPOLOGY OF RETAIL BRANDS

Retail brands now play a much more strategic role than they have done in the past, as is clear when one examines the different types of own brands on the market. In fact, given the existence of so many different types of retail brand, the term is too general and it is necessary to use more precise terminology to understand the role of particular categories of own brands in retailing strategies.

To reflect the different ways in which retailer brands can contribute to an overall product strategy, a number of typologies have been proposed. For example Pellegrini (1993) proposes a typology based on the degree of identification of the product name with the retailer, the positioning of the retailer brand vis-à-vis the manufacturer brands, the width of the range of products covered by the brands and the extent of backward integration required. Pellegrini identifies generics, controlled brands, counter brands, *produits drapeaux* ('flag products'), house brands and fascia brands as six separate types of 'own brands'. Although this typology is most relevant to the grocery industry, it provides an interesting starting point for the exploration of the diverse retailer product-branding strategies. This and other discussions have been used to create an inclusive and updated typology of retailer product branding shown in Table 12.1.

Generics, fighting brands, value or budget brands

Generic products are described by Pellegrini (1993) as non-branded merchandise, sold in plain packaging indicating the type of product only, with a low-price positioning. Even though non-branded merchandise is quite common (for example grocery products such as cereals, nuts and dried fruits sold loose by weight), the term generics was devised to describe supermarket-controlled products such as Carrefour's 'Produits Libres', which had a degree of identity with the retail outlet through the use of plain, but distinguishable packaging. Since the introduction of budget brands (also known as value or fighting brands) by the large UK grocery supermarkets, generics have become less commonplace and the term is less often used in connection with retail

Table 12.1 A typology of retailer product branding

Own-brand type	Description	Identification with the retailer	Positioning	Range of products	Degree of backward integration
Generics	Non-branded merchandise sold in plain packaging with low-price positioning; now replaced by budget own brands (see below)	Limited	Low	Limited	Low
Controlled brands/exclusive manufacturer brands	Brands owned by a manufacturer but exclusive to a retailer in a given market	None	Low/medium	Limited	None
Counter brands	Brands owned by a retailer, differentiated by product category, which do not identify the retailer and little attempt is made to associate the brand with the retailer's outlets	None	Low/medium	Limited	Low
Fighting/budget/ value brands	Products identified with the retailer but stress name of the good itself, sold in relatively simple packaging and with low-price positioning	Strong	Low/medium	Limited	Low
Copycat brands Re-engineered brands	Low-cost retailer-owned brands offering the same functionality of the branded product	Strong	Low/medium	Wide	High

Lookalikes	Offer similar quality and imitate many visual features of manufacturer brands	Medium	Medium	Limited	High
House brands	Name of retailer appears together with a separate brand name for different product groups or segments	Strong	Medium	Wide	High
Exclusive designer labels	Products designed exclusively for the retailer and carrying the designer's name	Strong	High	Limited	High
Fascia brands	The trade name of the retailer (or a name strongly associated with the retailer) identifies all products sold as private brands	Very strong	Medium/high	Wide	High

Source: Based on Pellegrini (1993).

branding. The purpose of value brands is to appeal to customers seeking low-priced basic products. The use of secondary labelling using terms such as 'Essential', 'Savers', 'Value' and 'No frills' is typical, and the branding 'get-up' is simple but still retains a connection to the retailer in which the product is sold. These ranges allow 'mainstream supermarkets' like Sainsbury's, Tesco and Waitrose to compete with 'discount supermarkets' such as Aldi and Lidl on a limited number of frequently bought products. They also can be used for promotional emphasis, and/or during periods of economic hardship when price becomes a more relevant attribute.

Counter brands and fighting brands are terms which can be used for branded products that have the same price positioning and emphasis on basic products, but whilst they are controlled by and exclusive to the retailer, they are not identified as owned by the retailer, so the customer is unlikely to make the connection with the retailer's corporate brand. The term fighting brand may also be used where a producer introduces a lower-priced brand with minimal advertising and promotional support to compete with retailers' own brands or generics, maintaining the price premium of their main brand.

Produits drapeaux ('flag products') is a term Pellegrini came up with for commodity-like, low-priced products with common packaging across categories, stressing the name of the goods inside, and carrying the brand colours of the retailer (its flag).

House brands, retailer sub-brands

Pellegrini (1993) uses the term house brands for products that carry both the retailer's fascia name (the name of the shop) and a separate sub-brand. In some instances the two brands are given a similar 'weighting' in the brand identity whereas in others a brand name is devised by the retailer and, although the association with the retail outlet is clear, it is not in high profile. This type of retail branding is frequently used when retailers wish to target specific customer needs with a range of products; a distinctive association with the fascia brand is strong. ASDA, Tesco and Sainsbury's all have house brands for their clothing ranges (George, Florence & Fred and Tu, respectively). Marks and Spencer use many sub-brands (for example Per Una and Autograph) to create distinctive product style-based ranges for different customer groups; however, it is clear that they are all Marks and Spencer's products.

Fascia brands, own-label products, private label

Fascia brands are what are often referred to simply as own-label products. Pellegrini included St Michael (the brand name previously used on all Marks and Spencer's products, but now only rarely on a limited number of product lines) as an example of a fascia brand; this is an unusual case and it is perhaps more helpful to consider this type of brand to have the same name or symbol on the products as the retailer's company name, with no other name or symbol used in addition. The terms 'own label' and 'own brand' are sometimes used holistically for retailer product branding, but in the UK market, it is surprisingly hard to find true examples of fascia branded products, where no sub-branding is present at all. McGoldrick (2002) suggests these are the standard store brands found in grocery stores, which use the retailer's own name. Where a retailer has a strong high-profile brand which is clearly understood by customers, a 100 per cent fascia brand strategy is appropriate, for example MUJI. Although many clothing brands use sub-branding to develop additional new markets, fascia brand reinforcement is common in the fashion retail sector. Here, a retailer brand can represent a particular style or handwriting which in designer clothing outlets becomes the main product attribute. McColl and Moore (2011) found that clothing retailers stress the importance of transferring values associated with the corporate brand name onto the merchandise.

Private label is a term that originates from the United States, where retailer-branded goods generally command lower market shares than in Europe (Euromonitor, 2000). The term is synonymous with 'own brand' in that it is used variously and generally to describe brands that are owned and marketed by retailers.

Lookalike retailer brands

An omission from Pellegrini's typology is the type of retailer brand which may or may not use a retailer's corporate name but nevertheless imitates many of the visual features (or cues) of a manufacturer brand. In April 1994, the issue of retailer lookalike branding, also referred to variously as me-too branding or copycat branding, was dramatically brought to the fore with Sainsbury's launch of Classic Cola, with a remarkable resemblance to the leading cola brand Coca-Cola. According to AGB's data, Sainsbury's Classic Cola took a 15 per cent share of the market in the week ending 24 April 1994, which compared with an own-brand share of 2.5–3 per cent for Sainsbury's previous own-brand cola, which was replaced by Classic. The chain's overall cola turnover grew from around £1.1 million in a normal week to £1.6 million, lifting its share of the total cola market sales from 20 per cent to 25 per cent. In value terms, Coca-Cola's share within Sainsbury's halved from 63 per cent to 33 per cent, while the own-brand share increased dramatically from 17 per cent to 60 per cent (Lewis, 1994, Drummond, 1994). Although dated, this example graphically illustrates the potential gains to retailers and the losses to brand owners as a result of the introduction of lookalike own-brand products. Two decades later this type of branding activity is still controversial (see Vignette 12.1).

One of the main functions of a brand is to denote ownership. Branded products generally have some kind of symbol, trademark, nomenclature or logo that can be registered by the owning and controlling company for protection from counterfeits under the law. However, lookalike branding is not the same as counterfeiting, which is illegal, but is the deliberate attempt to get a customer to associate a retailer-branded product with a leading non-retailer-branded product. The UK's Intellectual Property Office (www.ipo.gov.uk, 2013) defines a lookalike product as one 'sold by a third party which looks similar to a manufacturer brand owner's product and, by reason of that similarity, consumers perceive the lookalike to share a greater number of features with the manufacturer brand owner than would be expected simply because the products are in the same product category'. This type of retail brand development can put strain on the relationship between retailers and their suppliers. On the one hand, the retailer might be accused of stealing an established brand's equity or 'free-riding' on the basis of the similarity. On the other hand, producing for the retailer could be an option for the supplier, allowing them to find and grow in a new market under the retailer's label, without damaging their existing brand's image. In addition, more product alternatives may help to develop the category overall, which could benefit both brands. For product managers this is an important and strategic aspect of range planning and supplier relations.

VIGNETTE 12.1 IS LOOKALIKE BRANDING FAIR?

Lookalike branding is a practice that large FMCG retailers are well known for. There are many arguments that support opposing viewpoints and these are presented in the following table:

Arguments in favour of lookalike branding	Arguments against lookalike branding
The close resemblance of the lookalike own-label product to the original brand may confuse some customers but they do not mind as they end up with a good-value product. Most consumers are quite adept at distinguishing between brands and own-brand products.	The close resemblance of the lookalike own-label product to the original brand and it being placed side by side on supermarket shelves misleads consumers and they end up buying a product they do not like.
Many of the brands being imitated are made by the original supplier, so they shouldn't mind getting the extra business from retailers.	Retailers are attempting to ascribe by association the qualities of the imitated brands to the own-label product. Producing lookalike products is an attempt to trick consumers into believing that the own-brand products are sourced from the same manufacturer as the brands.
Similarities in packaging design are useful for consumers because they expect certain products to come in certain shapes and containers. The use of visual signposts and visual cues are necessary in the supermarket shopping process and help consumers to recognize products in that process.	Lookalike brands resemble leading brands products so closely that they imitate not only the trademarks, graphics, colours, lettering, words and packaging, but also the names of the branded products, and this is confusing to customers.
Own-brand products may be packaged similarly to brands, but they are not copies. Supermarket own-brand products provide a fair form of competition to the traditional brands.	Lookalike products are an attempt to steal the goodwill built up by a leading brand over a considerable period of time; retailers are taking advantage of the reputation that brands have built themselves.

Arguments in favour of lookalike branding	Arguments against lookalike branding
Brands have become synonymous with the categories of products that supermarkets are trying to sell, and argue that an own-brand product that looks nothing like a brand will not be recognized by consumers.	The increasing presence of lookalike products will diminish consumer choice in the future because they will act as a deterrent to innovation on the part of manufacturers and brand owners; the incentives to manufacturers to develop new products are clearly diminished by the likelihood of retailers subsequently copying the products, nullifying expected future benefits.
	If manufacturers lose sales as a direct result of lookalike products, they will be able to invest less in new product development in the future.
Similar-looking products are useful because they help consumers to make price comparisons within stores.	By attempting to associate the quality and the attributes of the brand to their own brands, supermarkets are effectively trying to gain a good brand name without the outlay normally required to achieve such a status. Whilst brand manufacturers invest heavily in new product development, packaging design, marketing and advertising, retailers incur none of these costs when launching lookalike own-brand versions.

The practice of copying is by no means restricted to FMCGs; there are many cases of design infringement by retailers in the clothing sector, and there are even cases where whole store designs have been copied. Although the morality of this practice is questionable, there are not many cases of manufacturers taking legal action against retailers. There are two main reasons for this reluctance. The first is the difficulties associated with proving 'passing-off' claims (a deliberate attempt to mislead customers) or proving claims that the retailer is directly benefiting from a brand's reputation (rather than their own). The second reason is the need to maintain a favourable working relationship with the retailer. The balance of power in the UK retailing industry is now firmly in the hands of a small number of dominant multiple retailers. Whilst retailers' own-branded products are competitors to the traditional brands, the retailers themselves are effectively customers to the manufacturers, and consequently manufacturers need to maintain good terms with them and cannot afford to risk being de-listed. Instigating legal proceedings against a multiple retailer would severely jeopardize

> the working relationship, and diminish the bargaining power of the manufacturer, particularly if that manufacturer is also an own-brand supplier to the retailer. It would also incur huge legal costs. There is a limit to the power of the large retailers, however; by the very act of incorporating similar packaging designs onto their own-brand products, retailers are acknowledging the fact that particular brands are very strong within their respective categories. In many circumstances, de-listing a particular brand would adversely affect the credibility of the retailer in question. This is why this aspect of branding has been described as a cold war.

Exclusive products or brands

Another type of own brand that is not included in the Pellegrini typology is the exclusively designed or endorsed product which is labelled accordingly. These could be products specifically commissioned by a retailer from a leading designer and sold exclusively by the commissioning retailer, bearing the designer's name to demonstrate the products' authenticity. Alternatively, a range of products might be endorsed by or developed by a retailer, or a retailer's supplier, in collaboration with a celebrity. For instance, Debenhams, the department store, works with a number of designers including Jasper Conran, Henry Holland and Jenny Packham to produce exclusive 'Designers at Debenhams' ranges. Sainsbury's collaborated with celebrity chef Jamie Oliver not only to advertise but also to develop a range of food products, and in fashion retailing there are many examples of celebrity-inspired collections, including the very successful range for UK clothing retailer Topshop produced in collaboration with supermodel Kate Moss. When the supermarket retailer ASDA made its pioneering strategic move into clothing, George Davis, a very successful designer, was the driving force and namesake for the George range. His authority in fashion gave the consumer confidence to buy clothing in supermarkets, and it was not long before rivals Tesco and Sainsbury's followed suit.

Exclusive brands and counter brands are often used when a retailer's corporate brand name is not credible or strong enough in a product category. Discount supermarkets use the counter brand strategy because customers may perceive their corporate brand to imply low price and therefore low quality, rather than value for money. With familiarity, however, the exclusive brands of Aldi and Lidl are becoming accepted as part of an overall strategy that gains loyalty from a diverse range of customers including those monetarily better off (Blythman, 2008).

An additional dimension can be added to Pellegrini's four criteria, namely that the type of own brand utilized depends upon whether it is a tactical response to market changes or a longer-term strategic development. In the typology presented in Table 12.1, generics, controlled brands and fighter brands are largely tactical responses by retailers, whereas copycat brands, house brands and fascia brands represent long-term branding strategies.

RETAIL BRAND DEVELOPMENT STRATEGY

The typology in Table 12.1 suggests a longitudinal own-brand development strategy, namely that retailers can start own-brand strategies by beginning with generics and then moving up the own-brand ladder as they gain experience and confidence in own-brand development. Wileman and Jary (1997) suggest a similar staged development of own brands over time in which retailers trade up in terms of quality and relative price vis-à-vis manufacturer brands, beginning with generics, followed by cheap store brands, which are a step above generics but still of inferior quality, offering a large discount against manufacturer brands. Re-engineered low-cost brands are the next step up, where a retailer proactively examines the product and packaging to see how costs can be reduced, whilst offering the same functionality of the branded product. The retailer makes no real attempt to pass off the product as a copycat of the branded product. For example, discount retailer Aldi has developed a set of 'exclusive' brands that allows it to deliver a price differential across the range of 20–30 per cent in comparison with supermarkets. The next stage is to offer par-quality store brands, which are aimed to match manufacturer brands in terms of quality and performance but at prices 10–25 per cent lower. The price discount is possible because retailers' marketing expenses are considerably lower and they can subcontract production of the store brands to manufacturers with excess capacity. In the final stage, retail brands take on a leadership role through positioning and innovation with a price parity or price premium relative to manufacturer brands, and hence better margins than traditional own labels (Dunne and Chakravarthi, 1999).

Whilst this development sequence is generally accurate for retailers who start off by selling only manufacturers' brands, fascia retailers are more likely to adopt an own-brand leadership strategy from the beginning rather than to evolve into one. That is, fascia retailers such as Marks and Spencer, Next and Gap have occupied that position from their inception. Similarly, discount supermarkets have adopted a policy of offering re-engineered own brands from the beginning and do not intend to evolve their own brands into positions of leadership vis-à-vis manufacturers' brands. Some retailers (for example Tesco and Sainsbury's) have developed a tiered own-brand strategy; with value brands aimed at price-sensitive shoppers, standard own labels that offer par quality designed to take market share from existing manufacturer brands, and premium sub-brands aimed at the top end of the market. The rise of premium own labels suggests consumers' acceptance of retail brands as being on a par with manufacturers' brands and the ability of retailers to deliver innovative quality products.

The discussion above suggests that key dimensions for own-brand development are the degree of innovation, positioning (that is the degree of identification with the retailer and its market positioning) and the strategic role of the own brand. These dimensions are used in Figure 12.1 to develop a matrix of own-brand development options which moves away from a simple descriptive typology. The matrix provides a clear rationale behind own-branding strategies. The matrix suggests that certain strategies are not viable, namely low positioning and high innovation, and low innovation and high positioning.

NEW DEVELOPMENTS IN OWN-BRAND STRATEGY

Whilst retailers continue to use copycatting and proliferate the variation of own brands across product categories, there is a danger that retailer product brands

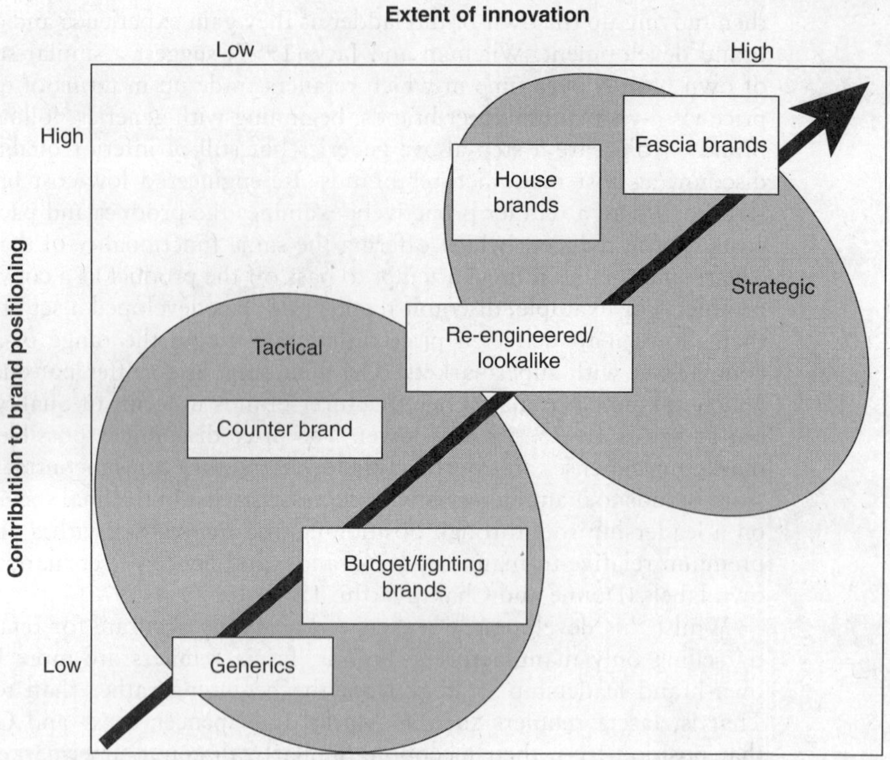

Figure 12.1 Key dimensions of own-brand development

can create inconsistent values. Hence, retailers also use own-brand packaging to project a clear corporate signature that can be seen, for example, in supermarkets' sub-brands that cross categories with distinct identities of their own. In terms of the typology used in Table 12.1, own brands are moving towards the house-brand phase.

The precursors of this trend are the economy and value lines, which make a bold unmistakable statement suggesting they are the cheapest products. Such clear positioning has allowed supermarkets to move the rest of their own-brand offer upmarket. Examples of this upward movement and extension of branding across categories are provided by Tesco's Finest line of chef-quality meals, which now includes fruit and vegetables and features the characteristic silver labels, small images and the same typeface across categories. This allows shoppers to instantly recognize that the products are of premium quality anywhere in the store. The increasingly sophisticated use of branding by retailers and their closeness to the customer means that own brands will continue to be a central part of product strategy (see Vignette 12.2). Sub-brands are a way of segmenting a wide consumer base or a way to enter a different market; for example Hobbs upmarket clothing and accessories retailer launched a sub-brand NW3 to appeal explicitly to a younger, more fashion-orientated consumer. Similar strategies are used by other clothing retail competitors Monsoon (Fusion) and Reiss (Reiss 1971).

VIGNETTE 12.2 THE HIGH-STREET RETAILER AS A DESIGNER BRAND? – TOPSHOP UNIQUE AND JOHN LEWIS & CO.

According to the Daily Telegraph Fashion Pages (2011), Topshop Unique is the collection where Topshop's design team let their fiercest fashion impulses run wild, the result of which is sent down the catwalk at London's Fashion Week in September and February. Showing alongside and being reported in the fashion press in the same breath as fashion heavyweights such as Vivienne Westwood, Paul Smith, Christopher Kane and Burberry Prorsum, the Unique collection does much more for Topshop fashion credentials than generate sales. In 2013, Topshop used a partnership with Facebook to allow people watching the live streamed show to share comments and photographs with friends, place an order and even customize the garments by viewing the items digitally in different colours. This furthers Topshop's positioning as the fashion brand for digital natives.

In June 2013, department store John Lewis, whose clothing ranges have until recently been considered rather unfashionable and traditional, made a similar move by showing their exclusive menswear own-brand John Lewis and Co. collection at a catwalk show during the S/S 14 London Collections: Men's. The range focuses on updated heritage fashion, mixing traditional styling with modern design details, and uses high-quality British fabrics in many of the garments. The venture continues the high-profile and increasingly fashion-forward positioning of John Lewis that has been taking place since around 2005.

Source: Mullany (2013), fashion.telegraph.co.uk (2011)

The relationship between retail product branding and the corporate brand

Implied in the retailer product-branding typology of Table 12.1 is the fact that retailer product brands have an impact on the corporate retail brand itself. With some strategies (such as generics and counter brands), the retailer attempts to maintain a distance between itself and its own brand. With other strategies such as house brand and fascia brand strategies, the retailer's brands are an integral part of the retailer's product and communications strategy. Hence, retailers have to be clear about where their product-branding strategy fits in with their overall branding strategies for the corporation (see Figure 12.2). This also implies that retailers must constantly monitor the relative contribution of their own product brands and of the brands of their suppliers that they do not own to the overall retailer brand image. For instance, it is widely regarded that one of the factors in Sainsbury's loss of UK grocery market leadership to Tesco was that the proportion of own brands in its stores had become too high. A similar experience befell the American retailer Sears in the late 1980s, when its excessive concentration on own brands led to consumer perceptions that its assortment was incomplete with a consequent negative impact on store traffic and profitability (Quelch and Harding, 1996). In 2008 Marks and Spencer introduced a small range of manufacturer's brands into its previously all retailer-branded grocery product assortment, as they found the absence of these brands was deterring shoppers from doing their main grocery shopping with them, and more recently the clothing house brand strategy has

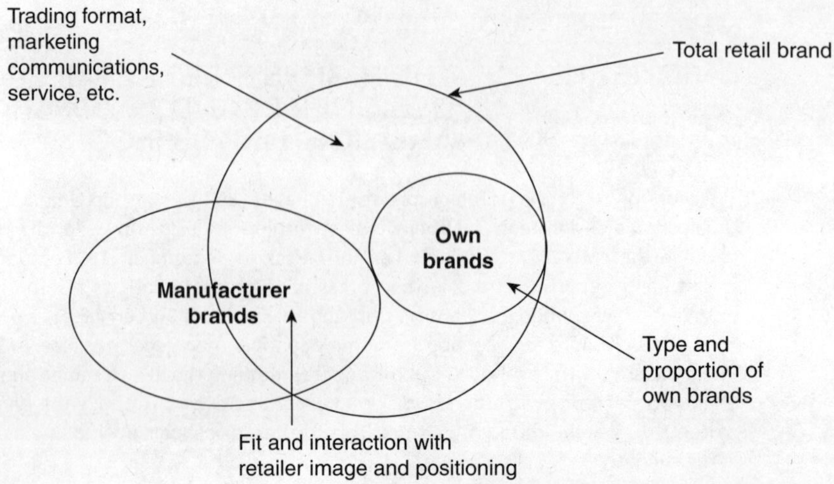

Figure 12.2 Factors contributing to total retail brand image and positioning

been criticized as confusing (Ruddick, 2013). Retailers also need to monitor and control their portfolio of own-brand types as they can impact on each other. For example it is suggested that one of the reasons for retailers withdrawing generics was that their association can have a negative impact on regular retailer's own brands (Burt, 1992). Category management, the process of managing products as categories rather than as individual brands or product lines (see Chapter 11), can help retailers manage the balance between their various product brands and manufacturer brands more effectively. However, problems are still likely to arise if there is too much emphasis on category profits or if categories are managed in isolation and without reference to the overall retailer brand.

From a customer perspective, it is generally accepted that brands have four main functions – identification, information, guarantee of product quality and symbolic (emotional) associations. Whereas identification and informational aspects of brands increase shopping efficiency, guarantees reduce consumer risk. Symbolic associations, on the other hand, provide psychological utility to consumers and allow them to make a social statement about themselves. In the main, the success of retail-branded products has occurred because retailers have demonstrated that they can perform the first three functions just as well as the brand manufacturers. However, except for fascia own brands, it is more difficult for own brands to compete with manufacturer brands in terms of symbolic or emotional associations. Also, manufacturer brands are much more likely to be innovative than retailers' brands. This is particularly likely to occur where a retailer offers a large number of their own brands, as it is unlikely to be able to support research and development costs in all of them.

The foregoing suggests that manufacturer brands have an advantage relative to own brands (excluding fascia brands) where symbolic associations and/or product innovation are important to customers. Conversely, where symbolic associations and product innovation are less important, there is an opportunity for retailers to compete successfully with manufacturer brands if they can demonstrate comparable product quality and provide value for money. As retailers become known and trusted as brands in their own right, the corporate brand itself builds symbolic and emotional value, which can then be transferred to new product developments. Marks and Spencer and John Lewis benefit from relatively consistent positive retail brand images because of the emphasis they place on good-quality products at competitive prices. Their socially responsible initiatives (Marks and Spencer) and high levels of customer service (John Lewis) additionally help their corporate brands stand out from other mainstream retailers. However, all retailers need to manage their corporate brand to ensure it has mostly positive associations. Unexpected events such as quality scares or reports about unfair practice can damage retail brands severely. Corporate social responsibility (CSR – see Chapter 18) and public relations activity (see Chapter 14) are increasingly important tools to use to help a retailer maintain positive brand values.

SUMMARY

This chapter has examined the growth of own brands in retailing. A typology has been presented which identifies the type of role that the own brand is required to perform in a retailer's overall branding strategy. Retailers have to make decisions on the balance between manufacturer brands and own brands as they affect the overall positioning of the retail brand image. Retailers are now considered brands in themselves rather than just purveyors of manufacturer's products, and are becoming very sophisticated in their use of branding techniques and innovative in their development of new products, leading the market in a number of product areas.

Although the field of retailer branding is complex and is the arena in which retailers and their suppliers work in an atmosphere of tension, it does not make too much sense from a managerial viewpoint to place an inordinate amount of attention onto the ownership of brands; ultimately, what is important for a retailer is the values that brands present to customers, the extent to which customers are prepared to become loyal to a brand and how brands might be used to differentiate one retailer from another. It is in these aspects of management that branding reveals its complexity and how different aspects or touchpoints may provide different or additional values from other retailers, but the main values of the corporate brand should underpin all brand facets.

There are diverse approaches by retailers to branding and this aspect of retail management continues to evolve, reflecting the evolution of the industry itself. A question many retailers are grappling with is the relationship between the retailer brand values represented by physical touchpoints and virtual touchpoints. As online retailing continues to play a significant part in the overall corporate retail strategy, the management of customer value interpretations, image development and ultimately loyalty to retailer brands at different levels will require omni-channel approaches.

QUESTIONS

1. What are the pros and cons of manufacturer and own brands for retailers?
2. 'Retailer's lookalike own brands amount to theft of goodwill built up by established brands.' Discuss.

3. Discuss the methods which manufacturers can employ to protect their brands.
4. Why do some retailers sell 100 per cent own brands and others do not?
5. How can retailers improve customers' perceptions of own-label quality?
6. How do retailers' own product brands and manufacturer brands contribute to the overall image of the retailer brand? Compare different retailers in different sectors.

REFERENCES AND FURTHER READING

Blackburn, J. (1994) 'Unique Branding Is a Thing of the Past', *Marketing*, 23 June, p. 20.

Blythman, J. (2008) 'The Rise of Lidl Britain during the Credit Crunch', *Telegraph*, (www.telegraph.co.uk), available www.telegraph.co.uk/news/features/3637902, 10 September [accessed 20 August 2013].

Burt, S. (1992) 'Retailer Brands in British Grocery Retailing. A Review', University of Stirling, Institute for Retail Studies, Working paper no. 9204.

Burt, S. (2000) 'The Strategic Role of Retail Brands in British Grocery Retailing', *European Journal of Marketing*, vol. 34, no. 8, pp. 875–90.

Burt, S. and Davies, K. (2010) 'From the Retail Brand to the Retailer-*er* as a Brand: Themes and Issues in Retail Branding Research', *International Journal of Retail and Distribution Management*, vol. 38, no. 11/12, pp. 865–78.

Burt, S. and Davis, S. (1999) 'Follow My Leader? Lookalike Retailer Brands in Non-Manufacturer-Dominated Product Markets in the UK', *International Review of Retail, Distribution and Consumer Research*, vol. 12, no. 2, pp. 163–85.

Dick, A., Jain, A. and Richardson, P. (1996) 'How Consumers Evaluate Store Brands', *Journal of Product and Brand Management*, vol. 5, no. 2, pp. 19–28.

Drummond, G. (1994) 'The Real Thing', *Supermarketing*, 30 September, pp. 20–2.

Dunne, D. and Chakravarthi, N. (1999) 'The New Appeal of Private Labels', *Harvard Business Review*, vol. 77, no. 3, pp. 41–8.

El-Amir, A. and Burt, S. (2010) 'Towards Modelling the Retailer as a Brand: A Social Construction of the Grocery Store from the Customer Standpoint', *Brand Management*, vol. 17, no. 6, pp. 429–45.

Euromonitor (2000) *Retail Trade International* (London: Euromonitor).

Fashion.telegraph.co.uk (2011) Live stream: Topshop Unique autumn/winter 2011 show from London Fashion Week, http://fashion.telegraph.co.uk/videos/TMG8333663/Live-stream-Topshop-Unique-autumnwinter-2011-show-from-London-Fashion-Week.html, 18 February [accessed 19 August 2013].

Grocer (1998) 'Imitation Has Limitations', 25 April, pp. 45–6.

Hobson, S. (1994) 'The Year of the Own-Label', *Supermarketing*, 14 January, pp. 22–3.

Intellectual Property Office (2013) 'The Impact of Lookalikes' (Newport: The Intellectual Property Office), available at www.ipo.gov.uk, 1 April [accessed 20 August 2013].

Kapferer, J.-N. (2012) *The New Strategic Brand Management*, 5th Edition (London: Kogan Page).

Kent, T. (2003) '2D23D: Management and Design Perspectives on Retail Branding', *International Journal of Retail and Distribution Management*, vol. 31, no. 3, pp. 131–42.

Lewis, J. (1994) 'Lords Back Owners against Retailers', *Marketing*, 3 March 1994, pp. 16–7.

McColl, J. and Moore, C. (2011) 'An Exploration of Fashion Retailer Own Brand Strategies', *Journal of Fashion Marketing and Management*, vol. 15, no. 1, pp. 91–107.

McGoldrick, P. J. (2002) *Retail Marketing*, 2nd Edition (Maidenhead: McGraw-Hill).

Mintel (2011) 'Private Label Food and Drink UK Report March 2011', http://store.mintel.com/private-label-food-and-drink-uk-march-2011 [accessed 20 August 2013].

Mitchell, R., Hutchinson, K. and Bishop, S. (2012) 'Interpretation of the Retail Brand: An SME Perspective', *International Journal of Retail and Distribution Management*, vol. 40, no. 2, pp. 157–75.

Mullany, A. (2013) 'Customize the Catwalk: Topshop and Facebook Partner on a Social Runway for London Fashion Week', www.fastcocreate.com/1681593/ [accessed 20 August 2013].

Myers, C. A. (2003) 'Managing Brand Equity; a Look at the Impact of Attributes', *Journal of Product and Brand Management*, vol. 12, no. 1, pp. 39–51.

Pellegrini, L. (1993) 'Retailer Brands: A State of the Art Review', *Proceedings of the 7th International Conference on Research in the Distributive Trades*, Institute for Retail Studies, University of Stirling, Stirling, 6–8 September, pp. 348–63.

Quelch, J. A. and Harding, D. (1996) 'Brands versus Private Labels: Fighting to Win', *Harvard Business Review*, vol. 74, no. 1 (January–February), pp. 99–109.

Rafiq, M. and Collins, R. (1996) 'Lookalikes and Customer Confusion in the Grocery Sector: An Exploratory Survey', *International Review of Retail, Distribution and Consumer Research*, vol. 6, no. 4 (October), pp. 329–50.

Rafiq, M. and Kirkup, M. H. (1999) 'Role of Own Brands in Retailer Branding Strategies', in L. Hildebrandt and D. Annacker (eds), *Proceedings of the 28th EMAC Conference* (Humboldt University: Berlin) (May).

Richardson, P. S., Dick, A. S. and Jain, A. K. (1994) 'Extrinsic and Intrinsic Cue Effects on Perceptions of Store Brand Quality', *Journal of Marketing*, vol. 58, no. 10 (October), pp. 28–36.

Ruddick, G. (2013) 'Walking Back to Happiness for Marks & Spencer?', *Telegraph*, http://www.telegraph.co.uk/finance/newsbysector/retailandconsumer/9975955/Walking-back-to-happiness-for-Marks-and-Spencer.html [accessed 6 April 2013].

Simmons, M. and Meredith, W. (1984) 'Own Label Profile and Purpose', *Journal of the Market Research Society*, vol. 26, no. 1, pp. 3–27.

Supermarketing (1994c) 'Classic Cola Boosts JS Own-Label Sales by 50%', 13 May, p. 16.

Uncles, M. D. (1994) 'Just How Different Are Retail Lookalikes from Traditional Me-Toos?', *Journal of Brand Management*, vol. 2, no. 4, pp. 204–7.

Wileman, A. and Jary, M. (1997) *Retail Power Plays: From Trading to Brand Leadership* (Basingstoke: Macmillan Business).

13 RETAIL PRICING

LEARNING OBJECTIVES

- To understand the relationship between price, cost and value, in a retail context.
- To appreciate the contribution that pricing makes to a retailer's overall market positioning.
- To explore alternative pricing strategies, and their suitability for different retail formats.
- To understand both long-term and short-term pricing strategies, and their relationship to retailers' objectives.
- To explore the notion of profitability from both product and store viewpoints, and to relate profit analysis to pricing.
- To introduce established frameworks that have been developed in order to gain an understanding of the complexity of pricing decisions.

INTRODUCTION

Pricing is a highly sensitive issue, for both retailers and consumers. In an era where pricing regulation has diminished, and price changes can be implemented instantaneously, retailers have considerable control over the prices that they offer to their customers. On the other hand, consumers are knowledgeable, well informed and confident, and when they can, they will seek out alternative retail outlets if they feel that they are paying over the odds. Online retailing has resulted in a higher level of price transparency for customers and for many purchases; the use of like for like product/price comparison sites is now ubiquitous. Pricing is a management issue, because of the unavoidable relationship between pricing and profitability, and pricing requires operational support in terms of price decision implementation, including shelf marking, point of purchase communications and product ticketing. Finally, pricing is also a strategic marketing management tool; playing an important part in both the formation of the retail brand image and competitive activity.

SETTING RETAIL PRICES

Unless a retailer is setting extremely aggressive promotional prices, the prices of goods sold in a retail outlet are higher than the price paid to the retail supplier. The difference between the two is the gross profit margin, often referred to as the markup. The gross margin can be expressed as a percentage of the cost price of the product, or more commonly as a percentage of the selling price. Gross margin level varies greatly between retail outlet types and between product categories. For example a supermarket may only apply a markup of a fraction of a per cent to some of their grocery product lines, whereas clothing retailers frequently operate on the basis of a gross margin of more than 100 per cent. The reasons for these variations will become clear in this chapter.

Retail costs

The prices that retailers pay for their supplies are only one of the many costs that have to be covered by the selling price of the product. Unless a retailer has other sources of income, the gross profit margin has to cover the costs of wages, the costs of distribution for multiple retailers, the running costs of the outlet including rent, rates and maintenance for store-based retailers and customer ordering centres for non-store retailers, the costs of running a central office and the costs associated with marketing activities such as advertising. The higher these costs are, the more pressure there is on the retailer to raise their gross profit margins to be able to contribute a net profit margin, which can then be used for reinvestment into the business, for example to pay for refurbishments, for overseas expansion or for rewarding shareholders. Different approaches to costing and profit assessment are discussed later in this chapter.

Price and demand

Traditional economic theory places emphasis on the relationship between the price charged for a product and the resulting demand for that product, and whilst an understanding of these general principles is important for retailers, this theory concentrates on an individual product item rather than viewing pricing within the context of a product range, and branded goods, thus ignoring the complexity of retail pricing from both the retailer and the consumer viewpoints.

The economist's view

In most product categories, demand rises as prices fall, whilst less is bought if prices rise, giving an inverse relationship between price and quantity demanded, as shown in Figure 13.1.

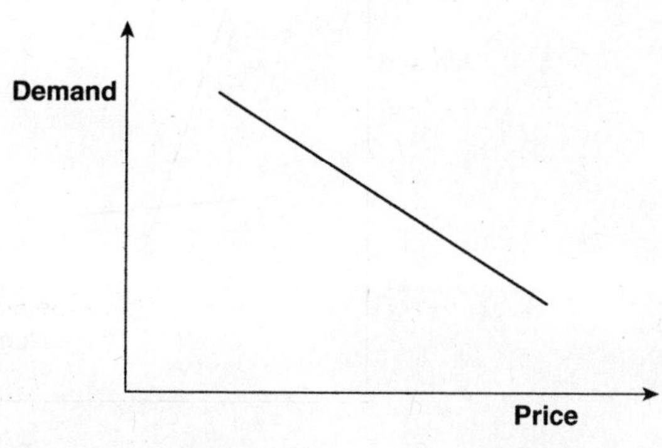

Figure 13.1 The relationship between price and demand

Some products are more sensitive to price changes than others. For example, even if the price of salt doubled, it is unlikely that the demand for salt would alter much. Likewise if the price for salt fell, it is unlikely that customers would buy much more (apart from perhaps on a temporary basis in order to stockpile). Salt therefore has a demand that is said to be inelastic, and unresponsive to price changes. Other products, however, have a much more 'elastic' demand, where sales are responsive to price fluctuations (Vignette 13.1). Demand for discretionary purchases such as clothing and home entertainment systems is more sensitive to price fluctuations. Figure 13.2 illustrates these differences.

VIGNETTE 13.1 THE LIPSTICK EFFECT

It is often assumed that during economic downturns all retailers will be adversely affected, but this is not the case. Expensive purchases such as cars, furniture and carpets may be postponed indefinitely but trading down rather than stopping spending is how most consumers prefer to act. Whilst mid-market retailers tend to suffer in recessions, the value and discount end of the market prospers, and small luxury items that 'cheer you up' (like lipstick and accessories) are bought more often. According to Elliot (2008) the 'lipstick effect' can be traced back to the Great Depression of the 1930s in the United States, when production fell by a half but the sales of cosmetics rose. The response to the economic downturn in 2008 was a healthy sales rise of around 5 per cent for the branded cosmetics producer L'Oreal. Even the retail giants have to fight hard to keep customers spending in recessionary times. In order to deter their shoppers from defecting to the discount sector, Tesco introduced a small range of lower-priced, house-branded goods (different from Tesco's own label – see Chapter 12) in August 2008. The items were modelled on the house-branded products of discount supermarkets such as Aldi and Lidl and were promoted with the strapline 'Tesco: Britain's Biggest Discounter'. Even Marks and Spencer, one of the highest-price food retailers, launched their 'Dine In for Two for £10' offers in response to expenditure cutting, highlighting a favourable price comparison with eating out in a restaurant.

Source: Elliot, 2008

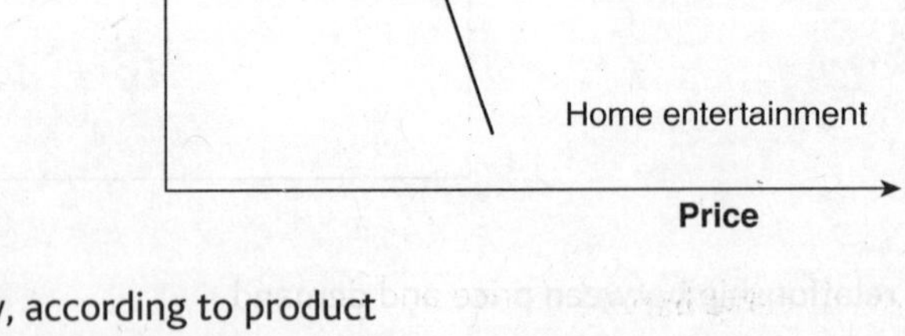

Figure 13.2 Demand elasticity, according to product

PRICE IN THE RETAIL MARKETING MIX

Ever since the abolition of the resale price maintenance legislation in 1964, UK retailers of most consumer goods have had the freedom to set their own prices, and have therefore been able to use pricing as a powerful marketing weapon. The wheel of increasing multiple retailer dominance (Figure 13.3) shows the combined effect on the industry of retailer-controlled pricing and the acceptance by consumers of lower-cost retail formats like the self-service supermarket (De Chernatony, McDonald and Wallace, 2011).

Prices are a visible and highly sensitive part of the retail marketing mix, and have a direct relationship with a retailer's profitability. However, prices are subject to individual interpretation in terms of value representation, and so are deeply affected by consumer behaviour. Value is an individual's interpretation of worth, and therefore measures the relationship between the price being charged for an item and the benefits received.

When it comes to making a purchase, most consumers work within price thresholds (Figure 13.4); if the price of an item rises above the upper price threshold, the consumer will not buy, perhaps choosing a substitute product or making do without the benefits that the product would bring. On the other hand, the consumer will normally work to a lower price threshold, under which they would not purchase a product because of concerns about product quality or the method of production.

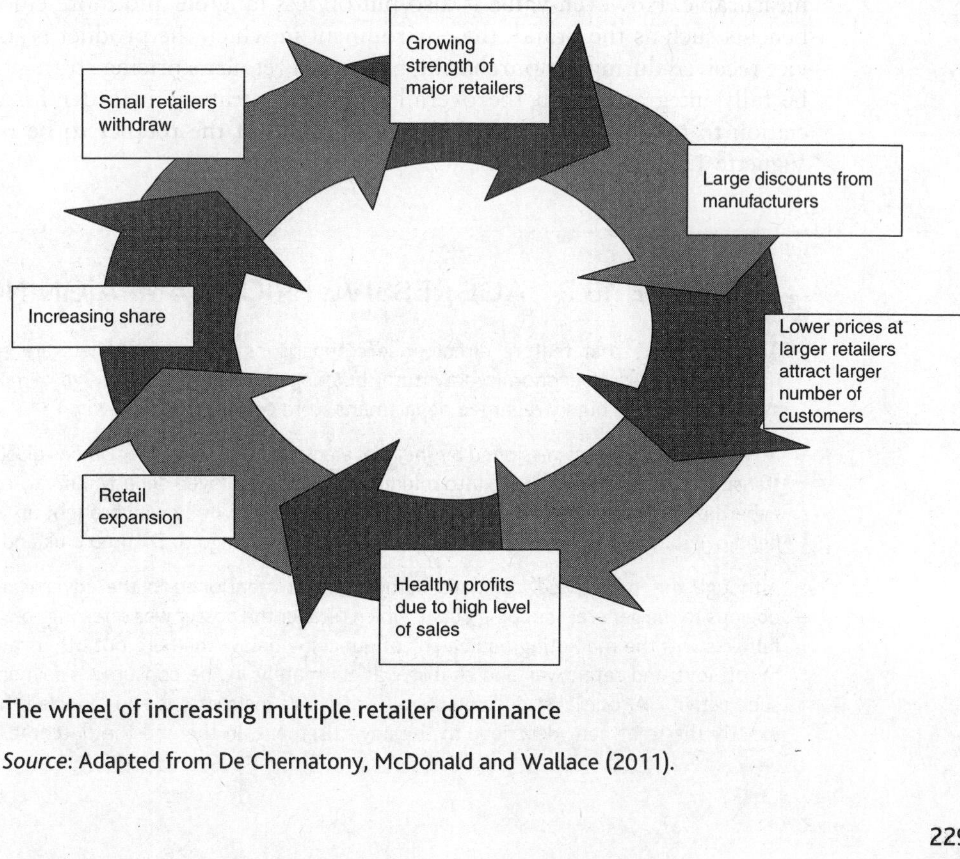

Figure 13.3 The wheel of increasing multiple retailer dominance

Source: Adapted from De Chernatony, McDonald and Wallace (2011).

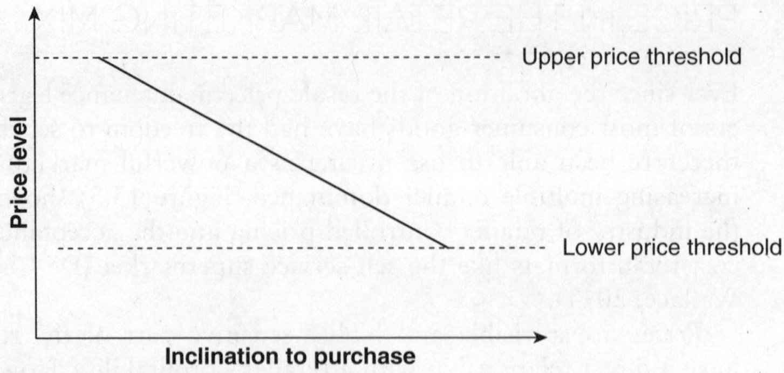

Figure 13.4 Price thresholds

The original purpose of retailers' own-label products (see Chapter 12) was to offer a low-cost variant, and as such they were perceived as lower quality. However, as retailer–supplier partnerships have developed and quality assurance improved, own-label products have been sold less on the basis of price, and more on the basis of quality and product innovation. Now many own-label products are perceived as being as good quality as the proprietary brand equivalent.

The benefits a consumer derives from a product bought in a retail outlet include physical attributes such as quality and functional features, which are tangible and measurable. However, value is also put on less tangible and more emotional product benefits such as the brand, the environment in which the product is sold and the service received during the purchasing process. A retailer's pricing strategy must therefore be fully integrated with the overall marketing strategy, in order for a value appreciation to take place and the price positioning of the retailer to be understood (see Vignette 13.2).

VIGNETTE 13.2 AGGRESSIVE PRICE CAMPAIGNING

Advertisements that feature direct price comparisons between retailers are seen more frequently in times of economic downturn, but one particularly aggressive campaign caused a storm at the UK's highly regarded department store company John Lewis.

An advertisement commissioned by the rival electronic goods retailer Dixons displayed on public transport read as follows: 'Step into middle England's best loved department store, stroll through haberdashery to the audio visual department, where an awfully well brought up young man will bend over backwards to single out a TV for you. And then go to Dixons.co.uk and buy it.'

Although the 'best loved' retailer's name was not mentioned in the advertising copy, it was obvious to the general shopping public which retailer the poster was referring to. Some observers felt this was the marketing equivalent of punching below the belt, but others argued that all's fair in love and retail war and that it was ultimately in the consumer's favour to encourage such activity. A journalist decided to follow Dixon's instructions and reported that he received exactly the treatment described in the advertisement. In the end the outcome for John Lewis was excellent, their reputation enhanced, free column inches in the press gained and the impression given that their long-standing reliability and excellent service can beat off tactical snipes by a struggling competitor. However, the competitive action also quickened the pace towards John Lewis extending its famous 'never knowingly undersold' price pledge to the online retail world.

Source: BBC 2 (2010)

For most consumers, price is only one element of all the things that provide value in the shopping experience. Location convenience, choice, lack of stress, pleasure, time efficiency and safety assurance are shopping variables that customers are willing to pay higher prices for. In addition, consumers are increasingly aware of unethical business and manufacturing practices in the supply chain that can result in products being very cheaply produced but thereby undesirable.

PRICE COMPETITION

Whilst an unregulated economy allows retailers to set prices as they see fit, a saturated retail market exerts considerable competitive pressure on retail pricing strategies. Where customers have a choice of outlet, offering the lowest price is an easily understood and effective marketing strategy. It is, nevertheless, a strategy that is easy for competitors to match, particularly in the short term. Price competition on a large scale can lead to price wars, where retailers cut their margins very low in order to maintain a competitive edge; however, price wars have a negative effect on profits of all the players in the industry, and are therefore avoided by retailers. In fact highly concentrated retail sectors such as grocery in the UK have been suspected of maintaining prices artificially high and have been investigated for uncompetitive behaviour in relation to pricing practices; however, evidence of anything other than competitive action that benefits the consumer has been very limited (Competition Commission, 2000, 2008).

PRICING STRATEGY

A retail pricing strategy usually operates on two levels. The first is the general approach to the overall pricing level, which positions the retailer in the market. For example, consider the price positioning of Lidl, Tesco and Selfridges Food Hall. Each retail outlet has a clear position when it comes to price: Lidl is a 'discount supermarket' offering extremely low prices; Tesco operates a medium-level 'value-for-money' approach to prices; and Selfridges is clearly in the category of retailers that takes a premium-pricing approach. Of course, these retailers have completely different retail marketing strategies and do not compete directly with one another; however, it is possible to buy food in all three outlets, and it is their long-term pricing strategy that most clearly sets them apart.

The second level of a retailer's pricing strategy is tactical. This usually relates to the need to manipulate prices to achieve specific short-term objectives such as an introductory price for a new product line, a defensive price cut in reaction to competitive threat or price discounts to clear redundant stock. The long-term market position pricing strategies will be considered first, followed by a discussion of tactical pricing techniques and short-term pricing considerations.

Long-term pricing strategies

Premium pricing

Retailers that operate a premium pricing strategy use sources other than price as differentiating factors in their retail marketing mix. High product quality and augmented customer services often go hand in hand with a premium pricing strategy, and consumers who value these aspects of the retail mix will not be deterred by the higher prices that need to be charged to cover the extra costs incurred by the retailer. In fact, many customers will gain psychological benefits associated with the symbolic status of shopping in such retailers. Retailers that use premium pricing include the department store Harvey Nichols (upmarket and fashion forward), the specialist store Fired Earth (tiles and furnishing fabrics) and the food store Whole Foods Market.

Seasonal pricing

Retailers who sell goods with a seasonal factor, such as clothing, will often need to add a time dimension to their pricing strategy. Where products have a tendency to become obsolete quickly, it is important for retailers to sell them while they still have some value to customers. Making decisions about when to drop prices is one of the most difficult areas of retail management, balancing the need for higher turnover with a reduction in profitability. Seasonal pricing strategies involve selling products at 'full price', and then 'marking down' or reducing the standard price of the product in an 'end-of-season sale'. For many retailers the sale period will attract a different customer profile because a wider band of consumers are able or willing to pay the reduced prices. This strategy is often referred to as a high–low pricing strategy. The selling of fresh produce involves a shorter-time-frame high–low pricing strategy.

A markdown is a reduction in the selling price, where the original price is displayed alongside the new price. In the UK a product should have been on sale at the original price for a period of 28 consecutive days in the previous 6 months in order for the markdown to be referred to as a price 'reduction' (Consumer Protection Approval Order 2005). Markdowns inevitably mean a reduction in profitability for the retailer; however, the extent of the loss is related to the amount of markdown taken and the volume of product requiring markdown. For example it is difficult for a clothing retailer to avoid having a few odd sizes and colours left at the end of the season, and a small markdown is likely to shift those that are left, but if a garment does not fit properly it may be necessary to take a large markdown on a very large volume of product items, cutting deeply into the retailer's profits.

In contrast to a markdown or price reduction, some items are sold at a very low price from day one. These offers may be referred to as a 'special purchase', and are usually the result of a supplier offering a retailer a special price for an item, which in turn is passed on to the consumer by the retailer. This type of product is sometimes offered alongside reduced-price merchandise in an end-of-season sale, so that the retailer can capitalize on a high volume of bargain-seeking store traffic.

Everyday low pricing

Many of the retailers who have undergone significant growth in the last two decades use 'everyday low pricing' (EDLP). Retailers who operate this policy, often referred to as value retailers, strive to offer very competitive prices on all of their product range, all of the time. Instead of the high–low variation of seasonal pricing, prices are kept low all the time and are normally only discounted when the product line is discontinued. EDLP is a popular strategy with the majority of retail customers because they feel they are receiving a fair deal; the pricing message is straightforward rather than being bound up in a complicated array of product/price offers (Vignette 13.3). It is not, however, an appropriate strategy for retailers who take risks with their product range, when it makes more sense to skim off profits on winning product items to pay for the markdowns on losers. EDLP makes it necessary for retailers to keep their selling costs low in order to maintain the pricing strategy as well as make a profit, and so they are less able to offer added value in terms of additional services and the store environment. The introduction of online retailing has put an additional emphasis on the need to be competitive, with price comparison sites such as Kelkoo, Price Checker, MoneySuperMarket and Shopzilla offering customers highly convenient price-checking services.

VIGNETTE 13.3 POUNDLAND: ENGINEERING PRODUCTS TO THE SINGLE-PRICE OFFER

Poundland is the biggest, single-price discount retailer in the UK, and its very straightforward retail formula of everything costing a pound is very appealing, especially in times of diminished disposable income. With over 400 stores in the UK and expansion into Europe planned, Poundland has a growing customer base in geographic terms, but also demographically; according to Morrell (2008) the number of customers from socio-economic groups A and B increased from 9 per cent to 11 per cent.

Poundland sell leading national brands alongside unknown makes in the typically 3,000-strong product offer, and because of the volume sold the company is able to work with suppliers to engineer products to the necessary £1 price point. For example, the company varies the number of batteries in a multi-pack according to the price of zinc, a major component in a battery. When the commodity price of zinc rises the number of batteries in a pack falls, and when the price falls the packs gets bigger, but to the customer the price of the pack is still one pound!

Source: Morrel (2008), Poundland.com (2013)

Entry prices

The term entry price is one that is often used in the context of product range management, and refers to the lowest-price offer within a merchandise category. For example the entry price for men's jeans at a fashion retailer may be £10, for a very basic pair of own-brand western style, regular stonewashed denims. From that entry price point, more value-added designs and branded jeans move upwards on price. Entry prices may be emphasized in promotional activity, and are likely to be price-checked regularly by competitors in their comparison research.

Discount pricing

Discount pricing is different from everyday low pricing, in that the retailer offers products at prices lower than the average high-street price. Retailers that are referred to as discounters vary in character. The term includes 'off-price' retailers who do not have continuity in their product range, giving an 'Aladdin's cave' appeal to the outlet. In contrast, discount supermarkets, or 'hard discounters' maintain a relatively consistent but limited range of products at very low prices. Discount retailing often involves selling 'seconds'-quality goods, ends of lines and previous season's merchandise, and is the basis of the 'factory outlet' retail concept which enjoyed healthy growth in the UK and the United States in the 1990s (Fernie and Fernie, 1997). A more recent retail development is the auction website, which allows customers to bid online for new or second-hand products. The phenomenal growth of the eBay organization is testimony to the appeal of the discount format, and their recent move into brand discounting via eBay outlet provides online competition to the factory outlet sector.

Pricing tactics

Within a long-term pricing strategy, a retailer may use pricing tactics that they believe will have a positive effect on the consumer. For example, a frequently used tactic is to set a price point at £X.99, so that psychologically a customer feels that a product is under the rounded pound price. In particular, price points such as £9.99 and £19.99 and £99.99 may be very effective for communicating the availability of products at low or good-value prices. However, other retailers feel that a rounded pound is a clearer price offer to their customers and is simpler to administer from a retail operations viewpoint. One widely held view is that forcing a sales associate to give a penny change from the till discouraged employee theft, a procedure that is less relevant in an increasingly cashless shopping society. Another pricing tactic that ties in with range planning (see Chapter 11) is the use of price lining. Here, a retailer will offer a selection of products at what they see as key price points for the product category. This activity is sometimes referred to as building a price architecture and is important in order to make the product offer more logical and meaningful to customers in terms of added value in a product for a particular price. A drawback associated with gearing products to selling prices may place restrictions on retail buyers, and could result in sales opportunities being missed for products that do not 'fit' into the pricing structure.

A retailer may offer a 'leading' price for a 'known-value' product item, again in order to communicate a best-value offer. Supermarkets use bread for this purpose, keeping the price of a basic white loaf at an extremely competitive price so that the rest of the shopping basket is viewed as well priced in accordance. The retailer is prepared to make little or no profit on these leading products in order to attract customers who will then buy other, more profitable items. Different products have different price sensitivities; in fact, research (McGoldrick et al., 1999, Evanschitzky et al., 2004) has shown that many customers have very low recall levels of most grocery items, but high-profile products like bread or milk are likely to be compared between competing outlets.

Short-term pricing tactics

The pricing strategies that have been described so far in this chapter have been ones concerning the overall price positioning of the retailer. They indicate to customers the kind of level of prices that can be expected in that particular outlet, and they reflect the rest of the retail marketing strategy. However, retailers also use a number of short-term pricing practices in order to boost the sales of particular products, or as defensive action in the face of competition.

Loss-leader pricing

This is a more radical version of the low-, known-value price tactic. Here the price is cut to an extremely low, or even loss-making level, and then heavily advertised in order to gain consumer interest. Sometimes referred to as predatory pricing, loss-leader pricing by its nature is a short-term strategy, and is usually only used in cases of extreme competitive action. One of its drawbacks is that this type of offer appeals particularly to bargain hunters, who are unlikely to become loyal customers and who will stockpile items, leaving the shelves empty for other customers, who then feel cheated by the advertising or publicity. One of the findings of the 2000 Competition Commission enquiry was that some supermarket groups sell a small number of products consistently at below-cost prices, and this was deemed to be unfair to smaller retail operators; however, a subsequent report, published in 2008, suggested that the pattern of below-cost selling by large grocery retailers did not represent predatory behaviour in relation to other retailers and that because much of this type of activity was temporary, it may benefit consumers by reducing the average price of a basket of goods across the grocery sector.

Multi-buy and linked purchase offers

In the retailing of fast-moving consumer goods, offers like 'buy one, get one free' (BOGOF) or 'buy A, get B half-price' are commonplace. They are particularly effective for introducing new products, boosting sales of particular product brands and categories on a short-term basis, increasing the value of each transaction and encouraging linked sales. Offering a variety of price promotions that clearly benefit the consumer will have a positive effect on an overall retail image; however, if the benefits of the promotions are not clear to the consumer, then promotional activity can be perceived as a waste of time, merely adding clutter to the store. Boots, for example, is famous for its two-for-one and three-for-two offers which encourage multiple purchases of specific items on a short-term basis, and contribute to the generation of a loyal customer base on a long-term basis (see Chapter 14).

Loyalty schemes

Many loyalty schemes are based on the premise that a price discount can be obtained by frequent visits to the same retailer. Some store cards offer a percentage discount once a particular level of spending has been achieved within a specified time period. Others provide some kind of cash or discount reward that accumulates over time. In 1995 Tesco launched the Clubcard, a tool that offered a combination of short-term rewards like vouchers and long-term benefits such as air miles or discounts on high-price ticket items. The chip-enabled card also enabled the company to link into a customer database. Having initially derided the idea of a national loyalty card as a gimmick, J Sainsbury launched its 'Reward' loyalty card a year later. ASDA, in the meantime, kept with its ASDA Price promotional campaign, and despite going through the process of trialling a loyalty card in a restricted number of stores, decided against a nationwide rollout. In 1999 ASDA even referred to the findings of a consumer survey conducted by Mintel as a basis for their in-store promotional message 'customers prefer low prices to loyalty schemes'. In 2002 Sainsbury's updated their loyalty scheme with the launch of the Nectar card, through which points are collected initially in their own supermarkets, in Debenhams department stores, at BP petrol retailers and through Barclaycard finance company. The points can be spent in a variety of ways, including popular leisure destinations and fast-food outlets. Increased flexibility in the collection and spending of loyalty points clearly appeals to customers, but most research concludes that it does not really increase loyalty. To date ASDA still do not have a stand-alone loyalty card although in 2011 the supermarket launched a credit card with loyalty incentives (Halliwell and Quinn, 2012).

Many loyalty schemes fall into demise due to the cost of administration in comparison to increased spending or tangible increase in loyalty. However, Tesco, Boots and Sainsbury's have benefited hugely from the understanding of shopping behaviour based on the analysis of individual purchasing cross-referenced to personal data (often referred to as data mining). This has led to increased sophistication in personalized and finely targeted promotional activity.

RETAIL PROFITABILITY

Whilst the overall price level in the retail outlet and price promotions are likely to be managed by the centralized buying and marketing departments of a retailer within the framework of a long-term strategy, the profit performance of most retailers is measured both by product and by store/outlet. Product profitability is a key responsibility of the buyers and merchandisers who manage the product ranges offered within each outlet (see Chapter 11); they will be working to profit targets set for each product line and/or product category, and so pricing, markdown levels and promotional activity are all integral to a retail product manager's remit, as well as controlling the buying-in cost of products by negotiating keenly with suppliers. Profitability in terms of the retail outlet relates to the relationship between sales made in the outlet and its running costs. This will be considered after product profitability.

Product profitability

Product profitability can be measured in a number of ways, which vary in degrees of complexity. The simplest measure is the gross profit margin of the product, often referred to as the markup as discussed earlier in this chapter. At one time the use of a uniform percentage markup was commonplace in retailing because it was simple to administer; however, the gross margin does not account for the level of sales generated on a product and the effect that the rate of sales has on the actual value of the profit contribution of different products. Table 13.1 illustrates this point.

A measure that overcomes the shortcomings of the uniform markup is the gross margin return on investment (GMROI), illustrated in Table 13.2. It is calculated by multiplying the gross margin percentage with the sales turnover ratio (for a specified time period). The GMROI measure effectively assesses whether a product earns its placing on a shelf, in terms of sales generated by investment in the stock.

One of the drawbacks of using GMROI to measure product profitability is that whilst it takes the sales turnover of a product into account, it does not allow for any of the retail costs associated with displaying and selling the product. The costs of selling a can of beans are assumed to be the same as the costs of selling a packet of frozen peas, but clearly the costs involved in selling a frozen product are higher than those of an ambient product: the fixturing is more expensive, the storage and transportation of the product are more expensive and the wages of the people who work in a 'freezer' environment (for example at a retailer's distribution centre) are higher than those for people who work in ambient conditions.

Through the 1980s in both the United States and Europe, a considerable amount of progress was made on making individual product profitability measures. As the opportunities to collect, store and analyse costing data became possible with improvements in data processing technology, so the profit implications of retailing different products became clearer. In effect, a profit and loss account could be generated for every product line within the product range, and by making adjustments to the product and its handling through the supply chain to display within the store, opportunities to improve direct product profitability (DPP) were taken.

A further refinement to the costing of products can be made by using activity-based costing (ABC). Here, not only are the direct product costs taken into account, but also an attempt is made to allocate indirect costs according to the activity required to source and manage that product. So, for example, instead of an overseas buying trip being absorbed into the general costs associated with the running of a buying office,

Table 13.1 Uniform markup

Product	Price (£)	Gross margin (£)	Gross margin (%)	Sales turnover	Profit contribution
Wine	4.00	1.00	25	5	5.00
Chocolates	4.00	1.00	25	1	1.00

Table 13.2 GMROI

Product	Gross margin (%)	Turnover ratio	GMROI (%)
Milk	10	12.5	125
Cola	12.5	10.0	125
Wine	25	5	125

the expenses of the trip would be charged to the product(s) that were sourced from the overseas market. The number of retailers who have the capability to refine costing data to this extent is limited, and the competitive nature of the industry means that retailers tend to focus on income generation for profitability rather than cost analysis.

OUTLET PROFITABILITY

As mentioned earlier, retail profitability is generally measured at both the product level and the outlet level. In order to implement some of the more aggressive pricing strategies mentioned earlier in this chapter, it is necessary to have strict control over the costs of running an outlet. Staffing costs are invariably the highest store cost, with rent or lease payments, rates, maintenance and refurbishment, heating, lighting and security all having to be covered. Some stores in a retailer's portfolio will have higher costs than others; for example high employment levels in the south-east of the UK inflate the level of wages for sales associates, whereas retailers in managed shopping centres like Westfield, London, have to pay a contribution to the management and maintenance of the centre. There are also the additional distribution costs associated with outlets in far-flung locations. There is an argument, therefore, for charging different prices at different retail locations. However, geographic variation in pricing poses significant problems such as those associated with refunds for returned goods, and it can cause bad publicity. There is the possibility of retailers exploiting a local monopoly by means of premium geographical pricing, a practice that was considered against consumer interest in the Competition Commission's (2000) report.

Where alternative channels are used for retailing (for example store, website and direct mail), a retailer has to carefully balance the need to maintain consistent image across outlets with the requirement to match channel competitors and provide rewards to customers who use cheaper methods of retailing.

One of the obvious attractions of online retailing is that the costs of running the retail outlet are considerably reduced. There is no need for expensive 'high-street' rental charges, and all the costs associated with running and staffing a store are avoided. The technological know-how associated with online retailing is now more readily available, and the quality of consumers' experiences using transactional websites has improved enormously over the last decade. The retailer without physical stores can pass cost savings onto consumers via low prices, which makes online retailing very price competitive. Nevertheless, in spite of the cost savings, online retailers still need to fund acquisition (supply-chain) costs, storage, packing and delivery (unless charged to the customer), and many online retailers that underestimated the cost and complexity of the infrastructure behind the website have run into difficulty. However, for multi-channel retailers there is less room for price flexibility. Shoppers expect a retail brand to have price integrity across its formats, and while 'online only' prices can help to generate cost-effective traffic, too much online discounting could begin to make the stores look expensive.

Perhaps the most pressing issue for online retailers is price transparency. The ease of comparison online means that customers are well informed on price, and especially for high-priced goods they are likely to have researched comparable items on price, attributes and benefits before coming face to face with a sales assistant. Mobile technology puts pricing information into consumers' hands at the point of sale, and so retailers that attempt to compete on price alone will need to undertake constant price monitoring of an increasing number of online offerings in order to maintain a leading position.

Many marketing textbooks propose a multi-stage approach to pricing, which is a useful framework for making pricing decisions about single items. In reality, most retail pricing decisions are more of a matter of fine-tuning prices within existing product ranges, and so a more appropriate framework for the analysis of retail pricing decisions is that proposed by McGoldrick (2002). This model is less concerned with the initial costing and demand aspects of pricing, and more focused on the complexity of pricing in a retail context, breaking down pricing into the four dimensions of time (for example seasonal markdowns), assortment (price architecture), comparison (with competitors) and geography. These dimensions have been explored within this chapter, and have implications for both short-term operational retail management and longer-term retail strategy.

SUMMARY

No matter what the economic situation, prices are central to consumer perceptions about and interest in retailers. Increased affluence does not make consumers less price sensitive; on the contrary, the ease of price comparison in online shopping has added to consumers' keen awareness of price and acute sense of value. It is therefore imperative that retail managers have an awareness of all the cost and profit implications of various decisions and actions relating to pricing and build an understanding of customers' price perceptions and reactions. Paradoxically, a large part of consumers' value appreciation involves many things other than price. In particular, shopping convenience, the right brand of product, a pleasant shopping environment and good customer service are all aspects of retailing that consumers are prepared to pay for, and so pricing cannot be isolated from the rest of the retail offer.

QUESTIONS

1. Explain the difference between 'price' and 'value'.
2. Outline the alternative long-term pricing strategy options that are available to retailers, indicating the type of retailer that might use the strategies you describe.
3. Discuss the concept of a 'promotional price'. To what extent would you consider a markdown to be a promotional price?
4. To what extent do you think online retailing has made customers more price sensitive?
5. Explain the meaning of the lipstick effect in relation to consumer spending in recession. How have you traded down in your shopping behaviour in times of financial hardship?

6. Conduct your own investigation into supermarket pricing within a grocery product category of your choice. In the light of your own investigation, do you think that the investigation by the Competition Commission (2000, 2008) was justified?
7. Maintaining low prices in the long term requires retailers to be keenly aware of cost control. Compare the *type* of costs that are incurred when using alternative retail formats.

REFERENCES AND FURTHER READING

BBC 2 Broadcast Inside John Lewis Episode 2, First broadcast 17 March 2010 http://www.bbc.co.uk/programmes/b00rhgx0/episodes/guide

Competition Commission (2000) *Supermarkets: A Report on the Supply of Groceries from Multiple Stores in the United Kingdom* (Norwich: The Stationery Office), available at http://webarchive.nationalarchives.gov.uk/+/http://www.competition-commission.org.uk/rep_pub/reports/2000/fulltext/446c3.pdf accessed 25 September 2013 Competition Commission (2008) *The supply of groceries in the UK market investigation* available at http://www.competition-commission.org.uk/assets/competitioncommission/docs/pdf/non-inquiry/rep_pub/reports/2008/fulltext/538 accessed 25 September 2013.

'The Consumer Protection (Code of Practice for Traders on Price Indications) Approval Order 2005' available http://www.legislation.gov.uk/uksi/2005/2705/made accessed 15 September 2013.

De Chernatony, L., McDonald, M. and Wallace, E. (2011) *Creating Powerful Brands* (Oxford: Butterworth-Heinemann).

Elliot, L. (2008) 'Into the Red: "Lipstick Effect" Reveals the True Face of the Recession', *Guardian*, 22 December.

Evanschitzky, H., Kenning, P. and Vogel, V. (2004) 'Consumer Price Knowledge in the German Retail Market', *Journal of Product and Brand Management*, vol. 13, no. 6, pp. 390–405.

Fernie, J. and Fernie, S. I. (1997) 'The Development of a US Retail Format in Europe: The Case of Factory Outlet Centres', *International Journal of Retail and Distribution Management*, vol. 25, no. 11, pp. 342–50.

Halliwell J. and Quinn, I. (2012) 'New Asda Card Ramps Up Loyalty Battle', *Grocer*, J July.

McGoldrick, P. J. (2002) *Retail Marketing* (Maidenhead: McGraw-Hill).

McGoldrick, P. J., Betts, E. J. and Wilson, A. F. (1999) 'Modelling Consumer Price Cognition: Evidence from Discount and Superstore Sectors', *Services Industries Journal*, vol. 9, no. 1, pp. 171–93.

Morrell, L. (2008) 'The Value Champion', *Mall Retailing*, November.

Poundland.co.uk (2013) 'Our History', http://www.poundland.co.uk/about-us/our-history/ [accessed 25 July 2013].

Walters, D. and Laffy, D. (1996) *Managing Retail Productivity and Profitability* (Basingstoke: Macmillan Business).

14 MANAGING RETAIL COMMUNICATIONS

LEARNING OBJECTIVES

- To distinguish between institutional and promotional objectives of retailers' communication programmes.
- To explore the differences between the communication objectives of retailers and those of manufacturers.
- To identify the elements of the retail communication mix and explore how they can be used to achieve the objectives of retailers.
- To understand how and why retailers and manufacturers cooperate on promotional campaigns.
- To understand the role of communications in influencing shopping behaviour.
- To appreciate the need for an integrated communications programme.

INTRODUCTION

As retailers strive to maintain credibility, their communications through various media have continued to increase in diversity in terms of the tools used and types of content and messages relayed. At one time it was manufacturer brands that dominated the relationship with the consumer and were the most active brand communicators; however, it is now easy for both retailers and producers to have direct and interactive relationships with existing and potential customers. Online retailing has changed the role of the retailer as intermediary, and now the website seamlessly brings together marketing communications and retail activity in one place, and acts as a facilitator for retailers and consumers to engage in immediate 'conversations'. Online retail space can now be considered a virtual brand medium through which customers interact, with the retailer and each other.

Although the main purpose of many retailer brand communications is to generate demand for a retailer's products, and move customers through the stages of the buying process, retailers also send messages that are more concerned with building long-term relationships with consumers, focusing on corporate image. This chapter will explore all the major elements of the retail communications mix used to manage these communications, namely advertising, sales promotions, public relations and personal selling. Loyalty schemes, database marketing and other customer relationship management techniques were discussed in Chapter 8 given their reliance on information technology. These are internal vehicles for many ways in which retailers communicate with customers, but the purpose of this chapter is to discuss how retailers manage the wider promotional mix to achieve their short-term promotional and long-term strategic objectives.

MARKETING COMMUNICATIONS OBJECTIVES

The objectives of marketing communications for retailers can be broadly be divided into those aimed at improving long-term performance (strategic objectives) and those aimed at improving short-term performance (operational objectives). Two main areas of strategic objectives normally apply to retailers, namely those related to image and market positioning and those relating to a retailer's role as a public service and their corporate social responsibility.

Retail image and market positioning objectives are intended to establish and reinforce the positive image and position relative to competitors, which the retailer wants to project in the customer's mind, with a view to creating and maintaining customer loyalty. Other long-term objectives relate to enhancing the retailer's reputation as a good citizen in the community, and to building customer goodwill towards the retailer. Many retailers have initiatives that are designed to help their local communities in the areas of health, education and the environment. For instance, since 2008 every large Waitrose supermarket branch has divided a donation of £1,000 each month between three local good causes that customers choose by placing a token in a box that represents a particular local organization in need. The more tokens a cause gets, the bigger the donation they receive. This is reflected by a similar online initiative where every 3 months Waitrose.com shares a donation of £25,000 between three national causes (www.waitrose.com, 2012). Increasing numbers of environmental initiatives such as recycling, reducing packaging and energy reduction are being implemented by retailers (McKinnon et al., 2010), and fair treatment of suppliers is also important for the retail image. Such initiatives are designed to create goodwill amongst the retailer's different constituencies – customers, the local community, employees and suppliers.

Short-term operational objectives can be divided into those aimed at increasing patronage from existing customers, and those aimed at attracting new customers. The latter can be further subdivided into those aimed at attracting new customers from the retailer's existing trade area, and those aimed at expanding the trade area by, for example, encouraging the use of an online shopping facility. Increased patronage from existing customers involves the use of promotional activity to encourage them to increase their expenditure with the retailer.

The selection of communication tools used in the pursuit of short- and long-term objectives has increased as the Internet continues to offer more variations using digital media. Traditional media such as television, print and billboards effectively carry messages from retailers to customers, whereas the Internet facilitates two-way communications between retailers and their customers, providing an additional dimension of interaction with individuals (see Table 14.1). While each element of a communications mix has individual characteristics that makes it more or less appropriate in specific

Table 14.1 Online implementation of communication tools (extended mix)

Communication tool	Online implementation
Advertising	Interactive display advertisements, pay per click, search advertising
Personal selling	Virtual sales staff, website merchandising, chat facilities and affiliate marketing; linked sale suggestions
Sales promotion	Incentives such as coupons, rewards, online loyalty schemes, social networks
Public relations	Online editorial, blogs, feeds, e-newsletters, social networks, links and viral campaigns
Sponsorship	Sponsoring an online event, site or service
Direct mail	Opt-in email using e-letters and e-blasts (stand-alone emails)
Exhibitions/events	Virtual exhibitions and white paper distribution; streamlined shows
Merchandising	Promotional ad serving on retail sites, personalized recommendations and e-alerts
Packaging	Virtual tours, real packaging displayed online
Word of mouth	Social networks, viral, affiliate marketing, email a friend, links, social shopping

Source: Based on Chaffey (2009), table 8.8, p. 462

circumstances, the concepts of integration and cohesion across the mix are important to prevent mixed or confused messages.

ADVERTISING

With the low comparative cost of online advertising and the continued importance of advertising in traditional media, this tool remains a heavily used method for relaying controlled messages to targeted groups of consumers. Advertising is a paid-for non-personal communication by a retailer through various media with a view to informing and/or persuading existing and potential customers regarding itself, and the products and services that it provides. Newspapers, magazines, billboards, radio, television and direct mail are the most frequently used offline advertising media by retailers, and these are now usually supported by Internet-based campaigns. The function of advertising is, primarily, to inform potential customers of the benefits of the retailer's offering, to develop the customer's preference for the retailer and to encourage purchasing activity.

There are two basic types of retail advertising: corporate and promotional. Corporate advertising focuses on the retailer as an organization and is designed to build and reinforce the retail brand. Its purpose is to improve long-term performance overall. Promotional advertising, on the other hand, attempts to improve short-term performance by focusing on the products that the retailer is selling and/or its prices. However, this dichotomy is somewhat superficial; promotional advertising needs to be delivered in a way that supports the retail brand. For example, in May 2012, UK general merchandise retailer Marks and Spencer launched a new range of low-priced grocery items under the sub-brand name 'Simply M&S' in order to encourage customers to use Marks and Spencer as their main grocery shop destination rather than a place to buy treats. The advertisement campaign that supported the launch used the strapline 'M&S quality now at prices you'll love', thereby maintaining the company's focus on quality while emphasizing the low price of the range (Russell, 2012).

Retailer and manufacturer advertising strategies

It has to be remembered that retailers are not alone in advertising to consumers; in fact, the highest expenditure on advertising to consumers tends to be producers rather than retailers. However, the communication objectives and the advertising strategies are quite different, and this can be a source of conflict between the two parties.

First, retail advertising often focuses on the short term and is used to publicize promotions and store initiatives (such as seasonal sales) designed to generate immediate sales uplift across a range of products. Manufacturer advertising, on the other hand, tends to have a long-term focus and is aimed at promoting and building the image of a product brand. Retail advertising is usually aimed at attracting customers to the retailer's outlet and maximizing store sales rather than the sales of any product in particular. Manufacturer advertising, on the other hand, is aimed at maximizing product sales, irrespective of where they are purchased. Also, retailers have traditionally used local media (newspapers, television and radio) to target customers, as most people tend to shop at stores near their homes and workplaces. Although Internet advertising is providing a relatively low-cost alternative that is appropriate for small businesses that can reach a national and international market via online retailing, national advertising is normally only affordable and appropriate for the large national chains. Large manufacturers, in the main, tend to use the national media as this provides them with the widest reach and their products are aimed at national rather than local markets.

Manufacturers also have the luxury of being able to focus on particular products as they have a relatively narrow range that they want to promote. This allows them to create communication programmes that focus on specific consumer benefits that project a consistent brand image for their products. However, given their extensive ranges, concentrating advertising on particular products is less appropriate for many retailers, and so retail advertising needs to develop messages that are consistent with the overall image of the organization and are more inclusive of the total offer. This conflict is further compounded by the fact that many retailers stress overall price benefits in their adverts. Manufacturers cannot control retail prices, and so they tend to emphasize product features and benefits so that consumers are less sensitive to price.

Cooperative advertising

Despite the areas of conflict discussed above, retailers and manufacturers or suppliers sometimes cooperate on advertising and share costs. Vertical cooperative advertising involves a retailer and a producer or (less commonly) a wholesaler and a retailer, sharing the cost of an advertisement. The producer will usually require the retailer to feature their brand name and/or products in the communication. The disadvantage of cooperative advertising for retailers is that they lose flexibility and there may not be consistency of image between the retailer and the third party. Also, advertising allowances are not always available for the most profitable of the manufacturer's products.

Horizontal cooperative advertising occurs where two or more retailers jointly fund the cost of an advertisement. Horizontal agreements often occur between small independent non-competing retailers, retailers located in shopping centres or franchisees trading under a common brand name. A major advantage of horizontal cooperative advertising is that the pooling of resources gives greater bargaining power in purchasing advertising space.

Factors affecting the choice of advertising media

The choice of media used for advertising depends on a number of factors relating not only to the ability of the media to reach the required target market, but also to its ability to deliver the intended message effectively. Some of the major factors that influence media choice are discussed as follows:

1. Coverage is the percentage of the market a particular medium reaches; for instance a local newspaper may be read by 50 per cent of the adults in a town. Reach is the actual number of target customers who come into contact with the advert. Internet coverage continues to improve and expand but the reach of an Internet advert is difficult to establish. However, by placing the advertisement on more Internet intermediaries (such as comparison sites) and search engine pages, the reach will increase.
2. Audience selectivity is the medium's ability to deliver a message to certain target audiences within the population. Many magazines, for instance, target specific markets such as gardeners, photographers or fashion enthusiasts. Geographical selectivity is also important. The ability of a medium to target a specific area is important to store retailers as a majority of their customers come from the immediate surrounding area. Although online advertising benefits from the use of online linkages from relevant sites, the Internet is a less selective medium from a retailer point of view, and so the general information on a retailer's website is important so that customers can locate and plan a shopping trip or choose to shop online (see subsection titled ' The website as an advertisement').
3. Frequency is the average number of times each person reached by the advert is exposed to the advert in a given time period. Media such as TV, where the viewer is exposed to the advert for a very short time, need several repetitions to ensure that the intended recipients receive the message.
4. Impact refers to the strength of the impression that an advertisement makes and its ability to influence purchasing behaviour. For instance, television and magazines are excellent media for building retail brand images with their high visual quality, whereas newspapers and the Internet are better at influencing purchasing behaviour in the short term as the advertisement placing is more immediate and flexible.
5. Flexibility, timeliness and the life of a medium are important considerations. Flexibility refers to the extent to which a medium can contribute to the execution of the advertising strategy. For instance, direct marketing allows advertisers to individualize the message and to enclose coupons, samples and so on. Television, on the other hand, can provide pictures, sound, words and music but the message is the

same for everyone. Timeliness refers to the lead times required to publish an advert in a medium; for instance a simple advertisement on the radio could appear the next day. However, lead times for advertisements in television and magazines can be long because of the popularity of the media and the complexity and sophistication of many visual campaigns. The 'life' of an advertisement refers to its longevity. Television and radio advertisements are gone immediately after they are aired and must be repeated a number of times if they are to be effective. Magazine advertisements may have a life of several weeks, as consumers tend to keep magazines and reread them from time to time. The Internet provides good flexibility in timing, lifespan, personalization and image quality.

6. Costs of the different media should be compared in both absolute and relative terms. The absolute cost of a medium is the total financial outlay of running an advert in it; the relative cost is the cost of reaching a certain number of people, usually expressed as cost per thousand (CPT). For instance, the absolute cost of advertising in a newspaper might be £3,000 for a full-page advert. If the newspaper has a readership of 500,000, then the CPT is £6.00 (£3,000 × 1,000 divided by 500,000). The cost per thousand measure is only useful for comparing similar media as different media differ in their effectiveness.

Timing of advertisements

A crucial factor in the success of advertising is the timing of the advert. There is no single best time for advertising because of the diversity of retailing activities. However, retailers need to consider when peak seasons occur in their business and the shopping patterns of their customers. Supermarkets, for instance, tend to advertise on Wednesdays because a high proportion of customers do their grocery shopping on Thursday, Friday or Saturday. Garden and DIY retailers, on the other hand, tend to concentrate their advertising in the early spring and summer months. Christmas TV advertisements have become something of an art form in the UK, using long and emotional scenes to encourage engagement, which reflects the importance of this trading period for many retailers.

Advertising effectiveness

Assessing the effectiveness of advertising involves evaluating the extent to which advertising objectives have been achieved. For instance, if the objective of an advertising campaign is to raise awareness, this may be assessed by measuring spontaneous and aided recall of the advertisement. If, on the other hand, the objective is to change the attitudes of customers, then it is necessary to conduct attitudinal research to assess the changes in customer attitudes towards the retailer. Many large retailers undertake continuous tracking studies of their promotional activities and their impact, which provides them with benchmarks for any new advertising programme. Measuring the effect of advertising on sales is difficult because sales are affected by numerous other factors besides the advertising itself, including choice, prices, availability and other promotional activities. However, a sales uplift is the normal expectation of advertising activity, and the size and duration of the uplift are indicators of advertising effectiveness.

Another major aspect of assessing the effectiveness of advertising is to judge how effective it was in reaching the intended market. Much advertising is wasted because the media used is not sufficiently focused on the relevant market. Advertising may also be wasted due to poor internal communication; for example employees are not aware that an item is for sale, or insufficient stock is available. At the same time, retailers need to be aware that their advertisements are seen not only by their customers, but also by their employees. Hence, any retailer purporting to show its employees in its advertisements needs to ensure that employees are being projected in a positive light. Advertising on the Internet has the potential to provide more detailed information, enabling a retailer to track visit activity, evaluate effectiveness in terms of converting clicks from advertisements to website visits to sales and analyse customer information from their online interaction.

The website as an advertisement

Many retailers have websites that resemble advertisements in many ways: images and text that communicate elements of the product range, which might also feature on billboards or in magazines; films which show the same 'campaign' footage as a TV or cinema advertisement; and price offers that persuade a customer to take advantage in a similar way to a newspaper advertisement. The difference is that the space is owned and controlled by the retailer rather than space which the retailer pays the various media owners for. Nevertheless, as a public-facing communication medium, the company website should be as carefully designed as any other form of marketing communication, especially as it offers the chance to include a plethora of detailed information about the product range, the services and the ethos of the company (corporate communications) and to be integrated with other elements of the communications mix (see Vignette 14.1).

VIGNETTE 14.1 WHITE STUFF

The UK-based clothing retailer White Stuff does not use conventional advertising; instead, each season the company chooses what they refer to as a 'wrap' theme, which provides a focus for all 'touchpoint' communication with the brand, from the website, catalogue and stores to emails and direct mail. The themes have varied from Gnomes to Squirrels and Budgerigars and represent a light-hearted way of integrating all the various aspects of the retailer's customer communication. Integration in marketing communication usually involves a repetition of visual triggers and the replication of graphics providing synergy and efficiency in the use of promotional resources. In 2011 the campaign theme was superheroes, using pop-art graphics and humour to engage customers.

INTERNET-BASED MARKETING COMMUNICATIONS

The Internet is providing the opportunity for retailers to make a closer connection between communication activity and sales. At one time retailers relied on external media to get a message of encouragement to engage to consumers, and then they would wait until shoppers entered the store to experience the outcome of the message. Online communications take a shopper directly from the relaying of the message to the point of purchase with one touch. A full and detailed discussion about online marketing communications is beyond the scope of this text but its importance in the era of ubiquitous multi-channel shopping cannot be overstated, and this section will provide a brief overview of the key principles of online marketing communications in order to give a basic understanding of the opportunities available to retailers, and some of the constraints of the medium.

Internet search engines (such as Google, Bing and Yahoo) are powerful entities that help to match keywords and key phrases used by potential customers in their search for a product or service to similar words in a website. The search engine uses highly sophisticated software programmes that ensure the most relevant web pages are returned in a search. Search engine optimization (SEO) is the process of managing key phrases to ensure the retailer maintains the highest position possible in what are referred to as 'natural listings' in a search result. In addition, a company can display an advert on a search engine, typically in the banners at the side ('sponsored links') or at the top of the listing page. When a consumer clicks on the advertisement, a charge from the search engine is made to the retailer for taking the searcher to the company's website (pay per click). Therefore, the more times an advertisement is clicked, the higher the charge for the ad placement, but an effective ad in terms of clicks will also retain a high position on the banner, thanks to the ranking by the search engine company, which wishes to maintain the most relevant information for their users.

Although SEO is a vital part of e-marketing, retailers are unlikely to generate the most traffic possible by relying on searches to 'pull' potential customers to their online stores. Advertisements in traditional media such as TV or magazines often explicitly or additionally encourage visits to retailers' websites. In particular, online retail service providers such as those selling insurance or travel advertise heavily on television. In addition, online marketing communications using other new media tools provide the 'push' to alert or remind a potential customer to visit a retailer's outlet. Especially, the use of social media and blogging are reported to have become really important tools for retailers as the popularity of the virtual conversation continues to grow, and some retailers have used online viral marketing campaigns very effectively to generate a 'buzz' about their company and/or its products. In 2013 Kmart released a viral campaign featuring the strapline 'ship my pants' (in other words arrange an online delivery for my trousers). The surprise that a traditional retailer would use the humour of almost swearing managed to generate a buzz of over 17 million views on YouTube. Kmart followed this with another viral campaign for petrol with the line 'big gas savings' (Brownell, 2013).

Interactivity is one of the most important characteristics of Internet-based marketing communications, creating a two-way dialogue between the retailer and customer, blending the marketing communications activity with purchase activity tracking in a way that helps the retailer to understand the responsive shopping and product-purchasing behaviour and preferences of customers. Like the loyalty card in the 1990s, retail technology that allows the analysis of online activity is providing a new level of activity and response intelligence that many retailers are currently grappling to make sense of. Once mastered, the potential to fine-tune offers to very small consumer groups or even individual customers is there.

PUBLIC RELATIONS

Public relations involves the creation and maintaining of interest and goodwill amongst a retailer's various publics such as customers, investors, employees, suppliers and local community. A major tool for generating interest in the company is publicity, which involves placing significant communications (usually news stories) regarding the retailer and its products in the media without paying for the time or space directly. This can take the form of a press release, which is the basis of editorial comment. Such coverage has more credibility than advertising amongst the retailer's customers and other publics because it is not directly paid for, and therefore regarded as an independent view. However, how the stories are reported, the depth of coverage and timing are out of the retailer's direct control.

Public relations activity for retailers can have objectives other than consumer sales. It may be necessary to limit the impact of negative stories about the organization, or to stress the benefits of the organization in its wider public arena. For example, when building new stores, it is often necessary for a retailer to promote the wider benefits of the development to local councils and community, such as additional investment into infrastructure and employment opportunities. Public relations activity often goes hand in hand with major advertising campaigns for retailers, which can generate additional comment in trade and national press.

A retailer might, for example, offer a specific publication an exclusive opportunity to preview and document the 'story' behind a major campaign. This could be particularly important when a retailer is changing strategic direction, to generate additional interest and understanding.

Many fashion retailers have public relations activity central to their communications mix. Press releases, fashion shows, seasonal launches' parties, the loan of samples for magazine photographic editorial content, product placement (in films or TV shows for example) and celebrity seeding (giving celebrities products to use in the hope they get photographed) are all part of what is seen as the natural promotional tool for fashion companies (Haid et al., 2006).

The usual way to measure the success of a public relations activity is to compare the indirect cost of generating 'free' column inches or airtime with the cost of advertising space in equivalent media. However, an evaluation of quality of the publicity generated is necessary to assess its true worth, for example how favourable an article in a newspaper is towards a retailer.

CORPORATE COMMUNICATIONS

A company website offers the opportunity to communicate with customers and other audiences with messages concerning many aspects of the business alongside an online shop: for example company history and heritage, product ranges and their specific benefits, aspirational images (such as marketing campaign visuals), corporate philosophy, social and environmental issues, store locator (if appropriate), contact details, employment opportunities, an interactive section (such as a chat room or blog) and links to other relevant sites such as social networks or trade associations. A press or 'media' section can be made available to registered media users such as journalists and editors to hold items such as press releases and approved corporate images.

After a disproved but high-profile piece of negative publicity concerning one of clothing retailer Primark's supplier's factories in a BBC Panorama programme in 2008, the company added a separate website on 'ethical trading', http://www.primark-ethicaltrading.co.uk/, with a direct link from the company's main website landing page. They also developed a separate page, http://www.primarkresponse.com/panorama/, featuring a filmed investigation that the company undertook to disprove the BBC's allegations. Primark's company website therefore reminds customers every time they shop online that the company is endeavouring to improve its ethical standards, and provides a link to an ongoing communication to counteract the unfounded allegations that provided negative PR for Primark.

A company blog and profile pages on social networks provide further opportunities for the dissemination of corporate communication. The two-way characteristic of social media and blogging means that as well as feeding relevant information to potential consumers, the retailer invites commentary from consumers. This provides the opportunity for a rich dialogue, which can be useful for gathering customer feedback. To use these tools effectively, however, investment must be made into the management of the dialogue. Consumers soon lose interest if a social media site is inactive or irrelevant. Social media participation acts like a combination of public relations and word-of-mouth communication, and helps to bring a retail brand to life in the virtual world. Lack of communication via social media may give the impression that a brand has little to say about itself or has something to hide, which may result in a negative image.

SALES PROMOTIONS

Sales promotions are incentives provided to customers for a limited period of time to stimulate trial or increase sales. The incentives are designed to add value to a retailer's products, and the limitation on the time period of the sales promotion encourages an immediate response from the customer. The most frequently used techniques include coupons, premiums, all store/seasonal sales, contests and sweepstakes, loyalty schemes, product demonstrations, samples and multi-buy offers (see Table 14.2).

Benefits and drawbacks of sales promotions

The major advantages associated with sales promotions include the following:

1. They are good at generating interest in the retailer and the promoted merchandise, effectively increasing sales volume in the short term.
2. They can be very distinctive because of the variety of promotion tools available, including online variations.

Table 14.2 Types of sales promotions

Coupons and online vouchers	Certificates redeemable for a specified amount of money on a purchase; coupons are most frequently used by supermarkets. Vouchers may be a fixed sum or a percentage and are often offered to customers via email. They are frequently used to incentivize multi-channel shopping
Price deals, refunds and rebates	Temporary price reductions; the price reductions may be printed on product packaging, or on the store shelf. Alternatively, rebates may be offered allowing customers to recover part of the cost of the product
Special packs/ bonus packs	Special packs give shoppers extra product 'free' instead of lowering the price
Multi-buys/ multi-save	Additional products given without extra charge; the most common form is buy-one-get-one-free (BOGOF), but 3 for 2 is also practiced by some retailers, for example Boots
Sales	Sales are price reductions implemented across the store; end-of-season sales are common in fashion retailing and are designed to get rid of stock quickly before the new season's stock arrives
Contests and sweepstakes	A contest is a competition requiring skill (for example quizzes, providing slogans etc.); sweepstakes are competitions where the winner is chosen by chance
Premiums	Premiums take the form of merchandise being offered for free or reduced cost as an incentive to buy a product; premiums can be free in-pack or on-pack gifts, free mail-in offers, or self-liquidating offers where consumers are asked to pay a sum of money to cover the cost of the premium merchandise; mail-in offers usually require a number of proofs of purchase, which help to drive sales and create brand loyalty
Demonstrations and sampling	In-store demonstrations are used by retailers to build excitement and to encourage impulse buying; free samples of the products may also be given out in the store to encourage trial of new products or brand extensions
Special events	Examples include fashion shows of the new season's merchandise, book-signing sessions by authors, and store visits by celebrities designed to generate store traffic and interest in the store
Loyalty programmes	Points are awarded (usually) for every pound spent on purchases in the store; the points can be redeemed for goods or services or for discounts on future shopping bills

3. Consumers may receive something free of additional value to themselves, which provides an extra incentive to visit the retailer and to purchase the promoted merchandise.
4. Sales promotions introduce novelty and fun into shopping.
5. They increase store traffic by attracting new customers and increasing the patronage of existing customers.

6. They increase impulse purchases.
7. They can help clear unwanted stock.
8. They help to maintain store loyalty.

The major strength of sales promotions is also their major weakness, namely that many sales promotions have only a short-term effect and can encourage customers to stockpile. Another major weakness, particularly for sales promotions that offer financial inducements, is that they can be expensive for the retailer and can lead to reduced margins. Effective sales promotions should at least recover the cost of the promotions. However, some promotions are loss leaders where products are sold at or below cost, and the promotion is designed principally to generate store traffic; profits are generated from increased sales from the rest of the store.

Many promotions are generated by suppliers, and therefore the cost is borne by the manufacturer brand owners. However, even where promotions are initiated by the retailer, the benefits to the supplier of increased sales and interest in their products means that promotions are often jointly financed. The precise split of the costs depends on the negotiating power of the retailer and supplier. Smaller suppliers may have difficulties if they find themselves being pressurized to finance retail promotions.

Sales promotions also require careful planning and collaboration with suppliers to ensure that customers are not disappointed because not enough extra inventory has been ordered of the promoted item to meet the extra demand generated. The success of a sales promotion may rely on a retailer's compliance on using suppliers' point-of-purchase materials (such as posters, banners, fixtures and leaflets) generated to support the promotion. However, this type of material can produce a cluttering effect in store, and so in fairness to both parties the operation of sales promotions should be properly negotiated for mutual gain.

Assessing the effectiveness of sales promotions

As sales promotions are, in the main, designed to achieve short-run improvements in store performance, they should be assessed in terms of the sales and profits directly generated by them. A simple method of assessing their effectiveness is to measure the weekly volume of sales before the promotion and compare it with the weekly sales volume during and after the promotional period; the sales volume prior to the promotional period provides a benchmark for comparisons. It is necessary to measure sales after the promotion because consumers may simply be stockpiling the product, which would lead to sales being lower after the promotion (referred to as the sales displacement effect) relative to the volumes before the promotion. For example, consider a supermarket featuring Clairol's Herbal Essences Shampoo/Conditioner on a 'buy one, get one free' offer for 2 weeks. Before the promotion, EPOS data indicated typical weekly sales of 10 cases. During the 2-week promotion, sales averaged 17 cases per week. However, 4 weeks following the promotion, sales were 5, 6.5, 8 and 9.5 cases per week. In the 5th and subsequent weeks, sales returned to the previous level of 10 cases per week. Thus, the net impact of the promotion was to increase sales by 3 cases, with the majority of the increase in sales being due to customers stockpiling for future needs.

The actual profitability of the promotion will depend upon how the costs of the promotion were shared between the retailer and supplier. It also depends on the effect of the promotion on the current and future demand of competing products, referred to as the substitution effect. For example, the promotion could have a negative impact on profitability if it leads to switching of demand away from high-margin full-price products to lower-margin promoted products.

The example above helps to illustrate some general points about sales promotions. First, promotions for non-perishable staples or necessity items will generally lead to stockpiling by consumers rather than increased consumption. Increased sales for these items will depend upon the degree to which they can attract customers from competitors, or their ability to attract customers from beyond the retailer's existing trading area. The fluctuation of sales (from 5 to 17 cases) also suggests that accurate forecasting and careful planning of promotions are necessary to avoid under- or overstocking of promoted merchandise. The indirect impact of sales promotions is much more difficult to estimate and requires more sophisticated analysis. This is because at any one time a retailer will have a number of sales promotions running concurrently, and other extraneous factors (such as competitor promotional activity) can influence the overall impact on store performance. A retailer's strategic position is also important to consider when managing sales promotions. A discount retailer will enhance its image by having many price-cutting promotions; however, a more upmarket retailer may find a discreet linked sale promotion more appropriate.

EVENTS

A wide variety of events are used by retailers to encourage customer engagement. Some events may be linked directly to the store. The UK department store Selfridges for example is famous for themed store-wide events. Other events may be associated with a product launch; editors and journalists are invited to the event in the hope that editorial space in the media is generated. Retailers are using increasingly diverse events to reinforce their images and maintain customer interest. The Spanish clothing retailer Desigual for example has used events many times to draw attention to store openings and to raise customer awareness in new international markets. Their Kiss Tour events which took place in 2010 in Paris, Berlin, London and Madrid encouraged the public to share their kisses at a rally which also included music and entertainment. Being a young, informal clothing retailer based in a country known for its warmth of character and sense of humour, Desigual's brand personality was reflected well by these events.

DIRECT MAIL

Traditionally, direct mailings by retailers to consumers took the form of personally addressed advertising delivered through the postal system (Fill, 2009). Retailers may send catalogues, leaflets or promotional offers to customers, or potential customers, and for many 'online only retailers' the use of a catalogue to drive interest has been an important part of their success. For example, early on in its rapid development, the online retailer ASOS used (and continues to use) a magazine that resembles a fashion magazine to re-position the retailer as a young, fashion-forward 'online department store', extending its appeal from its original emphasis on celebrity looks (As Seen on Screen).

Promotional offers however are often now sent by email either in addition to, or in place of, postal mail. Email marketing communication is a very effective tool for retailers, enabling them to send frequent and relevant messages to customer; however, in a lot of cases, there remains a great deal of scope for tailoring of content and personalization. For example most retailers send the same email messages to customers as 'cold prospects', thereby missing the opportunity to cross-sell, up-sell or encourage repeat purchase. The giant online retailer Amazon on the other hand makes good use of follow-up emails after purchases with email content tailored to the previous purchase (theretailbulletin.com, 2011). Once an online purchase is made, email addresses can be captured and used for after-sales marketing. Retailers' email communication also includes enquires sent from potential customers, which normally require a personalized response.

THE RETAILING ENVIRONMENT

The design, layout, signs, displays, decor, lighting, use of music and smell generate a store atmosphere and an image in the customer's mind. The store image thus communicated informs the customer about a retailer's pricing and service levels, and, for example, the fashionability of its merchandise offer. Once in the store, visual presentation of merchandise is used to influence customers in the final stages of the consumer decision-making process. Good presentation and store layout can be used to increase impulse buying and, by creating a pleasing experience, encourage customers to shop the whole store. In online retail environments the clarity, navigability and atmosphere of the website are all important in communicating appropriate messages to the customer. Retail design and visual merchandising are discussed in more detail in Chapter 10, but in an era of increasing customer design literacy the role of the retail environment in communicating both short-term and long-term messages must be acknowledged here.

POINT-OF-PURCHASE DISPLAYS

It is often suggested (Spanier, 2012) that over half of consumers' purchase decisions are made at the point of sale in a store. Hence, point-of-purchase (POP) displays are critical for influencing consumers in the final stages of the decision-making process, particularly where the customer is undecided or prepared to switch brands. In fact, Spanier (2012) suggests that retailers need to shift their thinking from POP being the last opportunity for communication as to being the one that will dominate the rest of the communications mix by being the link to previous communications.

POP materials include posters and banners, product displays, coupon dispensers, shelf wobblers (signs that dangle from shelves), floor stickers and touch-screen kiosks.

POP displays are often designed and supplied by manufacturers to attract attention and to provide consumers with information, and from a retailer's perspective POP displays are not always in keeping with the retailer's own image. Having numerous manufacturer POP displays can present a cluttered image and confused positioning for the retailer, and give precedence to the manufacturer brands over the retail brand. Hence, retailers are usually very selective about the POP displays that they employ; when integrated with promotional activity, they can create interest and excitement in the retail outlet.

PERSONAL SELLING

Personal selling involves salespeople communicating directly with customers in order to help them satisfy their needs through an interactive exchange of information. The degree of personal selling and personal service provided by retailers varies by the type of merchandise sold and the retailer's service strategy. For instance, retailers selling low-risk, low-priced merchandise, such as food retailers, do not employ large numbers of skilled sales staff to provide customers with detailed information about products and how to make most effective use of them. This is because the vast majority of the products are routinely purchased by shoppers and additional information is available on product packaging or provided by shelf cards. The type of information required by shoppers is likely to be about product availability, special offers, returns policy and so forth, which can be provided by sales assistants on request. On the other hand, for highly priced, complex or non-routinely purchased products, customers are likely to require and expect the assistance of a salesperson in making the right choice of product to satisfy their specific needs. This is because these are potentially high-risk purchases and customers seek to reduce the risk by seeking expert advice. Situations where personal selling is highly effective include the following:

1. Where the perceived personal risk of making the wrong choice is high, for example for cosmetics or health care.
2. Where the purchase price is high relative to the individual's income, for example a car.
3. Where customization is required by the customer, for example tailored clothing.
4. Where the product is complex and there are a variety of products to choose from, for example computers.
5. Where variable pricing is practised and discount negotiation takes place, for example travel or hotel bookings.

Schaefer (2011) suggests that multi-channel shoppers are much more informed when they enter retail outlets because it is so easy to accumulate information about goods and services online. Sales personnel will increasingly need listening and 'reading' skills in order to quickly establish how knowledgeable a customer is, and adjust their approach accordingly. Simply pouring out a standardized sales patter runs the risk of patronizing an informed customer who may know more about a product and its competitive alternatives than the sales advisor. Product knowledge training therefore continues to be of strategic importance.

Personal selling can help to convert outlet visits to sales, increase impulse buying by suggestion selling and increase transaction values by encouraging customers to trade up or to purchase complementary products. Good personal selling improves customer service standards overall, as discussed further in Chapter 15.

The selling process

The selling process in the retailing environment has the following basic stages:

1. Greeting and approaching customers.
2. Determining customer needs.
3. Presenting and demonstrating merchandise.
4. Answering objections.
5. Closing the sale.
6. Suggestion selling.
7. After-sales service

Greeting and approaching is an important stage in establishing rapport with the customer. A simple 'hello' or 'good morning' is less threatening than 'May I help you'. The key to a successful approach is to find out the customer's needs. Is the customer simply browsing or are they looking for a particular product? Do they have a price range in mind? Some well-chosen questions allow the salesperson to assess a product (or products) that fits the customer's requirements.

The approach stage is followed by presentation (and if necessary demonstration) of a product that may satisfy the customer's needs. If the exact product is not available, the salesperson may suggest a substitute or get the customer to trade up to a more expensive product with better features and benefits. In a retail setting, it is best to tailor the presentation to the needs of individual customers, responding to their varied needs and wants. Showing the customer too many products can be confusing and should be avoided, and the presentation should be made in an interesting manner emphasizing the important features and benefits of the product.

During the selling process the customer may have questions regarding the product which need to be addressed appropriately, or the sale may be lost. Having addressed any objections, the salesperson needs to close the sale, by getting the customer to purchase the product. Closing the sale can involve asking the customer to choose between products, choosing for the customer, assuming that the sale has been made and asking the customer how they wish to pay for the product or overcoming further objections by stressing the benefits of the product.

Once the customer has decided to buy the product, the salesperson can continue to sell by making additional suggestions of products that would enhance or get the best out of the original product. This is known as suggestion selling. Typical suggestion selling includes suggesting accessories for products, for example software for computers or extended warranties for electrical products. Effective personal selling requires that salespeople are enthusiastic, knowledgeable about the products they are selling, customer oriented and effective communicators. This requires that salespeople are carefully selected by the retailer to ensure that they have the right attributes for selling, which include people orientation, good communication and enthusiasm. It also requires that a retailer trains its salespeople to equip them with the necessary knowledge required to sell the products and in the different aspects of the retail selling process (see Vignette 14.2). However, because of the high turnover of personnel in the industry, retailers do not always train their salespeople to the highest standards, as it is seen as wasted investment. This short-sightedness can lead to lost sales and customer dissatisfaction.

VIGNETTE 14.2 SHOP-FLOOR AMBASSADORS

Upmarket designer brands need sales personnel who not only are extremely competent when matching customer needs to products, but also exude the brand themselves. As well as customer care and styling training, knowledge of the brand heritage and an understanding of a brand's culture need to be built. Asome (2006) refers to the term 'Chanelised' which sales staff have to go through before being let loose in the flagships of the famous designer brand Chanel. Grooming is important, but having the right personality for a brand is also a requisite. Marni designer clothing for example sells outfits that are very individual, like works of art, and the brand tends to employ sales personnel who have an artistic background such as designers or stylists. Many outlets for such goods are in cosmopolitan cities where the tourist trade is vital for business and so being multilingual is a real asset. Above all, building relationships with clients is the most important aspect of the role, knowing what their taste is, not only in terms of the brand itself, but also competing brands that might appear in the customer's wardrobe. Having the ability to interpret this season's looks for individual body shapes, thinking about what a customer has bought in the past and approaching clients when items arrive in store that the sales consultant thinks a loyal customer would like are all aspects of a high-value sales role. One-to-one personal communication is still the basis of this aspect of retail management, but a robust and creative approach to database marketing can help to ensure that the relationship is with the brand and not entirely with the person, which can be lost if that person moves on.

Source: Based on Asome (2006)

In today's era of multi-channel shopping, closing the sale may not be the end of the consumer purchasing process, and although it may seem frustrating to leave a sale uncompleted, it should not be considered to be a waste of time because the shopper may well later buy the product online. A customer may decide to take note of the product trialled in store and then buy online at home. After-sales service is also a very important part of the process, with stores accepting returned goods that were bought online. Retailers that have systems that allow a customer to shop across channels, for example ordering in store for home delivery, or 'click and collect' where a customer buys online remotely and then picks the product up in store, provide more flexibility in the purchasing process, which the retail salesperson can bring to the attention of the shopper. Personal selling is considered to be part of the services mix, which is explored in detail in the next chapter.

DIFFERENTIAL IMPACT OF THE PROMOTIONS MIX

Each of the elements of the retail promotions mix has different strengths and weaknesses, and in order to achieve the best results the different promotional activities need to be coordinated and integrated to convey a consistent message. Inconsistent messages communicated to customers can lead to confusion about the retailer's image and positioning with a consequent decline in store patronage.

Used in combination, the different promotional techniques can be used to enforce each other. For instance, whilst sales promotions are good at increasing sales during a promotional period, sales usually revert to their pre-promotion level once the promotion has ended. Advertising, on the other hand, is useful for building longer-term interest in the retailer and switching customers away from competing retail outlets and converting non-users. There is some evidence that if an advertising campaign precedes a sales promotion, the sales level settles at a higher level than at pre-promotion. Hence, retailers frequently use advertising to promote special offers. Online, and particularly mobile online, marketing can help to reinforce on- and offline promotional activity and encourage immediate response; for example email, texts and social networking messages can alert customers to promotions. Mobile applications can take this one stage further by providing the means by which customers can be alerted to promotions when they are in the store, while 'quick-response' codes included in static advertisements can take a consumer directly to the online point of purchase on a company website via a mobile device.

The appropriateness of the promotional technique also depends upon where the customer is in the buying decision process, or the buyer readiness stage, as shown in Table 14.3. In buying products, consumers often go through a number of stages called the hierarchy of effects, which takes them from (un)awareness of the product to knowledge, to liking, then preference, on to conviction and finally to purchase. Not all these stages are included each time a consumer purchases a product. The sequence is most likely to be followed in the case of high-involvement products, relatively expensive products and products that the consumer is purchasing for the first time. In the case of inexpensive, low-involvement products, the sequence may be reversed: that is, a product is bought and the liking and preferences are formed after the consumption of the item.

Table 14.3 Effectiveness of promotional mix elements in influencing different stages of the buying decision process

	Awareness, knowledge	Liking, preference	Conviction	Action
Advertising	High	Moderate	Low	Low
Public relations	Moderate	Moderate	Low	Low
Sales promotion	Low	Low	Low	Moderate/high
Personal selling	Very low	Moderate/high	High	High
Word of mouth	High	High	Moderate	Moderate

SUMMARY

In an era where consumers have become used to a constant flow of messages through a diverse range of media platforms, communicating with customers is a vital part of retail management. Retailers are not simply using their communications programmes to promote merchandise; they are also using them to establish the credibility of the retail brands in their own right, raising awareness and maintaining a positive image. Communications objectives can be characterized as promotional or institutional, depending on whether they are short or long term in orientation. The major tools for promotional communications are advertising, sales promotion, personal selling and direct marketing, while public relations and the selling environment itself, whether in physical stores or online, are more appropriate tools for delivering institutional messages. This chapter has discussed the major features and strengths and weaknesses of the different elements of the retail communications mix, and how they can be used to influence customers at different points in the buying decision process. The next chapter looks at a different aspect of the relationship between the retailer and customer by focusing on service.

QUESTIONS

1. Discuss what is meant by institutional and promotional objectives.
2. Why do retailers and manufacturers cooperate on advertising? Why is it not always in the interest of the retailer to engage in cooperative advertising?
3. How far do you agree with the view that sales promotions only have short-term effects and cannot be used to build the retail brand image?
4. How might a retailer evaluate the effectiveness of a sales promotion?
5. What is suggestion selling and how does it fit into the personal selling process?
6. Explain how different elements of the promotions mix can be used to influence the different stages of the buying process.

REFERENCES AND FURTHER READING

Ackland, H. (1999) 'Why Retailers Rule over POP Success', *Marketing* (London), 28 October, p. 41.

Asome, C. (2006) 'Shop Girls', *Vogue,* May, pp. 91–4.

Betts, E. J. and McGoldrick, P. J. (1995) 'The Strategy of the Retail "Sales," Typology, Review and Synthesis', *International Review of Retail Distribution and Consumer Research*, vol. 5, no. 3 (July), pp. 303–32.

Betts, E. J. and McGoldrick, P. J. (1996) 'Consumer Behaviour and the Retail "Sales": Modelling the Development of an "Attitude Problem" ', *European Journal of Marketing*, vol. 30, no. 8, pp. 40–56.

Brownell, M. (2013) 'Kmart's "Ship My Pants" Ad Sequel Promises "Big Gas Savings" ', http://www.dailyfinance.com/on/kmart-big-gas-savings-ad-viral/ [accessed 25 July 2013].

Chaffey, D (2009) *E-Business and E-Commerce Management: Strategy, Implementation and Practice*, 4th Edition (Harlow: Pearson Education).

Fill, C. (2009) *Marketing Communication: Interactivity, Communities and Content*, 5th Edition (Harlow: Pearson Education).

Haid, C., Jackson, T. and Shaw, D. (2006) 'Fashion PR and Styling', in T. Jackson and D. Shaw (eds), *The Fashion Handbook* (Abingdon: Routledge), pp. 172–87.

McKinnon, A. C., Cullinane, S., Browne, M. and Whiteing, A. (eds) (2010) *Green Logistics: Improving the Environmental Sustainability of Logistics* (London: Kogan Page).

Peattie, S. (1998) 'Promotional Competitions as a Marketing Tool in Food Retailing', *British Food Journal*, vol. 100, no. 6, pp. 286–94.

Peattie, S. and Peattie, K. (2000) 'Sales Promotion', in M. J. Baker (ed.), *The Marketing Book*, 4th Edition (Oxford: Butterworth-Heinemann), pp. 418–41.

Russell, M. (2012) 'UK: Marks and Spencer Launches "Simply M&S" Food Range', just-food, available at http://www.just-food.com/news/marks-and-spencer-launches-simply-ms-food-range_id119126.aspx, 11 May [accessed 8 September 2012].

Schaefer, M. (2011) *Capitalizing on the Smarter Consumer*, report published by IBM Institute for Business Value, http://public.dhe.ibm.com/common/ssi/ecm/en/gbe03390usen/GBE03390USEN.PDF [accessed 15 December 2012].

Smith, M. F. and Sinha, I. (2000) 'The Impact of Price and Extra Product Promotions on Store Preference', *International Journal of Retail and Distribution Management*, vol. 28, no. 2, pp. 83–92.

Spanier, G. (2011), 'At the Point of Sale Is . . . the Last Great Marketing Opportunity', *Evening Standard*, 25 July.

Theretailbulletin.com (2011), 'Retailers Missing Opportunities for Personalised Targeting and Cross-Selling Using Email Marketing', http://www.theretailbulletin.com/news/uk_retailers_missing_opportunities_for_personalised_targeting_and_crossselling_using_email_market_28-06-11/ [accessed 30 June 2011].

Waitrose.com (2012), Community Matters page, available at http://www.waitrose.com/content/waitrose/en/home/inspiration/community_matters.html [accessed 9 August 2012].

World Advertising Research Center (Warc) http://www.warc.com/

15 RETAIL SERVICES

LEARNING OBJECTIVES

- To understand the scope of service as a concept within retailing.
- To appreciate the various ways in which retailers can use services to differentiate their offer.
- To provide a distinction between short-term service initiatives and sustainable, long-term service differentiation.
- To understand the need to formulate a relevant service mix to meet the service requirements that are associated with different product categories, store and online formats and customer groups.
- To understand the relationship between services provision, operational costs and retail management approaches.
- To understand the relationship between customers' service expectations, their service experiences and potential shortfalls in the quality of service delivery.

INTRODUCTION

Retail management and service are conceptually inextricably linked. Service in retailing is a broad term; essentially, retailing is itself a service, providing the final consumer with a distribution service that provides efficiency in product retrieval (as shown in Chapter 1). Retailers also carry out a form of 'product editing' service, by formulating product ranges and assortments that are geared specifically to particular customer needs, and a stock availability service to allow consumers to buy products in suitable quantities at times when they need them. Retail service, or perhaps the more commonly used term 'customer service', can also refer to the variety of 'add-ons' to a core product or service purchase that can improve the consumer's experience during the shopping process.

The relevance and quality of the service mix is an effective way for one retailer to differentiate their offer from others, and because good retail service relies on long-term investment in training and developing people within retail organizations, it can be a sustainable source of competitive advantage (as discussed in Chapter 3). It is the purpose of this chapter to explore relevant retail services and consider how service level and quality can determine a retailer's market positioning. It will also consider service quality as an indicator of success in the achievement of customer satisfaction.

As indicated in Chapter 2, many retail organizations (for example restaurants, beauty salons and banks) are in the business of selling services as opposed to tangible products to their customers. While this type of retailing presents some additional challenges associated with the purchase, delivery and experience of the service, this chapter does not generally seek to make a distinction between the retailing of goods and services. Its purpose is to explore the scope of service in the retail setting in general, rather than to focus on the retailing of services specifically. We start the chapter with a categorization of retail services to explore the scope of this aspect of retail management.

PRODUCT-RELATED SERVICES

This is the type of service directly related to the product itself. It is an augmentation or 'add-on' to the product that helps customers feel that their needs have been fully met. For example if a customer needs to replace a malfunctioning freezer, that customer's needs will only be completely satisfied when the new freezer is installed in their kitchen. After the customer has purchased the freezer, a delivery time will have been organized, the delivery van will have arrived and the freezer would have been unpackaged, carried to the correct place in the kitchen and plugged in to make sure it functions. The packaging and the old freezer would then be taken away. The retailer's relationship with their customer certainly does not end with the close of the sale, but is continued as the product-related services are carried out.

The services that retailers offer to augment their product ranges will vary according to the nature of the products within those ranges. As well as some widely applicable service offers such as gift wrap and home delivery, Table 15.1 indicates a number of alternatives that are appropriate to specific retail sectors.

Some retailers go a stage further than providing an augmented product/service package. They actually differentiate their own retail offer from competitors by offering a higher and sometimes more complex level of service to match complex and highly involved customer needs. Examples could be given of a personal technology retailer that puts together a customized package of hardware and software for individual customers, an interior design service offered at a home furnishings specialist or a personal-shopper service offered by a department store. In a retail environment where customer needs are growing in their sophistication, it makes sense to be able to match

Table 15.1 Product-related service alternatives, by retail sector

Retail sector	Product-related services
Clothing	Changing rooms, alteration service, returns policy, personal styling
Electrical/electronic	Service warranty, home installation, sales support, online tutorials
Furniture/home furnishings	Home assembly, home trial, design consultation, measuring-up service
Automotive	Test drives, warranties, insurance, car service packages

these needs with a finely blended mix of products and services, which in the end allow a degree of personal customization for the shopper. The growth of Internet retailing has resulted in companies exploring and developing the one-to-one relationship with customers online with facilities such as personalized listings and customer input to product design, making the expression 'mass customization' meaningful.

CONVENIENCE-RELATED SERVICES

As consumers have become more time pressurized by busy lifestyles, retailers have responded by formulating a product and service package that is highly convenience orientated. The large grocery multiples have been particularly proactive in this area, and the following list indicates a range of convenience-related services that might typically be offered by a superstore retailer:

1. Bag packing
2. Home delivery
3. Cafeteria
4. Toilets
5. 24-Hour shopping
6. Cash machines
7. Variety of trolleys
8. Parent and disabled parking areas
9. Shuttle bus service

Some of the product categories on offer in a supermarket can be considered to be convenience orientated, in that they save a customer a separate trip to a specialty store; the in-store pharmacy, bakery and delicatessen could be considered in this way. In addition, many superstores offer the customer the opportunity to purchase 'service products' within the outlet. A dry-cleaner's, a bank, a post office and a shoe repair unit are examples of this type of retail service.

In the early 1990s leading grocery retailers all gave their service offer something of an overhaul, for a number of reasons. One reason was linked to responding to consumer changes – to keep satisfying the increasingly convenience-orientated supermarket customer (see Chapter 4); another was to maintain the image of a high-quality offer – an investment into higher service provision was seen to be a more strategic move than to cut prices; and a third reason was competitive – the supermarkets decided that service was an effective means by which to compete for market share. This resulted in something of a 'service war' in the UK, with each major grocery chain offering their 'unique' service bundle that might have included bag packing, carry-to-car service, parent-and-child parking spaces and even an umbrella service for rainy days! Some of these service offers were short-lived (such as brolly offers), but others, such as parent-and-child parking and the policy of opening more and more checkouts when queues were building (the 'one-in-front' policy), became an integral part of grocery supermarket operators' remit. This process, whereby a service provides temporary competitive advantage before being repeated in a competitor's offer, is described by the service life cycle.

THE SERVICE LIFE CYCLE

1. Introduction – a new service is introduced by a retailer giving them a competitive advantage.
2. Duplication – other retailers copy the new service, which removes the competitive advantage.
3. Stalemate – all retailers in a particular retail sector offer the service. Provision of the service becomes a cost, but removal of the service would result in competitive disadvantage.
4. Institutionalization – the service is taken for granted and expected by customers. It becomes a basic element of retail operations.
5. Replacement – another new service is introduced, or an existing service is improved or updated to provide competitive advantage again.

Source: Adapted from James et al. (1981) in McGoldrick (2002)

Recently, the service life cycle has been observed in the online shopping world, with innovative website-based service facilities giving a retailer first-mover advantage, only to be adopted by competitors. Facilities such as advice on what other customers bought together and time-slot delivery services are examples of website service enhancement that have become ubiquitous.

PAYMENT SERVICES

In order to provide a high level of convenience in the shopping process, the more methods of payment a retailer can offer, the better it is. If a customer cannot pay by their preferred method, then a barrier is created that might prevent the transaction being completed. This could result in the sale being lost completely. On the other hand, attractive payment methods and terms can be a way of enticing customers to proceed with a purchase. Flexible payment services are especially important for high-value transactions. Increasingly we live in a cashless society, so the methods and terms of payment that retailers offer need to have the flexibility to provide suitable arrangements for individual customers. The following list outlines some payment arrangements commonly found in retailing:

1. Cash
2. Cheque
3. Debit cards
4. Credit cards
5. Store account cards
6. Hire purchase
7. Monthly payment via direct debit
8. Monthly payment with additional guarantee period
9. Third-party payment service, for example PayPal

Payment arrangements that allow a customer to complete a purchase over a period of time provide an opportunity for retailers to build a relationship with that customer.

This is one of the strengths of mail-order operations, store-card schemes and loyalty cards. Customer details are collected, which can be used for further marketing initiatives.

Some loyalty cards double up as payment cards, which, in the eyes of the consumer, makes sense, because the debits and credits to their account with that retailer can be viewed as different aspects of the relationship between the two parties. Payment options are certainly subject to the service life cycle (see previous section). Today, the acceptance of debit cards is almost institutional in multiple retailers, and the exceptions that only deal in cash need to offer a clear benefit in return (such as exceptionally low prices). At the other end of the spectrum, cases have been known where cash has been refused in high-class eating establishments because the tills do not carry change! There has recently been a considerable debate in the UK about the future of personalized cheques. Banks are keen to eliminate cheques because they are less secure and more costly to process than card payments. However, cheques are popular with small businesses, and for elderly and less mobile customers they are a payment method that is the most convenient and familiar.

PRODUCT-AVAILABILITY SERVICES

Another aspect of retail service is that concerning product availability. When shoppers invest personal resources (time, travel costs and so on) to retrieve products, they expect their investment to pay off and are disappointed if it has not been worthwhile. If it is the retailer that was out of stock of an item, rather than simply a case of their own indecision, then the feeling of frustration is all the greater. Overall, the supply-chain initiatives described in Chapter 7 have raised the standards of customer service from a logistics point of view, so that as a general rule customers are more frequently able to find goods in stock. The out-of-stock situations that do occur should generally be viewed as a breakdown on the retailer's part, and therefore an opportunity for the implementation of an exceptional service to retrieve the situation, for example by making an arrangement to deliver the item to the customer's home when it does become available. The problem that modern retailers face is the high levels of retail provision (see Chapter 3), which allow a customer to switch to a competitor if they do not find a product available. In self-service situations this switching action may go completely undetected. In spite of the growth of volume and the improvements to infrastructure, online retailing continues to be criticized for poor order fulfilment and unreliable deliveries, which results in lost sales and customers. The use of analytics to track online activity (for example in-built programmes that measure the length of time customers spend on a web page or identify the point at which a sale was abandoned) will help retailers to understand where potential service downfalls are occurring.

In rare cases non-availability can augment the appeal of a retailer's offer. For example, luxury goods may require special orders for handcrafted items but the customer is prepared to wait a considerable period of time for the product because of its high desirability instilled by rarity. Fast-fashion retailers have trained their customers to 'buy it while they can' and accept that running out of a product line is a positive aspect of the retailer's marketing mix, with more desirable and up-to-the-minute designs being brought in to replenish stock rather than a repeat order.

INFORMATION SERVICES

The information that retailers provide about their products, and how they as businesses operate, can be considered as part of the retail service mix. This information can be imparted in a number of ways, for example in person, by telephone, on a website, in a leaflet or within a catalogue. The main criteria for good-quality information are accuracy, and presentation in a manner that is complementary to and consistent with the overall corporate image of the retailer. Most retailers have an informational website even if they do not have a transactional e-retailing operation (see Chapter 17), and this can be a very cost-effective way of communicating with customers. Retailers have used their websites to provide links to additional information that they feel is of interest to their customers, and it is this type of service that helps retailers to build a perception in customers that they are doing more than the basics in terms of service provision. This information can also build positive image perception and has become an important way of disseminating information about a retailer's corporate social responsibility (CSR) programme. Provision of information can therefore be viewed not only as a service, but also as a public relations exercise (see Chapter 18).

One type of information provision closely linked to the general area of retail customer sales service (see next section) is information about products that are complementary to the intended purchase. Although some customers could interpret this as a 'hard sell', Polonsky et al. (2000) found that, in general, customers believe companion selling to be an appropriate practice, and that it can contribute to a higher-quality customer-service provision. It has generally been acknowledged that adding services based on customer-generated information (such as product reviews, customer forums, combination sales information) has improved the online shopping experience.

CUSTOMER SALES SERVICE

One of the aspects of retail service that is most immediately apparent is the contact made between the customer and sales staff within the outlet. The type of contact can vary from a passive approach to a highly interactive one. The passive approach is characterized by customers making their own product choices and using a self-checkout station, with sales personnel only becoming involved when a customer specifically asks for help. An interactive approach is characterized by extended communication between the customer and the salesperson. Typically, this would involve an approach (from either party), an exploration of alternative solutions to the customer's needs, including information about product-related services on offer, the sale being closed and after-sale services, if appropriate, being offered. The Apple Store has proved to be an exemplar in this respect, with a huge availability of expert advisors on hand to provide friendly, detailed and tailored service to the customer, which carries on long after the close of the sale, including seminars and one-to-one tutorial services to help customer get the most out of their Apple product.

The level of customer sales service

Even for the same product item, consumers may encounter very different levels of service in different retail outlets. For example, ground coffee may be purchased in a vacuum-sealed package in a supermarket. On the other hand, a consumer may choose to buy coffee from a speciality store, in which case the service encounter might involve talking to the sales associate about the different strengths and aromas found in the various blends, being offered alternative blends to smell, waiting while the beans are ground, packaged, sealed and placed in an individual carrier bag and finally being offered the opportunity to place the purchase on their personal account!

The level of service found in a retail outlet is very closely linked to the prices charged. The type of service level described in the speciality store scenario above incurs a hefty labour cost, and in addition sales associates need to have high levels of knowledge and experience. This expertise can only be built in an organization that has a high level of staff retention and good training facilities. It is usual, therefore, for the level of service available in a retail organization to be linked to the retail format used, the staffing provision within the retailer and the margins applied to the product (Table 15.2).

Staffing provision and profit margins are concerned with the cost implication that goes with the provision of service within a retail outlet. However, there are two other very important factors in the customer sales service equation that retailers ignore at their peril. These are the service level that is appropriate for the type of product being sold, and the service levels expected by the target customer.

The type of product being sold

The more complex the blend of product features that go to make up a product, the more opportunity there is for a retailer to implement a high level of customer sales service and an explanation of the range of product-related services on offer. For example the purchase of a kitchen stove allows a retailer to impart extensive advice about the product benefits and align those benefits to customer needs in addition to the opportunity to sell a warranty, arrange home delivery and then install the appliance at the customer's home. Complex and high-involvement products, such as an electrical appliance, a wedding outfit or a car, typically have a high price ticket, and so the investment into the involved sale is likely to be worthwhile. However, not all high-involvement

Table 15.2 Retail formats and customer sales service

Retail format	Staffing levels	Need for product knowledge and experience	Profit margins
Supermarket	Low	Low	Low
Speciality store	High	High	High
Department store	High	High	High
Category specialist	Low	High	Low
Discount store	Low	Low	Low
Online store	Low	High	Low

products are expensive; for example Boots maintain a high level of product information available for all goods, many of which (such as skin creams or pharmaceutical products) are relatively low priced. However, Boots have a wide product offering, and customers remain loyal and keep their transaction levels high because they are assured that a consistently high service level will be received on request, even if the majority of purchases are routine. Although online retailing has become very popular, customer service is still a very relevant way of achieving competitive advantage (see Vignette 13.2).

Expectations of the target customer

The characteristics of the target customer may have a significant bearing on the type and level of service required in a retail situation. For example a retailer such as Mothercare that targets parents of young children has to ensure that its service provision is appropriate. This might include automatic doors, wide aisles, baby change rooms as well as baby-tolerant and knowledgeable staff. At the other end of a consumer's life cycle, retailers can improve service to third-age consumers by training sales associates to be clearly spoken and patient, by providing places for customers to rest and by publishing written information for customers in large print.

The first-time purchase is also a good opportunity for retailers to offer a high level of service, because as consumers become more experienced and knowledgeable themselves about a particular product item, they rely less on information from sources like retailers in their accumulation of relevant knowledge. In many instances a retailer will be wanting to 'lock in' a customer, so that when a similar need occurs in the future that retailer will be chosen for repeat purchases and store loyalty is built. This is particularly relevant to retailers of financial services and personal communications because many of their products have long-term implications for the customer and the retailer, and they are generally complex in nature. Retailers must be aware however, that in an era of information wealth, consumers do not wish to be sold to, but want to be known and respected, with a personalized shopping experience tailored to their needs and preferences (Schaefer, 2011).

Expectations and experiences

The work of Parasuraman, Zeithaml and Berry (Parasuraman et al., 1985, 1990, Zeithaml and Parasuraman, 2004) underpins much of the theoretical development relating to customer perceptions of service. They found that matching customers' expectations with their actual experience of service received leads to customer satisfaction. Conversely, if the experience does not meet the expectation, the customer would be dissatisfied with the service received. They found that it was not necessarily important to strive to achieve increasingly high levels of service, but that the quality of service received matched the expectations of customers in a particular context. Parasuraman, Zeithaml and Berry deduced that in order to provide a level of service that was satisfactory from the customer's point of view, there should be no gaps between the expectation and the experience. This led to the development of a model that helps service providers like retailers to identify where and why gaps might occur.

THE GAP MODEL

The gap model is very useful for retailers when they are trying to analyse where they may be failing customers on service. In a competitive retail environment where retailers are continually raising service standards, and thus raising customer-service expectations, an individual retailer needs to be able to monitor the satisfaction levels of their customers. Perfection in retail service provision would be the situation where expectations and perceived experiences are identical.

The preceding discussion in this chapter illustrates the extensive nature of service in retailing. In their research, Parasuraman et al. (1990) found that in most service-delivery scenarios the factors that customers use to judge the quality of service experienced could be categorized into ten identifiable dimensions; these have been adapted into the retail context in column 3 of Table 15.3.

The dimensions of service quality provide a framework (named SERVQUAL by Parasuraman et al., 1990) from which a retailer can then devise a research instrument to measure any difference between the expected and the experienced quality of service received. The SERVQUAL methodology uses a scaling technique, allowing

Table 15.3 Dimensions of retail service

Dimensions of service quality	Explanation of dimension	Dimension in retail context
Tangibles	Appearance of physical facilities, equipment, personnel and communication material	Appearance of outlet, displays, communications within the outlet and sales associates
Reliability	Ability to perform the promised service, dependably and accurately	Efficient checkout operations; accurate and safe payment and receipt; accurate and on-time home delivery
Responsiveness	Willingness to help customers and provide prompt service	Quickly identifying and responding to customers who require help; having an efficient helpline or customer service desk
Competence	Possession of the required skills and knowledge to perform the service	Well-trained sales associates, with relevant knowledge and skills; empowered sales associates who perform their tasks without referral to a supervisor
Courtesy	Politeness, consideration respect and friendliness of contact personnel	Sales associates genuinely interested in helping customers, friendly and respectful of all customers
Credibility	Trustworthiness, believability, honour of the service provider	Retailer's policy concerning services (especially returns) and reputation for customer service; approach of sales associates

Table 15.3 (Continued)

Dimensions of service quality	Explanation of dimension	Dimension in retail context
Security	Freedom from danger, risk or doubt	Presence of security staff, secure payment method, return policy and after-sales guarantees
Access	Approachability and ease of contact	Convenient location and opening hours; provision of customer facilities; outlet or department managers available if required
Communication	Keeping customers informed in language that they can understand, and listening to customers	Provision of information about products and services; explanation of payment methods and promotional offers; in-store signage; direct communications, e.g. direct mail or email; complaints procedures
Understanding the customer	Making the effort to know customers and their needs	Getting to know regular customers, either in person or electronically; understanding customer behaviour; responding to customer comments

Source: Adapted from Parasuraman et al. (1985, 1990).

customers to indicate the level of expectation and the perception of the service quality received.

The gap model suggests that there are four potential barriers to the service quality experienced by customers meeting (or exceeding) the level anticipated, leading to a mismatch between expectations and the service actually delivered (Brassington and Pettitt, 2000) (Figure 15.1).

The knowledge gap

This expresses the difference between the service that customers expect and the service that the retailer thinks customers expect. A retailer needs to research exactly what is important to customers, for example by establishing what are essential services in the eyes of the customer, and those considered to be optional extras. One of the challenges for the retailer is that different types of customers will have different expectations. For example, home grocery delivery might be an expected service for a less mobile customer but a fast checkout service might be more relevant to the busy lunchtime shopper. Only by carrying out consumer research can a retailer expect to monitor what type and level of service is expected by customers. Customers change over time, as alternative retail outlets change their service offerings and different retail formats emerge. Without this research and the opportunity for feedback, a retailer is bound to become out of touch, and the knowledge gap will start to appear.

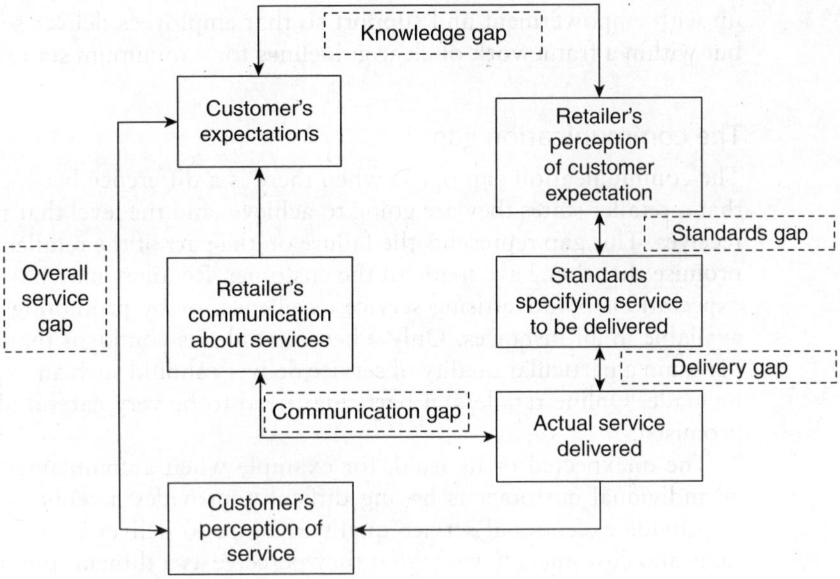

Figure 15.1 The gap model, adapted to retailing

Source: Adapted from Parasuraman, Zeithaml and Berry (1990).

The standards gap

The standards gap represents the difference between the service quality expected and the operational standards that the retailer achieves in its organization. Having closed the knowledge gap, by gaining a real understanding of what is required by customers, a realistic appraisal is needed in order to assess how this service quality level is going to be met. Commitment at the higher levels of management, and the acceptance of possible increases in costs in order to achieve higher-quality service (for example training and schemes to incentivize good service) are all part of this process. It is essential that those people within the retail organization who devise service delivery standards and procedures address knowledge gaps that become apparent from customer research, so that inappropriate and irrelevant procedures and practices are avoided, and resources are directed to the development and improvement of services considered relevant by customers.

The delivery gap

The delivery gap occurs when employees fail to deliver the required standard of service. Having formulated a plan to achieve an acceptable level of service quality, the retailer must now ensure that at least this level of service is encountered by every customer, on every purchase occasion. It is extremely important that employees are motivated to produce good service levels even though they may be having problems outside work, or when a customer is being particularly difficult. To ensure service deliverers have the knowledge and skills required, set procedures and good training are required, backed up with empowerment and support so that employees deliver services as they see fit, but within a framework of clear guidelines for a minimum standard.

The communication gap

The communication gap opens when there is a difference between the level of service that a retailer states they are going to achieve, and the level that the customer actually receives. This gap represents the failure on the part of the retailer to deliver the service promise that they have made to the customer. Retailers may have built up customers' expectations by advertising service excellence, or by promoting services that are not available in all instances. Only when a retailer is confident that their operations can maintain a particular quality of service delivery should such an explicit service promise be made. Online retailers in particular need to be very careful about delivery service promised.

The unexpected or unusual, for example when a complaint is received, or where an individual customer is having difficulty, provides a retailer with an opportunity to provide exceptional service quality. Failure to deliver on time, out-of-stock situations and customers having what they perceive as a difficult purchase are all instances where exceptional remedial service can turn a negative experience into a positive one for the customer. Retailers must be conscious of the tendency for customers to pass on commentary when service is bad, rather than when it is good, and with the growth of blogging, third-party forums and social networking, this commentary is fast and free.

These four potential sources of breakdown in service delivery contribute to the gap between expectation and perception. For example, a customer might indicate that in terms of responsiveness their experience in a supermarket had fallen short of their expectations because they had waited for an excessive period of time in the checkout queue. The retailer will then need to establish what type of 'gap' caused this dissatisfaction. Was it a knowledge gap, where the retailer was unaware of the extent to which customers dislike standing in queues, and overestimated the time that customers consider reasonable for queuing? Was it a standards gap; for example did the retailer have enough checkouts in operation or have they installed self-checkouts? Was it a delivery gap, in that all checkouts were in operation but the operators were very slow? Or could it have been a communication gap, where the retailer had made a promise of a very fast checkout service in an advertisement? The gap model points the retailer in various directions for further investigation into the specific nature of customers' dissatisfaction.

SERVICE DIFFERENTIATION

A strategy that is truly differentiated on service is one that is based on a long-term approach, as opposed to one where customer-service initiatives are introduced on a short-term basis either to achieve a short-term gain or to keep up with competitors. The relationship between costs and high levels of service was mentioned earlier in this chapter, but it must be stressed that good customer service does not have to incur higher costs – a courteous sales associate may well be on the same hourly rate as a rude one. The following management philosophies may be useful to adopt when developing a service-driven strategy.

Marketing orientation

The notion that the identification and satisfaction of consumer needs leads to improved customer retention underpins the marketing concept (Sivadas and Baker-Prewitt, 2000). It can be deduced, therefore, that retailers who are more marketing orientated are more likely to be sensitive to customers' service needs as well as their product needs. Marketing thought has embraced the idea that all products can be considered service providers in one form or another and that the value in a product offered by the marketing organization (for example the retailer) can only be unlocked by a co-creator of value, which is a different way of considering customers (Lusch and Vargo, 2006). The idea of a company or brand 'touchpoints' is a useful one to consider here; the branded service experience is as relevant as a branded product, and all aspects of a retailer, wherever the customer makes that contact, contribute to the customer's branded retail experience. Touchpoints include communications through formal (planned) and informal (unplanned) media sources, in-store experiences, Web-based experiences and home delivery experiences. Overall there is a growing opinion that marketing activity is what customers consider *is* the company (French et al., 2011), and so marketing orientation continues to be central to service differentiation.

Empowerment of the human resource

Nordstrom, a US department store, has found international acclaim for its service-differentiation strategy, which is founded on the empowerment of individual salespeople to implement customized service initiatives as they see fit on an individual customer basis, in the knowledge that the store, as a business organization, will support those initiatives. For example, a sales associate in a clothing department would be allowed to send outfits to a customer's home, for the customer to choose from, without any prior payment. The exceptional service from the retailer is based on the knowledge and experience of the employee concerning the cost-effectiveness of this action: for example knowing how high and frequent the transaction levels of individual customers are, and the extent to which individual customers are trustworthy (Spector and McCarthy, 1995).

Quality assurance

The notion of quality assurance is that the retailer has procedures in place that guarantee a particular level of service. For example, a training programme might indicate that customers are always greeted and that within five minutes their shopping needs identified. Training programmes ensure that consistent standards of service are provided to all customers, but they run the risk of stifling creativity in service delivery, and therefore an appropriate balance has to be achieved between standardization and customization (see below).

Staff development

Companies who operate a well-defined and understood programme of staff development will be able to identify the needs of personnel wherever they are employed within the organization. In particular, customer-service providers need to be trained in operational procedures so that they are efficient, and they need up-to-date product information so that they can advise customers appropriately. They may also be specifically trained in selling techniques. For example, the home-shopping customer advisors at White Stuff have a rail of current garments next to them, so that they can accurately describe the product detail to customers and advise on colour and style coordination on the phone. Many companies allow employees to identify their own customer-service developmental needs, which helps to motivate individuals and raise employee retention.

Service-orientated company culture

Companies that have a culture that embraces the 'customer is dictator' or a strong marketing orientation ethos will find it easier to introduce customer-orientated service initiatives. Sales associates are the people in the organization who are in touch with customers and are able to bring qualitative information about services that sales analysis may not reveal, and so encouraging employees to make suggestions to improve services helps to develop a team-working approach to customer service. This type of culture can be extended to employees of the organization who are considered to be 'internal customers'. John Lewis is an example of a retailer that has customer service at the centre of its business philosophy and a good record of employee retention (see Vignette 15.1).

VIGNETTE 15.1 SERVICE DIFFERENTIATION AT JOHN LEWIS

John Lewis, the long-established and highly successful UK department store group, can count the Queen of England among its customers, but the store has also been described as the People's Republic. It is a retail organization that has customer service at its heart. Its employees are courteous, well trained and well informed, and they have long-term customer loyalty rather than short-term sales gains as their ultimate goal. For example one customer might be advised to buy a cheaper laptop because it was more suitable for her needs, knowing that most customers have a child or parent (or both) who at some point may also need a laptop; another customer would be taken through the whole range of saucepans because that same customer could come back the next month to buy a new kitchen to put those pans in.

The long-term success of John Lewis is in every employee's direct interest, and this is what many commentators believe is the underlying source of the company's competitive advantage. John Lewis is a partnership, whereby the company is owned by its employees. All employees receive the same percentage share of company profits, and all employees can dine in the company restaurant. John Lewis has high staff retention; staff are involved in company decision making and are encouraged to be constructively critical of the organization through the company newspaper. Ultimately, John Lewis runs their business with the belief that good treatment of staff brings good treatment of customers. Without the need to answer to shareholders, it is a simpler relationship, between John Lewis employees and their customers only, which seems to bring long-term loyalty, trust and healthy sales figures. In spite of increased price transparency online, customers still say that they are willing to pay more for good service; however, overall service standards in retailing seem to be no better or worse than in the past. In this complex retail environment, John Lewis is providing what many other retailers seem unable to do.

Source: Based on Urwin (2009), *Retail Bulletin* (2011)

As mentioned previously in this chapter, while good service does not necessarily cost more than poor service, there are many aspects of a high level of customer service that do not come without additional costs. In fact, research (for example Pirron and Young, 2000) has indicated that a convenience-orientated service like a liberal returns policy may be routinely abused by some customers (see Vignette 15.2). A retailer must establish whether the resources put into their services offer is a worthwhile investment in terms of achieving strategic objectives, such as increasing transaction values or improving loyalty.

VIGNETTE 15.2 CUSTOMERS ARE NOT ALWAYS RIGHT

'De-shopping' and 'retail borrowing' are terms that describe a form of aberrant consumer behaviour that involves the conscious purchase of goods with the premeditated intention of returning them to the retailer after limited use, over a short period of time. It is suggested that the generous returns policies that many retailers have adopted to improve customer-service standards have encouraged this type of behaviour. King and Balmer (2012) estimate the activities of de-shoppers cost US retailers $16 billion a year and that it is a behaviour that is addictive and often learned by family and peers.

Retail borrowing seems to be carried out more often for social reasons (concerning an outfit for a special occasion for example) than for economic reasons (not being able to afford an item). Damage to goods is often inflicted in order to present a more 'credible' case for refund. Whilst retailers may be aware of high levels of customer abuse, they can be reluctant to challenge customers because of the damage a 'fight' over a refund might do to their image and reputation.

King and Balmer suggest four fronts on which to develop appropriate responses to this costly, demoralizing and unethical behaviour:

- *Training*, so that sales assistants are able to discriminate between de-shoppers and honest customers and manage returns effectively and fairly.
- *Communication*, both to shoppers and staff, about the problem can deter the activity because the de-shopper knows that the retailer is aware of their behaviour. Establishing a personal relationship can deter the 'borrower' by making them feel guilty about their actions.
- *Comprehensive, consistent and manageable policies and processes*, so that there are no gaps or weaknesses that an unethical shopper can exploit.

- *Watchfulness*, using surveillance technology, security systems and personnel who are trained to detect unethical shopping behaviour of any kind, which gives the impression that the retailer is not willing to tolerate it.

Sources: Based on Dean (2001), Pirron and Young (2000) and King and Balmer (2012)

SERVICES RETAILING

The discussion of retail service in this chapter has, in terms of the product range being offered by retailers, been general in nature. However, it is worth highlighting the fact that, in retailing, the 'product' being sold can be tangible goods orientated or service orientated itself. A useful way of exploring the nature of different retail products is by putting them on a goods–service continuum (Adcock et al., 2001). Retail products that are nearer the service end of the continuum are often characterized by the inseparability of the product's delivery and consumption (for example in the case of a haircut), the intangibility of the product at the time of purchase (for example a holiday or a personal loan) or the perishability of the product (for example a restaurant meal). They are also said to be heterogeneous in nature because service 'encounters' or experiences are likely to be slightly different for every customer and service delivery. This one-to-one nature of services retailing provides many challenges in terms of operational control, but can also be a real opportunity for differentiation by exceeding the standard of competitors and for the implementation of relationship marketing.

One of the difficulties associated with retailing services is control of the quality of service received by customers, and how the level of quality that can be expected in a retail outlet is communicated to customers. For example, in a hair salon the quality of the product is dependent on the stylist's performance, and how much the individual customer likes their new style. The satisfaction of the individual customer with the style produced, and the quality of the service product, can only be fully assessed when the styling is finished. However, customers are helped in their assessment of the essentially intangible product by tangible indicators such as the environment in which the styling takes place. If the salon is clean, with a fashionable decor, the stylists are carefully dressed and their styling qualifications accessible, this 'physical evidence' will send positive messages to customers about the level of quality they are likely to receive in the service product. Service quality in services retailing is important because rising living standards make customers want a higher standard of service to match their general lifestyle (Newman and Cullen, 2002).

Many services such as communications, banking and postal services either have been or are currently being deregulated, which has meant that service 'provision' has changed from being producer orientated to customer orientated. This has resulted in markets with offers from alternative sources competing on a mix of price, convenience, quality and service delivery, just like tangible-product retailers. Building brand awareness, trust and loyalty is extremely important in services markets because service products often are complex and expensive and require high levels of customer involvement (for example holidays, or personal investments).

The 'store' or environment where the service transaction takes place is a very important tool for service retailers to use to communicate their product to customers. For example, beauty services retailers tend to use white and cool colours (green and blue) and hard surfaces such as ceramics and glass in their decor, which helps to build an impression of hygiene and calm. The outlet may also show displays of the tangible element of the service (such as creams and lotions). Banks have softened their retail environment considerably over the years, to move from a focus on security to one on customer advice about financial management.

In order to ensure consistency in service levels in service product delivery, some service retailers use highly standardized approaches to customer interaction. Fast-food retailers have used this technique to ensure that a minimum standard of service quality can be guaranteed to all customers; procedures are extensive and strictly implemented, and staff are trained and continually assessed to ensure they maintain the standard required. In other service-retailing situations, technology can help to meet the needs of both customers and retailers. For example, booking systems are automated and flexible pricing can help service retailers to encourage use of their service (such as hotels and travel) at off-peak times, so that maximum revenue from the business' assets is achieved. With mobile communications, travel information and booking confirmation can be updated and accessed on the move.

CUSTOMIZATION VERSUS STANDARDIZATION

Both service and product retailers need to plan their operations so that the fundamental elements of the offering, such as preparation, stock control, processing and training, are performed away from customers, leaving the interaction between retailer and customer to be customer focused and dedicated. The extent to which retailers then customize the personal service given to individual shoppers can then vary according to the strategic aims of the business. In a mass-market fast-food situation, it is appropriate to have a standardized service quality, whereas in a department store like Nordstrom the freedom that sales personnel have to customize their service to individual customers is coherent with their upmarket and service-orientated positioning. The Internet however allows a two-way one-to-one relationship to be built with customers, and this has furthered the notion of mass customization, whereby tailored and personalized retail services are increasingly what customers expect and retail businesses should aspire to provide.

SUMMARY

It is no longer possible for retailers to limit their consideration of service to the interaction between the salesperson and customer at the moment of purchase. Customers are valuable commodities, who need to be nurtured and kept satisfied in an attempt to prevent them from straying to competitors. It is an old marketing adage that it costs more than five times as much to generate new customers than it does to keep existing ones, and that those loyal customers are more profitable customers. Providing a better level of service than competitors is an effective way to differentiate the retail offering, when there is little to distinguish between outlets in terms of products, prices and selling environments. Adopting a service-led strategy means that retailers have to focus all of their operations on providing a shopping experience that meets customers' expectations. Using the concept of gaps between these expectations and what customers may actually experience provides a methodology for identifying and correcting service-quality problems. Eliminating or minimizing these problems, and then building in services which make a positive impact on customers, generates the feel-good factor in customers and trust in the retail brand. Continuing to invest in services that customize the service offer to meet the diversified needs of a fragmented customer base is one of the most important ways in which retailers can generate competitive advantage while consistent service quality across the different shopping formats remains a strategic challenge as customers shop increasingly flexibly.

QUESTIONS

1. For a multi-channel retailer of your choice, provide an analysis of their services mix, using the categories of product-related, convenience-related, payment, product availability information and customer sales services.
2. Identify an occasion when your experience using a retailer did not meet your expectation? How and why did that gap occur? What recommendations would you make to the retailer in order for them to close the gap, and what might that retailer have done to redress the dissatisfaction that they had caused?
3. It is often said that there is a trade-off between price and service in retailing. To what extent do you agree with this?
4. Many retail 'services' are simply promotional gimmicks. Discuss this notion in relation to both store and online retailing, referring to the services life cycle in your answer.
5. Consider the viability of a retail strategy that uses service differentiation to create a sustainable competitive advantage. What implications does such a strategy have for resource allocation?

REFERENCES AND FURTHER READING

Adcock, D., Halborg, A. and Ross, C. (2001) *Marketing Principles and Practice* (Harlow: FT Prentice Hall).

Baron, S. and Harris, K. (2009) *Services Marketing – Text and Cases*, 3rd Edition (London: Palgrave Macmillan).

Brassington, F. and Pettitt, S. (2000) *Principles of Marketing*, 2nd Edition (Harlow: Pearson).

Collins, A., Henchion, M. and O' Reilly, P. (2001) 'Logistics Customer Service: Performance of Irish Food Exporters', *International Journal of Retail and Distribution Management*, vol. 29, no. 1, pp. 6–15.

Dean, J. (2001) 'What Cost Deshopping', British Shops and Stores Association website, http://www.british-shops.co.uk, 23 May, 1.

French, T., LaBerge, L. and Magill, P. (2011) 'We're All Marketers Now (marketers adjusting to deep customer engagement)', *McKinsey Quarterly*, July, no. 3, pp. 26–34.

Kelley, S. W., Donnelly, J. R. and Skinner, S. J. (1990) 'Customer Participation in Service Production and Delivery', *Journal of Retailing*, vol. 66, no. 3, p. 3.

King, T. and Balmer, J. (2012) 'When the Customer Isn't Right', Harvard Business Review Blog Network, available at http://blogs.hbr.org/cs/2012/02/when_the_customer_isnt_right.html [accessed 25 July 2013].

Lusch, R. F. and Vargo, S. L. (2006) *The Service Dominant Logic of Marketing: Dialog, Debate and Directions* (New York: M.E. Sharpe).

McGoldrick, P. J. (2002) *Retail Marketing* (Maidenhead: McGraw-Hill).

Mishra, D. (2000) 'Interdisciplinary Contributions in Retail Service Delivery: Review and Future Directions', *Journal of Retailing and Consumer Services*, vol. 7, no. 2, pp. 101–18.

Newman, A. J. and Cullen, P. (2002) *Retailing: Environment and Operations* (London: Thomson Learning).

Parasuraman, A., Zeithaml, V. A. and Berry, L. L. (1985) 'A Conceptual Model of Service Quality and Its Implications for Future Research', *Journal of Marketing*, vol. 49, no. 3, pp. 41–50.

Parasuraman, A., Zeithaml, V. A. and Berry, L. L. (1990) *Delivering Service Quality: Balancing Customer Perceptions and Expectations* (New York: Free Press).

Pirron, F. and Young, M. (2000) 'Retail Borrowing: Insights and Implication on Returning Used Merchandise', *International Journal of Retail and Distribution Management*, vol. 28, no. 1, pp. 27–36.

Polonsky, M. J., Cameron, H., Halstead, S., Ratcliffe, A., Stilo, P. and Watt, G. (2000) 'Exploring Companion Selling: Does the Situation Affect Customers' Perceptions?' *International Journal of Retail and Distribution Management*, vol. 28, no. 1, pp. 37–45.

Retail Bulletin (2011) 'New Survey Shows Customers Are Willing to Pay More for Good Service', available at http://www.theretailbulletin.com/print.php?id=17360 [accessed 29 July 2011].

Schaefer, M. (2011) 'Capitalizing on the Smarter Consumer', IBM Global Business Services, IBM Institute for Business Value, available at ibm.com/iibv [accessed 3 August 2011].

Sivadas, E. and Baker-Prewitt, J. L. (2000) 'An Examination of the Relationship between Service Quality, Customer Satisfaction, and Store Loyalty', *International Journal of Retail and Distribution Management*, vol. 28, no. 2, pp. 73–82.

Spector, R. and McCarthy, P. (1995) *The Nordstrom Way* (New York: Wiley).

Urwin, R. (2009) 'Life according to John Lewis', *Evening Standard*, 17 December.

White, F. (2000) 'Got Service All Wrapped Up?', *Retail Week*, 17 November.

Zeithaml, V. A. and Bitner, M. J. (2000) *Services Marketing: Integrating Customer Focus across the Firm*, 2nd Edition (Boston and London: Irwin/McGraw-Hill).

Zeithaml, V. A. and Parasuraman, A. (2004), *Service Quality* (Cambridge, MA: Marketing Science Institute).

16 INTERNATIONAL RETAILING

LEARNING OBJECTIVES

- To appreciate the factors influencing decisions to internationalize.
- To understand Dunning's eclectic theory and its relevance for international retailers.
- To consider the push and pull factors in the internationalization process.
- To explore the choice of markets of international retailers.
- To understand the rationale behind entry methods employed in internationalization.
- To justify standardization and adaptation approaches to internationalization strategies.

INTRODUCTION

The continuing globalization of the world economy coupled with mature and saturated home markets mean that international activity is a major management issue for most large retailers today, and is likely to continue being so in the near future. Internationalization in retailing is not a recent phenomenon; for instance Boots, the pharmacy, toiletries and beauty specialist found on almost every UK high street, not only opened its first store overseas in 1936, but was owned by an American company between 1927 and 1933 (Boots-uk.com, 2013). What is new, however, is the scale of the international activities of retailers and the importance of them strategically.

Historically, retailing has been an essentially small-scale, local activity. The highly capitalized, professionally managed, large-scale retailers that we see today are a relatively recent phenomenon. In the case of US and European retailers, for example, the size of the domestic market offered more than sufficient opportunities; however, recent stagnation at home has made overseas expansion a much more attractive growth strategy. Internationalization of retailers in recent years has been facilitated by the Internet and better transportation systems, which have made reaching global markets very easy and the control of international operations relatively straightforward. The purpose of this chapter is to examine the factors behind the increasing internationalization of retailers, the choice of markets, methods employed to enter them and trading strategies adopted within those markets.

INTERNATIONAL RETAILERS

Traditionally, the most active international players were luxury goods and specialist retailers. Nowadays, however, retailers of all types are active in international retailing activities (see Table 16.1), with fast-moving consumer goods (FMCG) and fashion both being important sectors. Retailers are also much more adventurous in that they are not only considering markets closest to them, but also operating more challenging and more distant markets. Part of the reason for this is that there are likely to be first-mover advantages for those entering relatively underdeveloped markets and the fact that there may be little opportunity for expansion in the retailer's own domestic market; however, market opportunities are currently the main drivers of international expansion.

EXPLANATIONS OF INTERNATIONALIZATION

Although the theory of retailer internationalization is still relatively underdeveloped, three major themes have emerged, namely Dunning's (1988) 'eclectic' theory of internationalization, the push–pull theory and the strategic management theory.

The eclectic theory

Dunning's eclectic theory of internationalization was originally based on manufacturing companies, but it has been used successfully to examine retailers' motives for internationalization. The theory attempts to explain why a firm will engage in foreign direct investment, rather than exporting or other forms of international activity. According to the eclectic theory, firms internationalize due to three factors: ownership-specific advantages, internalization and locational advantages.

Ownership advantages are transferable firm-specific advantages arising from proprietary know-how (unique assets) and transactional advantages that can be exploited for competitive advantage in the market. Transactional advantages refer to the ability

Table 16.1 Some foreign retailers trading in the UK

Firm	Retail trading name	Trading activity	Home country
Aldi	Aldi	Food discounting	Germany
Benetton	Benetton	Fashion	Italy
Cartier	Cartier	Jewellery	France
Costco	Costco	Warehouse club	USA
Gucci	Gucci	Leather goods	Italy
IKEA	IKEA	Furniture	Sweden
OTTO Versand	Grattan	Mail order	Germany
Toys 'R' Us	Toys 'R' Us	Toys	USA
Wal-Mart	ASDA	Supermarkets	USA
Zara	Zara	Fashion	Spain

of the firm to reduce costs by employing specific business systems, processes and technical know-how. Proprietary know-how can be in the form of patents, copyrights, brands and systems or process knowledge. The possession of these gives their owner an advantage over competitors. Proprietary assets that are legally protected such as brands and patents are easier to exploit in foreign markets. In the case of retailers, their main proprietary asset is their brand name, but at least in the early stages of internationalization these may have very little recognition in international markets, as many retailers have found to their cost. Owner-specific advantages such as merchandising techniques, expertise in a particular retail format (such as discounter or online), category dominance (buying expertise) and branding (product branding and retailer corporate branding) can be relevant in international retailing.

In retailing it is also very difficult to protect new ideas, as they are visible to competitors. However, firm-specific processes such as buying policies and strategies, information systems, customer relationship management, own-branding skills and supply-chain management are difficult to imitate for retailers. Where these processes result in firm-specific advantages in the form of economies of scale or customer loyalty, they are even more valuable.

Location-specific advantages refer to benefits derived from locating in foreign markets. These include lower labour costs, greater market opportunity (due to, for instance, market size or lower competition), the ability to circumvent trade barriers and diversification of risk. Unlike manufacturing, as the retailing product cannot be imported back into the domestic market, lower labour costs in foreign markets are not a significant motive for internationalization of retailers. Market size and growth, and diversification are the major motives behind much of the global expansion of international retailers.

Internalization advantages refer to the relative advantages of different methods of servicing international markets. The internalization theory suggests that where the transaction cost of non-equity involvement in international markets (such as exporting, franchising or licensing) is greater than the firm undertaking the activity itself, the firm will internalize the activity. For instance, a retailer wishing to franchise its concept internationally may find that the cost of marketing, setting up contracts and enforcing franchisee compliance may be greater than the returns in a particular country. They may, therefore, set up owned subsidiaries rather than franchising. For many retailers, exporting is not a viable option, given that they would be providing a distribution service of products that are available domestically. However, for retailers with strong own brands, exporting via online retailing is providing a low-risk route to new markets. For example specialist UK footwear retailer DUO won the Queen's Award for Enterprise: International Trade in 2012 by exporting footwear to customers in 132 countries via their online retailing networks (duo.com, 2013).

Push versus pull theories

Location-specific advantages in Dunning's framework clearly reflect the attractions, or the 'pull', of the new international market. Similarly, there are factors in the domestic market that are likely to 'push' firms into internationalization. Factors that push, pull or facilitate internationalization have received much attention in the discussion of internationalization of retailers. Push factors include saturated domestic markets, maturity of retail format, strong competition, trading restrictions and unfavourable economic conditions. Growth opportunities, potential scale economies, lack of retail provision and pre-emption of rivals are included among pull factors. Facilitating factors are identified as corporate philosophy and the vision of senior management, as well as the accumulation of in-company expertise through international buying and sourcing; however, expertise in online retailing is proving to be the most valuable facilitator for smaller retailers. External facilitating factors include lowering of trade barriers (for example the European Union, and the North American Free Trade Agreement), international alliances, compatible cultures, developments in international communications and transportation and the bandwagon effect (keeping up with competitors). Simplistic discussions of push–pull factors usually do not distinguish between environmental (external) factors and organizational factors internal to the firm. Much of the early research in this area tends to show that push factors have played a more significant part in the initial stages of internationalization (see for instance Kacker, 1985, and Salmon and Tordjman, 1989); however, pull factors such as high-growth emerging markets and the facilitating role of the Internet have made internationalization a viable strategy for many European and North American retailers (Dawson, 2007).

Strategic management approach to internationalization

A strategic management perspective of internationalization suggests that it is just one of a number of growth strategies that a firm can undertake. Knee and Walters (1985), for instance, extended Ansoff's product–market growth matrix (1965) and incorporated internationalization as a geographical expansion of the existing retail product into new markets (see Figure 16.1). International expansion is riskier than domestic geographical expansion; hence, domestic opportunities are more likely to be pursued first.

Internationalization strategies may also be pursued where product development strategies are either expensive (in comparison to internationalization) or not feasible without making a major change to the trading format. For instance, whereas large supermarkets (such as Tesco) have responded to limited growth opportunities in the food market by expanding their ranges to include non-food merchandise, this is not a strategy that can be adopted by limited-line discount food retailers such as Aldi. Major expansion of product ranges into non-food is not feasible for such stores because space constraints as well as the inevitable rise in costs would undermine the competitive advantage of the discount format. Hence, saturation of domestic markets led Aldi to embark on a strategy of internationalization.

An advantage of using the strategic management approach to internationalization is that it suggests management can be proactive and not wait for competitive pressures in the domestic market to arise before considering internationalization. For instance, innovative formats such as the Body Shop internationalized very early in

Market segments/customer base	Retailing product package: Existing	Related	New
Existing	*Market penetration*	*Product/tange extension. e.g.* specialization, new customer services, new outlet types	*product/ range development* (unrelated product range)
Related	Market extension (territorial expansion in domestic market)	Product/market development e.g. repositioning	
New	*Internationalization* using current format	*Internationalization* using new/adapted format	*Diversification*

Figure 16.1 Corporate strategy and internationalization

Source: Based on Knee and Walters (1985) p. 12.

their development because international opportunities were available to be exploited, long before the saturation of the domestic market.

MARKET SELECTION AND STAGES OF INTERNATIONALIZATION

Examination of retailer internationalization over time shows that there are a number of recognizable patterns. First, in the initial stages retailers are cautious and enter markets that are geographically and culturally 'close', and similar to the home market. In Europe, evidence of this is seen in the move of the French hypermarkets into Spain (for example Carrefour), and Swedish retailers into other Scandinavian countries (for example IKEA and H&M). Similarly, North American retailers have tended to enter the Canadian and South American markets before seeking markets further afield. Perceived cultural similarity is one of the major reasons for the large investment by UK retailers in the United States rather than in European countries, which are regarded as more distant culturally, with mixed results. Having acquired some experience of international operations, retailers tend to become more ambitious, and at this stage the growth opportunities are more important than geographical and cultural proximity. Retailers also begin to employ more than one strategy to enter markets. Marks and Spencer for example has used franchising, joint ventures, acquisition and organic growth to enter different international markets over time, with varying degrees of success (see Vignette 16.1).

VIGNETTE 16.1 MARKS AND SPENCER AND INTERNATIONAL ENTRY STRATEGIES

Marks and Spencer (M&S) began international retailing activities in the 1940s by exporting its St Michael own brand, which by 1996 amounted to around £116 million. Acquisition as an entry method was first used by M&S in 1973, when it entered the Canadian market with an acquisition of People's Department Stores Inc. (a budget-priced store) and D'Allaird's (clothing for older women) and Walker's clothing stores (which were later transformed into Marks and Spencer stores). Further acquisitions took place in April 1988, when M&S acquired the American clothing retailer Brooks Brothers for $750 million, and Kings Supermarkets. In 1975 M&S opened its first owned and operated European store in Paris. This was followed in the same year by a store in Brussels. Company-owned stores were also opened in Germany (1996), Hong Kong (1988), Ireland (1979), Spain (1990) and the Netherlands (1991). M&S began a major push into franchising around 1988. Since then the franchise operation has expanded enormously, and the company now operates in the Bahamas, Czech Republic, Dubai, Finland, Greece, Hungary, India, Indonesia, Kuwait, Malaysia, the Netherlands, Portugal, South Korea, Thailand and Turkey. The estimated sales turnover of the franchise business amounted to over £350 million in 2002. M&S experimented with joint ventures as an entry method when it opened its first store in Spain in 1990 in a joint venture with Cortefiel, a leading Spanish retail chain. M&S eventually bought out Cortefiel in 1999 to leave the store solely in M&S' hands.

On 29 March 2001, after a major review of its activities necessitated by its stagnating sales and sharply declining profits in its core domestic market, M&S sold off Brooks Brothers in the United States and all the European stores, and converted its Hong Kong stores into a franchise business. Although the US businesses were trading well, the company felt that they did not constitute a sound basis for developing M&S in the United States, and the losses incurred in Europe could no longer be afforded. M&S had already divested its loss-making Canadian operation in 1999. Luc Vandevelde, Chairman and CEO of M&S at the time, stated in the 2001 annual report that M&S' experience illustrates that 'to succeed internationally when entering mature markets, you must adapt your store formats to the competitive realities of those markets'. This hints at M&S' adoption of a largely standardized approach to international markets and its failure to adapt its strategies to local needs. In contrast, the success of its franchise businesses demonstrates the value of local market knowledge of franchisees in adapting the M&S approach and products to different customer needs.

M&S sold the remaining 26 Kings supermarkets in 2006, finally accepting defeat in the United States, which is sometimes referred to as 'the graveyard for European retailers', but the company continued to expand internationally using franchises in particular, and now operates 418 international stores in 51 countries, in Europe, the Middle East, Asia and Africa. M&S operates a joint venture with an Indian retail ownership group Reliance Retail, which allowed six new M&S stores to open in 2012. China is another important market where M&S have 14 stores in the Shanghai region and are developing an online business. France was also back on the list of countries served with stores supported with a dedicated website.

Acknowledging the need for flexibility in international markets, the 2013 company report states, 'our international strategy is built around a clear geographic focus, supported by the right business model for each market . . . combining our central planning with local market knowledge to deliver a more tailored product offer that better reflects local seasonality, culture and customer profile'.

Source: Various, including Sternquist (2007), Burt et al. (2002), Marks and Spencer annual reports (2001, 2002, 2013), Deloitte (2012), Faithfull (2013)

INTERNATIONAL OPPORTUNITIES

The increasing regionalism, or the tendency towards economic cooperation between countries within regions, particularly in the form of free-trade areas, is increasing internationalization opportunities for retailers. A free-trade area is an area whose member countries agree to have free movement of goods among themselves, without the imposition of tariffs or quotas. Two of the largest and most successful examples are the European Union (EU) and the North American Free Trade Agreement (NAFTA). NAFTA came into effect in 1993 and provides for the gradual removal of tariffs and quotas over a 15-year period creating a market of 390 million people. As a result there has been a great deal of investment by US retailers in Mexico and Canada.

In Europe, the completion of the single European market (SEM) and with it the transformation of the European Community into the European Union in 1993 has made the movement of goods much easier, resulting in a big increase in cross-border retailing within EU countries. With the relaxation of border and other trade controls, the 28 EU countries now constitute a huge market, with a population of over 500 million people. In the 1970s and 1980s much of the international retailing investment in Europe was in the more developed retailing countries such as France, Germany, Spain, Portugal and the UK, but then spread into Central and Eastern European countries, particularly the Czech Republic, Hungary and Poland. More recently, European retailers have been active in markets further afield, especially the so-called BRIC countries (Brazil, Russia, India and China). Much of the retail investment in Central and Eastern Europe and the Asia Pacific region is motivated by the fact that these countries are relatively underdeveloped in international retailing terms and currently have relatively high economic growth.

International opportunities inevitably come with risks, and retailers must therefore carefully analyse both the opportunities and risks before making entry decisions. Market attractiveness is an important concept where retailers draw up a set of criteria for measuring how different countries rate in terms that impact attractiveness for investment. Attractiveness can include quantitative measures and qualitative aspects that may be difficult to assess, but nonetheless could influence heavily on the success or failure of the retailer. These factors closely connect with the push and pull factors discussed earlier. Quantitative measures include large population size of low–middle age, high employment, high disposable income, geographic proximity, high economic growth and low operating costs including labour. Qualitative measures might include similar climate, high brand recognition and positive image, good retail and transportation infrastructure, number and nature of competitors, good labour talent and availability, appropriate lifestyle and shopping behaviour and economic and political stability. Some factors may be weighted more heavily than others according to the specific retail business. For example a growing young population, high disposable income, high employment, good infrastructure and a luxury lifestyle would be important factors for a designer fashion brand (such as Burberry), whereas for a grocery retailer an additionally important factor would be competitors: fashion is a retail sector that is usually less concentrated and so the presence of competitors is seen as positive, whereas in most international markets domestic grocery supermarket operators have established market share and are likely to retaliate strongly to a new international competitor. Some examples of markets that are considered to be attractive overall currently are China, India, Indonesia, Brazil, Chile, Uruguay, Peru, Mexico, Russia, United Arab Emirates, Oman, Kuwait and Turkey (Kearney, 2012).

ENTRY STRATEGIES

When moving into foreign markets, retailers have to decide the best method of entry. The main methods of expansion for retailers are shown in Figure 16.2 and discussed in the following:

1. *Company owned (also referred to as self-start entry, greenfield entry or organic growth)*. This involves building up a foreign retail presence from scratch. It is the method that is most likely to be used where a retailer has an innovative format and wants to retain maximum control over the venture. Organic growth also provides the retailer with control over the rate of growth and hence capital outlay. However, researching and developing sites can be time consuming and it is a resource-hungry activity. New retail formats such as online and pop-up shops are more flexible company-owned entry methods, and for strong retail brands the owned flagship store is a central tenet of the international strategy.

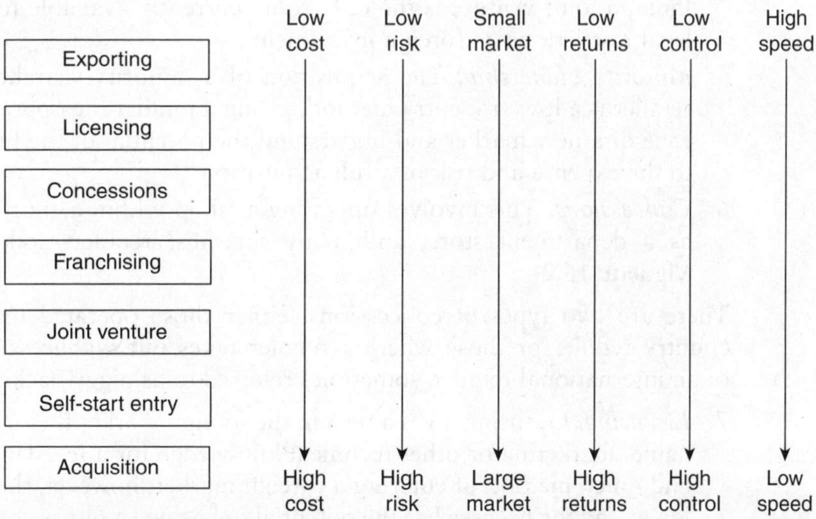

Figure 16.2 Entry methods for international retailing

2. *Acquisition.* Acquiring foreign retailers provides a quick method of entry but requires the most capital. Acquisition may be necessary in mature, concentrated markets where operations of a certain size are required in order to be competitive, as in the case of Wal-Mart's takeover of ASDA in the UK (1999). Suitable acquisitions are not always available because of the legal restrictions on ownership by non-domestic companies for example.
3. *Franchising.* Franchising is a frequently used method of international expansion, especially where the retailer is constrained by availability of capital or where markets are unfamiliar. Franchising allows the retailer (franchisor) to maintain a high degree of control over the marketing strategy, including what is sold within the store, whilst relinquishing control over day-to-day operations to a local partner (franchisee). Benetton and Body Shop provide examples of retailers that expanded internationally via franchising, and it is a market entry method that is often used in combination with complete company-owned outlets as in the case of Marks and Spencer, and Zara.
4. *Joint ventures.* Although some sources classify franchising as a type of joint venture, the term allows for a wide variety of agreements between companies, and in this context would include those of different international bases in a retail development. Both organizations share the costs and profits of the venture, but the exact terms of the agreement can be tailored to unique requirements with variations in terms of investment and control. Joint ventures work best where the partners bring complementary skills to the venture; however, failure of joint ventures due to disagreement over operational matters is very common. In some markets this is the only method available for entering markets. In other markets, such as Japan, markets may be so complex and expensive to enter that a joint venture is the best method of entry, as the partner can provide local market knowledge and share the risk of the venture. Boots used this method when entering Japan in 1999. Next and The Limited have also used joint ventures to break into overseas markets. To enter India, a joint venture is the only route currently available for retailers because of legal restrictions on foreign investment.
5. *Minority ownership.* The acquisition of a minority shareholding in an overseas retailer is a low-risk entry method, giving a retailer the opportunity to gain experience of a new market and understand the potential of the business without going to the expense and risk of a full acquisition.
6. *Concessions.* This involves operating a 'shop within a shop' in larger stores such as a department store, and many specialist retailers follow this strategy (see Vignette 16.2).

There are two types of concessions, either those operated in the store of a host-country retailer or those where a retailer takes out a concession in a foreign store of an international retailer, sometimes referred to as piggy backing.

7. *Licensing.* Licensing gives a firm in the foreign market the right to use the retailer's name, marketing or other technical knowledge for a fee. This is a relatively cheap and quick method of entering a foreign market; however, the expected returns are lower and the licensee has the potential to become a future competitor. This method of entry is used relatively rarely in retailing, although retailers of designer brands often sell licensed products in international markets.

8. *Exporting.* Although this is an important entry strategy for producers, the nature of retailing, namely that of providing a service, means that the term 'exporting' is not really relevant. However, retailers with strong own labels are able to export them where demand exists; for instance a company that only retails in its domestic market may wholesale in international markets and export that way. Marks and Spencer's initial venture into international retailing, for example, started with exporting their own-branded products.

VIGNETTE 16.2 REISS: A CAUTIOUS APPROACH TO INTERNATIONALIZATION, HELPED BY A ROYAL WAVE

Reiss is the eponymous fashion brand founded, owned and run by UK retail entrepreneur David Reiss. The company's early origins were in shirt manufacturing in the early 1970s, followed by wholesaling and retailing of menswear in the 1980s. The launch of womenswear as a mainstream retail category as opposed to capsule collection happened in 2000, since when the company grew steadily and organically until 2005, when it started a serious international retail expansion programme. Positioned as a bridge brand, with design-led, luxurious products and what are termed 'high-street prices', Reiss has carved a niche in the UK market as aspirational and stylish yet accessible and is currently enjoying increasing brand recognition and acceptance across the globe.

Easey (2009) refers to the influence of 'serendipity' on the fate of fashion brands, and Reiss has recently benefited from this effect with the kind of endorsement that the biggest marketing budget cannot buy: the preference of one of the most photographed women in the world, and a British royal too! First wearing the Olivia fitted flared coat, then the Nanette cream dress for the Mario Testino engagement portrait and the Shola dress to meet the Obamas (selling out within hours and then on eBay for 10 times the retail price minutes later), the Duchess of Cambridge has shown herself to be the most-valued Reiss fan, even though the brand has had other A-list customers such as Gisele Bündchen, Nicole Kidman, Sharon Stone, Meryl Streep, Kate Winslet and Nicollette Sheridan, which, particularly in international markets, is a must for brand acceptance.

Reiss has always had an international outlook. The wholesale business took the brand to retailers in Asia, the United States and Europe through the 1980s and 1990s, and overseas sales accounted for the majority of the wholesaling revenue in the mid-1990s.

After a number of successful years of wholesaling the brand in Japan through an agent, Reiss opened a franchised outlet in Tokyo in 1995, and appointed a licensee to manufacture and wholesale the Reiss collection in Australia. Really serious internationalization however took off in 2005 with a flagship store opening in New York's SoHo district and a franchised retail outlet in Dubai. Beverley Hills and Los Angeles followed in 2007 along with Malaysia, Hong Kong, New Jersey and Miami. Towards the end of 2005, there were reports of Reiss securing a deal to open 20 stores in China over the next 4 years. In 2010 Reiss appointed its first dedicated Head of International Operations, so that international plans could have more management support and further opportunities developed. In 2008 Reiss were reported to be aiming to have 250 stores globally by 2010, but the growth has slowed in the light of the world recession, and in fact in that year Reiss had 33 overseas shops including a newly opened store in Moscow. ▶

In 2011 Reiss launched a concession within the prestigious US department store Bloomingdale's. Pitched close to brands like Theory and Diane von Furstenberg, this adjacency suggests that Reiss has the potential to move closer to a luxury positioning. A sheepskin jacket retailing at £695 sold out in Selfridges in autumn 2011, and the success of the accessories category with handbags frequently selling at £300 would support a move from premium to luxury positioning in the global market. As well as giving Reiss high visibility in the New York through flagship at one of the most iconic multi-channel retailers in the United States, Bloomingdale's has many satellite stores across the US, which gives a potential opportunity to raise awareness in a huge geographic market that has often been found surprisingly challenging by UK-based fashion retailers. Recent reports suggest that the number of Bloomingdale's stores where the brand is stocked will rise from 7 to 14. In 2012 the company spoke of plans to double revenue through overseas expansion (Lovett, 2012) and further recent store openings include a second Hong Kong store and stores in Saudi Arabia. The company is taking the opportunity to open stores in high-profile cities in order to showcase the brand at the highest level in the belief that the Reiss product will travel to most corners of the world without major modification.

Source: Various including Bearne (2010, 2012) and Lovett (2012)

ONLINE RETAILING

Offering the opportunity for international customers to shop online is a low-risk and relatively low-cost method of entry and so has become a frequently used method to test international markets. In addition, the online shop is used in conjunction with other types of store operations as part of a multi-channel international strategy. Once the presence of a retailer is established in a particular country, for example a flagship store in a capital or major city, the Internet can be used to reach consumers further afield in that country. In order to establish a significant international online business, tailored websites, payment systems and logistical arrangements will be required for the specific international market. ASOS for example is expanding rapidly internationally and now has websites in a number of different languages. The Arcadia Group (that owns Topshop, Topman, Miss Selfridge, Wallis, Evans, Dorothy Perkins, Burton and BHS) has used both franchising and key flagship stores supported by significant marketing communications and online delivery to break into new international markets.

THE ROLE OF THE FLAGSHIP STORE IN INTERNATIONAL MARKETS

Flagship stores, particularly for retailers of luxury goods, but increasingly for speciality own-brand retailers, are a powerful and important platform for growth in international markets (Nobbs et al., 2012). By setting out the full product offer in an environment that enhances the identity and personality of the retail brand, the flagship is a statement and benchmark for future retailing activities. From there further stores can be opened (either owned or franchised), supported with online delivery, while wholesale activities and concessions may benefit from referred interest in the retail brand. The opening of an international flagship provides the opportunity for promotional activity such as a launch event, which in turn can turn into a flurry of publicity to generate press and consumer interest.

FACTORS DETERMINING CHOICE OF ENTRY METHODS

The actual method of entry into an international market will depend on a number of factors including cost, control, uniqueness of the format, availability of good locations, financial strength of the firm, size and competitiveness of foreign markets and political and economic risk associated with a particular country. For instance, larger formats (such as department stores) tend to be difficult to internationalize using licensing or franchising strategies due to their complexity and the initial capital outlay. Conversely, it is common to find that speciality stores often use franchising in their strategies. For innovative formats, acquisition is not an option, as such retailers are by definition different to existing businesses.

The size of the market is an important determinant of the entry strategy. Generally speaking, foreign direct investment (FDI) strategies like acquisition and self-start ventures are only likely to be used in larger markets. Smaller markets are most likely to be serviced using a non-FDI strategy ranging from a concession (store within store) to franchising. The competitive market conditions also have an important influence on entry strategies. For instance, Wal-Mart chose to enter the UK grocery market via the acquisition of ASDA; a major reason behind this strategy was the fact that the grocery market in the UK is highly competitive, with the top five food retailers controlling a market share in excess of 70 per cent. A self-start entry by Wal-Mart would have been ineffective as suitable large-scale sites are difficult to obtain due to the tight planning regulations in the UK, and would have been uncompetitive against the well-established networks of domestic retailers. As the world's largest retailer, Wal-Mart also had the capital to make such an acquisition, which also suited their aggressive international growth strategy.

In some countries, domestic legislation controls the types of entry methods employed by retailers. In other markets, whilst there are no legal impediments, the business environment may be so complex that working with a local partner is essential for the success of a retail venture. Other markets may be too politically or economically unstable to consider large investments, and so franchising or joint ventures may be more appropriate.

STANDARDIZATION VERSUS ADAPTATION STRATEGIES

When entering international markets, retailers have to decide whether to use their existing retail format or adapt it to the needs of the foreign market being entered.

The marketing concept holds that firms should be customer oriented and that marketing efforts will be more effective if they are closely adapted to the needs of each group (or segment) of target customers. In the international retailing context this means that because of the varying economic, geographic, demographic and cultural factors and characteristics of consumers in different countries, they are likely to have different wants and needs, spending power, shopping patterns and product preferences, and so an adapted retail marketing strategy is likely to be the best option. Although the advantage of such a strategy is that the retailing offer is more suited to the needs of consumers in the host country, the required changes in the retail mix may prove to be too resource hungry and not in line with the overall brand strategy.

Standardization involves using the same range of products, the same pricing, a common marketing communication strategy and a similar distribution/location strategy. Its major advantages include economies of scale in buying and economies of replication in store design and marketing communication themes, which results in lower overall costs. The rationale behind standardization is that similar products are wanted across all the markets that the retailer operates in. Examples of retailers using a mainly standardization strategy include Toys 'R' Us and Body Shop.

There are also other forces that make standardization an attractive and feasible alternative. Changes in communications, transportation and worldwide travel have led to the emergence of a global marketplace, and these same changes, it is argued, are leading to the homogenization of customer needs and wants and hence global markets. Theodore Levitt (1983), one of the foremost proponents of the standardization argument, argues that despite what customers say, what they really want is good-quality products at lower prices:

> If the price is low enough, they will take highly standardized world products, even if they aren't exactly what mother said was suitable, what immemorial custom decreed was right, or what market research . . . asserted was preferred.

Standardization proponents argue that the use of a common marketing programme on a global basis is the most effective method of marketing internationally in today's marketplace.

These arguments are based on the premise that there is a convergence of tastes and a convergence of income levels, which means that global markets exist for most goods and services and hence the advantages to be gained by adaptation are either small or non-existent. Similarly, the potential for cost savings in standardization are enormous. Standardization also allows the projection of a consistent international image, which is important in a world where consumers are more and more internationally mobile. Other advantages include simpler marketing planning and control.

Whilst the arguments for standardization are strong, it is extremely difficult to standardize the entire retail marketing programme. Standardization is in general more difficult for culturally sensitive items such as food and service products. Luxury and high-fashion items are easier to standardize because they are wanted for the unique values that they represent. Consumers of these products are also likely to be affluent, well educated and with a cosmopolitan outlook, and therefore represent a more homogeneous global segment.

It is also difficult to maintain equality in pricing across international operations since cost structures in different markets are quite different. The two major elements of costs for retailers are those associated with operating outlets, and distribution (logistical) costs, all of which vary considerably due to differences in labour and property markets and distributional infrastructures. In addition, the imposition of tariffs on imported merchandise, and different levels of competition add to the difficulties.

However, what retailers can do is attempt to achieve a similar positioning to their domestic market. For instance, a discounter such as Aldi will attempt to be at least 20–30 per cent cheaper than regular supermarkets in the countries that it operates in.

Promotional strategies may be difficult to standardize due to different regulations on advertising and sales promotion, availability of media and differences in communication styles. Location is also difficult to standardize since suitable sites may already be occupied or not available due to planning regulations. For instance, Toys 'R' Us normally locates its stores in out-of-town locations, but in France it has located them in shopping centres because planning permission was difficult to obtain in out-of-town locations.

The standardization versus adaptation argument is not an 'all-or-nothing' decision. The degree of standardization can vary from global standardization to adaptation for each market, and standardization in key markets to adaptation in key markets. A compromise between adaptation and standardization is a patterned standardization strategy that involves developing global marketing strategies whilst allowing for a degree of adaptation to take account of local market conditions. 'Think global and act local' is the idea behind patterned standardization. Thus, standardization is more a matter of degree rather than an absolute decision. Retailers should always be on the lookout for opportunities to standardize elements of the retail marketing mix, but understand that adaptation may be preferable depending on the operating conditions of the market.

PROBLEMS FOR NEWCOMERS

Newcomers to international retailing face a number of common problems. First, they will tend to underestimate cultural differences and their effect on trading internationally. Culture results not only in differences in customer needs but also impacts on styles of management and general business dealings with suppliers. Lack of supplier and distribution networks is another major problem. This may mean that the retailer has to import everything, thus increasing costs and impacting on efficiency. For instance, when Carrefour entered the US market in 1988, it had no distribution network and ended up using part of the store for storage purposes. This resulted in less space for its merchandise assortment and increased operational costs.

Most retail brands have little international carry-over. Even where customers recognize the retail fascia, they may not have a good understanding of the brand values. This means that new entrants need to put in a great deal of promotional effort to get their store noticed and to entice customers into the outlet. In effect, it may be necessary to rebuild the retail brand from scratch in the foreign market. This can also be seen as an opportunity to customize the brand more to the needs of the local market. UK retail giant Tesco for example has successfully internationalized in Europe and Asia, but has had difficulty making an impact in the United States, where domestic supermarket operators have a much deeper understanding of the grocery consumer culture.

Another common problem is to underestimate the strength of local competition or local reaction to market entry of foreign competition. For instance, in the early 1990s, when Aldi and a number of other continental food discounters entered the UK market, the large supermarket chains launched 'value' ranges of their own brands to compete with the low prices offered by the discounters. This had the effect of slowing down the expansion and restricting the market share that the discounters were able to achieve. Underestimating the fierceness of competition is one of the major reasons for the failure of numerous European retailers entering the US market.

Integrating the various parts of the international business, and integrating the domestic business with international business is another major area of difficulty for the international retailer; having domestic and international operations substantially increases the complexity of the management task. Integration is also made more difficult where foreign acquisitions have to be integrated into the structure of the existing business; problems often arise due to differences in management cultures and styles.

The difficulties mentioned can be overcome, and indeed there are many positive stories from which a number of success factors can be identified. Successful international retailers are likely to have distinctive skills or assets which they can leverage in international markets. These skills may be in the form of mass merchandising skills, buying or own-brand development skills or a strong or innovative retail concept that is relevant to the needs of the target market (for example IKEA or Zara). Success also requires exploitation of global scale and global sourcing to maximize supply-chain efficiencies and create value for the customer. Successful retailers also use local management to ensure that local customer needs are being met whilst ensuring that local management understands the brand values and business practices of the international retailer. Invariably, success in the international market requires long-term commitment.

SUMMARY

Compared with manufacturers, retailers have been historically slow to internationalize in the past. However, with increasing globalization of markets and the development of e-commerce and digital media, internationalization is a major feature of the retail industry and an important strategy for the majority of large retail organizations. In most developed retail markets, limited domestic opportunities exist for retailers due to high levels of competition, mature markets and restrictive trading conditions, which are the major drivers of retailers' decisions to internationalize. Low economic growth in European and US economies has also been a major push factor, while emerging and high-growth retail markets are providing interesting albeit challenging opportunities for retail investment.

Retailers need to carefully analyse both the opportunities and risks before making decisions on which markets to enter. In the initial stages of internationalization, retailers are usually cautious and enter markets that are geographically and culturally 'close', and similar to the home market. Over time, retailers tend to become more ambitious and seek opportunities further afield, and at this stage the growth opportunities are more important than geographical and cultural proximity.

Retailers have a number of choices when entering markets including fully owned self-start entry, acquisitions, joint ventures, franchising, concessions, licensing and even exporting. The actual method will depend on a number of factors including cost versus control, uniqueness of the format, availability of good locations, financial strength of the firm, market size and competitive conditions in foreign markets and the political and economic risk associated with a particular country. How fast a retail development can be put into operation is also likely to be an influencing factor. More experienced retailers may employ more than one strategy to enter markets.

A critical decision when entering international markets is the extent to which the existing retail format and marketing approach should be retained as a standardized strategy or whether to adapt the retail format to the needs of the new market being entered (adaptation strategy). However, this is not an all-or-nothing decision; retailers should always be looking for opportunities to standardize elements of their offer to save costs, but understand that some adaptation may be desirable depending on the operating conditions of the market.

Internationalization is not an easy task; even highly experienced retailers have been forced to withdraw from international markets. Some of the major reasons for failure include underestimating cultural differences, lack of supplier and distribution networks, overestimating the strength of their retail brands, underestimating the strength of local competition and lack of integration between the international business and domestic business. Despite this, retailers are likely to show increasing commitment to international markets, while benefiting from insights that online retailing in a global market can bring.

QUESTIONS

1. Explain what is meant by 'ownership-specific' advantages.
2. What is meant by 'internalization'?
3. Distinguish between push and pull motives behind internationalization of retailers.
4. The United States is a popular destination for UK retailers; discuss the factors that may motivate UK retailers to enter the American market.
5. Compare and contrast the relative advantages and disadvantages of franchising and acquisition as methods of entry into foreign markets for retailers.
6. What are the benefits of a globalization/standardization strategy? What are the disadvantages of such an approach?
7. Discuss the factors that lead to failure of many international retailing ventures.

REFERENCES AND FURTHER READING

Akehurst, G. and Alexander, N. (1996) *The Internationalisation of Retailing* (London: Frank Cass).

Ansoff, I. (1965) *Corporate Strategy* (London: McGraw-Hill).

Bartram, P. (1999) 'Saving St Michael', *Director*, February, pp. 34–7.

Bearne, S. (2010), 'Reiss Ramps Up Overseas Plans with New Head of International', *Drapers*, 10 December.

Bearne, S. (2012) 'Reiss Overhauls Website with Focus on Editorial', *Drapers*, 22 August.

Boots-uk.com (2013) 'Boots History', available at www.boots-uk.com/About_Boots/Boots_Heritage/Boots_History.aspx, accessed 20 September 2013.

Burt, S. L., Mellahi, K., Jackson, P. and Sparks, L. (2002) 'Retail Internationalisation and Retail Failure: Issues from the Case of Marks and Spencer', *International Review of Retail, Distribution and Consumer Research*, vol. 12, no. 2, pp. 191–219.

Corporate Intelligence Group (1994) *US Retailers in Europe – The New Wave* (London: The Corporate Intelligence Group).

Dawson, J. A. (2007) 'Scoping and Conceptualising Retailer Internationalisation', *Journal of Economic Geography*, vol. 7, no. 4, pp. 373–97.

Dawson, J. A., Larke, R. and Mukoyama, M. (2006) *Strategic Issues in International Retailing* (Abingdon: Routledge).

Deloitte (2012) 'Retail Global Expansion: Determining Your Method of Market Entry', Deloitte Development LLC, available at http://www.deloitte.com/assets/Dcom-UnitedStates/Local%20Assets/Documents/Consumer%20Business/us_retail_globalexpansion_030712.pdf [accessed 26 August 2013].

Deloitte (2013) 'Global Powers of Retailing 2013', available at http://www.deloitte.com/assets/Dcom-Australia/Local%20Assets/Documents/Industries/Consumer%20business/Deloitte_Global_Powers_of_Retail_2013.pdf [accessed 26 August 2013].

Doherty, A. M. (2000) 'Factors Influencing International Retailers' Market Entry Mode Strategy: Qualitative Evidence from the UK Fashion Sector', *Journal of Fashion Marketing and Management*, vol. 16, nos. 1–3, pp. 223–45.

Dunning, J. H. (1988) 'The Eclectic Paradigm of International Production: A Restatement and Some Possible Extensions', *Journal of International Business Studies*, vol. 19, no. 1, pp. 1–31.

(duo.com, 2013) About Us, http://www.duoboots.com/discover-duo/about-us/ [accessed 12 September 2013]

Easey, M. (2009) *Fashion Marketing*, 3rd Edition (Chichester: Wiley).

Faithfull, M. (2013) 'Retail Week's 25th Anniversary: How Have UK Retailers Fared Abroad?', *Retail Week*, 21 June.

Kacker, M. (1985) *Transatlantic Trends in Retailing* (London: Quorum).

Kearney, A. T. (2012) *Global Expansion: Keeps on Moving* (A.T. Kearney), available at http://www.atkearney.com/documents/10192/4799f4e6-b20b-4605-9aa8-3ef451098f8a [accessed 27 August 2013].

Knee, D. and Walters, D. (1985) *Strategy in Retailing, Theory and Application* (Oxford: Philip Allan).

Levitt, T. (1983) 'The Globalisation of Markets', *Harvard Business Review*, vol. 6, no. 3, pp. 92–103.

Lovett, G. (2012) 'Reiss Promotes Sharma to Bring Global Punch', *Retail Week*, 23 March.

Marks and Spencer (2001) Annual Report 2001 http://corporate.marksandspencer.com/documents/publications/archive/2001_annual_report.pdf [accessed 15 September 2013]

Marks and Spencer (2002) Annual Report and Financial Statements 2002 http://corporate.marksandspencer.com/documents/publications/archive/2002_annual_report.pdf [accessed 15 September 2013]

Marks and Spencer (2013) Annual Report and Financial Statements 2013 http://annualreport.marksandspencer.com/downloads/ [accessed 20 September 2013]

McGoldrick, P. J. and Davies, G. (eds) (1995) *International Retailing: Trends and Strategies* (London: Pitman).

Nobbs, K., Moore, C. M. and Sheridan, M. (2012) 'The Flagship Format within the Luxury Fashion Market', *International Journal of Retail and Distribution Management*, vol. 40, no. 12, pp. 920–34.

Salmon, W. J. and Tordjman, A. (1989) 'The Internationalization of Retailing', *International Journal of Retailing*, vol. 4, no. 2, pp. 2–16.

Sternquist, B. (2007) *International Retailing*, 2nd Edition (New York: Fairchild Publications).

Treadgold, A. D. (1988) 'Retailing without Frontiers', *International Journal of Retail and Distribution Management*, vol. 16, no. 6, pp. 8–12.

17 MULTI-CHANNEL RETAILING

LEARNING OBJECTIVES

- To appreciate how the Internet has enabled the emergence of the new retail format of the electronic retailer.
- To explore the use of the Internet as a new retail channel by existing store-based retailers and the emergence of multi-channel retailing.
- To understand what is meant by disintermediation (or the bypassing of retailers by manufacturers using the Internet), and its implications for retailers and manufacturers.
- To assess the impact of the Internet on shoppers' behaviour.
- To identify the key success factors in electronic retailing.

INTRODUCTION

In a relatively short space of time, Internet retailing (or more broadly speaking, electronic retailing) has firmly established itself as a viable alternative to store-based shopping. For instance, one of the earliest and best-known Internet retailers, Amazon.com, was launched only in 1995. Estimates for electronic retailing vary considerably, but it is estimated that global Internet sales reached $1 trillion by the end of 2012. In the United States, Forrester Research estimates that Internet retail sales in 2013 will be around 8.0 per cent ($262 billion) of total retail sales excluding cars (Sucharita and Gill, 2013) and rise to $370 billion by 2017. In the UK Internet penetration is the highest in the world, accounting for around 11 per cent (£30 billion) of total retail sales, and is expected to reach £58 billion (16 per cent) by 2018 (Mintel, 2013). Whilst this may not sound a great deal, a loss of 10–15 per cent of sales can make store-based retailers unprofitable (De Kare-Silver, 1998). All the indications are that this pace of development is likely to continue and will have a significant impact on store-based retailing. Whilst store-based retailers were initially slow to react to these developments, they now account for over 50 per cent of Internet retailing sales in the UK by adopting a multi-channel strategy, that is complementing their physical stores with Internet retailing. Multi-channel retailing is going to be critical to the future success of retailers in the fast-developing environment.

Electronic retailing is the sale of consumer goods and services via an interactive electronic communications network. Electronic retailing is variously referred to as Internet retailing, e-retailing or e-tailing, virtual retailing and cyber retailing. Until recently, the only generally available mass electronic communications network was the

Internet accessed via a personal computer. However, nowadays a number of alternatives are available including digital television, mobile telephones and tablet computers. This means that consumers can have access to Internet (and hence, Internet retailers) anywhere and anytime. The Internet is revolutionizing retailing in many fundamental ways, altering the relationships between manufacturers and retailers and retailers and shoppers. This chapter concentrates on issues relating to how the Internet is enabling new types of electronic retailers (or e-retailers) to emerge, the response of existing retailers to the Internet, the response of manufacturers to the Internet, the Internet as a new marketing medium and the response of customers to shopping on the Internet.

INTERNET PURE PLAYERS AS A NEW RETAIL FORMAT

Perhaps the most significant consequence of the Internet for retailing has been the emergence of a new retailing format of Internet-only retailers or pure players/cyber retailers/e-tailers (terms used interchangeably). One of the earliest and best-known examples is of Amazon.com (see Vignette 17.1). The distinguishing feature of these retailers is that they sell their products via the Internet only and do not have physical stores. They are thus independent of specific locations. Furthermore, unlike store-based retailers, virtual retailers do not carry any physical inventory; the Internet acts as an order-placing and transacting mechanism, and once the transaction is complete the product is delivered directly to the customer, circumventing the need for customers to visit a store.

VIGNETTE 17.1 AMAZON.COM: INTERNET RETAILING PIONEER

Launched in the United States in July 1995, Amazon.com quickly became one of the fastest-growing Internet retailers. Through its aggressive promotions, it has now become a major Internet retailer of music, toys and video games, clothing, electronics and groceries as well as the books with which it originally started. One of Amazon's key strengths is its easy-to-use interface incorporating a full search engine; however, users can also build a customer profile facility in order for Amazon to market its wares more directly. The site also features book reviews, interviews with authors and other similar services to facilitate product selection. In all these areas, Amazon aims to provide the biggest selection of merchandise available. For instance on its US site it offers around 3 million books. Amazon has taken this philosophy into other areas and now styles itself as 'Earth's biggest' store.

Amazon.co.uk was launched in 1998, and in order to improve the efficiency of delivery, two distribution units were opened in Bedfordshire in 1999. By 2013 it had seven distribution centres with a further three planned. Amazon has also built up dedicated websites in France, Spain, Germany, Italy, Austria, Canada, India, Brazil and Japan and plans to open further websites in a number of European countries.

Whilst Amazon could service the demand in those countries from its existing distribution network, the orders would take five to seven days to arrive rather than the following day from the local warehouses. Amazon feels that this is important for maintaining its reputation for service and it is also able to provide a more customized offering to its customers in those countries. Around 43 per cent of its sales now come from its international activities, which Amazon is looking to increase even further.

Much of the company's growth has been fuelled by substantial discounting, with many titles at 40 per cent discount. From the beginning Amazon has marketed itself aggressively; its marketing spend has consistently averaged around 25 per cent of its net sales in order to build market share. Amazon has also begun to diversify its activities and is involved in Web hosting (AWS Marketplace), and has recently acquired established online retailers drugstore.com (health and beauty), and Ashford.com (luxury and premium products). During the period 1995–2001, Amazon was not profitable and its losses amounted to around $2 billion. This investment was necessary to finance the high spend on advertising and promotion to build up the Amazon brand, the e-commerce and the physical infrastructure in order to achieve market leadership in its chosen areas. This meant that Amazon made losses for several years before making a profit. January 2002 marked a turning point, however, as Amazon reported not just an operating profit of $59 million, but also a net profit of $5 million in the fourth quarter. Since then it has reported a profit for the whole of 2002. Since then, turnover has grown to over $61 billion and Amazon made profits until 2012, when it made a small loss of around $40m due to acquisitions and further investment in the business.

Source: Hof (2001), McKegney (2000), Troy (2000), Anonymous (2001), Amazon annual report (2012)

The operating costs of Internet retailers are, therefore, much lower. According to one estimate, buying and maintaining a website costs a maximum of £50,000 a year, less than 5 per cent of the £1.25 million required to run a typical medium-sized retail outlet. According to another estimate, in traditional retailing the average transaction cost is approximately $15 per transaction, compared with telephone sales costing approximately $5, and the Internet cost being around $0.20–0.50 (Philipps et al., 1997). This means that margins on the Internet are about thrice the 6 per cent enjoyed by the average store (Pavitt, 1997). The costs of delivery are generally passed on to the customer, thus pushing up profits even further. Additional benefits are also realized in the form of customer information, complementary product and service offerings, ease of test marketing and international and new-market exposure.

Pure players also have advantages over catalogue retailers – the cost of running a website is a fraction of the cost of producing and distributing catalogues, and information on the website can be updated immediately. Also, unlike the physical catalogue, there is no real upper limit to the size of the virtual catalogue or the number of products represented. The assortment, therefore, is not limited by size of the store or physical size of the catalogue, and hence an Internet book retailer such as Amazon.com can offer 3 million books on its website compared with a fraction of that number carried by even the largest bookshop.

For time-pressured shoppers, the Internet provides the ultimate in convenience in that orders can be placed at any time of the day and not just when the shop is open. It also means that shoppers do not have to spend time and effort to visit the store, and avoid queuing, the most hated part of shopping for the majority of shoppers.

The downside for consumers is that they cannot physically handle the products and they miss out on the social aspects of shopping. Also, consumers have to wait for the product to be delivered.

Some prices on the Internet can be 5–10 per cent higher than on the high street, principally because of delivery charges, and consumers often have to buy in bulk to offset the costs of delivery (Pavitt, 1997). Product demand and competition can alter this; for example popular books and CDs in general tend to be cheaper on the Internet than the high street. However, the interactive nature of the Internet has spawned a number of Internet retailers offering alternatives to fixed pricing that is the normal practice in retailing. Priceline.com (http://www.priceline.com), for instance, allows consumers to propose prices for car rentals, airline tickets and hotel rooms, whilst auction sites such as eBay (http://www.ebay.com) provide an appealing format for bargain-seeking customers. However, despite the advantages that pure-play retailers have, multi-channel retailers (that is store-based retailers with Internet offerings) have gained a majority share of the Internet retailing market. This is mainly because customers are more willing to trust existing retail brands than less well known Internet-only retailers (see below).

TYPES OF MERCHANDISE SOLD VIA THE INTERNET

There are few products that cannot be bought via the Internet these days. However, the sectors that have shown the strongest growth and make up the vast majority of Internet sales include the following:

1. Computer hardware and software.
2. Books (including e-books), CDs/DVDs as well as music downloads.
3. Gifts.
4. Travel.

Three major factors in the success of Internet retailing are product/merchandise characteristics, retailing economics and trust in the retailer and consumer attitudes to purchasing on the Internet. Products that are likely to do well are standard, convenience, low-involvement, repeat, single, gift purchases. Hence, books, music, videos and gift items fit well into this category. It was initially thought that differentiated, high-involvement, new task, jointly purchased, self-consumption items would be harder to sell on the Internet. Fashion was a good example of this latter category, as shoppers wish to ensure that they buy just the right type of clothes and will want to try them on to make sure that they fit properly. However, the clothing and footwear sector has become the most successful, with online sales accounting for 9 per cent of the sales of the whole sector. This is mainly because Internet fashion retailers have introduced free returns policies to encourage customers to buy as well as making returns easier by allowing them to be returned to their nearest store. Also retailers such as ASOS have also made buying online more fun with the introduction of online catwalk videos, so that potential customers can see how the garments might look when worn. High-convenience, perishable, immediate consumption products are also less likely to be purchased via the Internet because of the inherent delay in delivery.

An important aspect of Internet retailing is that of consumer trust. For store-based retailers, trust is built up over time and embedded in the retail brand, whereas Internet retailers have to establish their brand identity and image from scratch. This is a major expense for most Internet start-ups, and establishing credible brands is not an easy task. Also, retailers require an economically viable trading model. For instance, in the grocery market one of the biggest costs is that of putting a customer's order together. This is a labour-intensive process and has prevented many would-be Internet retailers from entering this market. In addition, special refrigerated transport is required because of the perishable nature of some of the merchandise. This is in addition to the cost of the delivery and ensuring that the customer is at home when the order is delivered. Another major cost for non-store-based retailers is the high rate of returns. Return rates can be as high as 30–40 per cent, which Internet retailers need to build into their cost structures.

Some consumers are more prone to purchasing on the Internet than others. Time-pressured consumers are more likely to use it than those with less busy lifestyles, whilst consumers who like the social experience of interacting with other shoppers and retail staff and who enjoy store atmospherics are less likely to use the Internet.

THE INTERNET AS A NEW CHANNEL

For store-based retailers the key questions concerning the Internet are whether or not to use it and how to use it. UK retailers were initially rather slow to adopt the Internet; less than half of the top 100 retailers in 1998 had a website, and only 14 had transaction-based websites compared with 43 of the top 100 US retailers (Weatherall Green & Smith, 1999, Doherty et al., 1999). The majority of the sites were public relations sites. By the end of 2000, however, 91 out of the top 100 UK retailers had websites and just under half (42) of them were transactional. Nowadays the vast majority of retailers have some sort of Internet presence even if it is only a promotional website.

The arrival of the Internet means that retailers have to decide how to use it. They cannot afford to ignore it, and so the main options include the following:

1. Provide an information-only site.
2. Develop a transaction site.
3. Integrate online business with existing store.
4. Treat electronic retailing as a new channel.
5. Treat electronic retailing as new and separate business.

Information-only sites versus transactional sites

The first decision that an existing retailer has to make is whether its involvement with the Internet is going to be limited to an information-only site or whether it is going to allow customers to purchase via the Internet. As a minimum, existing retailers need to register their names as domain names to protect their brands and to keep their future options open. A full transaction site may not be appropriate because it does not fit well with existing operations or with the needs of target customers. For instance food discounters such as Aldi would find it difficult to maintain their low-cost base with the additional costs of maintaining a transactional Internet site and a new delivery system. Also, Aldi's value-conscious customers are less likely to be able or willing to pay the additional cost of delivery. At the same time, given that they are from less affluent backgrounds, they are less likely to have access to the Internet. Hence, predictably, Aldi's UK website (http://www.aldi-stores.co.uk) is an information-only website providing information on the company's operations in the UK, store locations, new and special offers, employment opportunities and a property section. Another retailer that has an information-only site is IKEA (http://www.ikea.co.uk). An interesting aspect of this site is that it allows customers to check if an item is in stock before they set off to the store and to create a shopping list. This type of site functions essentially as a source of information about the company and its products and as a public relations tool designed to create awareness and to support the retail brand.

Whilst retailers such as Aldi and IKEA may have no intention of turning their information sites into transaction sites, other retailers such as B&Q, the DIY retailer, have transformed their information sites into transaction sites. Transaction sites are a two-way communication system, allowing customers to place orders and retailers to contact customers. Building transaction sites requires far greater commitment from the retailer to the Internet. In addition to the cost of building and maintaining the site, delivery systems and secure online credit payment systems have to be put in place.

At first, most retailers were reluctant to build transactional sites. The first set of 'traditional' retailers to go online were catalogue retailers such as Argos (http://www.Argos.co.uk), which is understandable given that these retailers already had many of the prerequisites for online trading in place, namely a catalogue of products which could easily be converted into an electronic format and delivery systems designed for home shopping. Furthermore, they already had a customer base interested in home shopping.

Integration of online retailing

Although many more retailers now have transaction sites, they do not all necessarily provide the full catalogue of their products on their websites. In particular, this is not considered viable by larger retailers such as department stores, who have an extensive and constantly changing product assortment. Other retailers, such as Tesco, however, have successfully integrated their online stores with their existing physical stores (see Vignette 17.2). Integration means for instance that customers can order a product online and collect it in their local store. Click and collect, as this service is known, has become extremely popular with customers and is currently used by 40 per cent of the Internet shoppers. Meanwhile, other stores such as Sainsbury's view the online store as a new channel of distribution that requires its own systems. Some retailers, like Wal-Mart, have gone even further and organized their online business as a separate unit. This recognizes the fact that operational requirements and the needs of online customers are quite different. It also allows Wal-Mart to take advantage of the Internet and offer a much larger range of merchandise than in its conventional stores.

VIGNETTE 17.2 TESCO.COM

Tesco was the first major UK supermarket group to trial Internet shopping in December 1996. It did not roll out the service nationally, however, until mid-1999, and the long testing period is one of the major factors in its success. Tesco.com now has more than 750,000 registered online customers with 60,000 a week placing online orders totalling more than £5 million. Whilst the online sales of just over £250 million account for less than 1.5 per cent of its total annual sales of nearly £18,000 million, they are expected to double every 12 months. The company regards online retailing as a core part of its future strategy and expects it to become profitable. In the interim, it gives the company access to the most detailed information about its customers.

Tesco believes that a key component in its success has been the decision to fulfil orders directly from stores rather than from warehouses, as Sainsbury's does for example. In the early days 'pickers' would go round the store collecting ordered goods and then have them scanned at the checkout. Now the use of hand-held scanners has reduced collection time considerably. However, when orders start to exceed over 500 per week from a store, the ability to service the orders may be stretched and impact on the operations of the stores servicing the orders. For non-grocery items such as electricals, even Tesco employs dedicated warehouses, as many Tesco stores are not large enough to stock the full range of electrical items.

Tesco claims to be able to deliver to 90 per cent of the UK's population, far more than any of its rivals. Its nearest rival, Sainsbury's, covers 45 per cent of the UK. Whilst Safeway had closed down its online operation and ASDA is only just beginning to roll out its own online service, Tesco's wide coverage means that it is able to attract some of the highest spending and most profitable customers from its main rivals. Evidence shows that online grocery shoppers tend to spend on average a quarter more than the average of those shopping in stores. The delivery charge presumably acts as an incentive for bulk shopping.

Tesco has expanded its online operations, with Tesco Direct selling general merchandise. It has combined this with a click and collect service, which allows its online customers to collect their orders from their nearest store. Customers are also able to shop online using their mobiles as well as other devices such as tablet computers. Thus Tesco is becoming a well integrated multi-channel retailer. It sees multi-channel retailing as the future to its success and is investing £750 million in the 2013–14 financial year to support its multi-channel strategy. This has meant that Tesco's online turnover now exceeds £3 billion pounds.

Source: Hirst (2000), Rushe (2000), Tesco website (http://www.tesco.com); Tesco annual report (2012)

Multi-channel retailing is now evolving towards omni-channel retailing, which aims to provide a seamless consumer experience through all the retailer's shopping channels, namely mobile Internet devices, computers, stores, television, radio, direct mail, catalogues and so on. This requires integration across all aspects of the business. Hence, products, prices and promotions are not channel specific, but consistent across all channels. This is necessary as customers do not limit themselves to a single channel. For instance, they use the Internet to learn about and research products online but prefer to buy them from a store.

IMPLICATIONS OF INTERNET RETAILING FOR RETAIL BUSINESS SYSTEMS

For store-based retailers, involvement in Internet retailing has major implications for the way they do business, since Internet retailing involves a rather different retailing philosophy to their existing operation. Some of the differences are illustrated in Figure 17.1. First, store location is not an important variable in electronic retailing unless of course the stores are used to service orders, as in the case of Tesco. The product management task is simplified in some ways, as merchandising decisions are not constrained by store size. Logistics take on a new importance because of the need to develop home delivery systems, and mass sales-order processing requires new systems and skills. Given the intense competition, marketing takes on a new importance for attracting customers and brand building. The interactive capacity of the Internet also means that relationship marketing takes on a much more important role both for building loyalty and increasing sales via marketing of related products and services. Interactivity also opens up the possibility of personalizing (or individualizing) the service for customers.

The high degree of change required by store-based retailers has meant that they have been more cautious in developing Internet businesses. Also, the high potential consequences of getting things wrong for the existing business and the retail brand is another reason for a cautious approach. However, many store-based retailers have

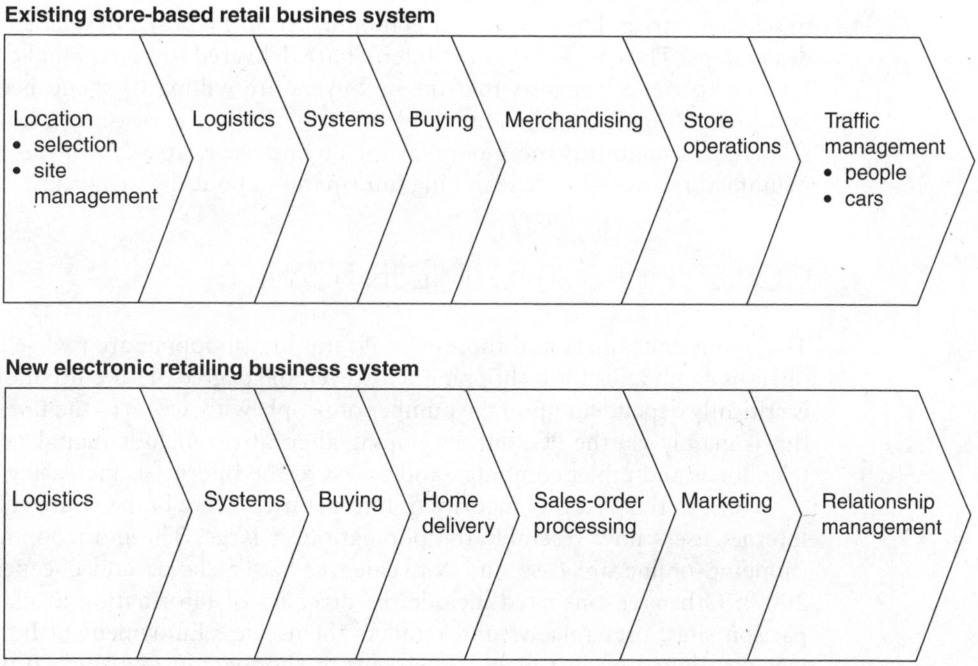

Figure 17.1 Internet retailing and changing business systems

Source: Based on De Kare-Silver (1998), p. 95.

realized that a multi-channel approach is essential in the new competitive environment and gives a competitive edge over only-store-based retailers and pure-play Internet retailers.

DISINTERMEDIATION

The huge reduction in the cost of access to customers that the Internet makes possible brings an additional threat to retailers in the form of disintermediation. Disintermediation is the direct selling of goods by manufacturers to consumers (that is bypassing retailers). While the prospect of disintermediation appears attractive, its implementation may be problematic for manufacturers. Most manufacturers are unwilling to sell online because of the nature of their product, and/or because of potential channel conflict. Disintermediation also requires additional heavy investment in the new channel that is unlikely to be profitable in the short term. The additional investment is not just in the Internet/electronic interface, but also requires infrastructural investments in the delivery of small orders. Such a strategy is risky in that it assumes that a significant proportion of customers are prepared to switch channels, which may well not be the case.

The majority of manufacturers selling online rank providing information, promoting brands and responding to customer enquiries above actual product sales. Some of the more active manufacturers in the use of the Internet are car manufacturers. Ford has the biggest market share in the UK market; it announced in 2010 that it was going to sell new cars online (www.fordretailonline.co.uk) whilst still selling cars through its dealerships. The cars sold via the Internet are delivered to 12 regional delivery centres. Ford's experience suggests that online buyers are willing to spend between £10,000 and £20,000 on a car. The direct sale of new cars to the consumer, however, remains relatively limited. It is more popular for buying used cars. Car buyers mainly use the manufacturer website for searching information about the products.

CONSUMERS AND THE INTERNET

Time-poor consumers and those who do not like shopping are two segments that are obvious candidates for e-shopping. However, the degree of take-up of online shopping is critically dependent upon the number of people with access to the Internet. Currently this is mainly via the PC, but developing alternatives include digital/cable TV, mobile telephones and tablet computer, and access to the Internet is increasing rapidly.

Whilst in the past the majority of Internet users were in the younger-age categories, Internet users now resemble the population at large. The most popular reasons for shopping online are ease and convenience, better choice and cheaper prices (OFT, 2007). Other reasons cited include the diversity of information available from comparison sites, user reviews and retailers themselves. Enjoyment of Internet shopping was mentioned by just over 50 per cent of shoppers in one study (OFT, 2007). The main reasons given for not shopping online are preference for shops and wanting to see/try the product before buying, not seeing the need for Internet shopping and lack of trust in Internet shopping (OFT, 2007).

The Internet is transforming the shopping process, and product information such as features, prices and availability can be easily obtained before purchasing. For instance, besides providing a brief content of the book, Internet book retailers may also provide a review and even interviews with the author to generate interest in the book. The Internet allows shoppers to compare prices fairly easily, either by visiting the websites of retailers individually, or by using one of the online comparison shopping services (or shopping (ro)bots) such as ShopGenie (http://www.shopgenie.com). ShopGenie seeks out the best prices for books, CDs, films, computer hardware, software and games. There are numerous other similar sites that assist comparison shopping and identify retailers with the required products.

With the widespread use of smartphones, the new phenomenon of showrooming has emerged. Showrooming is when an individual visits a physical store to examine the merchandise, then uses their smartphone to find the same product online and purchases the product online rather than in the store. Showrooming can thus result in lost sales and is said have been a major factor in the collapse of Jessops, the UK photography chain. Showrooming means that retailers need to be price competitive across the channels and find ways of getting customers to buy in store. One method of doing this is to use a price promise to not be beaten on price against. However, providing unique products and in-store customer experience is likely to be more effective.

SUCCESS FACTORS IN E-RETAILING

As a result of a number of high-profile Internet retailer failures such as Boo.com (fashion retailing), Boxman (Internet music store) and Clickmango.com (natural health products), it has become obvious that successful retailing on the Net is not easy. Whilst electronic retailing is relatively new, analysis suggests that successful electronic retailers will need competitive advantage in one or more of the following areas (Alba et al., 1997):

1. Strong branding.
2. Unique merchandise.
3. Complementary merchandise assortments.
4. Distribution efficiency.
5. Effective use of customer information.
6. Strong website design.
7. Good web links.
8. Good customer service.
9. Customer relationship management.

Strong branding

In comparison with store-based retailers (which essentially face local competition), virtual retailers encounter far more intense competition as customers have access to any number of virtual retailers on the Internet. In such an environment a strong brand image is of the utmost importance, which is one of the reasons why virtual retailers spend up to 25 per cent of their revenues on advertising compared with 3–5 per cent for conventional stores. A strong brand provides assurance to potential customers of the trustworthiness of the retailer, the quality of its products and the reliability of delivery and after-sales service, and that the information provided by customers will not be misused. This is important given that potential Internet shoppers are very concerned about credit card security, the fact that customers are buying products without examining them and that they trust that orders will arrive on time. Existing retail brands are in a strong position to transfer their brand values to the Internet, whereas new electronic retailers inevitably require large investment in brand building.

Unique merchandise

Offering unique merchandise allows retailers to differentiate themselves from competitors, builds customer loyalty and makes it difficult for shoppers to make price comparisons. One way of providing unique merchandise is to offer own-brand products, but this is difficult for new online-only retailers as consumers have relatively little knowledge of virtual retailers and their capabilities in delivering quality products. Hence, traditional retailers with online trading sites who already have well-developed own brands have a distinct advantage in this area. A good example of this is Amazon's e-book reader Kindle. Virtual retailers could also offer exclusive merchandise. However, manufacturers and brand owners will only want to be associated with trustworthy successful retailers, and again the strongly branded store-based retailers with virtual sites will have a distinct advantage in having already built a reputation with potential suppliers. Alternatively, virtual retailers could offer unique bundles of merchandise which could be purchased individually from other electronic retailers, but the bundling must either make purchasing more convenient for potential shoppers, or offer better value. Unless virtual retailers are able to achieve a certain degree of uniqueness in their merchandise offer, they will find it difficult to differentiate their offer from the multitude of competing offers and build up customer loyalty.

Complementary merchandise assortments

Given that there are no physical limits on the merchandise offered, electronic retailers can facilitate one-stop shopping and increase consumer convenience by offering a range of complementary merchandise. Such a strategy takes advantage of the fact that visiting a number of different websites is time consuming for shoppers just as it would be with store-based retailers. Virtual retailers can also take advantage of the fact that they can make suggestions based on the customer's current purchase (and previous purchases). For instance it is not uncommon for virtual retailers to tell shoppers what other products were bought in addition to the current one by other shoppers. Offering complementary assortments allows virtual retailers to build on trust established in one merchandise area and to transfer it to another area, thereby maximizing opportunities for cross-selling. Examples of virtual retailers offering complementary assortments include Amazon, which has expanded its merchandise range from books through music and films, electrical goods and computers, to clothing and groceries.

Distribution efficiency

A major factor hindering the spread of Internet retailing is the problem of order fulfilment. In addition to this, distribution costs are a major element of total costs. Efficient cost-effective systems, therefore, are an absolute necessity for successful Internet retailing. Efficient distribution systems not only lead to more satisfied customers, but also provide an important competitive advantage over other me-too Internet retailers. Many consumers have been put off from using virtual retailers because of problems of delayed arrival or non-arrival of merchandise ordered.

Effective use of customer information

The interactive nature of Internet shopping means that retailers can capture a myriad of information about the product preferences of individual customers, their response to promotions, frequency and amount spent on purchases and so forth. This allows retailers to personalize the merchandise and service offer and combine it with appropriate promotions to meet individual needs, thereby maximizing consumer satisfaction and sales. The amount and quality of data obtained in this way are not easily achieved by store-based retailers. Only mail-order retailers and retailers with loyalty-card schemes have access to a similar type of information about their customers. However, loyalty cards lack the interactivity that the Internet provides. Hence, virtual retailers that can best leverage this customer information to increase customer satisfaction and build customer loyalty are most likely to succeed in the virtual market. However, the information gathered by retailers must be used sensitively as privacy is a major concern amongst Internet shoppers. The best Internet retailers publish their privacy policy and provide a degree of control to shoppers over how the information they provide is used.

Strong website design

Just as store atmospherics and visual merchandising are critically important to store-based retailers, so the look of the home page, ease of navigation and quick download times are important factors for online shoppers choosing to visit a site. User convenience also needs to be at the heart of website design. For instance, grocery stores usually place milk and bread at the back of the store in order to encourage the shopper to shop the whole of the store, thereby increasing impulse purchases. Such an approach to online retailing would drive customers away. In fact, as grocery shopping online essentially amounts to a list of goods, the most frequently purchased items need to be at the 'front' of the online store. Personalizing the user experience by building individual profiles of customers by tracking their usage and taking them directly to the area of the website they most frequently use is an important method for facilitating online shopping. For instance, Tesco.com has an express shopper feature, which allows existing customers to view what they bought last time and to reorder with a couple of clicks.

Good web links

Just as location is important in physical retailing, it is similarly important in cyberspace, and one of the decisions virtual retailers have to make is whether to be located in cybermalls or not. Cybermalls offer potentially similar advantages to physical shopping malls by generating store traffic. Besides ensuring that the website is registered with the major search engines (such as Google, Yahoo, Bing and so on), there are a number of ways of generating traffic. One important method is to locate advertisements on websites that sell or provide information on related or complementary merchandise. An example of this is the banner advertisement that appears at the top of a host site; clicking on it links the user to the advertiser's website. Another method is the keyword advert which features mainly on search engines, where each time a search for a designated keyword is entered, an advert for a particular retailer or manufacturer appears. The advantage of this type of advertisement is that they are more targeted than traditional promotional methods as their recipients are existing Web users and interested in particular types of products. Inevitably, the cost per referral must be measured to ensure the effectiveness of these methods in generating traffic. Increasing generating traffic or driving traffic via the use of social websites such as Facebook is becoming increasingly important.

Good customer service

Inevitably a number of things can go wrong when shopping online. Orders not arriving on time is a frequent complaint of Internet shoppers, and Internet retailers along with mail-order retailers suffer from a high degree of returns due to products being unsatisfactory to customers for various reasons. Hence, good after-sales service is essential for success. However, most virtual retailers provide poor after-sales service, and this is one of the reasons why clicks-and-mortar retailers are performing better in this area, because customers know whom to complain to when things go wrong. Customers are also hesitant to purchase high-value items over the Net and may expect to be able to talk things over with a salesperson before making a purchase. Hence, the availability of customer-service lines is important for giving the service a human touch, assuring customers and helping them to complete more complex transactions.

Customer relationship management

In the highly competitive virtual marketplace, where the cost of switching for customers is very small but the cost for the retailer of retaining a customer is lower than recruiting a new one, relationship marketing takes on an added importance. Fortunately, the interactivity of the Internet medium means that it is easier to communicate with existing customers via email. Hence, existing customers can be informed of new promotions, products and benefits of shopping with a particular retailer. Some store-based retailers with loyalty schemes have transferred their schemes to the Internet as well, with the aim of building customer loyalty among their Internet customers.

SUMMARY

Internet shopping has grown considerably in the last decade and is likely to continue growing at a rapid rate for the foreseeable future. The growth of the Internet has enabled the new retail format of the virtual retailer to emerge and forced existing retailers to consider how best they can employ the new technology. Some have employed it simply as a way of providing information to customers, whilst others are using it as an alternative channel of distribution. The Internet has also given manufacturers access to consumers, allowing them to seriously consider disintermediation as an option. The Internet has also empowered shoppers by giving them more access to price and product information, and opened up new types of shopping such as auction sites and cooperative buying.

Store-based retailers need to seriously consider how they can employ the Internet in their business strategy ranging from information-only sites to multi-channnel/omni-channel strategy. Electronic retailing involves major changes in the traditional retailing business system and philosophy, and retailers need to consider them carefully before embarking on an online retailing strategy. Some key success factors in electronic retailing include strong branding, unique merchandise, complementary merchandise assortments, distribution efficiency, effective use of customer information, strong website design, good web links, good customer service and customer relationship management. Emerging evidence suggests that multi-channel retailing strategy is likely be more successful in the long run.

QUESTIONS

1. Discuss how Internet retailing is different from store-based retailing. What advantages do Internet retailers have over store-based retailers?
2. Why do some store-based retailers have information sites only?
3. Explain what is meant by disintermediation and its likely take-up by manufacturers.
4. Using CDs, cars and clothes shopping as examples, assess the potential of Internet shopping and the threat that it poses to store-based retailers in these categories. How can store-based retailers respond to the threat of Internet retailers?
5. How has the Internet empowered consumers in the shopping process?
6. Explain what showrooming is and suggest ways retailers can combat it.
7. Examine the Amazon.com and Tesco.com cases and explain why they have succeeded as Internet retailers.
8. Log on to a number of Internet shopping sites and discuss what features of website design you found attractive and features that you found off-putting. What advice would you offer to someone about to develop an Internet shopping site?

REFERENCES AND FURTHER READING

Alba, J., Lynch, J., Weitz, B., Janiszewski, C., Lutz, R., Sawyer, A. and Wood, S. (1997) 'Interactive Home Shopping: Consumer, Retailer and Manufacturer Incentives to Participate in Electronic Marketplaces', *Journal of Marketing*, vol. 61, pp. 38–53.

Amazon.com (2012) Annual Report http://phx.corporate-ir.net/phoenix.zhtml?c=97664&p=irol-reportsannual [accessed 15 September 2013].

Anonymous (2001), 'Special Article: Internet Pioneers: We Have Lift Off', *Economist*, 3 February, pp. 69–72.

Davis, G. (2000) 'Info-Only: Hit or Miss?', *Retail Week*, 19 May, p. 19.

De Kare-Silver, M. (1998) *E-Shock: The Electronic Shopping Revolution: Strategies for Retailers and Manufacturers* (London: Macmillan Business).

Doherty, N. F., Ellis-Chadwick, F. and Hart, C. A. (1999) 'Cyber Retailing in the UK: The Potential of the Internet as a Retail Channel', *International Journal of Retail and Distribution Management*, vol. 27, no. 1, pp. 22–36.

Doherty, Neil F. and Ellis-Chadwick, Fiona (2009) 'Exploring the Drivers, Scope and Perceived Success of E-Commerce Strategies in the UK Retail Sector', *European Journal of Marketing*, vol. 43, nos. 9/10, pp. 1246–62.

Doherty, Neil F. and Ellis-Chadwick, Fiona (2010) 'Internet Retailing: The Past, the Present and the Future', *International Journal of Retail and Distribution Management*, vol. 38, nos. 11/12, pp. 943–65.

Hart, C. A., Doherty, N. F. and Ellis-Chadwick, F. (2000) 'Retailer Adoption of the Internet: Implications for Retail Marketing', *European Journal of Marketing*, vol. 34, no. 8, pp. 954–74.

Hirst, Clayton (2000), 'Sainbury's Crosses North-South Divide in Net Grocery', *Independent on Sunday*, 19 November.

Hof, Robert D. (2001), 'Amazon's Go-Go Growth? Gone', *BusinessWeek*, 12 February, p. 39.

Mackintosh, J. (1996) 'Electronic Shopping Tipped to Boom', *Financial Times*, 28 June, p. 10.

McKegney, M. (2000), 'Amazon Blazes Trail in Europe', *Advertising Age*, 18 September, p. 78.

Mintel (2013) *E-Commerce – UK*, July (London: Mintel).

Office of Fair Trading (2007), *Internet Shopping: An OFT Market Study* (London: OFT), June.

Pavitt, D. (1997) 'Retailing and the Super High Street: The Future of the Electronic Home Shopping Industry', *International Journal of Retail and Distribution Management*, vol. 25, no. 1, pp. 38–43.

Philipps, F., Donoho, A., Keep, W. W., Mayberry, W., McCann, J. M., Sapiro K. and Smith, D. (1997) 'Electronically Connecting Retailers and Customers: Interim Summary of an Expert Round Table', in R. A. Peterson (ed.), *Electronic Marketing and the Consumer* (London: Sage), pp. 101–22.

Preston, G. (2000) *Internet Shopping in Easy Steps. Compact* (Southam: Computer Step).

Rosen, K. T. and Howard, A. L. (2000) 'E-Retail: Gold Rush or Fool's Gold?', *California Management Review*, vol. 42, no. 3, pp. 72–100.

Rushe, D. (2000), 'Grocers in Battle to Bag Online Shoppers', *Sunday Times*, 22 October, p. 17.

Stern, L. W. and Weitz, B. A. (1998) 'The Revolution in Distribution: Challenges and Opportunities', *Long Range Planning*, vol. 30, no. 6, December, pp. 823–9.

Stobie, I. (2000) 'European Consumers Seem Drawn to the Web', *Computing*, 30 November, pp. 76–77.

Sucharita, M. and Gill, M. (2013) 'US Online Retail Sales to Reach $370B by 2017', *Forbes*, 14 March, 2013.

Tesco (2012) Annual Report (2012) http://www.tescoplc.com/files/reports/ar2012/index.asp, [accessed 15 September 2013].

Troy, M. (2000), '"Earth's Biggest" E-Tailer Inching from Red to Black', *DSN Retailing Today*, 20 November, pp. 19–22.

Weatherall Green & Smith (1999) *A Beginners' Guide to E-Commerce: An Introduction to the Impact of E-Commerce for Commercial Property and Retail Investors* (London: Weatherall Green & Smith).

Williams, D. (2010) 'Ford Is the First Car Manufacturer to Sell Its Cars Online', *Telegraph*, 20 June.

USEFUL WEBSITES

http://www.aldi-stores.co.uk

http://www.amazon.com

http://www.amazon.co.uk

http://www.argos.co.uk

http://www.computerprices.co.uk

http://www.ebay.com

http://fordretailonline.co.uk

http://www.ikea.co.uk

http://www.priceline.com

http://www.shopgenie.com

http://www.tesco.com

18 LEGAL AND ETHICAL ISSUES IN RETAILING

LEARNING OBJECTIVES

- To become familiar with the basic provisions of the consumer protection legislation in the areas of product safety and liability legislation, display of prices and consumer credit.
- To gain an overview of the basic provisions of employee protection legislation as it relates to employee rights, the national minimum wage and part-time workers' rights.
- To understand what is meant by corporate social responsibility and why retailers undertake CSR initiatives.
- To understand the concepts of the ethical consumer and ethical sourcing.
- To explore the initiatives that retailers have taken to position themselves as ethically and socially responsible.

INTRODUCTION

All businesses have to comply with the law of the land. Legal issues affect all aspects of a retailing business, and some of the areas of legislation that specifically affect retail strategy, such as planning and competition regulation, have been discussed in earlier chapters. Most retailers, however, realize that it is not sufficient merely to comply with legal requirements; there is increasing pressure on retailers from consumers and other members of society to behave in an ethical and socially responsible manner. This is encapsulated in the corporate social responsibility (CSR) concept, which involves the retailer undertaking activities which benefit society overall, above and beyond its legal obligations. The drivers behind the growth of CSR activities include growth of consumerism (the consumer movement for the protection of consumer rights) and the emergence of the ethical and environmentally conscious consumer. These issues and the response of retailers are discussed in the later sections of this chapter. The chapter begins, however, with a discussion of UK consumer protection and employee protection legislation. The purpose here is not to describe in detail each individual law that applies to retailing, but to give an overview of some of the major types of legislation that affect retailing businesses. For a more detailed discussion of laws relating to retailing, readers are referred to a specialist textbook such as Thomas (2003). In addition, whilst much of the legal framework of the UK is similar in principle to that in many other developed retail markets, each country will have its own regulations and legislation, which can impact on international retail strategies.

CONSUMER PROTECTION

In the UK, as in many other western countries, an extensive amount of consumer protection legislation has been built up over time. There is legislation covering all aspects of retailing much of which relates to specific products (for example alcohol, food, drugs and medicines), product safety, pricing, sales and sales promotions and advertising. In the UK, consumer protection, which had previously been afforded by law of contract and common law, has been largely superseded by specific consumer protection legislation, which has been further supplemented by European Union legislation. The aim of much of this legislation is to provide consumers with certain basic rights that can be enforced through the courts if necessary. The recent growth of consumer protection legislation can be attributed to the pressure exerted by consumerism (or the campaign by consumer groups and others to protect consumer rights). An early piece of consumer protection legislation in the UK was the Sale of Goods Act 1893. More recently, consumer rights were laid out in the Sale of Goods Act 1979 and then amended in the Sale of Goods (Amendment) Act 1994, Sale and Supply of Goods Act 1994 and Sale of Goods Act 1995. These acts specify that buyers have a fundamental right to expect that the goods they buy are

1. of satisfactory quality,
2. fit for all intended purposes and
3. as described.

Retailers must offer a refund to customers where faulty goods are supplied provided that the retailer is notified in a 'reasonable time' that the goods are not acceptable. Alternatively, customers may choose to accept replacement or repair of the goods, or a credit note. Retailers may also be liable for any losses incurred as a result of customers using faulty goods. A customer has up to six years to bring proceedings against the retailer (Limitation Act 1980).

Consumers have additional rights when they buy anything by mail order or any other method where they do not meet with the trader directly. Whether shopping via the Internet, TV or telephone or from a catalogue or magazine article, the buyer will be protected by the Consumer Protection (Distance Selling) (Amendment) Regulations 2005. In simple terms, the buyer is entitled to

1. clear information,
2. the right to cancel an order within seven working days for any reason and
3. a full refund if they do not get the goods/services on time.

For contracts other than for the sale of goods (for example in the retailing of services such as hairdressing), the Supply of Goods and Services Act 1982 details the rights of purchasers and the duties of sellers. In addition to the rights provided under the sales of goods legislation, this act requires that services performed under contract must be performed with reasonable skill and care. Customers are entitled to sue the service provider if there is a breach of contract.

PRODUCT LIABILITY

The Consumer Protection Act 1987 provides for liability for damage caused by defective products, and incorporates into UK law the 1985 European Union Directive on Product Liability. The act requires that goods supplied must conform to the general safety requirement. Products fail to satisfy the general safety requirement if they are not reasonably safe given all circumstances, including their intended use, storage, usage instructions, safety standards and so forth. The act also makes provisions for approved safety standards to enable compliance with general safety requirements. This has led to the development of a number of specific safety standards for specific products that are published by the Trading Standards Institute, under the auspices of the Department for Business Enterprise and Regulatory Reform. To further enhance consumer safety, the act requires retailers and others involved in the supplying of goods to publish notices warning consumers of unsafe goods previously supplied by them. The act also provides powers for the suspension of sale and seizure of unsafe goods.

Liability under this act falls mainly on producers, importers and own-brand suppliers, either individually or severally. Intermediaries such as retailers may also become liable if they cannot identify the suppliers of the defective goods. This should not normally be a problem for retailers if they maintain good records. However, even if they inadvertently sell counterfeit products, retailers would be responsible for any loss or damage caused by these products. There may also be a problem if the products are bought in the 'grey' market, that is not directly from the original producer.

Food safety

Because of the perishable nature of food and the potential hazard to human health resulting from substandard food products, there is extensive legislation covering all aspects of food retailing including preparation, storage and labelling of merchandise. There are a number of pieces of legislation that all food businesses in the UK must be aware of: in particular the Food Safety Act 1990, the Food Hygiene Regulations 2010 and the Food Premises (Registration) Regulations 1997.

The Food Safety Act 1990 makes it an offence to render food injurious to health and prohibits the sale of food that is unfit for human consumption. It also makes it an offence to sell food that is not what the customer is entitled to expect in terms of content and quality. At the same time, the act prohibits the presentation of food that is false or misleading through advertising or labelling. It also controls the types of claims made for food. For pre-packed foods, ingredients must be listed in order of weight and the name or address of the packer or labeller must be displayed.

Pre-packed foods also require clear marking of a 'shelf life', indicated by either the term 'Use by . . . ' or 'Best before . . . '. The use-by label is used on highly perishable food products such as meat and dairy products to indicate that the food is high risk and could cause food poisoning if consumed after the date indicated. It is illegal to sell products that have exceeded their use-by date. However, 'Use by' does not always mean that the product must be consumed by that date. If a food can be frozen, its life can be extended beyond the use-by date. On the other hand, the best-before date, which generally appears on foods that can be kept for a longer period, is more an indicator of quality than safety. Hence, when the date expires, it does not mean that the product is dangerous, but it may no longer be at its best. The Food Standards Agency (FSA, www.food.gov.uk) is a central body which works with businesses and local authorities to enforce food safety regulations and promote food safety and hygiene across the UK.

Food labelling also enables consumers to make informed choices regarding the products that they buy. For example in 2012, new European Community legislation on gluten-free labelling came into force, which clarified terms used on food marking and packaging. This makes it much easier for people with an allergy to gluten to ensure that they buy products that will be suitable for them.

In order to protect consumers further, the Food Safety (General Food Hygiene) Regulations 1995 and the Food Hygiene Amended Regulations 2010 lay down procedures and guidelines for the handling and storage of food products. Under the regulations, retailers must have effective food safety management measures (or 'controls') in place to ensure that food is produced safely and that the health of customers is not put at risk. The controls required include measures to protect food from risk of contamination, training of employees in hygiene and food preparation, cleaning of equipment that comes into contact with food and storage of food.

The Food Premises (Registration) Regulations 1995 require that any new food business must register with the local environmental health department 28 days before opening. Also, if there is a change of activity at the food premises, it must be notified to the local environmental health department within 28 days of the change. Once registered with the FSA, a retailer will receive updates about regulations and legislation in this area and will be subjected to inspections to ensure compliance with regulations.

The enforcement of regulations on food safety and quality is primarily the responsibility of local authorities in the UK, and in particular of environmental health officers (EHOs) and trading standards officers (TSOs). Where food law enforcement does not rest with local authorities, it is carried out by the Food Standards Agency (set up by the Food Standards Act 1999). For more detailed information on issues relating to food standards, see the FSA website (http://www.food.gov.uk/) and the Trading Standards Institute website (http://www.tradingstandards.gov.uk/).

Displaying prices and the law

The way that prices are displayed have an important bearing on consumers' decisions, and hence specific rules are laid down for their display, so that consumers are given accurate information regarding a product's cost before purchasing. The Prices Act 1975 and the orders made under the act require the display of the selling price of most goods. The orders also lay down requirements for display of unit prices for many foodstuffs, and petrol and diesel fuel. Prices must be displayed either

1. by a price ticket on each individual item, or
2. by a nearby shelf edge label or
3. by a nearby price list.

Unit prices must be displayed in the following cases:

1. If goods are sold loose (not pre-packed) from a quantity on display, for example fruits and vegetables; the price per kilogram (kg) must be given.
2. If pre-packed goods are of the same type but with varying quantity, for example pre-packed chunks of cheese of varying weight; the price per kilogram (kg) must be given as well as the selling price.
3. If the retail outlet has an internal retail sales floor area of more than 280 square metres, the product quantity must be marked (mainly foodstuffs and cosmetics), or if the product is made up in a legally prescribed quantity (for example bread as prescribed by the Weights and Measures Act, 1985).

All prices must include VAT unless the sales are mainly or exclusively to business customers, for example wholesalers. Delivery and other charges payable before the goods can be obtained must either be included in the price or displayed separately with equal prominence.

During sales and promotions, price reductions may be shown by way of a notice provided that the reduction applies to all goods, or, if not, it must be clearly identified which goods it applies to. If the same price does not apply to all methods of payment (for example credit cards or cash), the circumstances when the price does not apply and the difference, either cash or percentage, from the marked price must be displayed clearly and prominently at all payment points and at all public entrances to the premises.

Misleading prices

The Consumer Protection Act 1987 makes it a criminal offence for traders to give misleading price indications relating to goods or services. It is an offence even if the indication of price was correct at the time but later becomes misleading. For instance, a price ticket stating 'Was £99.99. Reduced to £69.99!' is misleading if the goods were never provided at the higher price. It is also misleading if a retailer fails to show 'hidden extras' (such as delivery charges) or to make it clear when a price is conditional on, for example, another purchase.

The Consumer Protection (Code of Practice for Traders on Price Indications) Approval Order 2005 made under the Consumer Protection Act 1987 provides guidance as to what constitutes misleading price descriptions. Price comparison should always state the higher price; statements such as 'usual price', 'normal price' or 'regular price' should make clear whose usual, normal or regular price is being referred to. In comparison with the retailer's previous prices:

1. The previous price should be the last price at which the product was offered during the last 6 months.
2. The product should have been offered at that price for 28 consecutive days during the last 6 months.
3. The previous price should have been offered at the same store where the reduced price is offered.

However, an offence is not necessarily committed if there is a departure from these guidelines so long as the consumer is provided with a clear and positive explanation as to the period for which and the circumstances in which the higher price applied (see Vignette 18.1).

VIGNETTE 18.1 WHEN IS A FIXED PRICE NOT A FIXED PRICE?

In 2012–13 Which? campaigned on behalf of consumers for mobile phone retailers to stop using the term 'fixed price' or 'fixed rate' in their long-term customer contracts. In fact, Which?'s research found that not only were prices being raised mid-contract, and being blamed on the 'recession' or 'inflation' or 'covering of costs', but customers were being advised that the price would not go up when the contract small print allows for that to happen. Mystery shopping research conducted by Which? in 2013 found that when asked if the contract price could increase without warning during a 12- or 18-month contract, 57 per cent of staff in a variety of mobile phone shops still insisted that the price would stay the same during the term of the contract, while 'hidden' contract clauses can not only allow the companies to raise the costs of fixed-rate tariffs, but they can also prevent customers leaving the contract.

Source: Based on Hawkes (2013)

The code also deals with introductory and promotional price offers, sales and comparisons with other retailers. The comparisons must be fair and meaningful and must not mislead. Introductory and promotional offers should state for how long they apply, and in the case of introductory price offers they should not be for so long that they appear to be the normal price. Retailers should only quote an 'after-sale' or 'after-promotion' price if the same products are offered at that price for at least 28 days in the 3 months after the period of the offer or after the promotional stock runs out. In the case of 'sales' and 'special events', where a retailer indicates that products are for example 'half of marked prices', the marked prices should be the retailer's own previous price and the rules on comparison with the retailer's previous price should be followed. However, where a retailer displays a notice of the type 'up to 50% off', at least 10 per cent (by quantity) of the merchandise offered must be at the maximum price reduction indicated.

Price comparisons

Retailers who compare prices of their products with those of other retailers should do so with care and ensure the following:

1. The other retailer's price quoted is accurate and up to date.
2. The name of the other retailer is given clearly and prominently with the price comparison.
3. The location of the shop where the quoted price applies is given.
4. The price quoted applies to the same product – or to substantially similar products and that any difference is clearly stated.

The main stipulations of the code also apply to advertising and promotional material, mail-order catalogues and online trading operations. Therefore, it is in the interest of the retailer to check promotional materials, catalogues and online material constantly for accuracy, given that it is an offence, even if the indication of price was correct at the time of publication but later becomes misleading, if customers could be reasonably expected to be relying on it and the retailer does not take reasonable steps to prevent them from doing so.

REGULATION OF CONSUMER CREDIT

Another extremely important piece of consumer protection legislation in the UK is the Consumer Credit Act 1974 (updated in 2006). This act provides the legal framework to regulate consumer credit and consumer hire and covers most forms of consumer lending. The main aim of the act is to establish 'truth in lending', that is to ensure that borrowers are given full and accurate information, to enable them to choose the best credit agreement for their purposes, and to inform them of their legal rights. The act requires that businesses that offer goods or services on credit to consumers must be licensed by the Office of Fair Trading.

It is not only businesses offering credit that must have a consumer credit licence, but also if they have any connection with transactions where customers are given time to pay. Retailers will require a credit licence if they

1. Sell on credit.
2. Hire or lease out goods for more than 3 months.
3. Lend money.
4. Issue credit cards or trading cheques.
5. Arrange credit for others.
6. Offer hire-purchase terms.

In addition to licensing, the act also regulates entering into credit agreements, default and termination of agreements and advertising and canvassing of credit. Under the legislation, any credit or hire agreement made by the retailer must

1. Show the total charge for credit including administration and other charges.
2. Tell the customer the annual percentage rate (APR) of interest on the total of the loan including administration and other charges. The APR is based on the present value of the loan given the length of the agreement and payment terms.
3. Show the cash price of the goods or services.
4. Give a customer signing a credit agreement at home (that is not at the retail premises, in the case of catalogue retailers for example) 5 days as a 'cooling-off' period to change their mind. Most firms give customers 14 days to change their minds.
5. Supply customers with a copy of the credit agreement to keep and inform them of their legal rights under the act, including the right to settle in full at any time during the term of the agreement.
6. Not lend money or offer credit to customers under the age of 18 years.

The act also gives powers to courts to intervene in the case of extortionate credit agreements. A credit agreement is extortionate if the debtor is required to make payments that are grossly exorbitant, or contravene the principles of fair dealing. The update in 2006 gives consumers more rights to challenge unfair agreements, dispute charges and get resolutions easier through the use of an independent ombudsman.

Advertisements of any type offering credit or hire facilities to consumers are controlled by the Consumer Credit (Advertisements) Regulations 2010, which relate to the Consumer Credit Act 1974. The aim is to ensure that customers receive a true picture of the nature and cost of credit terms being offered. To this end, the act requires that advertising relating to credit must use plain and intelligible language, be easily legible/audible and specify the advertiser's name. For more detailed and up-to-date information on the regulation of consumer credit in the UK and other legal aspects of running a retail business, readers are directed to the business advice section of the Office of Fair Trading website (www.oft.gov.uk/business-advice/).

As well as the legal framework in which retailers have to operate, there are many industry bodies which regulate the sector by determining an expected standard of operation. The Advertising Standards Authority (www.asa.org.uk) for example is an industry self-regulatory body that investigates consumer's complaints about advertisements across all media, including those on websites, and applies codes of practice, to ensure that advertisements are legal, decent, honest and truthful. The British Retail Consortium (www.brc.org.uk) also provides guidelines for retailers; for example their guidelines for responsible retailing of children's clothing make reference to sexualizing and gender stereotyping.

EMPLOYEE-RELATED LEGISLATION

For many years the major piece of legislation regulating working conditions in retail outlets in the UK was the Shops Act 1950, which laid down controls on shop-opening and -closing hours and employment conditions for retail staff. However, many of its provisions became dated over time, particularly in relation to Sunday trading. The Deregulation and Contracting Out Act 1994 and the Sunday Trading Act 1994, which allowed Sunday shop opening in England and Wales, gave new employment rights for Sunday working and repealed the Shops Act 1950. These and other employee rights are now consolidated in the Employment Rights Act 1996, whose provisions are not limited to the retailing industry. This is an extensive piece of employment legislation and deserves close study. The basic rights and protections that the regulations provide are as follows:

1. A limit of an average of 48 hours per week (over a 17-week period) that a worker can be required to work (although workers can choose to agree to work more than this, but the agreement must be in writing).
2. A limit of an average of 8 hours of work in 24, which night workers can be required to work.
3. A right for night workers to receive free health assessments.
4. A right to 11 hours of rest a day.
5. A right to a day off each week.

6. A right to a rest break if the working day is longer than 6 hours.
7. A right to 4 weeks' paid leave per year.

The Sunday Trading Act 1994, which allowed Sunday shop opening in England and Wales, gives shop workers additional employment rights concerning Sunday working. Shop (and betting workers) have the right

1. Not to be dismissed for refusing to work on Sundays.
2. Not to be made redundant for refusing to work on Sundays.
3. Not to suffer any other detriment for refusing work on Sundays. Detriment can include, for example, denial of overtime, promotion or training opportunities.

However, these rights do not apply to those contracted to work only on Sundays, and shop workers can be required under their contract of employment to work on Sunday. However, shop workers can, if they wish, opt out of Sunday working by giving 3 months' notice in writing. They also have the right to opt back into Sunday working.

Three areas of legislation that have an important bearing on retailers are the national minimum wage, the improved rights of part-time workers and equality. As a result of the National Minimum Wage Act 1998, a national minimum wage has been in operation in the UK since 1 April 1999 and applies to all types of businesses. The rate is set by the government through consultation with the Low Pay Commission. The rates vary according to age and whether or not a worker is an apprentice. Employers are committing an offence if they do not pay their employees at least the current hourly rates laid down under the national minimum wage legislation (see www.gov.uk/national-minimum-wage-rates for up-to-date information).

The Part-Time Workers (Prevention of Less Favourable Treatment) Regulations 2000 introduced new rights for part-time workers similar to those of their full-time counterparts. The legislation means that part-time workers are entitled to the same hourly pay rates, access to company pension schemes, annual leave and maternity/parental leave on a pro rata basis, contractual sick pay and access to training.

Retailers must also ensure that their employment, promotion, recruitment and training practices do not discriminate on the basis of race, age, gender, sexual orientation or disability. The Equality Act 2010 consolidated previous laws in these areas and has simplified the requirements of employers. Retailers must also ensure that they provide a safe environment for their employees. The relevant legislations in this area include the Health and Safety at Work Act 1974 (and subsequent regulations) and the Fire Precautions Act 1971. Public liability insurance is required, as is employers' liability insurance if staff are employed.

BUSINESS ETHICS AND SOCIAL RESPONSIBILITY

Whilst laws and the legal framework set minimum standards for business behaviour, retailers must also take into account ethical norms and social responsibility in their operating practices. At one level, laws can be considered as the explicit formalization of the ethical and moral standards of a society. However, it is not possible (or even considered desirable) for societies to set down detailed laws and codes of conduct for all aspects of a business activity. Legislation in general tends to be reactive (that is it responds to business activities that are considered to be harmful to consumers, employees, other businesses or society generally), as it is generally difficult to anticipate future business practices resulting from economic, technological and social changes. In these circumstances, organizations need to behave in an ethical manner consistent with the ethical norms of society as well as complying with legal requirements.

As high standards of ethical behaviour are regarded positively by society, this is likely to have a positive impact on the reputation of the business and thereby influence the attitudes of current and future customers, employees, suppliers and other stakeholders towards the organization. Conversely, businesses that merely comply with the legal requirements or behave unethically are likely to find their reputations adversely affected with negative consequences for their businesses.

Corporate social responsibility (CSR) involves retailers undertaking activities that benefit society overall. Retailers undertaking CSR initiatives recognize that their activities have an impact on the wider society, that they must manage this impact and that they have responsibility to the local communities in which they operate and to society in general. Most retailers publish CSR statements, and whilst it is not a legal requirement at the time of publication of this text, many large multiple retailers produce extensive reports relating to the relationship between their business and society (see Vignette 18.2).

VIGNETTE 18.2 TESCO AND THE HORSEMEAT SCANDAL

At 11 p.m. on 17 January 2013, Tesco Customer Care put out the following message on social network Twitter: 'It's sleepy time so we're off to hit the hay! See you at 8am for more TescoTweets.' Whether this was an ill-judged joke or simply bad luck on the timing of an innocent remark (as claimed by Tesco in their profuse apology later), it was an action that typifies the saying 'when you are in a hole, don't dig yourself in deeper'. For this remark was made at a time when DNA testing of processed meat products was beginning to show that many supermarket products labelled as beef were in fact contaminated with horsemeat (and hay is what horses sleep in) . . .

On 16 January 2013 Tesco had revealed that it had withdrawn 26 product lines in response to the news that the Food Standards Agency of Ireland had found traces of horse DNA in a number of burger products including two Tesco product lines.

On 11 February Tesco Everyday Value Spaghetti was found by Tesco's own DNA testing to contain 60 per cent horsemeat and was withdrawn from sale. On the same day the UK Government Secretary for the Environment announced plans to test all processed beef in the UK. He called in representatives from all producers, retailers and distributors in the UK and told them to test all processed beef products across the supply chain and that testing should take place every 3 months with results being sent to the Food Standards Agency. He suggested that the presence of horsemeat in products labelled as beef was an issue of fraud and mis-labelling.

On 15 February the UK's Food Standards Agency (FSA) released the results of a set of tests taken from producers and retailers of processed beef products. They found that 29 products from the 2,501 tests contained undeclared horsemeat at or above 1 per cent. These included products from Aldi, the Co-op, Findus, Tesco and various catering establishments including those supplying schools.

On 16 February the CEO of Tesco, Philip Clarke, insisted a supply chain with more transparency and traceability would not lead to increases in prices, and said details of the product-testing programme would be posted on a new website.

On 27 February Philip Clarke pledged to bring meat production 'closer to home' and work more closely with British farmers in response to the horsemeat scandal. He said he could not guarantee 'right now today' that all of Tesco's products contained exactly what was on the label, but 'that is our objective' (BBC News, 2013b).

Tescos, like may other large multiple retailers, has been producing CSR reports for a number of years, but in 2013 it moved to a more holistic approach under the title of Tesco and Society Report, which in the Chairman's foreword states,

> We have been reflecting on our values and how to use our scale for good. Our values need to build on what we believe in. So when we talk about our value of using our scale for good in society, we think in terms of creating opportunities, having respect for both people and products and supporting choice for everyone. When we talk about our business, these values underpin how we relate to customers, work with colleagues and what we sell.

The horsemeat scandal appears to have given these values a hard test.

Source: BBC News (2013a, 2013b), Tescoplc.com (2013), Glotz (2013), Blake (2013)

The main areas in which retailers have undertaken CSR activities are community initiatives, environmental protection and ethical sourcing. Community initiatives include gifts in kind, charitable donations, sponsorship of community events, educational initiatives, fund-raising, sponsorship of the arts and other such acts and many other types of initiatives. Environmental initiatives include reduction of carbon dioxide (CO_2) emissions, energy usage reduction, reduction of transport, reduction of chlorofluorocarbons (CFCs) and hydrochlorofluorocarbons (HCFCs) in refrigeration, waste management and recycling, introduction of organic products and the avoidance of genetically modified (GM) products. Ethical sourcing includes fair-trade initiatives (designed to help emerging economy producers get a better deal for their products), and the implementation of international labour codes of conduct to prevent the exploitation of workers.

Much of the recent impetus behind CSR initiatives has come from customers. However, retailer involvement in CSR initiatives is not new. For instance, over 150 years ago the Co-operative Movement was set up to trade ethically and in a socially responsible manner. More recently, Body Shop and People Tree are examples of companies that have based their trading philosophy around ethical trading, fair trade, environmental sustainability and human rights. The major drivers behind this impetus are the development of consumerism, the emergence of the ethical consumer and environmentalism, concepts that are developed further in the following subsections.

CONSUMERISM

Consumerism refers to the activities of consumers, consumer organizations (and other independent organizations), governments and businesses aimed at promoting and protecting the rights of consumers. These are countervailing activities against the maxim of *caveat emptor* (buyer beware), designed to ensure that producers and retailers behave ethically and responsibly in their dealings with customers and society. These activities range from campaigning for consumer protection legislation (as discussed above) to consumer boycotts. Consumerism is increasing because consumers are better informed, more experienced and more sophisticated about what they expect from the products that they buy. Consumers are no longer simply concerned with the price, product features, delivery and service aspects of products; they are also environmentally, ethically and socially aware and want products that reflect their concerns.

Numerous consumer organizations also exist to promote the interests of the consumer. For instance, in the UK the Consumers' Association has been active in promoting consumer issues since 1957, and now trades as Which? (www.which.co.uk). Which?, funded solely by subscriptions and having charitable status, issues product test and reviews to enable consumers to make more informed choices about the products they buy, instigates campaigns and informs consumers of their rights. Similar organizations exist in other countries.

The development of consumerism has been given further impetus by the development of the Internet. It has allowed consumers and consumer interest organizations to articulate their demands and organize themselves more effectively globally. For example the ethical consumer (magazine and website www.ethicalconsumer.org) lists boycott calls for all products based on a variety of categories including environment, human rights, animal rights, workers' rights and irresponsible marketing.

Ethical consumers

Whilst there is no widely accepted definition of what constitutes an 'ethical' consumer, it is used here to describe consumers whose purchases are influenced by their ethical beliefs on such matters as animal welfare, fair trade, labour standards, human rights and so forth. By making positive choices about goods and services that are considered to be ethically produced and avoiding those that are believed to be unethical, the ethical consumer considers the wider impact of their purchasing. The term 'green consumers' is sometimes used to describe those who align themselves to the environmentalist movement, and so are concerned with the protection of the environment resulting from the production, distribution and marketing activities of businesses and consumption activities of consumers. There is considerable overlap between these groups, and this can be seen in the concern over chemicals used in denim processing which can harm both workers and the environment. Green consumerism contributes to the formation of an ethical consumer in that its objective is to minimize the damage to environment and to preserve it for future generations. An ethical consumer however may have additional concerns.

Given the close alliance between the two concepts and the difficulty of distinguishing between them, the Co-operative Bank's report (2011) defines ethical consumerism as the 'personal allocation of funds, including consumption and investment, where choice has been informed by a particular issue – be it human rights, social justice, the environment or animal welfare'. Using this definition, the report estimates that at least once a year 55 per cent of the UK population have chosen a product or service on the basis of a company's responsible reputation and 55 per cent have avoided a product or service on the basis of a company's responsible reputation, 45 per cent have bought primarily for ethical reasons and 75 per cent have supported local shops or suppliers. The report also suggests that sales of ethical goods and services have remained resilient during the recession in the UK, totalling £46.8 billion in 2010 (this compares to retail expenditure on ethical products at £1.3 billion in 2000 reported by the same source).

ENVIRONMENTALISM

Whilst the consumerism movement is concerned with protecting the rights of consumers, the environmentalist movement is concerned with the protection of the environment resulting from the production, distribution and marketing activities of businesses and consumption activities of consumers. It is concerned with the societal impact of business activities and not just the impact on individual consumers. Environmentalists are concerned with what economists refer to as externalities, or the costs of business and consumer activities to the community.

Retailers' responses to environmental concerns can be divided into two broad areas, namely those concerned with the products that they sell and those related to retail operations. Examples of the type of product initiatives that have be taken by retailers include the introduction of organic foods, the removal of CFCs from aerosols, the selling of Forest Stewardship Council (FSC)-certified wood products and more recently the stocking of ultra-low-sulphur petrol. Product-related initiatives provide direct evidence of a retailer's commitment to environment-friendly policies. In addition, by purchasing environment-friendly products, customers provide evidence of consumer commitment to environmental concerns. With their dominance in grocery markets, supermarkets are in the position to take a lead in this field; however, if they decide not to do so, the growth of ethical product markets can be restricted.

In terms of value, the biggest environmentally friendly product sector is the organic food market. According to the Soil Association, which promotes the interest of organic farming and food production and certifies products (www.soilassociation.org), the UK organic market had sales of £1.67 billion in 2011 (compared with £802 million in 2001 from the same source). The majority of the sales are through the large supermarkets, but increasingly specialist and online retailers such as Ocado are augmenting their share. In particular, organic food is increasingly favoured by younger (under-35) consumers in the UK. Unlike other ethical products which continued to grow in popularity through the recession in the UK, sales of organic products peaked in 2008. The Soil Association suggest that supermarkets can make falling demand for organic products a self-fulfilling prophecy by cutting space given to organic ranges, and thus reducing availability of the products to consumers. Without the support of supermarkets, farmers are less likely to take the long-term decision to invest in organic production systems.

Retailers' environmental initiatives in their retail operations can be classified into reusing, recycling and reducing, sometimes referred to as the 3 Rs. See for example Vignette 7.1 about green supply chains. Using refillable containers by both retailers and their customers is one method of reuse that can be employed. Sainsbury's for instance uses 3 million returnable crates in its distribution system per week, thereby reducing the amount of cardboard boxes used to move merchandise through its supply chain. Offering products in refillable containers to customers is operated on a very limited scale and confined to areas such as soap powders, detergents, cooking oil and wine. Recycling or reclaiming materials from used products is increasing amongst retailers as not only is it environmentally friendly, but it can also make financial sense. In addition to their own internal recycling activities, the major supermarkets also provide recycling facilities on their premises for the use of customers. These range from collection points in-store for used plastic carrier bags, to recycling banks for a wide range of materials including bottles, cans, clothes, paper and shoes. The recycling banks are normally operated by the local authorities, which take space in retailers' car parks.

Environmental initiatives designed to reduce resource usage include reduction of carbon dioxide emissions, reduction in energy usage, reduction in transport usage and the reduction of the waste produced by retail operations. Many of these activities are also encouraged by tax incentives and regulation. These include landfill taxes on the waste produced by retailers and the Packaging (Essential Requirements) Regulations 1998 (the UK's implementation of the European Union Directive on packaging), which require retailers to minimize packaging, and design packaging for recycling (subject to safety, hygiene and acceptance by consumers).

Some large multiple retailers have made attempts to demonstrate leadership in environmental initiatives. In particular, Marks and Spencer have adopted the high-profile Plan A initiative, embracing sustainability in all aspects of its business (see Vignette 18.3).

VIGNETTE 18.3 MARKS AND SPENCER'S PLAN A

Plan A was launched in 2007 as a set of sustainability targets for the next 5 years. The initiative was given high profile in all the company, including store windows communications as a commitment to improvements for the benefit of the environment and society. In 2013 the company reported that it had achieved the majority of the targets set including what they refer to as the 'big two' of becoming carbon neutral and sending no waste to landfill.

Plan A covers every aspect of the business, and embraces all stakeholders. Employees in stores, warehouses and transport have not only been considered as instrumental in implementing Plan A but they are encouraged to take a more sustainable approach to life outside of work. For example they are given discounts of M&S green services, supplying electricity and gas, loft insulation and solar energy, and discounts with other companies for bikes and eco-holidays. There is a staff well-being website, and every employee is allowed a day's paid leave a year to work with a charity while outstanding volunteer work is recognized at annual awards. As such, Plan A is considered to be the company's most successful motivational and change management programme to date. All suppliers are invited to an annual one-day Plan A conference, where it is made clear that they are part of Plan A as members of the Marks and Spencer supply network. An external Sustainable Retail Advisory Board was set up in 2011 to bring a wide variety of expertise and experience to Plan A together with independent opinion and comment. Even an element of the directors' bonuses is based on their achievements and leadership in areas of sustainability.

The Plan A Report gives a detailed performance summary, categorized under seven 'pillars' or themes, with 180 separate commitments. Performance is rated as achieved, achieved and ongoing, on plan or in rare cases behind plan or not achieved. The seven pillars are as follows:

1. Involve our customers in Plan A.
2. Make Plan A how we do business.
3. Climate change.
4. Waste.
5. Natural resources.
6. Fair partner.
7. Health and well-being.

Marks and Spencer are benefiting from the effect of Plan A both quantitatively and qualitatively; for example the 2013 report specified that 2012 Plan A contributed £185 million in net financial benefits for reinvestment into the business, whilst new recruits quote Plan A as being a reason for wanting to work with the retailer.

Plan A has brought Marks and Spencer many industry accolades, including The Queens Award for Enterprise: Sustainable Development 2012, The National Business Sustainability Award 2012, The Retail Week Best CSR Initiative 2013 for the Shwopping (clothes exchange) campaign and the Guardian Sustainable Business Awards in 2011 (Employee Engagement) and 2013 (Built Environment – Cheshire Oaks store).

Source: Based on Marks and Spencer (2013), Wills (2011)

Minimal environmental impact and the use of sustainable sources are now common in retail design. In 2012 Sainsbury's opened a store that housed many sustainable design features including a recyclable timber frame and indoor panels; renewable source timber cladding for the external walls; double-glazed skylights over the sales area to allow natural light into the store, with internal lights linked to sensors to dim or switch off according to the natural light source; movement detectors in the delivery area to automatically dim lights when not in use; a biomass boiler powered by locally sourced wood pellets providing renewable hot water and heating; rainwater harvesting for flushing toilets and even 'bee hotels' (to encourage the local population of solitary bees) and bat-friendly lighting in the car park (www.chqarchitects.co.uk, 2013). Peglar (2010) demonstrates a number of case studies of retailers that have used eco-conscious store designs including some luxury designer stores.

ETHICAL SOURCING

Ethical sourcing is concerned with ensuring that products sold by retailers do not exploit workers and producers in the production and supply chains. There are two important initiatives in this area, namely the Ethical Trading Initiative (ETI) and fair trade. ETI is concerned with ensuring that retailers and other businesses take the responsibility to work with their suppliers to implement internationally accepted labour standards in the workplace. Fairtrade, on the other hand, tries to ensure that producers (especially small producers in developing economies) are paid a fair price for their produce that at least covers the true cost of production.

Set up in 1998 with the help of the UK government's Department for International Development, the ETI is a tripartite alliance of companies, voluntary organizations and trade unions which is committed to developing and promoting a widely endorsed set of standards embodied in codes of conduct for good labour standards. These standards are formalized in the ETI's Base Code of Labour Practice, which is based on the standards of the International Labour Organization (ILO). The main provisions of the code are as follows:

1. Employment is freely chosen.
2. Freedom of association and the right to collective bargaining are respected.
3. Working conditions are safe and hygienic.
4. Child labour shall not be used.
5. Living wages are paid.
6. Working hours are not excessive.
7. No discrimination is practised.
8. Regular employment is provided.
9. No harsh or inhumane treatment is allowed.

The base code sets minimum employment standards for a company's suppliers. ETI members are expected to adopt the code (or incorporate it into their own employment codes) and require their suppliers (or subcontractors) to meet the set standards and monitor their performance in adhering to the code. The implementation of the code must be effective, transparent and independently verifiable. Much of the early work on the development of codes of conduct for labour occurred in the United States, where a majority of large organizations have now adopted such a code. Most major UK clothing retailers, department stores and supermarkets are now members of the ETI, ranging from Primark, INDITEX (owners of Zara) and ASOS to Superdry and Burberry. Critics of the ETI suggest that a code of practice is of limited value unless it is enforced through a transparent supply chain, and that practices like unannounced auditing by properly trained and not corrupt inspectors should be adopted and that non-compliance should results in harsh penalty.

In the main, ETI-type initiatives are aimed predominantly at the formal sector in developing economies, where producers already have access to export markets across the globe. In contrast, Fairtrade has the aim of alleviating poverty in developing countries by providing small, marginalized and disadvantaged producers access to global markets. These are often small-scale farmers, or independent plantations involved in producing commodities such as coffee. The initiative also involves paying producers a fair price that provides them with a sufficient return to cover their basic needs and a margin for investment. When requested, partial advance payments are also made to allow producers to buy the necessary inputs without falling into debt. Long-term relationships and contracts are established between parties to provide a stability of earnings for producers. This is extremely important in commodity markets, where prices tend to fluctuate wildly. In return, producers are required to ensure that their activities are sustainable, working conditions are acceptable and they contribute to the development of their communities. The Fairtrade campaign has its origins in the 'trade, not aid' philosophy for helping emerging economies.

There are a number of organizations across the globe that promote fair trade. A widely used mechanism for doing this is to award a Fairtrade mark to products that meet the recognized standards of fair trade. In the UK the Fairtrade Foundation (http://www.fairtrade.org.uk/) was set up in 1994 to bring Fairtrade products into British supermarkets, awarding the Fairtrade mark to items that meet its criteria for fairly traded products. All the leading supermarkets in the UK sell Fairtrade products. The two largest UK importing organizations of fairly traded merchandise are Traidcraft and the Oxfam organisation. Oxfam sells a variety of products largely through its own retail outlets, while Traidcraft sells its fairly traded gift products, food and beverages, clothing and accessories and home wear through a network of voluntary organizations and mainstream retailers, as well as directly to consumers via their website or catalogue.

In 2013 the Fairtrade Foundation licensed over 3000 Fairtrade-certified products for sale through retailers and catering outlets in the UK. Around 26 per cent of roast and ground coffee and a third of all bananas sold in the UK are Fairtrade, and the market for all Fairtrade products in 2012 was £1.5 billion (www.fairtrade.org.uk, 2013). The Fairtrade mark assures consumers that whatever a retailer charges for a Fairtrade product, producers have received an agreed fair price for the goods, together with a social premium to invest in the future of their community.

Despite high growth rates, the size of the fairly traded products segment is still small compared with the overall retail market. In part this is due to the low availability and premium prices of these products. Nevertheless, the increasing interest of consumers and retailers in fairly traded products as well as associated organizations such as the Fairtrade Foundation means that the number of fairly traded products will continue to grow. In 2004 research conducted by the Fairtrade Foundation suggested that recognition of the Fairtrade mark was at around 20 per cent of the general public, whereas in 2013 78 per cent of consumers recognized the symbol, according to the same source. Providing that retailers continue to support Fairtrade products, the market for these goods will expand; the high awareness of the mark would suggest that most mainstream supermarkets would now be perceived negatively if they did not stock a good range of Fairtrade products.

CSR AND ENVIRONMENTAL REPORTING

In order to demonstrate to consumers and other interested bodies that they are conducting their business in a socially responsible and environmentally friendly manner, major retailers are increasingly producing corporate social responsibility (CSR) and environment reports that are independently audited. Although the majority of the FTSE 100 and Fortune 500 companies now report their environmental performance, social impact or both, the reporting standards vary (Morhardt, 2010). Typical CSR reports are available on the websites of most major retailers, and are clearly designed to position retailers as socially responsible organizations and thus build goodwill amongst customers and the rest of society. Although the evidence of a link between CSR activities and performance is mixed (Pava and Krausz, 1996), a study by Connelly and Limpaphayom (2004) found that the combination of high disclosure and high CSR performance has some correlation with a firm's favourable financial performance. Supermarkets are deemed to be the sector of the FTSE 100 companies that produce the best-quality reports and perform best on a set of elected environmental criteria (Environmental Leader, 2012).

Positioning an organization as a socially responsible company raises customer expectations and opens the organization to a wide range of scrutiny and potential criticism that may not be manageable. The discipline of CSR reporting can be used to ensure that the retailer is not over-promising and over-claiming their commitment to society and the environment. This also raises the question as to how responsive retailers should be to concerns of consumers and other stakeholders regarding the environment and social and ethical issues. The answer depends on the retailer's corporate philosophy regarding its role in society. If it believes that businesses exist to maximize profits (given its legal and contractual responsibilities), a retailer will not undertake CSR activities unless they are profitable. However, if it believes that it needs to conform to social norms and ethical values in the conduct of its business, or if it believes that it needs to take into account the impact that its activities has on other stakeholders besides its shareholders and customers, it will undertake CSR activities (even though they are not profitable) because the retailer feels that it is their duty to do so. Finally, if the corporate philosophy incorporates the belief that the firm should contribute towards the betterment of society, then it will undertake CSR activities because it believes them to be the right thing to do.

SUMMARY

Retailing is an activity that closely connects with consumers, and arguably if a retailer is not trustworthy or acts immorally, consumers are free to take their custom elsewhere. However, in mature and increasingly concentrated retail markets, retailers are powerful entities and can lapse into abusing their power, while consumers may have little choice but to continue shopping with them. A substantial and complex legal and regulatory framework has therefore developed in order to protect stakeholders, including customer protection, employee legislation and supplier treatment. In addition to their legal obligations, retailers also need to take into account ethical norms and their social responsibility when operating their businesses. Legal obligations can be seen as the formalization of the minimum ethical and moral standards of society, but, increasingly, consumers and other members of society expect retailers to behave in a socially responsible manner, encapsulated in the concept of corporate social responsibility (CSR). CSR involves the retailer undertaking activities which benefit society overall, above and beyond its legal obligation. The drivers behind the growth of CSR activities include growth of consumerism (the protection of consumer rights), the emergence of the ethical and environmentally conscious consumer and the increasing ease by which information about relevant issues is generated and disseminated via digital media.

Retailers have responded to these concerns and are continuing to do so by developing products that meet these concerns and by changing the way they operate. Some retailers are going as far as differentiating themselves on the basis of operating sustainably and ethically; however, for large and mature retail organizations that are beholden to shareholders, this can be very challenging. Retailers are engaging increasingly in ethical sourcing practices and cooperate with industry codes of practice; however, supply chains of retailers are also under increasing scrutiny as exploitation of workers in manufacturing and producing organizations for well-known retailers continues to be exposed. The degree to which retailers adopt CSR initiatives depends on their corporate philosophy; however, it is increasingly obvious that retailers that ignore the ethical and social concerns of their customers do so at their peril.

QUESTIONS

1. Explain the main rights that buyers are given by the Sale of Goods Act 1979 and subsequent amendments. What additional rights do consumers have when they do not purchase goods directly from the retailer (for example by mail order)?
2. According to the Consumer Protection Act 1987, who is liable for faulty goods?
3. Explain why, in your opinion, there are extensive regulations regulating the displaying of prices.
4. What is APR? Why do legislators insist that the APR be stated in all credit agreements and that it appear more prominently than any other rate?
5. What is corporate social responsibility? How does a retailer benefit from undertaking CSR initiatives?
6. Explain the similarities and differences between ethical consumers and green consumers.
7. What is ethical sourcing? Distinguish between ethical trade initiatives and fair trade.
8. Identify and discuss the legal and ethical issues that are raised in the account of events in Vignette 18.2.

REFERENCES AND FURTHER READING

Balabanis, G., Phillips, H. C. and Lyall, J. (1998) 'Corporate Social Responsibility and Economic Performance in the Top British Companies: Are They Linked?', *European Business Review*, vol. 98, no. 1, pp. 25–44.

BBC News UK (2013a) 'Horsemeat Scandal: Tesco Reveals 60% Content in Dish', available at www.bbc.co.uk/news/uk-21418342[accessed 10 September 2013].

BBC News UK (2013b) 'Tesco Pledges to Sell Meat from "Closer to Home",' available at www.bbc.co.uk/news/uk-21597596 [accessed 10 September 2013].

Blake, M. (2013) 18 January, available at dailymail.co.uk/news/article-2264394 [accessed 13 August 2013].

Brave, J. (1993) *Law for Retailers*, 2nd Edition (London: Sweet & Maxwell).

Co-operative Bank (2011) Ethical Consumerism Report 2011, http://www.co-operative.coop/PageFiles/416561607/Ethical-Consumerism-Report-2011.pdf [accessed 20 August 2013]

CHQ Partnership (2013), 'Dawlish', available at http://www.chq-architects.co.uk/dawlish [accessed 14 August 2013].

Connelly, J. T. and Limpaphayom, L. (2004) 'Environment Reporting and Firm Performance: Evidence from Thailand', *Journal of Corporate Citizenship*, no. 13, pp. 137–49.

Environmentalleader.com (2012) 'Marks and Spencer, National Grid Top FTSE 100 Carbon Reporting Ranking', available at www.environmentalleader.com/2012/11/13/marks-spencer-national-grid [accessed 14 August 2013].

Glotz, J. (2013) 'Horse Meat Scandal: 26 Tesco Lines Withdrawn', available at http://www.thegrocer.co.uk/fmcg/fresh/meat/horse-meat-scandal-26-tesco-lines-withdrawn/235629.article [accessed 13 August 2013].

Hawkes, S. (2013) 'Phone Operators Slammed for Misleading Customers on Price', *Telegraph*, available at www.telegraph.co.uk, 18 June [accessed 16 August 2013].

Marks and Spencer (2013)*Your M&S Plan A Report*, available at http://planareport.marksandspencer.com/docs/33722_M&S_PlanA.pdf. [accessed 14 August 2013].

McWilliams, A. and Siegel, D. (2000) 'Corporate Social Responsibility and Financial Performance: Correlation or Misspecification?', *Strategic Management Journal*, vol. 21, no. 5, pp. 603–9.

Morhardt, J. E. (2010) 'Corporate Social Responsibility and Sustainability Reporting on the Internet', *Business Strategy and the Environment*, vol. 19, no. 7, 436–52.

Murphy, P. E., Laczniak, G. R. and Prothero, A. (2012) *Ethics in Marketing: International Cases and Perspectives* (Abingdon and New York: Routledge).

Pava, M. L. and Krausz, J. (1996) 'The Association between Corporate Social-Responsibility and Financial Performance: The Paradox of Social Cost', *Journal of Business Ethics*, vol. 15, no. 3, pp. 321–57.

Peglar, M. (2010) *Green Retail Design* (Cincinnati: ST Books).

Piacentini, M., MacFadyen, L. and Eadie, D. (2000) 'Corporate Social Responsibility in Food Retailing', *International Journal of Retail and Distribution Management*, vol. 28, no. 11, pp. 459–69.

Schlegelmilch, B. (1998) *Marketing Ethics: An International Perspective* (London: Thomson International).

Strong, C. (1996) 'Features Contributing to the Growth of Ethical Consumerism', *Marketing Intelligence and Planning*, vol. 14, no. 5, pp. 5–13.

Tescoplc.com (2013) Tesco and Society report, available at www.tescoplc.com/society [accessed 15 August 2013].

The Co-operative Group (2011) *The Ethical Consumerism Report*, available at www.goodwithmoney.co.uk/ethicalconsumerismreport [accessed 14 August 2013].

Thomas, W. T. (2003) *Law for Retailers*, 2nd Edition (Chalford: Management Books 2000 Ltd).

Waddock, S. and Graves, S. (1997) 'The Corporate Social Performance – Financial Performance Link', *Strategic Management Journal*, vol. 18, no. 4, pp. 303–19.

Wills, J. (2011) 'M&S – Wholly Embracing Staff in Plan to Become the World's Most Sustainable Retailer', *Guardian*, 26 May, available at www.theguardian.com/sustainable-business/staff-plan-worlds-sustainable-retailer [accessed 16 August 2013].

USEFUL WEBSITES

http://www.co-op.co.uk/index.html (The Co-operative Group website)

http://www.fairtrade.org.uk/ (Fairtrade Foundation website)

http://www.food.gov.uk/ (Food Standards Agency website)

http://www.oft.gov.uk/Business/default.htm (Office of Fair trading website)

http://www.soilassociation.org/ (Soil Association website)

http://www.tradingstandards.gov.uk/ (Trading Standards Institute website)

http://www.which.net/campaigns/contents.html (Consumer Association website)

www.ethicalfashionforum.com (Ethical Fashion Forum website)

www.ethicaltrade.org (Ethical Trading Initiative website)

www.fsc-uk.org (The Forest Stewardship Council website)

www.ilo.org (International Labour Organization website)

www.ethicalconsumer.org (The Ethical Consumer online magazine and organization)

www.which.co.uk (Which?/The Consumers' Association)

INDEX